JOE DIMAGGIO

"Greatest Living Player" : "Greatest Player Ever"--Center Field
"Greatest Living Player"-- Center Field
JOE DI MAGGIO

JOE DIMAGGIO
Baseball's
Yankee Clipper

Jack B. Moore

PRAEGER

New York
Westport, Connecticut
London

Library of Congress Cataloging-in-Publication Data

Moore, Jack B.
  Joe DiMaggio, baseball's Yankee clipper.

  Originally published under title: Joe DiMaggio,
a bio-bibliography.
  Bibliography: p.
  Includes index.
  1. Di Maggio, Joe, 1914- . 2. Baseball
players—United States—Biography. 3. Baseball—
United States—Bio-bibliography. I. Title.
GV865.D5M66 1987   796.357′092′4 [B]   87-2369
ISBN 0-275-92712-1 (pbk. : alk. paper)

A hardcover edition of *Joe DiMaggio* is available from Greenwood Press
(Popular Culture Bio-Bibliographies; ISBN 0-313-23917-7).

Library of Congress Catalog Card Number: 87-2369
ISBN: 0-275-92712-1

First published 1986

Paperback edition 1987

Praeger Publishers, 521 Fifth Avenue, New York, NY 10175
A division of Greenwood Press, Inc.

Printed in the United States of America

The paper used in this book complies with the Permanent Paper Standard issued by
the National Information Standards Organization (Z39.48-1984).

10 9 8 7 6 5 4 3 2 1

Copyright Acknowledgments

The author would like to thank the following for graciously giving permission to reprint
copyrighted materials:

Portions from *Lucky to Be a Yankee* by Tom Meany. Copyright 1946 by the author. Reprinted
with the permission of the publisher, Chilton Book Company, Radnor, Pennsylvania.

The frontispiece photo and caption were supplied by the New York Yankees.

This time
for Judy

CONTENTS

PREFACE

The inclusion of Joe DiMaggio as an important symbol in Ernest Hemingway's 1952 novella *The Old Man and the Sea*, and his selection in 1969 as baseball's greatest living player, suggest a measure of DiMaggio's impact on American sport and society. His 56-game hitting streak, his mid-season comeback from injuries for the important three-game series with Boston in 1949, his relationship with Marilyn Monroe, and the allusion to him in the popular song "Mrs. Robinson" provide proof of the unusual abilities as an athlete and as a man embodying the special qualities of a hero that made him an exceptionally respected American. First capturing public awareness as a minor league outfielder, he became the best known player on the most famous team of his day, and ultimately developed into a figure reputed to possess many of the most desired qualities in American life—skill, victoriousness, courage, the ability to endure pain, resilience, cooperativeness, decency, and dedication.

The purpose of this book is to note the known, salient facts of Joe DiMaggio's life on the field and off, to analyze the reasons underlying his enshrinement as a myth, and to investigate the literature written about him, in which most of the details of his life have been transmitted and through which his ascendency as a sports and culture hero can be followed. I have tried to distinguish between fact and fancy in this biography, something not always easy to accomplish when dealing with a great many sources that have not. But I have recognized that even stories of doubtful veracity have a function in exploring and explaining the attitudes people hold toward a figure of history.

I have tried to account for the rare, almost unique stature DiMaggio has achieved in becoming a symbolic hero in American life. The truly significant public heroes in our society, the ones who will endure, are not easy to identify. But it seems likely that DiMaggio will remain—as has Babe Ruth for example—a hero of sport and of the culture outside sports as well for a prolonged period. Finding out how such a hero with socially mythical overtones is produced in our time is another focus of the book, for the processes of modern myth-making reveal much about our culture.

In writing about DiMaggio's life, the literature concerning him, and the symbolic figure both have made him into, I use a number of terms whose meaning I would like to clarify. Some of these words incorporate complicated concepts I could not possibly investigate at length here. When I refer to DiMaggio's life I mean the factual events of his life (as accurately as I can ascertain them). When I refer to his story or narrative I mean the mixture of fact, near-fact, and embroidered fact or fabrication that his public has come to accept as the truth about him. His narrative is the story generally told about him, though parts may be fictional. That DiMaggio was born in Martinez is a fact, that his father strongly objected to his thoughts of a baseball career is part of his narrative. Many facts of his life, though, are not strong parts of his narrative, such as the time he was connected to a break-in purportedly to obtain divorce proceeding evidence on Marilyn Monroe.

I use the terms image, celebrity, star, hero, legend, and myth frequently. I realize that in much contemporary commentary the terms are greatly overused and thereby debased, and yet I know of no better substitutes for what I want to discuss. By image I mean the identity of a person established by what others think about them: the picture of them in others' minds. This picture may duplicate what the person actually is like (however that might be objectively determined) or it may reflect a distortion or reshaping of the person. By celebrity I mean someone who receives a significant amount of publicity in the media. Celebrities need not do anything of particular importance or value, but they must be written about, spoken about, or shown often enough publicly that they become (even for a short time) recognized persons in a community. A star is viewed as a lead performer. A sports star is a player hailed as a chief performer either in a game or an extended series of games, and is ordinarily a winner. A hero is one who has performed with recognized, substantial abilities over a period of time, to the extent that some portion of the populace—which can include other players—feels emotionally close to them, greatly respects them, and perhaps wishes to emulate them. I am fully aware of the irony of applying the term to individuals who have not performed risky acts in the cause of some goal that society determines is noble—a person like Rosa Parks or the explorer Robert Scott.

Here I should acknowledge that I am also aware of other ironies relating to the treatment of baseball players as heroes, and the stories about them as legends. While some writers and many fans (the groups are not mutually exclusive) have imposed childish fantasies upon sports and baseball in particular, and have thereby cheapened the reality of games by changing them into impossibly important events, their collective and deeply felt adulation is part of what turns sport into myth. Any athletic contest can contain both a distorted—because inflated—surface and a true and pure performance; baseball or any professional sport can be viewed as heroic, romantic adventure and as a very tough job. Baseball is a national symbol, a boy's game, and a hard, big business.

I use both myth and legend to describe heroic individuals about whom a body of stories has accumulated and been transmitted to the public. These terms have been particularly cheapened by loose designation, but I believe if they are justifiable in being assigned to any performer, they are valid for identifying DiMaggio. Individuals who become a myth or legend are endowed with a cultural radiance or resonance and seem to possess striking abilities superior not just in degree, but in kind, to other persons. Their magnitude is of a different order. Thus they come to represent the highest realms of achievement, very special, transcendently human achievements; their abilities have projected these people into an almost more-than-human realm. I also use myth and legend to represent the stories that accumulate about such a heroic person: some of these stories may be true, others may not. For some reason, all are desired by the mythical hero's public.

I hope I have written this book for a mixed audience of readers; those interested in and knowledgeable about sports, and others who perhaps are not so interested in sports, but concerned with the American culture. At times I have provided information that might be well-known to one group but not the other (keeping in mind that interest in sports does not disqualify a reader from interest in the greater culture outside sports).

Finally, I would like to thank again all those mentioned in the text who supplied data, submitted to interviews, or otherwise provided important assistance to me while I researched and wrote this book. Some, unmentioned in the text, I would like to thank now: Maury Crane, Madelaine DiMaggio, Gene Elston, Carl Lundquist, Tamsin Moore, Russel Nye, Mike Ochshorn, Pat Schuster, Randy Scott, and Joseph St. George. Kip Ingle, Ken Nigro, and David Szen of the New York Yankees' office gave me greatly needed assistance, as did many librarians at the University of South Florida library.

I would specifically like to acknowledge the aid of the University of South Florida's President's Council Faculty Awards Program for providing the needed funds which enabled me to conduct interviews and do research in California and New York.

JOE DIMAGGIO

1

A HERO'S LIFE

Many versions of the story of Joe DiMaggio's parents have been told. The most likely facts are that both Giuseppe Paolo DiMaggio and his wife Rosalie Mercurio were born in or around Palermo, Sicily; Giuseppe in 1874 and Rosalie in 1879. The exact place of birth may have been Isola Della Femmine, a small island northwest of Palermo in the Golfo di Carini, where the two grew up. The village's population was about 1,900 during the 1890s, when Giuseppe and Rosalie married. Giuseppe worked as a fisherman as had his ancestors for generations past, and like them, he worked without much profit—it was a hard life. In 1896 he fought in Italy's unsuccessful war against Abyssinia (Ethiopia) and, according to family legend, emerged more gloriously from the disastrous battles—the defeat at Adowa was one of the most notorious in modern Italian history—than many, for he was apparently awarded a citation for valor.[1]

Like so many Italians, he left the steady treadmill of poverty after the war and shipped off for the economically greener new world of America in 1898. Unlike most he headed for California. Rosalie's father already lived in Collinsville, a small town north of San Francisco, where he thought his hard-working son-in-law could make a better living. Like so many other immigrants, Giuseppe did not immediately pick up nuggets of gold in the streets, nor could he find immediate employment as a fisherman. Moving south from Collinsville to Martinez, California, he worked as a section hand for the railroad for the typically low wages of around ten cents an hour. But he saved enough to bring Rosalie over in 1902, along with his daughter Nellie who had been born September 1, 1898, shortly after his departure.

In time Giuseppe secured work at his regular trade and fished the waters off San Francisco. He continued to live in Martinez with Rosalie who gave birth there to seven more children, roughly one every two years: Mamie (September 25, 1903), Thomas Paul (January 12, 1905), Marie (June 17, 1906), Michael Paul (June 17, 1908), Frances (July 13, 1910), Vincent Paul (September 6, 1912), Joseph Paul (November 25, 1914).[2] In 1915 the family moved to the North Beach section of San Francisco, an already long-established enclave for Italian-Americans, many of whom were engaged in some aspect of the fishing business. The family's last child, Dominic Paul (all the boys were named Paul after Giuseppe and his favorite saint) was born there February 12, 1917.

Life in San Francisco was easier for the DiMaggios than it had ever been before, but it still demanded hard work and cooperation to lift and maintain the family standard of living above the level of poverty so many similar Sicilian families experienced back in Italy, and that some yet knew in the vaunted land of opportunity. The DiMaggio clan ate simply and well, but they lived for two decades in the same, often crowded, four-room house on 2047 Taylor Street for which Giuseppe paid $25.00 a month. He had to labor hard each workday, and needed the help of his sons as he sought, along with thousands of other early rising Italian San Franciscans, the fish (in Giuseppe's case mainly herring, smelt, salmon, and particularly crabs) that spawned such profit in the community, though it did not always bring individual families great wealth.

The DiMaggio family never knew want, but the older boys knew tough labor and Rosalie and the girls were skilled at practicing economies that would conserve resources. They lived as did many ordinary, nonaffluent American households in the 1920s and 1930s, the younger children wearing the outgrown clothes of their older brothers and sisters and all experiencing how it felt to lack money for small pleasures their friends could afford. As an adult, Joe DiMaggio would remember, for example, that he could not afford to attend two movies he particularly wanted to see. The first was the highly publicized talking picture, Al Jolson's *The Jazz Singer* (released late in 1927), the second, *All Quiet on the Western Front* (released in 1930, when Joe would have been about 16). After all, as Quentin Reynolds wrote in one of the first widely distributed articles about the star player, "Poppa DiMaggio had to feed and buy confirmation suits for Thomas, Mike, Vincent, and Dominic and he had to go for hair ribbons and pretties for Nellie, Mamie, Marie, and Frances."[3]

Giuseppe prospered enough, however, that eventually he was able to buy his own boat, the *Rosalie*. The two older boys, Tom and Mike, fit into the scheme calling for hard, productive, cooperative work on the boat. Tom even declined a tryout with the Hollywood Stars of the Pacific Coast League to remain at the family's traditional job (he was also injured at the time). But even while the family continued to live in its predominantly Italian North Beach enclave, it was becoming increasingly and inevitably Americanized. Though Rosalie and Giuseppe would not become naturalized citizens until 1944 and 1945, respectively, and Tom spoke English with traces of an Italian accent,[4] all the children save Nellie were citizens at birth. The boys particularly and quite naturally began easing or breaking away from some of the old ways. Joe's aversion to working on his father's fishing boat has become a famous part of his childhood story, but apparently big brother Vince gave little thought to following the family job from the time he became a young adult, and certainly by the time Dominic was growing up, the pattern had been broken.

In America a young boy like Joe DiMaggio could only have worked the boat at odd times anyway, for he was expected to attend school most of the year. There are stories that the smell of fish or the movements of the boat made him sick. Probably in his father's eyes, Joe Jr.'s reluctance to help at sea or even around the docks was a sign of both laziness and rebellion. Doubtless young Joe was no better then at masking his discontent than he would become as a grown baseball star notorious for his sulks. This led to confrontations from which his more tenderhearted mother tried to protect him. The arguments were what anyone would expect between a hard working father who never had it easy and a son who was surrounded by relative affluence even though his personal share was not very great; the conflicts between an immigrant who still could not read English and his American son who wanted to go with the other guys to see Al Jolson sing "Mammy."

Still, DiMaggio has always been publicly loyal to both his parents. In *Lucky to Be a Yankee* he mentions but does not stress conflicts with his father, and notes with distinct pride the pleasure his father eventually felt because of his son's baseball triumphs. Even when lamenting instances of his family's lack of money, DiMaggio has continued to view his childhood as tender and affectionate and his father as "a good father." He declared in a 1949 article written by Jack Sher that his father was "always very nice to us kids. He loved kids, he was that sort of guy. I can remember him coming home from work, drinking a glass of wine, then playing with us. His hours were long. He used to have to get up at four o'clock almost every morning." In the same article he recollected "we had some rough times. . . . But there was always enough bread in the house, even though our clothes were hand-me-downs, and we never had any extras. My mother always worked very hard, too. I can't recall a time when she was not working." Later, when he hit it big as a Yankee star, one of the first things he did with his money was buy his parents a new home. He would be a dutiful son, if not a hard-working adolescent.

When not forced to scrub the decks of his father's boat or perform odd jobs to bring some money into the family—such as hawking newspapers, a task that Dominic could perform much better than he—the unspectacular young DiMaggio attended school with neither noticeable delight nor high frequency. Here too he dissatisfied his father and probably even his mother, for while the Italian-American community in which the DiMaggios lived did not stress higher education necessarily as a preeminent way to get quickly up the American economic and social ladder, these new Americans could clearly see that a basic education helped attain success and acceptance. But the torch of learning did not seem to brighten the path of ambition for the Italian-American youngster at Hancock Grammar School, Francisco Junior High, nor at Galileo High School. His memories of schooldays as he would later recollect them for one reporter or another seemed skimpy and drab. In Maury Allen's *Where Have You Gone, Joe DiMaggio?*, one of his North Beach friends remembers the shock he and Joe felt at Galileo, the first regional school they attended, seeing how much better dressed the children of middle-class Anglos were. DiMaggio's strongest vision of high school appears to have been his departure. In his first year there (the tenth grade) he was assigned an ROTC class when he wanted physical education, and he responded by cutting school for half a semester. Then when he was ordered to return and told to see the principal, the principal never showed up in his office (DiMaggio said), so DiMaggio left school permanently. The year was 1931, one of the roughest periods of the Depression, and in the eyes of his hard-working father and even his much-forgiving mother, undoubtedly a most unwise time for him to drop out and hit the streets, seemingly a recalcitrant, lazy, and wrong-headed boy.

According to Allen's biography "so shy around girls that he would rush out of his own home whenever his sisters had female friends over. . . . afraid his sisters might introduce him and thereby force him to talk"; a flop at various jobs that he had attempted, such as newsboy, as he was growing up; moody and seen as a loner even by his friends, DiMaggio experienced his greatest satisfactions and popularity as a kid through his abilities at playing games. He did not know it of course when he quit school and worked on the docks or delivered groceries or crated oranges, but a game would be the miracle key—perhaps for him the only key—to his golden success.

He was never crazy about playing baseball but he was always good at it. Nearly all the boys in San Francisco played baseball, for it was the unchallenged king of team sports. Football was a distant second; but if a boy dreamed of hitting the big time, he would have to think about enduring college. Such attendance was unusual for most Americans and an exotic fantasy among Joe's Italian buddies. Baseball became an almost essential part of their Americanization. In both his books, DiMaggio states that he played his first competitive baseball games when he was ten, or around 1924; the year when Ty Cobb lost out as batting champion to Babe Ruth. Tris Speaker, the other dominant outfielder of the era had retired three years previously, but "Big Train" Walter Johnson finally arrived in a World Series game against the New York Giants, managed by John McGraw in his last World Series, after seventeen years of high powered pitching. Johnson struck out twelve but lost a heart-breaker in the twelfth, 4-3. So some giants of the old game had departed when DiMaggio began his development as a boy player, some were in their prime, and some demi-gods that he would play with himself as a rookie, such as Lou Gehrig, were little more than rookies themselves (Gehrig hit .500 in the twelve at-bats he took for the Yankees in 1924).

If baseball was beginning to be big business during the twenties, the kind of sandlot ball DiMaggio played was paleolithic compared to the Little Leagues of today replete with moms hawking hot dogs and dads solemnly mispronouncing the names of nine-year-old pitching whizzes. "We played on a cleared space of ground which we called the Horse Lot, because it was used by a dairy firm as a parking area for its milk wagons," DiMaggio remembered in *Lucky to Be a Yankee*. "We used rocks for bases and most of us played bare-handed because we couldn't afford gloves." Often their ball was more bicycle tape than horse hide and twine. And as a perfect example of local acculturation and children's creativity, they used an oar handle as a bat. As had his older brother Vince, who also quit school to work in a fruit market, Joe played infield mainly, and achieved recognition as the "best kid in the neighborhood in baseball," according to Allen's biography. On the 130-pound team of Francisco Junior High, and later on various semi-pro squads, Joe was tops. Still, he did not play ball with a passion and did not recognize it as his vehicle for traveling beyond the streets of the North Beach Italian-American community. He played street football too, and at one time tennis crowded out baseball as his consuming athletic interest. Inspired by local greats Maurice McLaughlin and Bill Johnston, he dreamed of a career as a tennis star. In *Lucky to Be a Yankee* DiMaggio states that around 1928, when he was fourteen, he "almost stopped playing baseball" completely. Inevitably, his interest in tennis waned (tennis is an expensive sport in terms of equipment and lessons, no sport for ethnic Americans), and kids kept after him to play on their baseball teams. Disregarding his moodiness and lack of sociability, they recognized his talent, and so seemingly without much excitement on his part, baseball continued to be his game. According to Bob Broeg, Joe and Dominic would sometimes play catch after dinner, each trying to outsparkle the other.

Joe usually played the infield and most frequently at third base, where kids ordinarily place good hitters with strong arms who are not quite as skilled as the boys who play shortstop. Joe starred with various youth teams in league play, the first being the Boy's Club League when he was fourteen. In *Lucky to Be a Yankee* DiMaggio said "an olive oil dealer . . . named Rossi"[5] took the team from that league, bought them good equipment, and the team responded by winning a championship. DiMaggio hit two home runs in the deciding playoff game, and was awarded two "gold" baseballs and merchandise worth about $16.00, his first pay for play. With the Sunset

Produce Team he hit .632 in eighteen games and was given the best pair of baseball shoes he had ever owned. By this time he was a shortstop, and late in the 1932 season, received his first professional offer for a tryout with the San Francisco Missions in the Pacific Coast League. He had been spotted by the Missions's manager Fred Hoffman, a former journeyman back-up catcher for the Yankees (1919-1925) and the Boston Red Sox (1927-1928), when his team played against the Mission's farm team, the Mission Red A's. Were Joe to be successful in the tryout, his contract would be for $150.00 a month, or about $25.00 more than the regular contract payment.

Joe was inclined to accept, but he wanted to ask the advice of his oldest brother Tom, who was a young Americanized Italian, perhaps a stronger figure in the family by this time than Joe's father, and who had once himself been offered a chance to become a professional baseball player. Tom was hard-working, responsible, and practical. Joe also wanted the advice of his brother Vince, who had also quit school and in 1932 entered professional baseball. All along Vince had suggested to his apparently reluctant younger brother that he consider trying to earn real money at baseball. Vince had been hired by the Missions' San Francisco rivals, the Seals, and in 1932 he had batted .347 for Tucson until called up by the Seals. He thought Joe should try out for the Seals. Joe went to the Seals's park (the Missions were on the road) mulling over Hoffman's offer.

What ensued became one of the most famous sequences of his legend. Writers delight in dramatizing versions of it, and if DiMaggio's career is made into a film, it is certain that some form of it will be spun into the narrative. One suspects that the tale has been told and retold so many times, that so many echoes of it have been heard and recorded and played back and distorted and listened to, that even if the principal actors in the scene could be reassembled for its recreation, they would no longer always be able to distinguish amplification and modification from true sound.

DiMaggio was at this time seventeen years old, fully grown in height and neither spindly nor wiry but still not quite fully fleshed out. His face was thin and big-beaked and his big teeth protruded in a sharp overbite. He had a face somewhat like a wedge: not the least startling aspect of the classic success story he would become has been his physical transformation from a homely kid into a truly distinguished looking, handsome man, the ugly duckling story all over again.

Neither Philip Roth nor Robert Coover, whose fictions *The Great American Novel* and *The Universal Baseball Association, Inc.* contain fabulous baseball players such as Frenchy Astarte and Rag (Pappy) Rooney, ever created a better name for the legendary and yet real scout who seemingly plucked DiMaggio from obscurity and started him on his highway to glory: Spike Hennessy. Similarly, the name of DiMaggio's first professional manager rings with epic resonance: Ike Caveney. In *Lucky to Be a Yankee*, DiMaggio says that Hennessy saw him looking for Vince through a knothole in the fence around the Seal's playing field, and knowing Joe "as he would have known any kid who played ball on any sandlot in San Francisco" said to him "Never stand on the outside looking in, unless it's jail. . . . Come along with me, kid." Hennessy "practically" dragged DiMaggio into the office of Seals president Charlie Graham, introduced DiMaggio as Vince's brother, and Graham offered the scared kid a "fistful of passes" so he wouldn't have to peer through the knothole any more. Graham then asked if Vince did all the playing in the DiMaggio family, and Hennessy answered in such detail that Joe realized "how closely Hennessy had been watching our sandlot games." Graham then offered Joe a tryout with the team, which made him forget the Missions' offer. *True* comics for May, 1948, actually depicts an old wood fence with boards about six and a half feet high with a knothole in it the right height and size for Huckleberry Finn. Pot-bellied Hennessy catches an undersized, runty Joe at the knothole and tells him he should "never stand on the outside looking in, kid. Come with me." Joe, scared, says "I wasn't doing anything wrong," and is led to (presumably) Charley Graham's office. Graham tells Joe he knows he didn't do anything wrong and that "I've seen you play and I think we can use you. How about third base?" Then he, Joe, and Hennessy head for the Seal's dugout as Joe says (well he might) "What a break!"

The ever-imaginative Gene Schoor fleshed out the basic plot of this interlude in three works with dialogue detailing what might have been said during the scene. In *The Thrilling Story of Joe DiMaggio* (1950) Graham asks "the shy boy" if he "can play like your brother Vince?" and Hennessy interrupts with "This kid is going to make the big leagues. . . . I've seen him play sand-lot ball . . . He's got the stuff." In two later books, (1956, 1980) Schoor wrote dialogue suggesting that Graham and Hennessy had previously discussed DiMaggio "around the office here a couple of times." In all probability, since California was becoming an increasingly fertile location for the production of professional baseball players, and since San Francisco had two minor league teams looking for players, the young hero would have been well known in local baseball circles. In his 1936 *Collier's* article Quentin Reynolds did not mention the jailhouse line so popular among later writers, but simply has Hennessy say "Listen, kid . . . I'll get you into the ballpark so you can see the games. In fact, I'll fix it so you can work out mornings with the team." Dan Daniel, one of DiMaggio's first and closest New York writer friends, quotes DiMaggio in his 1950 booklet on him, to the effect that even before he went to the ballpark to seek brother Vince's opinion on the Missions's offer, "I was aiming at the Seals." Daniel also states that before seeing DiMaggio at the Seals's ballpark, Hennessy had watched the young player "in a few sandlot games." So the future hero's discovery was not quite so miraculous as legend explains. In fact, Vince DiMaggio has stated that "No, Spike Hennessy did not discover Joe at the knothole."[6]

What was perhaps more amazing is that DiMaggio apparently was not paid for his brief first season in minor-league play, though three games from the end of the campaign he broke into the lineup. Augie Galan, later an excellent clutch hitter for a number of National League teams, was the Seals's regular shortstop. He wanted to leave the team a few days early to travel to Honolulu with "Prince" Henry Oana, an outfielder (and later, a pitcher). Since the Seals were in sixth place and out of pennant contention, manager Caveney agreed with Galan's request. The usual version of the story states that Caveney then asked "Who's going to play shortstop Saturday and in Sunday's doubleheader?" According to DiMaggio himself in *Lucky to Be a Yankee*, "Vince spoke right up. 'My kid brother can play short,' he said." DiMaggio hit a triple his first at-bat—triples were to become good omens to him—and though he did not field well and had trouble with the throw to first, his three-game average of .222 was enough to confirm the Seals' opinion that he was worth an extended tryout next season. And though he began 1933 battling other rookies for a place on the team, he became by the end of the year, and for the remainder of his playing days, a virtually unparalleled star in exploit and reputation.

Money has always been a mark of DiMaggio's worth to his teams, an element of his career that over the years has brought him extra attention, not all of it positive. In 1933 his contract was either for $225.00 or $250.00 a month, both considerably more than the $125.00 ordinarily offered Seals rookies. In *Lucky to Be a Yankee* DiMaggio gave the smaller figure, but in 1950 he told Dan Daniel "I refused the customary $125 and finally won a $250-a-month contract for myself." Surprisingly, for a shy rookie DiMaggio was a hard bargainer his early years, but he knew his value, and was apparently toughened in salary talks by his brother Tom who had considerable experience in wage disputes in the fishing industry. Though often underpaid by modern standards, and according to the exploitive and tight-fisted practices of his day's management, he was always relativly well rewarded for his skills.

He started the season on the bench in 1933. After several weeks Ike Caveney apparently uttered other words that sound now as though they were written by some particularly prescient scriptwriter. Ed Stewart, another rookie, was not hitting well and Caveney said something unmomentous like " 'Go out to right field, Joe' " (*Lucky*) or " 'Go up there, DiMaggio' " (Reynolds, 1936). Gene Schoor (1956) underscored the moment's portent by doubling the lines assiged Caveney. " 'Hey, DiMaggio. Get in and pinch-hit for Stewart,' " Caveney yells, but what he says does not "penetrate for a moment." DiMaggio continues to sit on the bench. " 'DiMaggio!' Caveney called sharply. 'Get up there and hit, will ya! You're holding up the game.' " Joe walks, then to his surprise is told to replace Stewart in the unfamiliar position of right field. Another part of the story which evolved was that he regretted taking his older brother Vince's rightful place. Dan Daniel reported that "Joe's superseding his brother Vince on the Seals still is a most poignant memory for the Clipper." But Vince was disabled with a sore arm when Joe began playing daily with the Seals, and though in truth Vince would be traded away before the season's end, Joe could not have realistically blamed himself for what would always be for Vince an erratic career whose highs and lows resulted from his own mixed abilities and not Joe's shining talent.

An amazing aspect of DiMaggio's career was the exceptionally high level at which he operated from the very start. With the exception of his truncated year's-end performance in 1932 he hit his peak very quickly and stayed there, as a hitter first and then as a fielder, thrower, base-runner, and finally as a team leader. Except for minor slumps and a few scattered days of blunders in the field, he maintained that peak until he left baseball for three years during World War II. Very soon after he began playing daily his exceptional skills became quite clear. Fans went crazy for him, and of course his father was now won over to see the value of Joe's formerly worthless activity by the adulation and money his son received. Papa DiMaggio, as the now retired immigrant fisherman was often called by sportswriters who glorified the DiMaggio family's tightly-knit old-country clannishness, started to learn at least enough English to revel in his son's triumphs in the newspapers. Vince was the first to bring money home, but Joe brought more, and brought it more steadily since he played more steadily. Joe was OK—his Americanization was no disaster. Dan Daniel reported Pop DiMaggio saying "Smart boys, stepping out on their own. Guess they knew what they were doing. I always said my boy Joe had wonderful shoulders. He could pull up a net when he wanted to. Now they tell me he pulls in people at the ballparks to see him hit a little ball over a fence. A great country this is." Mama DiMaggio could also bask warmly now in her beloved son's popular achievements.

He played three full seasons with the Seals, and by the time he left them for the New York Yankees he was perhaps the best known player in minor-league baseball. Playing in right field, he hit .340 in 1933, with 28 home runs, 45 doubles, thirteen triples, and perhaps most impressive because it suggests the kind of clutch hitter he was, 169 runs batted in. He riveted special attention to himself almost from the start by launching a hitting streak early in the season which, after about twenty games, fans and sportswriters watched with mixed delight and apprehension. Described as late as 1939 in a *Life* magazine cover story as "a tall, thin Italian youth equipped with slick black hair, shoe-button eyes, squirrel teeth and a receding chin," and by his own admission not even knowing what a "quote" was (he thought perhaps it was a drink), he ended by hitting in 61 consecutive games and greatly increasing attendance wherever he played. Gene Schoor and others have credited him with lifting the Depression-wracked Pacific Coast League from the verge of collapse. Whether this is so or not, obviously this was a heady time for the eighteen-year-old boy. His behavior remained what it had always been, quiet and reserved except among his very closest intimates, of whom there were few. He remained within himself, looking out and observing, learning about the exciting but very different and high-pressured world around him. When major leaguers such as fellow San Franciscan Joe Cronin (eight years his senior) came by and spoke to the Seals's rookies about how to live properly in the big leagues, he listened intently, for he knew he was just an eighteen-year-old kid who did not know how to act. In *The Hot Stove League*, Lee Allen tells of the trouble newspapers had spelling DiMaggio's name, for it would be printed that year as Demaggio, and De Maggio, even in the *Sporting News* ("Baseball's Bible"). But what the nationally distributed *News* said May 25, 1933, about the young star was quite accurate. "This hard-hitting kid seems to have no weakness at the plate, and in addition to his prowess with the bat he knows how to play the outfield much better than some experienced flychasers." Not until August 5, 1933, however, did they spell his name correctly.[7]

The life of a hero contains many often told stories whose frequency of repetition suggests the hold they have for whatever reason over teller or told. During DiMaggio's minor-league streak, as in his later even more impressive major-league streak, several incidents occurred that provided the pattern for embroidered narratives in later years. One such incident happened in the 43rd game of the streak when DiMaggio faced ex-Yankee Tom Sheehan, known as "a bush league Grover Alexander" because of his cunning as a pitcher. Sheehan's team, the Hollywood Stars, was far ahead and with the count no strikes and two balls on DiMaggio, Sheehan and his catcher Johnny Bassler debated what to do. A walk would bring San Francisco fans screaming to their feet. A fastball laid down the center would offend Sheehan's professionalism. Eventually Sheehan decided to throw his best pitch, which DiMaggio whacked for a double. As Bill Corum told the tale (in Robinson, 1941) before DiMaggio used it in his 1946 autobiography, Sheehan then stopped the game and walked to DiMaggio at second base. "Son," he said, "you hit my curve ball when I didn't want you to. A fellow who can do that belongs in the big leagues": an augury delivered by a wise old man.

So DiMaggio's first full year as a professional player was a spectacular success. He was an acknowledged star on his team, suddenly a recognized citizen of the community. His fame was particularly gratifying to his many fellow Italian-American San Franciscans—Mayor Angelo Rossi himself presented him with a watch at the Seals's field commemorating his 61-game hitting streak. Joe's father was ecstatic. Gene Schoor wrote (1956) the old man's quaint dialogue: "Hey, Mama, Giuseppe got two hits today. But he no hit a home run. Wat's the matter with that boy?"

As he would later when he became a Yankee, DiMaggio followed his exceptional rookie year with another high performance season in 1934, playing in fewer games (101 to 187 in 1933) because of an injury, but still hitting .341, with eighteen doubles, six triples, twelve home runs, and 69 runs batted in. The injury introduces another strand of the fabric that ultimately became the DiMaggio legend, another favorite sequence in the hero's epic narrative. Still the family boy, he was riding in a crowded jitney to his sister's house for dinner after a Sunday doubleheader. His left foot possibly fell asleep, and when he stepped to the street he went down as though shot, in terrible pain. It would be a shot (in De Gregorio, 1981, DiMaggio says his knee "popped like a pistol") heard round the baseball world, for by this time all the major-league teams had heard plenty about him and would have wanted to purchase his contract from Charlie Graham. DiMaggio had the leg treated, but poorly, and he continued to have trouble with it until finally he had to be benched for it to improve. The hurt leg made DiMaggio's future questionable, for in baseball few returned intact or unimpaired from such a wound. Injuries and wounds would become a staple of DiMaggio's story, as would also (until the very end) the overcoming of injuries. As the famous umpire Jocko Conlon wrote in his autobiography *Jocko*, "Once you had a bad leg, it was nearly impossible to get a major-league club to take a chance on you. The only one I can remember back then who did get a chance was Joe DiMaggio."[8]

While others questioned DiMaggio's fate at this critical and dark point in his career, the New York Yankees, (in his legend obviously) the one team in the world he was destined for, remained firm in their belief in his promising future. As with other minor strains connected to the DiMaggio story, this theme has a number of variants. In his autobiography Yankee president Ed Barrow claimed that the decision to purchase DiMaggio was concluded at a minor-league meeting held in the fall of 1934, in the inauspicious-sounding town of French Lick, Indiana (later famous as the hometown of Larry Bird). "I made the decision to gamble on DiMaggio," Barrow claimed. "Joe Devine had been watching DiMaggio right along. He said he was outstanding. I had dispatched [Bill] Essick to look over DiMaggio also. Essick had poked around on his own. . . . 'I think he's worth a chance,' I said, and on Essick's recommendation we bought him for $25,000. I consider that the best deal the Yankees ever made." In *Lucky to Be a Yankee* DiMaggio also credits Essick (who he told Red Smith (1979) lived across the street from the family for several years) with maintaining faith in his ability to come back from the injury: "That I got to the Yankees at all, or even stayed in baseball, was due to the persistency of Essick," DiMaggio said. Dan Daniel claimed that the knee injury decreased DiMaggio's "value in the open market by something like $100,000" and "had scared 15 big league clubs away from him," something of an overstatement since Joe Cronin, then player-manager for the Boston Red Sox, has stated that he would have advised his team to buy DiMaggio if the Yankees hadn't. Still, the injury was serious and for a time crippling, and represented a trial for the young player to overcome and something for his fans to worry about and agonize over. The Yankees must have had more than passing confidence that his body was sound when, after numerous medical tests, they signed DiMaggio, because the price paid was substantial—the $25,000 Barrow mentioned, plus five ballplayers for Charley Graham, who needed them: outfielder Ted Norbert, first baseman Les Powers, infielder Ed Farrell, and pitchers Jim Densmore and Floyd Newkirk. Powers, Farrell, and Newkirk were good enough to play at least briefly in the majors. Dan Daniel (1950) said that Farrell refused to report to San Francisco, and so the Yankees had to pay an extra $5,000 to compensate Graham. Finally, either because Graham needed his services or the Yankees felt he would benefit from another season's polishing or both, DiMaggio was to remain at San Francisco an extra season. Yankee fans and the New York reporters who were already anxious to observe the gifted rookie in action would have to wait—an experience they would become familiar with during DiMaggio's major league career.

De Gregorio reports that Essick told Barrow in 1934 to "Buy DiMaggio. . . . I think you can get him cheap. They're all laughing at me, but I know I'm right." If "they" laughed, they must have stoppped soon after the 1935 season began. According to Gene Schoor, (1956) Tom DiMaggio again haggled with Graham over Joe's 1935 salary but the two finally came to acceptable terms, and Joe performed better than ever at bat, on the basepaths, and in the field. He lost the League batting title by less than a percentage point, hitting .398 with 49 doubles, eighteen triples, and 34 home runs in 172 games. He also stole 24 bases in 25 attempts. The *Sporting News* voted him the league's Most Valuable Player. If ever a player seemed ready for the big time, it was he. The Seals' manager in 1935, great hitter Lefty O'Doul, had given DiMaggio hints to improve upon his already high ability at the plate, and DiMaggio demonstrated his skill under all kinds of conditions, against all kinds of pitchers including major leaguers and occasionally touring black stars such as Satchel Paige (against whom DiMaggio did as well as most, which meant not very: a scratch single in five tries according to his own testimony recorded in *Great Negro Stars*). He seemed ready for the Yankees and the Yankees seemed ready for him.

Though many aspects of baseball seem reassuringly changeless, the game has been modified in numerous ways since 1936, a time before expansion, night games, and television. The players were far fewer and were sold from club to club less often, the teams seemed more permanent, the features of the game were easier to focus upon; thus the drama of the daily confrontations was more basic with greater purity of outline. Less was known about the teams as business institutions and less about the players as human beings who worked for a living. To paint the image of baseball and its participants at that time you would need only a few strong colors (excluding, notably enough, brown). This was the baseball world into which DiMaggio fit. Part of his significance as a player is that he was one of the few stars to bridge this older time of baseball and play into the new era.

Since Babe Ruth joined the New York Yankees in 1920, they were the most successful and consistently well-publicized team in professional baseball. During the Ruth years (1920-1934), they finished first seven times, second six times, and third twice. They were World Series champions four times. In 1923 they finished sixteen games in front, in 1927 nineteen games, and in 1932, thirteen games. Ruth was the game's dominant player during his career, but he was supported by platoons of pitchers and batters on the Yankees who were famous for their own skills, such as the pitcher Herb Pennock, a great outfielder Bob Meusal, and the incomparable Lou Gehrig. With the exception of the movie business located in Hollywood, New York was also the entertainment and communications center of the country: vaudeville, radio, and journalism found their capitals in New York City. Then, even more than now, if you could make it there you'd make it anywhere. In that sense, DiMaggio was indeed lucky to be a Yankee, just as he had been lucky to play for his only other professional team in San Francisco, a smaller but still glamorous center of cultural life on the Pacific side of the country, heavily populated with Italian-Americans. Unlike Ruth and nearly all of the other early stars of baseball, DiMaggio was anxiously awaited when he arrived in the majors. His minor-league career had been auspicious and his exploits had been reported by a far more extensive, well-developed New York and national press than had existed when players such as Willie Keeler, Walter Johnson, or Babe Ruth began performing in the big time. From 1933 on, he had no seasons of obscurity.

DiMaggio's first year with the Yankees can only be described as a spectacular success. A great performance was expected of him as it often is from exceptionally promising rookies, who in most instances do not fulfill these high expectations. DiMaggio did. With the Yankees pennantless since 1932 and Ruth-less since 1934, (though ruthless for many years previous to that) the New York writers were like thirsty men in a bar who found DiMaggio to be cold beer for their parched gullets. Establishing himself almost immediately as a star on a star-filled team, DiMaggio was further constructed into an evolving legend from the very beginning of his arrival into the Yankee training camp in St. Petersburg. In this development of his myth, the 1936 season would emphasize certain elements that became refined or magnified to fit into his continuing story in later years. Chief among these were of course his superb all-around ability, his shyness and taciturnity, and his belonging to a large, Italian-American family. Perceived by the Yankee public as the potential successor to Babe Ruth, partly because he was quite consciously seen in that light by Yankee management and portrayed in that mold by New York sportswriters, DiMaggio, like Ruth, was to become a symbol of the athlete as winner, the player who made the difference, and brought victory to his team. Almost totally unlike the flamboyant, irresponsible bad boy Ruth (in legend if not in fact an orphan), DiMaggio would share with him the aura of the victor. A hero of the 1920s, Ruth embodied the image of the winner who pulled his team ahead through consummate and unparalleled individual power, as Benjamin Radar (1983) has suggested.

DiMaggio was highly skilled, but not an overwhelming juggernaut like Ruth. Instead, DiMaggio, even during his first year, would become known as the team player, a more spectacular Lou Gehrig. Completing the picture of DiMaggio that became etched in baseball spectators' minds that first year was what might be called his rookieness, which helped to endear him to the Yankee public and defused possible criticism of what later would be termed his aloofness or sulkiness. Further, his strong early image as a callow rookie offered a deep contrast to his later stature as an enduring veteran.

Even before he joined the Yankees, DiMaggio revealed again his, or brother Tom's, shrewd and hard-headed desire to obtain top money for his talent. As the *New York Times* reported on February 2, 1936, "Joe DiMaggio, young San Francisco Seals' outfielder, returned his unsigned contract to the Yankees today, because the contract failed to specify the usual 25 percent increase over the sum paid by the Coast League Club. He probably will demand $8,000 for his first season with the Yanks." Then on February 13 in the same paper came the news that "DiMaggio, Outfield Recruit, Wires Acceptance of Terms to Yankees. Coast Star Ends Threat of Holdout for Sum Said to be 8,000." Years later, a publicty handout prepared by the Yankees listed his first salary as $7,500 and in *Lucky to Be a Yankee* DiMaggio claimed it was $8,500. Whichever amount is correct, clearly DiMaggio was not joining the Yankee fold with his vision completely bedazzled by Yankee luster.

DiMaggio drove to the Yankee training camp in St. Petersburg with two other San Francisco Italian-Americans on the roster, second baseman Tony Lazzeri and shortstop Frank Crosetti. Steven Reiss in *Touching Base* (1980) has pointed out that the 1930s was the great blossoming time for Italian-Americans in baseball. Up to 1906 their participation in professional baseball was statistically unrecordable. By 1920 only 2 percent of the major leaguers were of Italian-American descent, but by 1941 the proportion had increased fourfold. Newspapers blatantly used colloquial language to identify them. Lazzeri was "Poosh'em up, Tony." Vince DiMaggio was early called the "Walloping Wop."[9] The trip Lazzeri, Crosetti, and DiMaggio took has also become one of the minor anecdotes writers love to repeat in the DiMaggio legend, where it becomes a journey emphasizing the young hero's rawness and at the same time his quiet self-assuredness. Only after the trip had begun—and in 1936 it would have been, while no pioneer's trek, still a grueling experience sometimes—did Lazzeri and Crosetti learn that DiMaggio could not share the driving with them, since he did not know how to drive. In *Lucky to Be a Yankee* DiMaggio relates their mock-anguish over his inexperience. But DiMaggio also says that he otherwise got along fine with the two big leaguers, and figured that he would have "no trouble" gaining the acceptance of the other Yankees. In Gene Schoor's (1956) account of the trip, Lazzeri like the hero's loyal *comes* in legend, prepared DiMaggio for his future test with the Yankees by offering him the wise advice to remain modest and quiet during his apprenticeship period.

According to Ed Barrow, the Yankee's business manager at the time, DiMaggio received similar advice from San Francisco sportswriter Tommy Laird, whom Barrow called the "most rabid and vociferous of the DiMaggio boosters" responsible for much of the "ballyhoo" about the Yankee's "New Era" star. DiMaggio probably would have naturally behaved in the ways that mentors like Lazzeri and Laird suggested—not to brag and to keep his mouth shut around the New York writers—but their instructions also reveal the conscious manipulation of behavior and therefore of image that DiMaggio was subjected to, and perhaps more importantly, accepted early in his career. Even DiMaggio's entrance at the camp was affected by this manipulation, for though his arrival was eagerly awaited by the New York writers who naturally anticipated ample opportunity for fresh copy (and thereby greater justification for their Florida holiday), Barrow says the threesome quite consciously had a leisurely dinner in one of nearby Tampa's Spanish restaurants "so they would get to training camp late, to miss reporters." Knowingly or not, the players were withholding the hook which was soon to dangle before and be snapped at by the copy-hungry writers. When the reporters finally caught their quarry the next day, according to Barrow, at first 'they didn't know whether they liked the new rookie or not," so reserved was he in his manner.[10] At first, most came to attribute the distance he tried to place between himself and them to his shyness and newness to the big time, behavior actually flattering to the writers since it would place them in the role of powerful inhabitants of a great world. They could sympathize and perhaps even take pleasure in his shyness (which he once said he thought "developed when his parents used to tease him about his mistakes in speaking Italian as a youngster; rather than risk the teasing, he kept quiet").[11] Later, some would attack him for being cold and aloof.

Most of the copy sent from DiMaggio's first Yankee training camp shows that the metropolitan reporters were at least receptive if not totally charmed by his personality and, more importantly at this stage of his career, highly impressed by his abilities. He had a sensational spring training, completely fulfilling the advance publicity about him. Even before the training games began, the *New York Times* reported on March 3, 1936, "The eyes of the fans were riveted on the sparkling Joe DiMaggio, California's latest gift to the big leagues. He responded with a couple of drives into left field which disappeared out of sight among the wavering palms.'' On March 4, the *Times* described holdout pitcher Red Ruffing giving ''DiMaggio his undivided attention when the latter was batting. Like everybody else, the pitcher was impressed.'' Already DiMaggio was demonstrating the full range of his talent and not just his hitting skill. The *Times* headlined on March 6 that ''DiMaggio Shows Speed Afoot and Powerful Throwing.'' The accompanying article focused attention on manager Joe McCarthy's ''unconcealed admiration, for the swiftness of his young star in pursuit of balls, and the power of his arm in returning them to the infield.'' For nearly every day of his training, the *Times* and other New York papers reported DiMaggio's exploits and conjectures about where he would play—possibly in centerfield but more likely (March 15) in left because that was the ''easiest'' outfield position in Yankee Stadium. That he would play somewhere was a foregone conclusion: ''DiMaggio Assured of Outfield Berth With Yankees, McCarthy Announces'' (March 15).

He was already beginning to attract the sort of printed chatter ordinarily associated only with celebrities. A letter to the March 21 *Times* registered the ''distress'' one of DiMaggio's New York Italian-American fans experienced hearing the rookie's name pronounced incorrectly over the radio. The editor's soberly facetious reply was that Joe himself said ''Dee-Mah-jee-o'' was correct. The pronunciation controversy, pointless in itself but revealing the newly and quickly won status of the ballplayer and reflective of his Italian following, continued in the March 28 edition, with an arch exchange of letters containing arcane references to items such as early editions of Tennyson's ''The Daisy'' used as corroborating evidence. To terminate the debate, a *Times* editor used the authority of the paper's sports editor, the erudite John Kieran, who would achieve celebrity status himself two years later as a performer on the popular ''Information Please!'' radio show. In a personal interview DiMaggio told Kieran that ''De-Mah-joe'' was correct. Thus the *Times* settled the argument conclusively twice with two authoritative and conflicting pronouncements delivered but one week apart.

Mostly, however, the *Times* reported DiMaggio's exploits at bat and on the field, and by itself could have provided ample headlines and texts for one of those montages so popular among biographical filmmakers who fill the screen with swirling newspapers extolling a hero's triumphs. March 18: ''DiMaggio Has Great Day. His Four Safeties Include a Triple in First Interclub Game.'' March 20: ''DiMaggio's Heavy Hitting Helps Yanks. . . ,'' ''Yanks Crush Reds as DiMaggio Stars.'' The ''Italian lad'' was ''glittering'' in the field, ''a glutton for work,'' ''irrepressible'' as he was ''once again . . . in the limelight,'' ''brilliant,'' and ''a shining light.''

While DiMaggio never pleased all the New York or out-of-town writers, he seems to have been fortunate in establishing and maintaining excellent relations with many of the best and most influential of them. Whether this is completely because of qualities inherent in him that the best writers have almost invariably recognized, or because with them he forced himself to overcome his reserved or icy manner, would be a complicated matter to untangle. Throughout his career he would inspire deep loyalty from some of the finest sportswriters, from Jimmy Cannon for example, to Red Smith and Robert Lipsyte. At the same time, some of the lesser known writers have described him [to the author] in terms of a kind of dead zone they have encountered who was simply blank to them. Their response could be caused by their inordinate and excessively intrusive demands upon him or by his lack of interest in them. One of the most respected sportswriters who recognized DiMaggio's greatness early, and who would establish a mutually satisfying friendship with him (they both liked each other and could benefit professionally from their relationship) was Dan Daniel of the New York *World Telegram and Sun*. Daniel seems to have been a transitional kind of sportswriter; less of a personality than some of the greats of the 1920s such as Grantland Rice, less of a pundit, too, less of a phrase-maker, less colorful and idiosyncratic, but probably more knowledgeable. He was an excellent, hard-working sports journalist who wrote good, steady, but not particularly memorable prose. He eventually wrote a very informative pamphlet on DiMaggio and as an official scorer during DiMaggio's 56-game hitting streak, called a debatable play in DiMaggio's favor and was respected enough that no one loudly disputed his decision. Daniel is typical of the kind of writer who somehow penetrated DiMaggio's defenses or who was permitted to get close to the star, and who liked what he saw close up, in terms of both talent and character.

From the start of DiMaggio's training, Daniel praised him and helped set forth an image of him as a worthy Italian-American successor to Babe Ruth. On March 2, 1936, his story about the Yanks was headlined "DiMaggio Steals Show as Yankees Launch Training. Coast Rookie Has Style of Joe Jackson. Explains Preference for Right Field Though Slated for Left." Daniel's opening remarks stressed what would become familiar elements of the rookie's image, his humble Italian-American origins, his innocence, and his preeminent skill. "Joe DiMaggio, from the spaghetti society of romantic San Francisco, who never has seen New York, but may be destined for a vital role in its baseball fortunes, today stole the show as the Yankees started their twelfth consecutive training season in St. Petersburg." Despite Joe McCarthy's ostensible attempts to mute specu- lation about "Giuseppe," as Daniel familiarly referred to the rookie, "in the public mind, DiMaggio seems to be rated the successor to Babe Ruth." Throughout spring training, Daniel and the *World Telegram and Sun* continued to follow DiMaggio's impressive progress in picture and text.

One of the subjects Daniel often referred to was DiMaggio's destined position. Today, of course, DiMaggio seems inevitably fated for center field. In 1936 the matter was not so certain. On March 2 Daniel wrote that Joe would like to play right field, where he said he played in San Francisco "until the last month of the season, when I shifted to center." On March 4 he reported however that "McCarthy Now Says DiMaggio's Place in Outfield Unsettled." His story explained that "During the winter Marse Joe kept reiterating his intention to send DiMaggio to left, with Ben Chapman in center and George Selkirk battling" to play right field. Now, McCarthy said he wanted to wait and watch "before talking about Giuseppe's ultimate post." Yankee plans for DiMaggio's position were undoubtedly tied to their feelings about the turbulent Chapman, who had played center field for them in 1935, and who had never batted lower than .289 since his arrival in 1930. Chapman was a holdout during spring training, and DiMaggio would have been a handy club for the Yankee management to use to bang down his salary demands. Furthermore, Chapman was far from the most popular player with management, always a prickly individual and moreover, to Ed Barrow's displeasure, a Southerner. Barrow held an animus against Southern players, whom he considered hot-tempered and self-defeating.[12] On March 10 Daniel wrote that "Chapman Awaits Call from McCarthy" (whose only public comment was that Chapman should sign at the offered terms) and that McCarthy had ordered DiMaggio "to concentrate on center field. Apparently it is Marse Joe's plan to open the exhibition season against the Braves on Saturday with Giuseppe in Ben's old berth."

Daniel continued throughout the training period to provide copy that inspired headline writers at the *Sun* to produce those big, bold letters of praise that seem created for the scrapbooks of idol-worshippers. The words for March 20 were "DIMAGGIO BIG CAMP LURE. SENSATIONAL RECRUIT GIVING YANKEES NEW POWER AT BAT AND BOX OFFICE." Daniel's accompanying text could also have supplied lines for a cinematic montage of DiMaggio's life, now being reported nationally, day by day, game by game, and practically swing by swing: "Never before in the history of the Yankees has a recruit fresh from the mines [minors] created the furor which DiMaggio has stirred up."

DiMaggio's place in Yankee history was clearly planned beforehand—he was to succeed Babe Ruth, their former "Sultan of Swat." Of course such a plan is not easy to carry out. Earlier in the century when heavyweight champion Jim Jeffries retired and eventually was replaced by the supremely confident, arrogant (to white audiences) Jack Johnson, prizefighting's boondocks were avidly reconnoitered to find the "great white hope" who would restore the king's crown to white control, but none was found while Johnson was in his prime. Occasionally in sport, new champions are sought out and miraculously found to replace the old. DiMaggio was one of these. He would ultimately replace—or come close to replacing—the greatest Yankee in history. The spotlight was already on him when he stepped on the stage, his star turn expectantly awaited, and he did not disappoint his audience. In some ways this is even more surprising than the overnight success of an unknown. In Yankee history, the pattern would be repeated when Mickey Mantle arrived as a star following DiMaggio's departure.

New York's *Daily News*, then a favorite tabloid for the city's lower middle-class and for all readers with a taste for scandal or lowbrow politics and culture, provided its audience with clear evidence of DiMaggio's place in the Yankee succession. An article appearing on March 3, 1936, told about the "record crowd of popeyed citizens" who turned out to gawk at "all but seven members of the entire Yankee squad" at St. Petersburg, of whom "the most popular by far was the $75,000 [sic] rookie Joe DiMaggio," who at this stage of his career wore the number "18 on his back." The same issue featured an interview with Ruth titled "Yanks Won't Win!" which summed up Ruth's feelings about his old team's pennant chances. Ruth, released by the Yankees in 1934 without having been offered the managerial position he sometimes seemed to crave (though he appeared temperamentally unsuited for it), had played 28 games in 1935 for the Boston Braves. He also occupied a murky coaching position that seemed to suggest that he might one day become manager, but that actually made his connection to the team tenuous except as a part-time player. He hit a feeble .181 including six home runs, three of them on one day, a glorious remembrance of things past. In 1936 he was at liberty and the picture accompanying his interview showed him golfing in Florida, where the active Yankee players were preparing for their season. His essentially sympathetic remarks printed in the paper revealed a veiled sense of reservation, if not quite rancor, toward the team he had led to so many championships.

"Babe Ruth," the interviewer began, "predicted the Yankees out of the pennant although he said it busted up his big washtub of a heart just thinking about it. . . . He sized up Joe DiMaggio, the Italian rookie billed as 'the Second Babe Ruth' by saying he honestly hopes the kid has a great season." But, Ruth commented, "He must first show something in the Stadium. Remember that left field is plenty tough on his type of hitter. He'll be nervous and pressing." Ruth then added accurately, though somewhat uncharitably enough, "Only one out of a 100 makes good and they all look like $1,000,000 under a palm tree." Between golf swings he continued to talk about his putative replacement. "It's the bunk," he grunted, "about Lou Gehrig needing someone to help lift the burden so he can really hit. A good hitter will hit on a winning or losing club and Gehrig's all of that." The interview (and one must always allow for reporter's license: Ruth's comments might have been distorted) ended ambivalently, both criticizing DiMaggio and demonstrating awareness of his sensitive predicament. Referring to DiMaggio's "habit this morning of carrying his weight on his right leg when belting a ball," Ruth commented "Doesn't sound so hot, but give the kid a chance." Then he grinned and said "Those grandstand critics are a pain."

DiMaggio was presented to readers almost as a center of indifference amid all the publicity about him. The *Daily News*, for example, several times during spring training referred to him as "the dead-pan Californian" with a "free and easy swing," or "Dead Pan Joe . . . wielding a 36-inch telephone pole" who "smacked half a dozen into the wind."[13] So his image was set forth as a supremely gifted, naturally graceful, quiet competitor—not a brash rookie.

Wire service reports also sent news around the country of DiMaggio's talent and the high expectations the Yankees had for him—expectations that he was fulfilling at least in spring training. The shyness that seemed so apparent and painful to him—Gene Schoor (1956) reports him saying of his relation to sportswriters at the time "I couldn't seem to get friendly with them. Every time they'd want to talk to me, I'd kind of freeze up"—was greatly overshadowed by the skill with which he played. Perhaps considering the affable Ruth's place in the hearts of most of the writers, shyness was the best trait the rookie could have exhibited so as not to seem an upstart. In the reams of copy they wrote about him, it is clear the writers accepted DiMaggio, and moreover, in the writers' reports, so did his teammates. On March 8, for example, Associated Press writer Eddie Brietz reported that "the most talked about baseball rookie since Dizzy Dean blew in from Houston has been voted 'all right' by his teammates on the New York Yankees." Far from hazing Joe or cold-shouldering him, the regulars were reportedly seeking him out and introducing themselves to him. In later accounts the superb veteran pitcher Red Ruffing is sometimes depicted as needling DiMaggio, but in this early wire service report he is simply quoted as asking pleasantly enough "where is this DiMaggio?" By March 16, United Services writer Sid Mercer was already quoting Joe McCarthy's prediction that the Yankee prospects were good for 1936, and himself added, "and we haven't even mentioned Joe DiMaggio."

DiMaggio was hitting over .600 and fielding and throwing brilliantly when he was injured. Tripling his first time up (his good omen), he performed at an almost incredibly high level until benched by the injury, foreshadowing others, that would keep him from the lineup opening day. When "an error by the well-nigh perfect Mr. Joseph DiMaggio let in Boston's only runs in the second inning," the March 22 *New York Times* reported that "the amazement of the onlookers and the Yankee bench was measured accordingly." On March 23 however, the *Times* indicated that DiMaggio was "Out With Blistered Foot," and that his services would be lost "from three to ten days." While playing the Braves, DiMaggio had injured his left foot when third baseman Joe Coscart fell onto it. The inexperienced player kept the foot under a healing diathermy machine for too long and the resultant burn would heal slowly. Strangely enough this could be viewed, because of the publicity it engendered and the expectations it whetted, as a fortunate occurrence, for it temporarily removed DiMaggio from play at the peak of his performance, when he was at a level he could not have sustained. Though it seemed impossible, the Yankee fans' appetite for his reappearance increased. Daily articles and notes appeared in the newspapers chronicling DiMaggio's progress, often teasing with hopes of an early return, then dashing those hopes. On April 1 the *Times* stated that he "will not likely be seen in any of the road exhibitions," though on April 2 he was reported "in uniform and" working out "lightly in batting practice . . . the object of keen interest from [Ben] Chapman, whose position he menaces." Chapman finally signed his contract April 4, but by then there was probably other writing about him on the Yankee wall: he would shortly be traded. On April 11, though DiMaggio was still not playing, the *Times* reported his number had been changed from 18 to 9 on the team scorecard, and on April 12th and 14th, Manager Joe McCarthy and John Kieran were stating that the Yankees' pennant chances were greatly improved by the still wounded athlete.

All this publicity fed like a stream the dam of interest in the Yankee's prize rookie. Though naturally disappointed that they could not get their potential star immediately into action, Yankee management was aware of the force of publicity building up. In his autobiography, Ed Barrow notes after a section discussing Babe Ruth's departure, that the ballyhoo connected with DiMaggio, the "foremost among the 'new Yankees,'" helped introduce the team's "New Era." Barrow was annoyed that DiMaggio missed opening day "because a tremendous public interest had been built up in him and I wanted to cash in on it at the gate."[14] On April 29 the *Times* reported that "Joe DiMaggio, cured of his left foot complaint, will return to action as soon as Manager McCarthy considers him ready for play." On May 2 fans were informed the "Coast Italian" would "get into action tomorrow . . . in left field." Finally, on May 4, the *Times* reported the previous day's game with the St. Louis Browns. The sports page carried a big picutre of "DiMaggio of Yankees Driving Out Triple in the Sixth Inning," and headlines declared that "Joe Plays Brilliantly in His Big League Debut." On May 6 the *Times* described another Yankee victory over the Browns the previous day, when "DiMaggio was the attraction for 8,000 persons, including several thousand schoolboys." He was still in left field, but soon replaced Ben Chapman, who was traded to the Washington Senators. Not all the details of his image were fixed yet. He wore the number nine for the season, not the five he would make famous; he batted third, not fourth; the unmodified contours of his face, the nose that reminded Dan Daniel and others of Cyrano de Bergerac's, and the protruding, sharp-looking front teeth still made him look like a homely kid and not the handsome, distinguished man later fans would recollect. But his skills were all in place.

In 1936 he played in 138 games. He collected 206 hits, of which 44 were doubles, fifteen were triples (he tied for the league lead with teammate Red

Rolfe and Cleveland's Earl Averill), and 29 were home runs (fourth after Lou Gehrig's 49). He hit .323, with 125 runs batted in. DiMaggio's only memorable flop of 1936 came in his first All-Star game, where he failed to hit in five at-bats, several times with men on base (it was a tight game which was finally won by the National League 4-3). In the first inning he hit into a double play against Dizzy Dean, and in the ninth with the tying run on second he popped up to second. In the field he misplayed one line drive that went for a triple, and made an error permitting Billy Herman to advance to second base, from which he ultimately scored the game's winning run.

That was on July 7. By July 13, however, he was on the cover of *Time* magazine, a rare bit of publicity for any baseball player, even rarer for a rookie. He was a favorite with the spectators, especially Italian-American fans, and the coolness which some writers later complained about did not seem at this time to affect his high popularity. A controversy about DiMaggio sparked by one of John Kieran's columns, in the September 12 *New York Times*, underscored DiMaggio's excellence as a first-year player: it centered on the issue of whether DiMaggio would become a truly great star over the years. The editor of the letters column in which the controversy was carried on remarked "this DiMaggio debate must have been instigated by the Post Office Department or the pen and ink manufacturers. The mail vote is heavy." Jimmy Cannon, who partly through his strong personality and partly because of the power and sensitivity of his literary style became one of the most influential of the New York sports reporters, remembered DiMaggio that first year as did many of the writers who knew him: "On the first road trip he took around the league, he was a quiet kid but friendly. There were some who insisted he was inaccessible then and suspicious. But I found him easy to be with. . . . We had a lot of laughs that first season although Joe went to bed early on the road."[15] Reports of DiMaggio's inaccessibility typically are related second hand by writers other than those involved, or reported by writers who did not know him those first years. In *The Decline and Fall of the New York Yankees*, Jack Mann says that "In his first years as a Yankee, his basic coolness was interpreted by the followers as arrogance, and then resentment was fanned by New York columnists who made a public issue of his failure to give mawkish recognition to the mawkish recognition he received, and deserved."[16] But it is very difficult to find eyewitness reports during DiMaggio's first year of his alleged "arrogance" or even his "coolness." His perceived reticence was most often interpreted as part of his shyness, a rookie's appropriate reservation.

DiMaggio ended his first year with a superb World Series which one of the Yankee's best all-time teams won against an almost equally gifted New York Giants squad, 4-2. The Giants featured such players as Bill Terry at first base, Mel Ott in right field, Dick Bartell at shortstop, and Hal Schumacher, Carl Hubbell, and Freddie Fitzsimmons as pitchers.

DiMaggio hit .346, a mark he would not top in World Series play, and made what has become one of the legendary catches of his career. President Franklin Roosevelt attended the second game, played at the Polo Grounds, when the Yankees clobbered the Giants, 18-4. Prior to the last out, the public address announcer stated that spectators should remain in their seats after the game, until the President had been driven from the field in his special car. With two outs, Hank Lieber, the Giants' powerful outfielder, smashed one of Lefty Gomez's pitches high, hard, and straight away. DiMaggio raced back nearly as far as he could range in the Polo Grounds' spacious center field, almost to the steps exiting the field and leading up to the players' clubhouse, where he caught the ball for the game's final out. Not knowing whether to continue up to the dressing room, DiMaggio saw his teammates standing still as requested, so he froze at the foot of the steps. The President's car passed within several feet of him, and while some accounts relate that Roosevelt gave Joe what became Roosevelt's famous high sign, in *Lucky to Be a Yankee*, DiMaggio humbly says Roosevelt's grin may have been for the cheering crowd in the bleachers.

Bill Terry, the Giants' player-manager, was reported saying about DiMaggio "I've always heard that one player could make the difference between a losing team and a winner and I never believed it. Now I know it's true."[17] This remark underscores another important element of DiMaggio's evolving image and identifies a key piece of the picture establishing him as not just a star but an enduring hero. He is strongly portrayed as being a member of a winning team, in fact the key player for the most successful team in baseball history. Prior to his joining the club, from 1932 to 1935, the Yankees had not won the pennant even though they were a good squad. They did win ten of the thirteen years he played with them. Playing for a team with a winning reputation already, he was credited with making them even better winners. Being successful with a losing team, as for example Tris Speaker ordinarily was, does not establish a player as a loser, and surely such a player as Speaker is remembered for his towering skills and not for the fact that the teams he played for were often unsuccessful. But to play as DiMaggio did for a consistently winning team, under pressure, is to be almost totally identified with success. This identification itself could also work against a hero, making his exploits appear almost mechanical. In fact, writers sometimes described DiMaggio's abilities as being machine-like. But other elements of his character and performance, such as the injuries which kept him from so many opening day games, would ultimately dissipate the aura of automatic perfection surrounding DiMaggio's performance as year after year, the Yankee "wrecking crew" dominated baseball.

In 1936 the Yankee batting order featured Bill Dickey (.362), Lou Gehrig (.354), Red Rolfe (.319), George "Twinkletoes" Selkirk (.308), Jake Powell (.299), Frank Crosetti (.288), and Tony Lazzeri (.287). Among their pitchers were Lefty Gomez (13-7), Red Ruffing (20-12), Monte Pearson (19-7), and "Fireman" Johnny Murphy, the relief specialist (9-3). All had distinguished careers in the majors. Gehrig was of course the active Yankee whose name most often appeared linked to DiMaggio's in these early years, just as Babe Ruth's was the name from the past most frequently coupled with his replacement's in the hearts and minds of the Yankee followers. In retrospect, surprisingly little antagonism or resistance among the followers was focused on DiMaggio as the new hero. His skill was so generally consummate and steady that it would have been difficult to assail his reputation merely for failing, say, to hit as many home runs consistently as Ruth or Gehrig. Ruth had been gone for several years, making the transition to DiMaggio worship easier, and furthermore, Ruth was not gracious in retirement. Bitterness is not the best response for a sports hero, no matter how justified his complaints might be. A player like Ty Cobb might always be idolized for the pure artistry of his skills and even for the unrelenting nature of his mean but total competitiveness. But he would not be loved. Ruth had been loved and he would be loved again, particularly when he was no longer publicly acrimonious, and especially when he was weak and dying. But in 1936 that was still in the unanticipated future.

Gehrig's role in DiMaggio's legend—or DiMaggio's role in Gehrig's legend—is a different matter. Today, Gehrig's image possesses a strange, sad luminosity, partly perhaps as a result of the popular and melancholy motion picture, *Pride of the Yankees*, that was made of his life. His sad, slow, public death dominates the remembrance of him among those who never knew him as a superb player day after day. His major record that everyone knowledgeable about sports records knows, his 2,130 consecutive games played, is of course most visably an endurance record, and this combined with the agony of his dramatically dwindling muscular ability—the "Iron Man" brought weak as a baby before he died—has cast a shadowy and ironic light upon the raw data of his bright attainments (a lifetime batting average of .340, 493 home runs in seventeen years, 162 triples, 535 doubles). But even before his sudden decline,when he was at his peak, there was a quality about Gehrig that made him like a great performer who even when playing in starring roles was thought of as a character actor and not a leading man. The only year he won the Most Valuable Player award was 1936. David Voigt remarked that he was "close to being the Galahad of the era. Incredibly durable [the opposite of DiMaggio] and efficient and terribly determined to better himself, Gehrig personified the Protestant ethic in baseball."[18] But as Mann wrote, "never in baseball history have so many been so unexcited about so much. . . . By the end of the season the name of DiMaggio was first on the lips of the Yankee followers, and Lou Gehrig's magnificence was being taken for granted again."[19] Though Gehrig's statistics were superior to DiMaggio's in 1936 (Gehrig batted .354, hit 49 home runs, batted in 152 runs), "He who had walked so long in the Babe's shadow, now walked in the shadow of the rookie DiMaggio.''[20] In the forever entwined narratives of the two players' momentarily connected lives, DiMaggio's domination of Gehrig as the Yankee star adds poignance to Gehrig's sad story, and sharpness to DiMaggio's intense tale of success. But DiMaggio could never be blamed or disliked for replacing Gehrig, because he himself was so shy and never brash as a rookie. And further, DiMaggio brought victory where Gehrig, great as he was, had not when he was the team's star after Ruth.

Certainly few thought of Gehrig in San Francisco, where Joe returned from New York after the Yankees' 1936 triumph. He would remain associated with these two cities his whole life and in some ways they embody aspects of his success. He would always be the hometown boy (San Francisco of all American cities seems most like an old village) who would not betray his roots or leave his family (in fact he brought his mother and brother Tom but not his father to New York to the 1936 Series), but he would also become a cosmopolitan success, an integral part of big-time eastern urban modern life. A picture of him returning home in 1936 that *Life* ran as part of its 1939 cover story illustrates his success in the two distant city worlds: he rides mounted on top of a seat in an open car, his hair slicked back looking almost painted on, smiling happily but for the moment of the photo his eyes looking a bit dazed, wearing a magnificent full-length camel's hair coat with an extremely tasteful three-piece suit and tie underneath. Mayor Rossi sits crowded with his head near DiMaggio's elbow, with a child of the DiMaggio clan at his knee. It is a picture of success and satisfaction. Of this time he wrote in *Lucky to Be a Yankee.* "I had had a good season, a group of wonderful fellows as teammates, and I'd certainly have a bunch of stories to tell the old gang at Columbus Avenue and Taylor." It had been slightly under eight months since he had seen them.

Off seasons in San Francisco were generally times of comparative quiet and reclusiveness for DiMaggio. This first year as a resting World Series champion, he dutifully bought his parents a new home, and brought greater security to his retired father. Although the country was still far from out of the Depression, with about 8 million unemployed in 1936, and unrest and turbulence clearly manifest in the large number of sit-down strikes engaged in throughout 1937 by desperate industrial workers, baseball enabled DiMaggio and his family to live financially in a bubble during these years. He and Tom thought they would expand that bubble by holding out again for a larger raise than the Yankees offered him for his first, great year. The relatively calm dispute continued until mid-March, 1937, when DiMaggio signed for, according to Gene Schoor (1956), about $17,500, and according to a newspaper handout prepared by management in DiMaggio's files, $15,000.[21] Either sum, though still far from his commercial and athletic value to the team, virtually doubled his 1936 salary. He again missed the opening games, because of infected teeth and tonsils, and did not appear until May 1, but once he began performing it was obvious that the fabled sophomore jinx was not going to strike him. Playing in 151 games, he hit .346, with a league leading total of 46 home runs and impressive extra base and runs batted in totals. The Yankees, improved by the addition of Tommy Henrich and with young Joe Gordon at second in place of Tony Lazzeri, won the pennant again by a large margin though not so great as in 1936, and beat the Giants once more in the World Series, four games to one. His home run production for a time out-paced Ruth's the year he hit 60, and one homer in particular was so long that the eponymous "veteran observer" sportswriters, like a Greek chorus, declared it was as long as anything Ruth had ever hit. In 1937 DiMaggio transcended (while keeping) his celebrity status and grew further into his position as a hero—a performer with substantial abilities proven over a significant amount of time.

The Yankee team was establishing itself as a new incarnation of the old-time all-time great Yankee squads of the 1920s, the Ruth era. The new Yankees of DiMaggio's day were a more modern club in their corporate image, but like their older predecessors they were becoming more than just winners, they were evolving into a dominant presence, a touchstone of superiority and greatness, like the Notre Dame teams of Knute Rockne or the Boston Celtics of recent years. Here is a pattern that would also repeat throughout DiMaggio's life—he would become a legend within another legend. The two symbiotic stories would feed upon each other, each enabling the other to grow, to live longer in the minds of people. Today the Yankees of those middle-late years of the thirties seem a transitional team, linking (as does DiMaggio in some ways) older baseball times with more modern—the old Murderer's Row to the Bronx Bombers. They had players such as Lazzeri and Gehrig, who had played when Ty Cobb and Tris Speaker were still active and able. But now the Yankees were becoming the model of modern industrial efficiency, producing many of their best players from their own farm teams, such as the 1937 Newark ("Wonder") Bears, and starting to staff their club with an increasing bureaucracy of effective parts of what would increasingly be thought of as a business-like machine. But unlike a machine they still had roots, and these were in the past, in the rough and tumble times of baseball as a kind of ruthless free-for-all played by grown men with their eye on the buck but who were also committed to the sport with an unsophisticated spirit of adventure and enterprise—the difference between the Hollywood world of silent films and the banker's California of today, the difference between old-time vaudeville with its complicated human circuits big time and small, and corporate television.

So DiMaggio's fellow team members have a place in his narrative as well as the team officers who controlled them. As David Voigt has written of these 1936-37 Yankees, "In a tough age which called for tough men in baseball, the Yankees were toughest. They were managed by a perfectionist, bossed by a president who hated second place, and owned by a man who could say, even with a seventeen game lead in 1936, 'I can't stand this suspense. When are we going to clinch it?' "[22]

While most of the players were very serious competitors, one famous member who was not was DiMaggio's roommate, Vernon ("Lefty," "Goofy") Gomez. Gomez, an excellent pitcher with a lifetime 189-102 record, including 24-7 (1932) and 26-5 (1935) seasons, was a featured player in DiMaggio's continuing star story, more or less the wise fool in the hero's retinue, funny Sancho Panza to DiMaggio's somber Don Quixote. In reality, not only an excellent player (a star in his own right) but a witty man, in his retellings of DiMaggio's life he manages to both deflate what might otherwise become pretentious in the story and to lend DiMaggio or point out that he possessed a likeable humanity the sportswriters often missed because of his shy seriousness. A typical Gomez anecdote has him throwing to a puzzled DiMaggio on a pickoff play instead of to Crosetti or Lazzeri, because he was directed only to "throw to the wop" (turning the idolized, idealized ethnic hero into just another Italian). In the talks he gave around the country travelling as a member of the Wilson Sporting Goods advisory board, he related how during DiMaggio's hitting streak, Joe was calm "but every day after 44 I threw up *my* breakfast" (the side-kick acts like the human being the hero cannot be). Gomez enjoys talking about how much the young DiMaggio loved to read comic books. He would send Gomez out to buy them for him (the great man reads comic books, which makes him like us). But the flaw is innocent, boy-like, which is the sort of flaw the hero can possess, a bit of Babe Ruth's little bad boy image. DiMaggio always seemed comfortable around Gomez who could act out the goofy things Dimaggio could never permit himself to do, even if he had thought of them. As an older player, DiMaggio would often be special friends with some madcap Yankee whom he may have admired for his ability to behave comically or antisocially in ways he perhaps admired but would not emulate. Since he was older than these players, Billy Martin and Joe Page, for example, he could also be their mentor. Gomez was instead one of Joe's teachers, one of the many he observed and listened to as he was growing up privately, while growing up in public.

Another important figure in the Yankee picture in these early years, and another minor legend that has been assimilated into DiMaggio's story, was Yankee business manager and president, Ed Barrow. Born in May, 1868, during a wagon train stopover in Springfield, Illinois, Barrow was like the team he helped assemble, a transitional figure spanning the rough, early days of professional baseball to its emergence as an efficient, modern corporate enterprise. Barrow's life as he related it has a wonderfully old-fashioned tone. In his autobiography he told about the exhibition fight he almost had with "Gentleman" Jim Corbett (legends constantly mingle with each other), that he was proud night baseball—"not a wholesome trend"—did not arrive at Yankee Stadium until after he left, and that he signed Honus Wagner to one of his earliest contracts with the Paterson team of the old Atlantic League in 1896. Barrow also made clear his interest in modernizing baseball, claiming that he was the first to mark distances from home plate to the outfield stands, and the first to put numbers on players' uniforms. It is easy to sentimentalize figures from the past, especially when the past is a period of nostalgic attraction, but Barrow was no sentimental "Pops" figure. He was a shrewd, tough, often tight-fisted executive who typifyed the old iron-fisted single leader-at-the-helm rather than the modern, blow-dried, organization executive. He was a hard man, as DiMaggio had already discovered by 1937, and he would get harder.

"Marse" Joe McCarthy, the Yankee manager, often seemed stiff to the public, but DiMaggio and most of his other players would always praise him highly. Barrow thought he was "baseball's greatest manager." Wes Ferrell, a very good no-hit pitcher who played for a number of teams 1927-41, including the Yankees in 1938-39, said he "thought McCarthy was a great manager. Still do. He was all business running his ball club, very professional. You didn't see guys running around all night and then kicking your game away the next day. . . . When I got up to the stadium, he called me into his office" and said "We've got one rule around here. . . . We don't second guess the manager."[23] Firm but fair is the general appraisal of McCarthy. He may have banned his players from playing cards in the locker room because to him baseball was baseball's only business, and he may have dampened premature victory celebrations, but as Spud Chandler told Donald Honig, he was a "terrific manager. You couldn't help but respect him, and he demanded respect, and he received it from every player on the club."[24] The Yankees of that era seem to have accepted his insistance that they behave decorously in public. No one argued with him in 1939 when he found them horsing around in their Pullman car and told them to "cut that out. . . . What are you—amateurs? I thought I was managing a profess-ional club. You're worse than college kids."[25] He was perhaps the ideal manager for young DiMaggio; cool, concerned, paternal, but emotionally undemanding. DiMaggio always had praise for McCarthy. He told Jimmy Cannon "if you put out for him, he never let you down. . . . I never heard a player beef about one of Joe's moves. . . . Everybody on the club knew Joe knew more baseball than anybody playing for him. And another thing. Joe never showed up a ballplayer."[26]

From the start of spring training, 1936, McCarthy had been quietly enthusiastic about DiMaggio and able to communicate his confidence in him. To others, McCarthy might be a cold tyrant. Some writers accused him of being a push-button manager who merely had to arrange the wealth of Yankee talent into a workable batting order to produce his championship teams. But McCarthy had maintained a sincere regard for DiMaggio and his skills early on. Years later he said of this time: "I wanted him to be comfortable before I put him in center. . . . He needed the room in center to roam, especially in Yankee Stadium, the toughest center field in baseball. Only the great ones can play it. And he did everything so easily. You never saw him make a great catch. You never saw him dive for a ball. He didn't have to. He was already there to catch it." [27]

These were only a few of the figures associated with DiMaggio in the early good years. The 1937 season was a particularly satisfying time for him, with a spectacular regular season and a good all-star game (in which five Yankees participated) where he made his first all-star hit—off Dizzy Dean—and a good World Series in which he hit his first World Series home run, and Lou Gehrig hit his last. In the first game against the Giants, he singled with the bases loaded to augment the avalanche of runs under which the Giants were buried, 8-1. Furthermore, Vince now performed regularly and acceptably for the Boston Braves in the National League, and younger brother Dom was beginning to star with Joe's old team the Seals. As far as his playing was concerned, who could ask for anything more? He was a star and a celebrity—known for his athletic exploits, and known, as Daniel Boorstin suggests in *The Image*, for being known, for generating publicity. When he met that year with other star-celebrites such as Joe Louis, another quiet ethnic super-hero of the 1930s (as *Life* kindly stated in its 1939 cover story on DiMaggio, both were "lazy, shy, and inarticulate"), the news was reported all over the country—from New York to San Francisco.

In 1937 he also met his future wife Dorothy Arnold (Dorothy Arnoldine Olson) while making a film called *Manhattan Merry-Go-Round* in Astoria, Long Island. Curiously enough, DiMaggio's autobiography is confused on precisely when this momentous event occurred, placing the date both in 1936 and 1937. Most certainly it was the latter time. The movie opened in California early in November. Starring singer Phil Regan and exvaudeville headliner (soon to be the Cisco Kid's sidekick) Leo Carillo, with guest appearances by Cab Calloway, Ted Lewis, and Jack Benny among others, its feeble plot was a simple vehicle to provide opportunities for numerous guest stars to perform. According to *Variety* November 10, 1937, "so much talent and novelty has been compressed within the limits of the film that customers dare not sneeze for danger of missing something." The Republic film also contained numerous "dialectics" (dialects), mostly "upper Second Avenue American-Italian." However, "Joe DiMaggio speaks excellent center-field English." According to the *New York Times*, December 31, 1937, he delivered "a self-conscious monologue about baseball with the benefit of some newsreel cuts." Otherwise, *Merry-Go-Round* was a "mildly infernal machine" for "the amusement of children" that went "round and round, getting no place at all." No cast listing mentioned Dorothy Arnold.

Books and articles about DiMaggio never deal at length with DiMaggio's first wife or first marriage. Their wedding ceremony in 1939 was pandemonium, but beyond that public ritual, his fans showed little appetite for incorporating this part of his life into his continuing story. Ordinarily, marriage constitutes a major chapter in a man or woman's life, but not much more than paragraphs have been written about DiMaggio's relationship with Dorothy. More appeared in the press concerning their seemingly constant impending divorce than their life together. Usually, as in Dan Daniel's monograph, she is described (in a caption under a photo showing her happily shoving wedding cake into her open-mouthed bridegroom's face) as a "former film actress." Sometimes she is termed an "ex-starlet" or "one-time show girl." One of the more realistic treatments of her by George De Gregorio reports that she met DiMaggio "not long after she left Duluth, Minnesota, her hometown, to seek a career in show business. She was singing in a New York nightclub and had a stock movie contract with Universal Studios."[28] Even Maury Allen, whose *Where Have You Gone, Joe DiMaggio?* contains so much oral reminiscence, is extremely sketchy about this part of his subject's life. Hardly anyone who writes about DiMaggio even mentions that he was reported engaged to another woman during his rookie years. It would appear that the hero in love was not a favorite topic among his fans who wanted a near-celibate celebrity. Ironically, when he became a father that would be reported: the star as dad was far more acceptable than the star as lover or hubby. One might even conjecture that these feelings reflected DiMaggio's own.

DiMaggio had a different kind of baseball year in 1938. It was not because he did not play well (because he did), though his statistics were not quite so impressive as the previous year (he hit .324 with 32 home runs), and it was not because he did not play again for a winning team, because he did. The Yankees triumphed over Boston by nine and one-half games and crushed the Chicago Cubs in four World Series games. Nor was the season exceptional in that he missed its opening. What changed was that he sat out the season's start because of a salary dispute and not an injury. And when he finally played he was booed. In later years it would seem that the hurt to DiMaggio's ego in the aftermath of his holdout was far greater than the pain of any previous wounds he had suffered.

Fans whose concept of DiMaggio began to emerge around the time of his 56-game hitting streak in 1941, or after his return to baseball from military service in 1946, are not generally aware that part of his picture during these earliest playing years was colored by nearly annual attempts to haggle for as much money as possible for his skills. Before the relatively recent possibility of free agency, players held out for more money less frequently, and those were rarely marginal performers. Preseason reports of spring negotiations between management and personnel were filled with brash claims of dissatisfaction by players, and rejoinders (at first) of paternalistic surprise by team presidents and general managers. Team managers supported their bosses most often, but frequently with an eye toward not alienating the players whose abilities and loyalty their jobs partly depended on. In retrospect these salary dances take on a peculiarly futile aspect, for though greats and near greats such as Babe Ruth or Ty Cobb, or more recently in Yankee history Red Ruffing or Ben Chapman, might squeeze a few dollars from management, the players had in the last resort only retirement and loss of livelihood to threaten. Like roosters strutting in the barnyard for more feed, ultimately they had to step into the coop and do their jobs or face the pot (which was inevitable anyway). The image is of course unfair to the players, who were, because of baseball's special monopoly industry status, often more like hens desperately staving off the frying pan by laying egg after egg than preening roosters. At best, team officials were often benevolent despots who could be charmed out of more money by cooperative (and productive) workers, or, they might match the steps of the players with a dance of their own by offering a low salary the marginal player might or might not accept, and then be delighted if the player came to those terms. Certainly Yankee negotiators did not typically offer large raises, or what players considered large enough increments, without much preliminary dickering.

Though appearing shy and reticent off the field, DiMaggio was always a very businesslike player whose loyalty to the Yankee tradition aside, was tough in salary negotiations. Even before he joined the Yankees he complained that he was not being paid sufficiently. It has been claimed that his brother Tom or even Joe Gould, the Broadway character and fight manager, were behind his salary claims, but clearly even if he were acting under advisement, he was accepting the advice offered because it represented his own feelings. Though De Gregorio's account of the shadow-boxing between DiMaggio, Ed Barrow, and Yankee owner Colonel Jacob Ruppert is a detailed one, it is perhaps written too much from the point of view that DiMaggio's quest for more money was simply a result of his swollen ego caused by the glowing reception of his first two years with the team and fueled by recent player of the year awards from New York and Philadelphia writers. From January, 1938, until mid-April, dickering turned more sourly into bickering which the press sporadically noted. DiMaggio felt that his talent deserved higher pay than the $25,000 offered him, irrespective of what anyone else on the team was making (Gehrig was at first also a holdout though he signed a month before DiMaggio for a reported $39,000). As De Gregorio reports the conflict, Ruppert was absolutely firm that his offer was fair and would not be changed. DiMaggio was an ingrate to ask for more. He should be practicing and not sulking in San Francisco. He would not get the $40,000 Ruppert said he was seeking. Ed Barrow said that if he did not sign soon he would be suspended. According to Larry Merchant, "a check of three newspapers—*Post, Times* and *Mirror*— showed that none of the leading sports columnists thought the holdout was worth more than a passing mention," possibly because the writers knew DiMaggio had few—in fact no—realistic alternatives to signing.[29] Finally he capitulated. Even with the popular restaurant he now owned in San Francisco, which would eventually become a tourist attraction and after he retired (and had sold his interest in it) practically a shrine, he knew his one chance for a significant life was as baseball player, and the Yankees controlled that chance. As early as March 12 he had been quoted in the *New York Times* as observing, "I suppose it will end up with the ballplayer signing the contract. It usually does." The $25,000 he would be paid (minus fines for failing to be in shape to play the games he missed at a rate according to the April 26 *Times* of $148.81 a day) would be the second highest on the Yankees. De Gregorio points out that in 1938 the immortal Carl Hubbell, in his eleventh season, was paid $2,500 less by the New York Giants. One could also say that relative to the many Americans still suffering from the Depression, both were overpaid—or that compared to the profit their teams extracted from their appeal and productivity, the stars were grossly underpaid.

Large numbers of spectators, Yankee rooters and Yankee haters, were angered in 1938 by DiMaggio's holdout, and their displeasure brought real and at first puzzling misery to him. Though he began almost immediately to perform at his usual peak level, DiMaggio was often booed when he played, a situation not alleviated even by his brief hospitalization after the day of his return when he and Joe Gordon collided in shallow center field going for the same fly ball during the sixth inning of the Yankee's game with Washington. Larry Merchant reported that Charley Segar of the New York *Daily Mirror* wrote "DiMaggio showed no indication that he was more than shaken up . . . occasionally breaking into song while waiting for the conveyance to take him to the hospital"—possibly, Merchant comments, "Brother, Can You Spare a Dime.?"[30] Some later accounts, including DiMaggio's own in *Lucky to Be a Yankee*, perhaps overstate the extent of the fans' booing, and usually fail to mention that equal numbers of admirers usually tried to indicate to him their approval by cheering for him. There is no doubt, however, that the period was a new and trying experience for DiMaggio, and probably marks the end of his innocent rookie period. At first DiMaggio simply let his play speak for itself. As Dan Daniel reported in the New York *World Telegram and Sun*, May 4, he doubled twice, one of them being "one of the longest doubles in the history of the stadium." His friend Daniel also noticed however that he was a "bit shy on condition. . . . He dropped into an out at third base like Pavlova performing the 'Dying Swan.'" By his third game of that season he had hit two home runs, and yet on May 3, Jimmy Powers of the New York *Daily News* printed the rumor that "dugout players try to cover-up, but there are plenty of Yanks who speak none too cordially . . . if at all . . . to DiMaggio."[31]

After a while DiMaggio began wondering out loud about his treatment. On May 5 under the headline "DiMag Cannot Understand Why He is Booed," he confessed to Dan Daniel that "when he was booed in Washington Joe DiMaggio could understand this phenomenon. He was on alien territory . . . But the hoots of the Stadium customers who sit behind the dugout of the visiting club have Giuseppe up a tree. Every time he comes up these lads give him the Bronx cheer. Which is drowned out by demonstrations in other parts of the house." On May 6 a *World Telegram* headline declared that "DiMaggio Steals Hitting Show. Excels Mates Despite Loss of Spring Drill. Joe's Bat Silences Critics at Stadium." In the six games since his return, DiMaggio had hit three home runs, one triple and three doubles in 24 at-bats, while hitting. 458. The article indicated, "the erstwhile booers became amalgamated with the DiMaggio Marching and Cheering Club." But apparently all DiMaggio could hear were the jeers which the May 5 paper said continued to "puzzle him." Generally the New York sportwriters were sympathetic to DiMaggio once he returned, for as Bob Cooke of the *Herald Tribune* wrote "It's pretty hard to hold a grudge against a guy who takes abuse without complaint, public or private, and who continues to play the kind of ball DiMaggio has been playing."[32] Cooke may have overstated DiMaggio's reluctance to complain. Clearly his remarks to Daniel constituted a complaint, but he had played with all his usual skills during this time of unaccustomed pressure from his former supporters. The boos continued for a longer time than would have ordinarily been expected, given the high calibre of his performance—usually nothing silences detractors in the stands more than success—but invariably the noise was drowned out by cheers of loyal fans and those mollified by his obvious successes. In the May 31 *Times*, John Drebinger reported that during a doubleheader with Cleveland before a massive crowd of 85,533 "it was difficult to tell whether the cheers dominated the jeers when DiMaggio took his first turn at bat, although all seemed agreed it was by far the noisiest demonstration ever accorded any ball player for merely stepping up to the plate." Fan reason, or self-interest, finally prevailed, however, for "once the Great DiMaggio cut loose with that first inning double, the cheers gained the ascendency and, after a few more blows fell, carried the day." By June 3 (as reported in the *Times* the following day), when a crowd of 12,000, half of them "Lady's Day guests, . . . cheered DiMaggio to the echo" unreturned by boos, the occurrence "was something of a novelty." Soon only DiMaggio continued to hear them in his memory, but there the sound was strong, for as he recollected, "All I ever heard were the boos."[33] In *Lucky to Be a Yankee* DiMaggio refers to this year as "a season I wanted to forget. . . . I knew that it wasn't doing me any good to draw the boos of the fans and I resolved that I would never again be their target."

He concludes that the fans' "right to express their opinion on all his affairs" is "not entirely unreasonable" since they "pay to see a ball player perform'' and this ''contributes to that player's income.'' But it also seems fair to conclude that privately, DiMaggio was deeply disturbed by the fans' invasion of his life—the comment one hears from DiMaggio's friends over and over again is that he is a ''very private person'' and so he would naturally resent open criticism. The greater he became in the eyes of his public, the less he could live like a normal human being able to determine his own circumference of privacy. He would have probably preferred to receive recognition solely for his exploits, his athletic skills, but the public apparently wanted to judge him for more than his playing abilities. Around this traumatic time he became a changed hero, perhaps even resentful of the public's desire to eat his image. In *Lucky to Be a Yankee* he concluded that after his troubles in 1938, ''whatever contract discussions I had with the ball club in the future'' he would try to have all problems settled before the start of training. What he probably decided to do was keep his life private, as much as he could, and prevent the public from observing what he did not want it to. Though a normal determination for an ordinary person, it is probably an impossible desire for a celebrity, star, and hero.

In later years DiMaggio remembered 1938 far more bleakly than did those who wrote about him. His reputation as a player who was hard to dicker with would soon be overshadowed in the minds of amnesiac fans by his image as a great player who was frequently injured. To the writers and fans, 1938 was a great year overall. The Ruppert Rifles, as they were sometimes called, dominated almost as much as they had in 1937 when one sportswriter referred to the league as ''Snow White and the Seven Dwarfs.'' In a moment of euphoria after the Yankees swept the World Series from Chicago, McCarthy said the team was his greatest.[34] It probably wasn't, but it was an excellent squad, and DiMaggio was becoming its leader. New players such as Tommy Henrich and Joe Gordon began seeing him as the player in charge, taking over for Lou Gehrig who had always been self-effacing and whose phenomenal skills were beginning to decline. His .295 batting average in 1938 was his lowest since 1925, the only year until his retirement when he would hit under .300. Gehrig played well enough (though not to his satisfaction) in the 1938 series, as did another all-time star. The Cubs' Dizzy Dean had a chronically sore arm, but it did not prevent him from pitching a brave and cunning game which he ultimately lost. Dimaggio hit a home run off Dean in the game and thought himself fortunate. Dean said that his arm felt at times as though his ''bone were sticking out of the flesh after the sixth inning,'' that he ''couldn't have knocked a glass off a table.''[35] Gehrig grew steadily weaker, and while Dean continued pitching off and on until 1941 (in fact came back for one bizarre appearance in 1947 with the weird St. Louis Browns), 1938 was his last year near the top. DiMaggio was young and in his prime, one of the very few star athletes of the thirties who would be a star in the forties and fifties also.

The Yankees of the 1920s and the Depression were becoming the modern,

DiMaggio Yankees. Colonel Ruppert, a colorful and integral part of old Yankee history, died January 13, 1939. In many ways he belonged to the world of New York society that Edith Wharton described so beautifully and devastatingly in her novels. Born only two years after the Civil War ended, Ruppert was far more the patrician than his Yankees business manager, Ed Barrow, but they appear to have been equally tough when dealing with ballplayers. A bon vivant who enjoyed being known throughout his entire lifetime as one of the most eligible bachelors in the city, Ruppert's colonelcy at the age of twenty-two was a result of a two-year stint he enjoyed in the New York National Guard. He relished the title and conducted his affairs with the Yankees as though he were their general. Like Babe Ruth, he was another figure from baseball's early days who would provide young DiMaggio with connections to an older tradition. He also could have provided the young Italian-American from San Francisco with glimpses of a classy if not class-ridden world the developing hero was beginning to participate in. The first baseball season after Ruppert's death revealed that DiMaggio had passed beyond his apprenticeship not just as a player, but as a young man in the big world outside baseball.

The Yankees of 1939 played even better than the 1937 or 1938 squads, finishing the season with 106 games won, seventeen games ahead of second place Boston. DiMaggio avoided salary squabbles and spring training injuries and thus started the season for the first time in his career—though a leg injury he received when his spikes caught in the turf of Yankee Stadium after just eight games reduced his total games played to 120. The Bronx Bombers were beginning to replace the Ruppert Rifles as outfielder Charlie (King Kong) Keller joined the team and hit .334. DiMaggio's position as the team's chief star was sadly reinforced May 2 when Gehrig asked Joe McCarthy to remove him from the day's lineup against Detroit. He would die little more than two years later, the "Iron Man" wasted by a form of polio, Amyotrophic Lateral Sclerosis, that has come to be known as "Lou Gehrig's Disease."

Babe Dahlgren (Gehrig's replacement), DiMaggio, and Joe Gordon, hit three home runs each on May 11, a day when the team knocked a total of thirteen. Five Yankees batted over .300 and once again they swept the World Series in four games, this time against Cincinnati, marking the first time a team had triumphed four consecutive years. As late as September 8 DiMaggio was hitting .408, but slumped because of an eye allergy and still ended the season at .381 to gain his first batting title. He was the second Italian-American to do so (Ernie Lombardi had taken the title one year previously in the National League). One of DiMaggio's few recorded criticisms of Joe McCarthy questioned why he was kept in the lineup despite McCarthy's knowledge of DiMaggio's blurred vision.[36] DiMaggio also hit 30 home runs, plus one in the All-Star game in which the American League team, dominated by six Yankees, beat the Nationals 3-1. DiMaggio was voted the Major League Player of the Year by the *Sporting News*, and won his first Most Valuable Player award.

Two events on the field that year stand out in DiMaggio's and baseball's history. The first was his famous catch off Hank Greenberg's soaring clout at the Stadium, late in the season against Detroit. Of all retellings of this tale, including Greenberg's own in Lawrence Ritter's *The Glory of Their Time*, Spud Chandler's remains the freshest. Chandler, a great pitcher who joined the team after DiMaggio, looked up to him as a team leader. "It's hard," he told Donald Honig in *Baseball When the Grass Was Real*, "to believe that a fellow could hit a ball as high and as far as Greenberg did and have it caught. When the ball was caught, Greenberg was at second base—that's how far he'd run before it came down. . . . DiMaggio . . . took off with the crack of the bat, on a dead run, going at kind of an angle toward the fence. I don't think he ever looked back; he just seemed to have it in his head where the ball was going to come down. Right at the fence, at the 460 mark, he just flicked out his glove and caught the ball." The story epitomizes DiMaggio's graceful and exceptional fielding ability, but to Chandler it also represented the approach to the game DiMaggio exemplified: the catch "occurred late in the season in 1939. We were way behind in the game at the time, and nothing was at stake. But that's the way Joe played ball—everything was at stake for him, all the time."

The second event involved a notorious World Series blunder that DiMaggio capitalized upon. Charlie Keller was the batting star of the games, but DiMaggio hit a respectable .313 and due to good base-running scored an important run during Ernie "Schnozz" Lombardi's infamous "snooze" or "swoon" at home plate. Lombardi, an excellent catcher and a .306 lifetime hitter in his seventeen seasons in the majors, is unfortunately now best remembered for his slowness on the bases (fans swore they saw him thrown out at first on hits into right field) and the momentary "nap" he took. It was the tenth inning of the fourth and final game when Keller had smashed into him at home plate (in pitcher Johnny Vander Meer's version, after being hit in the groin by the ball thrown to him by Ival Goodman, that had originally been a single by DiMaggio that Goodman mishandled). Lombardi is a good example of a fine player who never attained a public image equal to his abilities.

DiMaggio's increasing fame and his evolving image as a hero these years were of course a direct result of his athletic exploits. Both his fame and image were fed not only by the standard daily articles on sports pages all over the country which related his achievements, but by the unusual attention he received in nationally distributed articles in books and magazines. In his very first season *Time* magazine ran a feature story on him. In 1939 another of the then most popular magazines, *Collier's*, included in its July 29 issue a report supposedly written by him entitled "Pitchers I Have Hit." (The "twirler" DiMaggio says he "least want[s] to see'' is Cleveland's Mel Harder.) More significantly the country's most read (or looked at) major periodical, the pictorial *Life*, featured him on their May 1, 1939, cover, together with a curious, lengthy, half-comic, and sometimes tasteless and error-filled account of his spectacular career, emphasizing his superior talent, his Italian background, and his family heritage. More and more, DiMaggio's fame and image were leaping beyond the sports pages. Several years before his spectacular hitting streak, he was something of a household name. A popular author such as Rex Stout could use his name in the 1938 Nero Wolfe mystery *Some Burried Caesar* and presumably expect readers to catch his small joke.

Joe DiMaggio, who had entered the American League in 1936 as the rawest of rookies, though one with exceptional skills, who had been depicted as having led a life in San Francisco sheltered from contact with any kind of urbane culture, was now becoming amazingly enough a symbol of the gentleman celebrity. In the United States such a characterization can be very capricious and temporary of course, especially since no accepted criteria for the type exists—unlike England, for example, America possesses no guaranteed ancestry, no definitive school, nor in the instance of performers or popular figures, no King's or Queen's list of distinguished commoners which could in a quasi-official fashion bestow gentility upon a popular hero. In America the matter is decided by a kind of media folklore whose calibrations are fuzzily determined but glaringly visible in press accounts. Around 1939 it was easy to observe DiMaggio's ascendency beyond being a rookie, beyond being another star performer, to the status of a national hero with class. Babe Ruth lacked class, Jack Dempsey lacked it (though he had his nose fixed partly to achieve it), Gene Tunney when he was champion had it but was in the public's vision a person who was frozen and stiff. Earlier in the century for blacks, but not for whites, Jack Johnson had it, and late in the 1930s Joe Louis was developing it. In 1939 DiMaggio had progressed to the point where the ex-kid from San Francisco was now actually on a list of the nation's allegedly ten best dressed men (Joseph E. Davies, at the time Secretary of State Cordull Hull's aide, was first). Throughout his career, DiMaggio's clothes would remain a symbol of the first-class gentleman's status he had achieved. Younger ballplayers such as Billy Martin—who had style but no class—envied his clothes. Yankee attendants and other players were reported commenting on the splendor of his double-breasted tailor-made suits.[37] DiMaggio's clothes represented how far he had come—a rookie without even a high school education, son of an immigrant who still could not read English. In a talk that the *New York Times* reported on October 20, 1939, Warden James A. Johnston of Alcatraz Prison told the New York Advertising Club that the best work they could do was to get kids to emulate men like Lou Gehrig (who had recently been named to the Municipal Parole Commission by Mayor Fioreilo LaGuardia), ''and Joe DiMaggio. . . . The children want them . . . they really do. They do them good. So why not give them more Gehrigs and DiMaggios?''

In some ways the public who recognized him as a hero also thought of him as their meat, and as a private person he must have resented this though he kept his resentment to himself. Some sources say that on November 19, 1939, approximately 30,000 fans in San Francisco massed inside and outside of the cathedral in which DiMaggio married Dorothy Arnold. The event turned into more of a spectacle than a solemn celebration of union.[38] The bride's party even had trouble getting into the church prior to the wedding. Only a gentleman could have retained his dignity in the face of such pandemonium, but one wonders if DiMaggio did not loathe the intrusion upon his life, even while recognizing that "this lack of privacy . . . is not entirely unreasonable."[39]

When DiMaggio began his fifth season with the Yankees, again starting late because of a knee injury, he was entering a period which was changed from his earliest years with the team. Historians do not agree when the absolute low point of the devastating depression was attained, nor precisely when the nadir was passed and the country as a whole anyway, if not many of its poor, began experiencing general prosperity. Neither can it be precisely ascertained when the nation's leaders began to be more concerned with the possibilities of international war than with battling the internal enemies of unemployment and social misery. But certainly by 1940 the worst of the Great Depression was in the past, and just as surely the threat of direct American involvement in a world war was more imminent. By 1940 the nations who would become our new enemies—Germany, Italy, and Japan—had already attacked countries that would in 1941, become our allies. Appeasement of Germany, which a Gallup poll in 1938 indicated most Americans approved of in the instance of the Munich Pact signed September 30 of that year, was no longer a serious possibility after Germany's invasion of Poland on September 1, 1939, and the subsequent declaration of war upon Germany by France and Great Britain. In December of 1940, Franklin Delano Roosevelt, recently elected President for the third time, delivered a speech declaring his intent to make America a "great arsenal of democracy" in the fight against fascism.

Much farther down the scale of historic significance, baseball, as it entered the 1940s, was a game changed from what it had been during the early thirties, though of course its changes were slow and natural; for example, personnel turned over gradually as players aged and as their abilities grew or declined. Certainly the old stars of the early 1920s no longer remained, though a few of those who arrived mid-way or late in the decade were still performing well: for example, Jimmy Foxx who played from 1925 until 1945, though unspectacularly at the start and finish; Carl Hubbell, who achieved 253 lifetime regular season victories with the New York Giants from 1928 until 1943 with only one losing season; Mel Ott, also of the Giants from 1926 until 1947. Most of the players who would become legends or stars in the 1940s were in place: Bob Feller, Hank Greenberg, and Ted Williams, though Stan Musial would not enter the National League until 1941. There were also players around such as the Chicago White Sox's Luke Appling a steady performer of rare gifts, who from 1930 until 1950 performed consistently with excellence but never for a championship team, whose skills never received the publicity they deserved. By 1940, the age of Cobb, Walter Johnson, and Tris Speaker was gone; the age of Ruth, Gehrig, and Hubbell was over; the age of DiMaggio, Williams, Feller, Musial, and other 1940s stars had arrived. And of these, DiMaggio had been a star the longest, for the most successful team.

Now, in 1940, he was married and a long way from the "naive kid of 21" which, in his autobiography, he says he was in 1936. Role model for children, envied best-dressed celebrity, his name was linked with the names of other New York and San Francisco celebrities, sportswriters, and savvy restauranteurs such as Jimmy Cannon and Toots Shor. Very much a part of a traditionally male world of metropolitan insiders, he had changed as much as the decade, outwardly at least. Something new in 1940 was the Yankee's third-place finish: a game behind Cleveland and two games behind Detroit. The Yankees started badly and could never make up the early losses despite a rush to the top toward the end of the season. DiMaggio's performance was at its usual high level, providing personal compensation for his sharp disappointment at the defeat of the team whose lead player he had become. For the second consecutive year he won the league's batting championship, hitting .352. He was third in home runs with 31 (Hank Greenberg, Detroit's star, hit 41), and third, again behind Greenberg, in runs batted in with 133.

A minor annoying incident, but one which revealed the strange and inconsistent sacrosanctity of baseball, which the public was always pre-vented when possible from viewing as another American industry, occurred shortly after DiMaggio returned to the Yankee lineup following his early season injury, midway through May. DiMaggio and Joe McCarthy were ordered to appear before baseball's commissioner Judge Kenesaw Mountain Landis to explain reports Landis had seen stating that DiMaggio shared part of his Yankee salary with a business agent, an act that would have horrified Landis. In other words, did DiMaggio have a paid agent? Landis is another example of a legendary figure whose name has become part of the DiMaggio legend. Nearly always referred to as baseball's czar and in fact consistently praised in the press for acting like a tyrant in a world apparently peopled by little boys who needed occasional paddling, Landis is often credited with restoring public confidence in the game following the infamous "Black Sox" scandal of 1919 which publicized charges of players bribed to fix the World Series. He was always called "Judge," and even his homespun name reeked of solid homely native virtues. He was in fact, a poor though well-known jurist, whose crabby decisions were often overturned by higher appeals courts. In 1917 he had sentenced the radical Big Bill Haywood to twenty years in prison (Haywood jumped bail and died in Russia) and felt no grief sentencing Victor Berger and six other socialists to jail for supposedly impeding the First World War effort (a decision overturned later by the United States Supreme Court). The flamboyant journalist-historian John Reed described him at the trial of some Industrial Workers of the World ("Wobblies") in April, 1918: "Small on the huge bench sits a wasted man with untidy white hair, an emaciated face in which two burning eyes are set like jewels, parchment-like skin split by a crack for a mouth; the face of Andrew Jackson three years dead."[40] He was appropriate as baseball's monarch, since he fully supported baseball's monopolistic exploitation of its labor force, though on individual occasions he might free farm players from the servitude forced on them by stockpiling owners. DiMaggio and McCarthy were small potatoes for him to mash, and after an hour's talk with the old man, DiMaggio announced that "my salary never has been and never will be shared with a manager or agent."[41] Thus a threat to the kingdom of baseball was averted.

Fine as his performance was in 1940, DiMaggio exceeded it the next year. It is always difficult if not impossible to ascertain when a sports star becomes a legend, but in 1941 it is clear that through his 56 consecutive game hitting streak, DiMaggio performed a legendary feat, if he did not yet attain the personally legendary status he would later have bestowed on him. It would be a mistake to assert that the streak made DiMaggio into a star or hero, for he was already that, already arguably the game's dominating player. Not because of his skills alone but because he performed at such a high level with a winning team in an exceptionally visible location. The streak made him into a different kind of a star or hero and celebrity.

The year began well for him. His wife Dorothy was pregnant through most of it with the baby, Joe DiMaggio Jr., that she would give birth to on October 23, not long after the World Series. This made Joe happy because though he now lived part of the time in a world entirely different from that of his parents, he held many of the old standards and values. Marriage meant a family, and the wife, no matter how glamorous, was to become the mother. DiMaggio and Barrow disagreed again over Joe's salary and Joe missed the opening of spring training, but the $37,500 he ultimately signed for was not far from the $40,000 he had apparently sought. He hit safely in the Yankee's last nineteen exhibitions, began the regular season healthy, and continued his consecutive streak over the first eight league games. He was undisputed leader of the squad, and used his usually understated authority wisely, for example by aiding the rookie Phil Rizzuto to get the number of practice licks at bat which some of the other veterans were crowding him from in the standard manner of older boys hazing the new guys. Off the field, DiMaggio's image as a classy dresser, a symbol of his success that pleased him, was again reinforced by his inclusion in "Professor" William Taub's list of the ten best-dressed athletes, an award noted with some humor by John Lardner in the March 3 *Newsweek*. While a few of the other choices seem somewhat questionable (prizefighters Billy Conn, Max Baer, and Joe Louis, for instance), DiMaggio's recognition was probably legitimate, and a sign of his arrival as a gentleman of substance at least along the Broadway turf that occupied in the 1930s and 1940s even more territory in the American state of mind than now. "That DiMaggio is a poem," Lardner reports Taub declaring "dreamily . . . 'well do I mind that time when he first came to my laboratory, with a store suit and a bit of hay in his hair.' "

Writers delight in recounting the streak that made 1941 memorable in both DiMaggio's life and the life of baseball in a way that no other year would be, though of course in baseball history other seasons would possess unique achievements. But 1941 would forever be the year DiMaggio hit in 56 consecutive games. For writers or sports commentators, many qualities of the streak contributed to its overwhelming interest as an event inspiring not just day by day reporting, but countless repetitions of its major details years afterwards. It was an event that could be focused upon in anticipation of its continuation; writers could prepare to cover it in advance, just as readers or listeners were increasingly anxious to read or hear about it, day after day, as the streak continued. So, interest in it compounded as it proceeded. At the same time, it was distinctly time bound and compressed—unlike career records such as Ruth's magnificent all-time home run record or Gehrig's consecutive games total, which were impossible to focus on with drama as they were transpiring. Unlike a batting average record, the streak had to be maintained with success every day. Each game became a separate battle that absolutely had to be won.

Not only was the accomplishment reported across the nation as it was taking place, but it has become a favorite set piece, like a song sung by a folk troubador about a famous epic fight, among later commentators who were attracted by its innate significance as an athletic achievement, by the drama it created, and by its inherent shape as a story that builds but does not continue endlessly.

Several distinct parts are most frequently recounted by writers who deal with the narrative in any fullness. Many of these contain an element of mystery about them or of improbability that blends fact with fancy. The incredibility of DiMaggio's streak legitimizes this blend: the reality of the almost unbelievable event was attested to by presumably factual stories in newspapers and on the radio that added up to perhaps as much scrutiny as any nonmilitary event during that very real year. Who could blame writers, or readers, or listeners for accepting occasional fancy as fact, when so many of the facts were so extraordinary?

Most full accounts of the streak note that both the Yankees and

DiMaggio were playing poorly prior to its start. The Yankees were in fourth place playing .500 ball and five and one-half games behind Cleveland. Gene Schoor began his book (1956) with a stilted dialogue supposedly between DiMaggio and Max Kase, sports editor of the New York *Journal American*, in which Kase tells Joe "you know for the past twenty games you've been hitting only .184. If you hadn't started the season with a tremendous splurge that's about what you'd be hitting now," instead of the .299 which is Kase's notebook tabulation for DiMaggio. Al Silverman's account relates that in his last thirteen games, DiMaggio had batted only .237. After the Yankees' loss on May 15 to Chicago, when DiMaggio had hit one for four after two previous hitless games against Cleveland, his batting average for the season dropped to .304. Silverman also reports that the following day's headline about the game in the *Journal American* declared the "YANK ATTACK WEAKEST IN YEARS." By the termination of the streak, the Yankees would be seven games ahead of the Indians, thus underscoring DiMaggio's contribution to the team's success. His batting average during the 56 games would be .408.

Accounts vary concerning when the streak first began to be noticed in some significant fashion. DiMaggio said nobody, including himself, paid attention until it had passed game twenty, though doubtless he was aware earlier that he had hit in a certain number of games consecutively. As Dan Daniel, who would play a small but important role in narratives of its continuation, said in 1950, "Joe was deeply interested in his streak from the very start, being a good player, and always loving to hit, and above all to help his team." Silverman noted that John Drebinger of the *New York Times* wrote on April 2 that DiMaggio had hit in eighteen straight contests.

Of course the more games he hit in, the more he, his teammates and opponents, writers and spectators, paid attention to what he was doing. But at that time, although records were kept on hitting streaks, the achievements were not nearly as well-known as they would become after DiMaggio was in the process of equalling and then bettering them. In that sense he created the significance of the consecutive games hitting record. At first, writers had to dig through record books to discover the milestones DiMaggio was aiming at—most consecutive hits for a Yankee, for the American League, for a major leaguer. Even then, the incompleteness of reporters' investigations at first caused the declaration of a false goal, George Sisler's 42 consecutive games for the St. Louis Browns in 1922. A writer discovered that in 1897 another of baseball's immortals, "Wee" Willie Keeler of the Baltimore National League club had hit in 44 straight games. Though Keeler's record, as it now was called, was set under distinctly different playing conditions favoring the batter, it was finally determined that this was the goal DiMaggio had to surpass.

Al Silverman's book *Joe DiMaggio: The Golden Year, 1941*, contains the most complete collection of stories connected with DiMaggio's life and performance while he was setting his greatest record. Silverman touches upon and often provides detailed information about the individual events many writers have retold, embellished, and occasionally made mistakes about, including DiMaggio himself. In *Lucky to Be a Yankee*, DiMaggio told the interesting tale of how in game 44 his brother Dom robbed him of a hit and nearly ended his streak, "kind of rubbing it in to be robbed of a record by your own brother, especially when he was coming over to my house for dinner that same night." Arthur Daley of the *New York Times* enjoyed repeating this story, and it has passed forever into the folklore of DiMaggio's history. In the May, 1948, issue of *True* comics, there is even a picture of Dom catching his brother's drive. But it was a catch Dom never made, of a ball Joe never hit.

There was constant anxiety each day in the drama of the event itself, and enough real-life color to satisfy any sports enthusiast and, beyond the fans, to intrigue the general public as well. Early in the streak DiMaggio experienced one of the worst days of his athletic life—a day he played when because of an injury he should not have—when he made four errors in one doubleheader May 30, against the Boston Red Sox. He had a painfully stiff neck and should have been benched to help him recuperate, but he convinced Joe McCarthy (who had been told about the injury by DiMaggio's roommate Lefty Gomez) that he should remain in the lineup. In game 30, DiMaggio was striving to break Roger Peckinpaugh's (1919) and Earle Combs' (1931) Yankee record of 29 straight games. As Silverman retells it, DiMaggio "topped what looked like a routine groundball to shortstop Luke Appling." But the ball "took a bad hop and caromed off his shoulder." Teammates and fans looked up to the official scorer's box to see if the play would be called a hit or an error. The scorer, Dan Daniel, thought about it—who knows now what he thought?—and finally signalled "hit." It would be DiMaggio's only hit that day.

In game 36, DiMaggio was hitless in three at-bats against the St. Louis Browns' Bob Muncrief. His last at-bat he singled sharply to left. After the game, Luke Sewell, the Browns' manager, asked Muncrief why he did not walk DiMaggio. "That wouldn't have been fair to him—or to me," Muncrief said. So in the telling of the story, and probably in its living, rules of competition resembling those in old courtly traditions heightened and regulated the daily battles. When sport is played at its best, in story anyway, the participants must display themselves at their best.

But life and tradition both admit, in fact insist upon, occasional touches of human frailty to spice the narrative and remind onlookers that their heroes after all operate in a human world. In game 40, the Yankees faced Johnny Babich of the Philadelphia Athletics. Babich had played for the Yankees in the minor leagues, but they had never brought him up to the majors, and according to Silverman, he "had a reputation as a Yankee killer." Babich plays a villainous role in streak narratives, and is punished accordingly. Having beaten the Yankees five times in 1940, his revenge, so the story goes, would be complete only if he could thwart DiMaggio. In the third inning Babich pitched to the hitless DiMaggio for the second time and threw him three straight balls far out of the strike zone. The fourth pitch would also have been a ball but DiMaggio had received the hit sign, and as Silverman says, the ball "went on a vengeful line directly at the pitcher. . . . through his legs and out into center field." DiMaggio had hit safely and Babich was "white as a sheet." Heroes should disavow petty vengeance, but occasionally it is necessary to rebuke the minor Mordreds of the world. Had Babich played with courtesy, as had submarine pitch specialist Eldon Auker of the Browns in game 38, he would perhaps have been treated more as a lesser champion contributing nobly to the great quest. In the last of the eighth against Auker, the Yankees, who were leading and thus might not get to bat again, had one on first with one out when Tommy Henrich was allowed to bunt to decrease the chances for a double play and give the hitless DiMaggio another chance. Henrich bunted successfully sending Red Rolfe to second and leaving first open. Would Auker walk DiMaggio? Silverman reports Henrich thinking "Auker's a big man, he won't walk him. He'll pitch to him." And he did. And DiMaggio doubled to left on the first pitch thrown.

Magic and thievery overcome were part of DiMaggio's penultimate triumph, the tying and surpassing of Sisler's record. His third time at bat against the Washington Senators' knuckleball specialist Emil "Dutch" Leonard, DiMaggio doubled, tying Sisler. Between the first and second games, however, someone stole DiMaggio's bat. While never a particularly superstitious player, unlike for example performers who believe placing one bat above another robs the lower of potential hits, DiMaggio was upset over the loss of his bat, one that as always, he had honed with a soupbone and rubbed down with olive oil and rosin, and then burned slightly to improve his grip on it. Silverman likens the bat to Roy Hobbs's talismanic "Wonderboy" in Bernard Malamud's *The Natural*. Offered other bats by Henrich, the bothered DiMaggio still hit safely in the second game, setting a new record for American League hitters. For a time he would have to continue his adventure unaided by the marvelous bat. Not until July 3 would it be miraculously returned to him, according to Silverman, after he received a telephone call from a man from Newark, New Jersey, who admitted that one of his friends had stolen the bat as a souvenir, meaning no harm.

As the streak continued national attention given to it mounted. An editorial in the New York *Herald Tribune* for June 30, 1941, noted that DiMaggio had tied Sisler's record and also recognized the cynosure he had become. *Life*, in its September 29 issue, published a full page painting by Edward Lanning of "Joe DiMaggio Tying Record for Hits," depicting a house packed with fans including Fiorello La Guardia (who was in fact there) in the foreground. Even *Time* could not cheapen the magnitude of his athletic accomplishment through its pompous, overblown style. They reported on July 14 that "the Yankee Clipper left in his wake the broken fragments of one of baseball's immortal records" (a record that had only recently been exhumed, according to Silverman, by a San Francisco writer named Jack McDonald). Once again emphasizing DiMaggio's ethnic origin and the geographic and social distance he had travelled during his career, the article declared that "in 102 years of baseball few feats have caused such nationwide to-do. Ever since it became apparent that the big Italian from San Francisco's Fisherman's Wharf was approaching a record that eluded Ty Cobb [who hit in 40 straight games in 1911], Babe Ruth, Lou Gehrig and other great batsmen, Big Joe's hits have been the biggest news in U.S. sport. Radio programs were interrupted for DiMaggio bulletins," *Time* alleged, a claim that other books and articles have repeated, although little documentation of such unusual interruptions exists. Whether folklore or fact, writers have emphasized the national interest in the streak by noting this detail. Dave Anderson for example, wrote that after DiMaggio hit in his 42nd game, breaking Sisler's record, "All over the country radio announcers interrupted programs to say [apparently all using the same words] 'Here is a sports bulletin: Joe DiMaggio of the New York Yankees today set. . . .'" Perhaps they did.

Interest in the streak continued, but not at such an intense level, after DiMaggio passed all known standards and launched out upon a frontier of accomplishment only he had ever travelled to determine the limits of the new record. Along the way he faced his old enemy Johnny Babich again, but this time singled off him his first time at bat. On July 6 he stood at attention in Yankee Stadium with the other players and fans (attendance was 60,948 for the day's doubleheader with Philadelphia) to honor Lou Gehrig, who had died June 2. A few speeches were delivered, a plaque in centerfield was unveiled, and then "Taps" was played.

In game after game DiMaggio continued to hit safely, somtimes a home run as in game 50 against the St. Louis Browns, sometimes a single rolling so slowly down the line the inrushing third-baseman could not field it in time. He even hit in the All-Star game (which did not of course count in his record). Wherever the Yankee played, DiMaggio's streak was advertised as a lure at which spectators eagerly bit. Publicity attending DiMaggio's quest for an ultimate sports record was fully orchestrated in the media as had no ongoing sporting record attempt ever been before—literally orchestrated by Ben Homer for Les Brown's "Band of Renown" in the popular song declaring "Joe, Joe, DiMaggio, we want you on our side." In good Hollywood tradition, according to Dave Anderson, the song was "scribbled" on "a tablecloth" by its writer, Alan Courtney, a New York disc jockey, while he sat one evening in a nightclub while DiMaggio was still working on the streak, another instance of the public's wild interest in

DiMaggio's performance and media capitalization upon that interest. While the Yankee and opposing team managements did place advertisements to attract customers to DiMaggio's games, and of course fed stories to the newspapers, no central office controlled publicity about his daily efforts. The orchestration for the event was full, but spontaneous, and undirected; a result of the efforts of people who had something to gain from the public interest in the streak. And yet, unlike similar publicity campaigns in the media today over significant sporting events such as the World Series, the Super Bowl, or the Olympics, exploitation of what DiMaggio was accomplishing seems disorganized and untheatrical, natural, unaccompanied by the kind of slick dramatics television uses to smother even the most authentic contests.

DiMaggio's streak was finally broken in game 57 at Cleveland, the evening of July 17, before an announced crowd of 67,468, for many years the largest crowd to see a night game. There is barely a pitch of the game—at least a pitch thrown at DiMaggio—that has not been written about, hardly a minor or important feature of the play unanatomized: Al Smith of the Indians had the same last name as the pitcher against whom DiMaggio got his first hit of the streak, Edgar Smith; Ken Keltner, the Indian's third-baseman, made two good (great, sensational!) plays to put DiMaggio out (rob him of hits) twice; on his last at-bat, DiMaggio hit a grounder to Lou Boudreau and the ball took a bad hop that somebody else might have missed at second, but Boudreau turned it into a double play.

So perhaps every imaginable detail of the game has been recorded and turned over and weighed and carefully examined. But even legends that are based on fact often end in mystery.

As the story is told, when DiMaggio and Lefty Gomez took a cab to the ballpark the night of July 17, the cabbie prophetically told Joe, "I got a feeling your streak's gonna be stopped." In another version the strange cabbie says "I got a feeling . . . if you don't get a hit the first time up, they're going to stop you tonight."[42] Ever the scriptwriter, Gene Schoor (1956) reports his cabbie saying, "I hate to tell you this, Joe, but I was telling my wife tonight, 'Honey,' I said, 'I think they're finally gonna stop DiMag tonight.'" In all versions Gomez responds angrily, but not DiMaggio, who as a proper hero accepts his fate, as the more mortal Gomez, the realist, the jester, rails against ill-fortune. DiMaggio did not even mention the incident in his autobiography, just as when the real final out was made in Cleveland ending his unparalleled achievement, he simply "rounded first base, picked up his glove and trotted to center field. There was no kicking of dirt, no shaking of the head." Twenty-seven years later he said that inside, 'I wanted to keep going. I felt a little downhearted. . . . It was like going into the seventh game of the World Series, and losing it. I wanted it to go on forever." After the game he borrowed $17.00 from Phil Rizzuto because he had left his wallet in the clubhouse and did not want to return, and he walked into a bar alone. The next day when "in papers all over the country . . . there were head shots of Smith, Bagby [Cleveland's second pitcher the evening before], and Keltner, side by side, like three assassins of a king,"[43] DiMaggio began another, more modest after-ripple of a streak that lasted sixteen games. Though Ted Williams hit .406 in 1941, the year was DiMaggio's and he won the Most Valuable Player award. His .357 was the league's third highest, his 30 home runs fourth highest (Williams was first again with 37), he was second in doubles with 43, led in total bases with 348 and, most importantly, in runs batted in with 125.

The Yankees beat the Brooklyn Dodgers in the World Series in five games. DiMaggio hit only .263 while Red Rolfe hit .300, Charlie Keller .389, and Joe Gordon .500, but it was not a bad series for him, especially since the Yankees won, and he played a good role in one of baseball's fabled contests. In the fourth game the Dodgers were leading 4-3 in the top of the ninth, with Hugh Casey pitching strongly in relief. With two outs and fans and some Yankees starting to move toward the exits, the count three and two on Tommy Henrich, Henrich swung and missed on an inside, breaking pitch. But the Dodger catcher, Mickey Owen, missed the pitch, possibly a spitball (endless reasons have been given in endless postgame bull sessions), and by the time he could scramble to it Henrich was on first. So the game was not over: Henrich was on first, and the players and fans returned to their seats. Something surprising and terrible was happening to the Dodgers before the eyes of the appalled team and their rooters. DiMaggio singled and Keller doubled, scoring both teammates—DiMaggio, the complete ballplayer, was a highly skilled base-runner—then Bill Dickey walked and Joe Gordon doubled and the Yankees were ahead 7-4. They made no mistakes in the half-inning remaining, and won that game and the next one, significant now only because as Silverman claims, "it was the only time in his whole career that Joe DiMaggio ever got into a visible argument on the playing field." Whitlow Wyatt had brushed him back with a couple of pitches. Running out a caught fly ball, DiMaggio said something to Wyatt who said something to DiMaggio and the players moved toward each other, but they never got close to touching and after the game they spoke in a friendly fashion to each other.

After he became an established player, DiMaggio habitually lingered in the locker room long after the games, sipping coffee brought to him by the Yankee clubhouse attendant Pete Sheehy. The locker room was a good place in his domain. There he was supreme with his fellow players, safe in a quiet male world, isolated from nearly everything outside baseball. Although he must have been glad to leave the locker room world for the birth of his son on October 23, he must have missed its insulated camaraderie between the seasons of 1941 and 1942. Following the surprise attack by Japan on Pearl Harbor on December 7, 1941, Congress declared war on Japan, Germany, and Italy on December 8. The war impinged upon

DiMaggio's life and emotions just as it did upon the lives and emotions of most other non-combatants, bringing anger over America's seemingly forced involvement in it and anxiety because of our early, steady, devastating losses. On a more personal level it caused unrest over what would happen personally to him because of it. After a while it was certain the game would be continued though modified in various unimportant ways (spring training in Asbury Park, New Jersey, no mention of the weather during game broadcasts), because baseball was important to the nation's morale, and because it was one of the features of American life that seemed most American, that America was fighting to maintain. But he wondered if his career would stop temporarily or permanently because of it.

It became evident he would play in 1942 at least, but DiMaggio was not just a player, he was a husband and son too, just as baseball was not really a world separate from the rest of American commerce but was only fantasized sometimes into that dimension by the people who played it, wrote about it, or watched it. On the West Coast the real world DiMaggio and his family lived in was changing, or perhaps revealing itself as it probably always had been; it was not a place where the pastoral and slow-paced beauty of baseball set a standard that the cities surrounding the ballparks generally reflected. In an article the *New York Times* found fit to print on February 12, 1942, under the headline "WEST COAST WIDENS MARTIAL LAW CALL," Lawrence E. Davies mentioned that recent investigations in and around San Francisco among ethnic communities had disclosed "large quantities of contraband material such as fifth columnists might find helpful" such as ' guns, radios, ammunition" (staples of life otherwise to many a good American). There was already a call to move Japanese-Americans (usually just referred to as Japanese) inland, where they might better "engage in 'productive agricultural labor.'"

In the same article, reference is made to the problem that agitated the DiMaggio family during this time, the parents' status as nonnaturalized Americans: pressures to uproot some Italian families from areas designated as off-limits to non-citizens. "In this city," Davies wrote, "Joseph P. DiMaggio, Sr., father of three baseball stars, all of whom are American citizens, took out his first citizenship papers during the day, along with Mrs. DiMaggio. They live, however, outside the 'prohibited' Fisherman's Wharf area, so that Attorney General Biddle's recent order [of removal] will not require them to move." DiMaggio Sr., however, would not become a citizen until 1945, after Italy had capitulated and Allied Forces were slightly more than 100 miles from Berlin.

So the war against the Axis powers began unsettling DiMaggio's private life, as it did the lives of most Americans of the time in small ways and large. After the greatest season of DiMaggio's life, Ed Barrow tried to use the war as an excuse to cut DiMaggio's salary by $5,000 in 1942. DiMaggio, who always attempted to obtain top dollar for his play, was shocked.

Barrow in turn pretended to be amazed at DiMaggio's request for a raise. Eventually DiMaggio received about a $5,000 increase, but not until after he and Barrow had battled privately and in the press. Barrow had issued a classically self-serving managerial news release stating how appalled he was that while American "soldiers are making $21.00 a month," DiMaggio had the nerve to "want a big raise."[44] This rip in the pleasure dome did not offend fans as much as the squabble in 1938 had, because DiMaggio signed before the season began, but Barrow probably knew fan sentiment would be with him, with management, against the player whom fans did not consider a member of the labor force. DiMaggio never mentioned the incident in his autobiography, and the public of 1942 seems not to have retained detailed memory of the unpleasantness for any longer than it took to be terminated, but DiMaggio's image was affected nonetheless. The comic book *Trail Blazers* for July, 1942, which featured "The Authorized Story of the Unbeatable Yanks" contained one page devoted to DiMaggio. No mention is made of his hitting steak the year before but the story emphasizes the Yankee gamble to buy him, the restaurant he owned, the good salary the Yankees paid him, and one panel depicts him leaping into the air, preparing to stamp both feet on the ground like a petulant child, with a balloon over his head saying "I want $25,000." The caption underneath says, "Joe used to yell for more money, but he is quieter now—." The message is similar to one that a parent might send a child in a particularly moralistic fable.

The 1942 season itself would have been splendid for most players and was good for DiMaggio, but in some ways was statistically his worst since becoming a Yankee. For the first time in his life, he was on the cover of the *Sporting News*'s *Who's Who in Baseball.* He played in all 154 games for the only time in his major league career, but hit only 21 homes runs (making him fourth in the league), batted in only 114 runs, his lowest total so far (second in the league), and hit only .305, nineteen points below his previous worst year, 1938. He also managed to be fourth on the slugging percentage list, second in total bases, second in runs scored, and second in triples. In most categories, Ted Williams hit better than he. The World Series was a fitting anticlimax to the season. Although DiMaggio hit .333 the Yankees lost to the St. Louis Cardinals with Walker Cooper, Enos Slaughter, Marty Marion, Stan Musial, Terry Moore, Whitey Kurowski, Mort Cooper, Johnny Beazley, Howie Pollet, and Max Lanier, four games to one.

The first phase of DiMaggio's career ended with 1942. He was 28 years old and seemed to be, physically, at his peak. For seven full seasons, despite injuries, he had never played fewer than 120 regular games a year, batting a cumulative average of .339, and averaging 31 home runs a season. His arm was sound and greatly feared, his fielding was fabled. After three years in the service he returned and in the six major-league years left to him he dipped below the 120 game mark twice, missing half a year due to injuries. His cumulative average was .304, and his home run productivity dropped by nine a year. His fielding, always graceful, became less reliable as he slowed down, and his arm gave way to the point that he knew he had only one good throw left per game. But his central role in leading what would again become baseball's preeminent, dominant team seemed not to diminish, as though the intangibles writers and teammates always claimed he contributed, became augmented as his playing skills declined. Certainly his image acquired a greater richness of dimension during this period when he so often played in pain or with less sharp and overwhelming physical domination than before.

Generally, books and articles about DiMaggio pay little attention to the time between 1942 and 1946 when he was not performing as a professional baseball player. His marriage unravelled during these years, and his career in the service, though doubtless bringing pleasure to the armed forces personnel who saw him play with various teams, was undistinguished. He did what he was told without griping, even with determination, but frequently he was sick with stomach ailments, and never really established any rhythm of enterprise or activity that would have provided either himself or the Army Air Force with a steady sense of fulfillment in what he was accomplishing. The time spent in the service is unremarkable in terms of the DiMaggio story that most fans are interested in; it represents a blank, a forced abandonment of the direction his life had taken as a star athlete since the 1933 season. It took three seasons, from what most probably would have been prime performing years, during which he accomplished absolutely nothing relating to what his fans had come to expect from him. In his autobiography DiMaggio alludes to his wartime years in three very generalized paragraphs. In Schoor's 1956 biography little more than two pages are expended on the subject, concluding with "The war was over now" and returning to the meat of the book that DiMaggio's fans wanted. If the war years were filled with anxiety and tedium in DiMaggio's mind, he has never admitted it. However, they seem to have aged him physically and perhaps emotionally as well. It is hard to see how they could have been happy for him.

Like many a soldier he lost his wife during the war, though the war doesn't seem to have been the cause of the breakup. Before DiMaggio enlisted on December 3, 1942, Dorothy Arnold DiMaggio had already engaged a lawyer whose job was to file a divorce suit.[45] On January 13, 1943, DiMaggio and his wife were reported reconciled in Reno where Dorothy had gone to establish residency. Once in the Air Force, DiMaggio was at first stationed near Los Angeles where he could periodically visit his wife and son, but the visits did not help the disintegrating marriage and in October, 1943, his wife sued for divorce on grounds of cruelty. In May, 1944, she obtained the divorce and custody of Joe Jr. On May 13 the *New York Times* reported that she claimed DiMaggio had wrecked their marriage by his "cruel indifference." He had "never acted like a married man." Having a child, she thought, would make him "realize his responsibilities as a married man," but "even the baby's arrival did not change him." The charges are obviously one-sided, reflecting the laws of that day which demanded a public and humiliating declaration of a partner's gross dereliction. Nevada was the state famed for these "easy" divorces, requiring only a brief residency and relatively vague reports of minor shameful marital behavior.

DiMaggio's unimpressive but hardly unique batting average with his two wives—0 for 2 as surely some tabloid must have recorded it—reflects the imbalanced and uneven nature of his development as a person. A high school dropout, the son of immigrants who often did not speak English at home and were members of a very tightly-knit provincial community within a larger city whose life they only rarely participated in, DiMaggio had suddenly been transformed into a local hero who was well paid for a young man at the time, a minor league star, then in his first year in the majors a star in the biggest city in the country, playing for the most famous team in the most popular professional sport in America. By the time that male adolescence ends and young manhood begins, DiMaggio was living an incredibly high-pressured, highly rewarded, and yet cocooned existence. For seven or eight months a year he was under constant public scrutiny for his athletic exploits, lived almost totally in the society of men who traveled at least half of the time on the road, and who were surrounded by well-wishers and worshippers who could turn, almost overnight, into vicious critics. DiMaggio, who admitted when he came to organized baseball he did not know what a "quote" was, lived in the company of some of the best known public figures in a highly cosmopolitan atmosphere. As a boy he had been exceptionally shy with girls, and the women he knew best were his sisters and his mother, for whom he seems to have had great respect. What he knew of marriage and the family came from his parents and his traditional family. But many of the men and especially the women who would have been attracted to his big-time baseball world would not have been, ordinarily, like his parents, brothers, or sisters. His education as a young man had been decidedly eccentric and irregular.

Clearly, neither of the two women he married, Dorothy Arnold and Marilyn Monroe, were very much like Rosalie DiMaggio or his homebody sisters. Few American women in any case would have been trained for life as Rosalie had. The women Joe seems to have been most attracted to shared little of Rosalie's perspective and one can only assume he did not want them to: glamorous starlets, seemingly sophisticated young women, would have been attractive to him because they represented the new, bright world that he now belonged to in his public life. Dorothy was very pretty and for a time she seemed happy to leave the drab existence of her midwestern childhood for a shot at the movies or nightclub work. A sparkling young woman, she did not seem destined for life as a homebody when DiMaggio met her.

When Joe met Marilyn Monroe she had clearly emerged from a bleak and truly depressing life in California's emotional flatlands. She was dazzling, outgoing, very sexy, and she hoped to god she was on the rise—she was climbing. Although DiMaggio's development was irregular, he was a man of solid accomplishments and a stable home background that emphasized traditional values and traditional roles. Having married these lovely and (in different ways) talented, aspiring women, he seemed not to have known what to do with them. Both were types of a newer kind of woman DiMaggio had no early experience with (though what experience would have prepared him for Monroe is not easy to say). He had his own life strongly determined, his male baseball star's life on the field or talking with Toots Shor, Walter Winchell, and Jimmy Cannon at special tables in nightclub restaurants. While beautiful women were a gracious adornment to this scene, they were allowed to contribute nothing substantial to it. DiMaggio seems to have been a much better suitor than he was a husband. When he was not married to Dorothy or to Marilyn Monroe, he seems to have gotten along much better with them—that is, when he did not have to live with either of them steadily and they did not have to perform as domestics or cooks and stay-at-homes for him.

With Monroe, especially, he would ultimately learn to expect or demand less from her, as long as they were not married, and then he could be truly supportive of her needs (some of them anyway). At home with Dorothy or Marilyn, he seemed to them a dull man, but not, as far as the acrimonious language of divorce settlements reveals, mean-spirited. The kind of woman he wanted to marry (and did twice) just does not appear to have fit into his concept of wifely behavior. Strangely enough, in some ways he behaved as a husband in many ways as his father had. Both spent a great deal of their time at work, and when they were not working they were often in the company of other men of their community. But DiMaggio's life was so much more extended than his father's had been; his job precluded anything like a normal family life more than half the year; his community was more far-flung, a community of one or two intersecting interests (mainly baseball and other sports), not a community of shared place and culture, as was his father's. So while the superficial aspects of his life were similar to his father's, the substance was vastly different, and perhaps more compli-cated. Rosalie DiMaggio could share her husband's life in ways that Dorothy was not allowed to share Joe's. The fault was not so much his as it was a terrible condition of the society that formed around him as he grew up so unevenly as a young baseball hero.

Joe DiMaggio and Dorothy Arnold appear to have loved each other before, during, and after their marriage, but their lives were not shaped to fit together for long. Sometimes they reconciled and sometimes they fought (over Dorothy's demand for increased child support in 1952, for example.) On October 16, 1952, Judge Elmer Doyle denied Dorothy's petition, lecturing her that she had "made a mistake" divorcing DiMaggio. Both, it would seem, had made the mistake of marrying the other. The war did not kill their marriage and may have even prolonged it slightly. The success that lifted him from his ordinary life in San Francisco and made him a star, a hero, and a celebrity while he was still a very incomplete man, no more proficient in social wisdom that most of his buddies, helped destroy his marriage more than the war did.

The war did, however, curtail his career, though it may have allowed him to play catch-up with his life. He performed, when at all, only on the fringes of public consciousness. Throughout his Air Force hitch DiMaggio was treated deferentially as far as the war-time system permitted, as were other leading athletes such as the Army's Joe Louis. While used for morale building purposes most of the time he was on active duty, and therefore in no danger of death or mutilation in battle, DiMaggio was still subject to the orders and discipline of his superiors and had to push himself to perform on the schedule most expedient for the Air Force. A center of attraction wherever he played, the games and baseball instruction sessions he participated in were only sideshows to the war and he knew it. If he hit well or cracked a home run, crowds of enlisted men might yell, but these displays of ability would be unrecorded officially and meant nothing to the outside world, where most fans and reporters were unaware of precisely what he was doing. So for the first time in his adult life he worked unspectacularly, far from important playing fields. Even more than his job on the Yankees, his life was determined for him by his bosses, for whom he was a special but not a critical employee. Still, the Air Force, as an institution, did not hover about his life to the extent that his baseball employers did. They could not focus as much upon him, nor spotlight him in the same way Yankee management did. In a way he had an independence in the armed forces which was lacking when he was under the eye of his team's management. In some ways he was also treated as a more responsible adult than he had been as a baseball boy.

At first, back in the winter of 1943, it was not clear when, where, or even if DiMaggio would enter the service. De Gregorio says that a newspaper controversy DiMaggio engaged in with Prescott Sullivan from the San Francisco *Chronicle* underscored "DiMaggio's confused state of mind."[46] Sullivan tracked DiMaggio to Reno, where DiMaggio had followed his wife to effect a reconciliation. Sullivan tried to get DiMaggio to declare his service induction or marital plans, but DiMaggio would only reply brusquely and enigmatically. Several days later, DiMaggio even denied Sullivan's account of their conversation and did so, according to Sullivan, obscenely. Eventually, DiMaggio and Dorothy patched up their disintegrating marriage temporarily, and DiMaggio was reported in an Associated Press release as saying that his future in the military was "in the hands of my draft board," implying that he was not going to enlist. On

February 16, 1943, his draft board in North Beach announced that DiMaggio was enlisting in the Air Force under a special ruling, since individual enlistments had been formally halted at that time. How long this plan had been considered is not known, but DiMaggio clearly still did not want his private life intruded upon any more than necessary in the matters of his enlistment and his marriage.

For a time he was assigned to the Santa Ana Army Air Field and played for their baseball team. As might be expected, DiMaggio was held responsible for success against the opposition they faced, mainly local college teams, and he would be booed if the squad, hardly a sparkling aggregation, lost or performed poorly. Playing close to Dorothy and Joe Jr. should have made his time more pleasant because he could visit them frequently, but personal contact did not improve the relationship, and by October, Dorothy was suing Joe for divorce and custody. Eventually his baseball fortunes fared better, though this in no way compensated him for the breakup of his marriage. As a staff sergeant he was sent to Honolulu to join the Seventh Army Air Force team, one of the super squads built up during the war by commanders whose competitive urges propelled their interests beyond mere morale building and motivated them to play athletic empire builder. In an interesting reminiscence of those days, a correspondent for the *New York Times*, on December 5, 1982, recalled the summer of 1944 in Honolulu when such players as Mike McCormick of the Cincinnati Reds, Walt Judnich of the St. Louis Browns, and Gerry Priddy of the Washington Senators played with DiMaggio along with future major leaguers Ferris Fain and Charlie Silvera, all "ground-based airmen without wings . . . assigned to the Seventh Air Force, whose commanding officer, Brig. Gen. William Flood, was a baseball enthusiast who made sure that none of the athletes would get dishpan hands." In June the group played before 20,000 fans against a Navy team, and when DiMaggio hit a home run reportedly 450 feet long, the "crowd went nuts." The Navy team was also loaded with carefully hoarded ex-major leaguers, such as Johnny Mize and Pee Wee Reese. DiMaggio was the center of attention, however, hounded by autography hunters but apparently feeling no great excitement himself. Why should he? Air Force vs. Navy was not the Yankees against the Giants in the World Series. By this time he had again developed stomach ulcer problems and was visibly "homesick for his actress wife, Dorothy Arnold" (who in fact was no longer his wife). One night a great dance was held after one of the games, but DiMaggio did not participate. Instead, he reportedly sat in a car "a couple of hours" by himself.

In August, 1944, DiMaggio was hospitalized for the ulcers, and in September he was reassigned to the Air Transport Command, a ferrying service shuttling wounded troops to California and fresh recruits and supplies back to Honolulu. He called his ex-wife whenever he could, seeming to be still in love with her, and missing his son terribly. His ulcer ailment did not improve and in October he was sent back to the California mainland to the Fourth Air Force Hospital. Following a three week period of observation and attempted cure, he was given a three week furlough. He flew immediately to New York City to visit Dorothy, his son, and his old cronies at Toots Shor's. His weight was down from over 210 to 187 and he was on a soft food diet. Still, he looked snappy in his tailored uniform. He was assigned to the Redistribution Center in Atlantic City, New Jersey, then a summer resort town where the Yankees would practice in the spring of 1945. For six months he served at the physical training section there. A photograph in Dan Daniel's monograph shows him with a bat on his shoulder, looking good in his uniform, with his sergeant's jacket still on, standing in front of a group of t-shirted, grinning soldiers. The caption states that he is "acting out a lesson in batting," though one suspects if he were really doing this, he would first remove his coat. More likely he is acting out, acting out a lesson. But he must have provided some relief and excitement for the thousands of services personnel shuffling in and out of the recreation center. Atlantic City's fabled therapeutic salt air had no effect upon his ulcer, however, and in August, 1945, he was sent to the Don Cesar, a once flamingo-colored, splendidly garish, gorgeous pink hotel on the Gulf at St. Petersburg Beach; a marvelous structure suggesting speakeasies and Scott and Zelda Fitzgerald (who in fact once stayed there). Like DiMaggio, it was now in the drab service of its country, as a convalescent hospital for wounded servicemen. Apparently, DiMaggio's ailment was a duodenal ulcer which was first diagnosed in 1940, before the war. It was a bothersome, nagging condition fed by tensions he felt but did not like to reveal. On September 14, DiMaggio's service days were over, and on November 20, 1945, DiMaggio, best-dressed as ever, signed his 1946 Yankee contract in New York City. The team's new owners were Larry MacPhail, Dan Topping, and Del Webb, all wealthy men lacking, except MacPhail, the strong background in baseball that had played so great a part in Ed Barrow's career. DiMaggio was thirty-one when the season began, not nearly as bad off on his return as Rip Van Winkle had been when he came back to find everything changed, though he would share Rip's loss of a wife, and Rip never had to start playing again immediately with all the younger guys and an ulcer inside him.

Al Silverman reports DiMaggio saying that the war years "never seemed to move at all." He thought they "would never end." Of course using Ed Barrow's logic when he wanted to cut DiMaggio's salary in 1942, you could say DiMaggio should have considered himself lucky. He had pulled a soft tour and he came back to his old job at his old salary. He had a few of the problems plaguing the characters in the 1946 Academy Award winning film about returning veterans who had given up *The Best Years of Our Lives*, but not nearly as sharply developed as in them. It would be ludicrous to compare his erosion of skill to the loss of limbs experienced by Harold

Russell; more realistic comparisons would be that like Dana Andrews his marriage was a failure, and like Frederic March, he was returning to his old-time post but with a different, aged, perspective. Also like March, his employers wanted him to reassume the responsible position he had once been so commanding in. That would be another pressure that Rip Van Winkle never had to live through. The effect of these conditions upon DiMaggio's image was to make him a more human figure with human shortcomings. Still a superstar, his performance would no longer be as consistently magnificent as before. His sulks would be more pronounced. A grown-up playing a kid's game, his reported perfection would be tempered by obvious frailties. But curiously, his heroism as a player would become even more legendary.

So he changed as the baseball world around him changed. Like so many World War II veterans, he had to adjust to new conditions upon his return. At first he got along well with his new owners, none of them men like the old-fashioned baseball frontiersman Barrow, or the aristocratic Ruppert. MacPhail, Topping (on his fourth marriage in 1946; one ex-spouse having been the once popular movie ice queen Sonja Henie), and Webb (who belonged to fourteen golf clubs across the country) were men with many interests outside baseball. They tended to be colder and more shifting in their attitudes toward Yankee personnel. And as De Gregorio says, "the Yankees served them, if not as a plaything, then as a vehicle for publicity and public relations goodwill in bigger enterprises." MacPhail however, was easier to deal with financially than Barrow, and after the war DiMaggio never again had to squabble for more money. The triumvirate did things differently. For the first time the Yankees had a February pretraining period outside the country, in Balboa, Panama Canal Zone, prior to St. Petersburg. Dan Daniel (1950) reported the happy mood attained there on one night anyway, when improbably enough, DiMaggio and Joe McCarthy crowned the queen of a carnival at the Club Atlas.

McCarthy's gaiety did not last long into the season, however, and in May, claiming he felt ill but also tired of arguments arising from what he considered to be the interference of MacPhail, he quit. DiMaggio, who had seen only one Yankee manager through 1942, played under three in 1946—McCarthy, Bill Dickey, and Johnny Neun. Another new feature of the season was that for the first time the Yankees flew in airplanes on some of their away trips, special charters. On the evening of May 28, 1946, the Yankees played their first home night baseball game, an act that could be seen as symbolic of the new Yankees no longer under Barrow's traditional control, for he had always opposed the phenomenon. DiMaggio singled for the only run the Yankees made in a losing cause.

Like a typical veteran, DiMaggio's adjustment was successful in some ways, and unsuccessful in others. He fit back in, was again the team leader, and fitfully displayed his old talents. But neither he nor the team attained their pre-war level. Public attitude toward him was ambivalent. Many Americans wanted him to return to his old scene better than when he had departed it for the war and rooted for his recovery, just as the audiences attending *The Best Years of Our Lives* wanted those returning veterans to slip back into their old positions, improved by their military experiences. "The Army must have done it," *Time* stated in its April 8 issue. "The Great DiMaggio, who once made news if he showed up for any spring hitting at all, hadn't changed much physically. The sheen of his black hair was flecked with grey: his weight (a pre-war 205) was down to 190. But his dispostion, like his ulcers, was better. He still knew that he was the greatest baseball player alive, but now he talked as if he were only as good in his business as many others are in theirs." Where pictures before the war often showed him with his mother, father, and sisters, *Time* showed him with his son, for whom he was reportedly (unlike his own father) having a special, small baseball mitt made.

He was not however, by any measurable index, "the greatest player alive," not in 1946 anyway, and the fans could see his diminishment of skill. His friend Jimmy Cannon wrote of this time that "the attitude of the galleries in St. Petersburg, the first spring Joe was back from the war indicated his greatness as a ballplayer. They conceded him perfection but they took it out on him when they detected a temporary flaw in his skill."

DiMaggio himself was aware of the need to change his attitude toward the game if not his performance in it. Gene Schoor quotes him as saying at this time, "I'm tired of being called a sourpuss. I want people to like me, and I try to like them. I'm learning to take all that stuff, and I guess maybe, if I could relax and smile a little more, it would be better all around."

Behind the scenes, the 1946 Yankees were a team in turmoil. In an interview with Maury Allen, MacPhail claimed that McCarthy was "drinking too much and . . . wasn't eating right." Vic Raschi, who was to become one of the Yankee's best pitchers in their not-yet-achieved new era, told Allen that "No rookie ever broke into a more confused situation than me" in 1946. "There I was a rookie, my first day with the Yankees, and I was on the mound."[47] The Yankees were in what could be termed a transitional period. A few of the players who had starred for them in war-time baseball were producing far below their previous levels. Their first baseman, Nick Etten, always clumsy on the field, had hit 22 home runs in 1944 to win that title, but managed only nine in 1946 against better pitching, and batted a feeble .232. George Stirnweiss, a utility infielder who captured the batting title in 1945 with a low but decent mark of .309, hit only .251. The old-timers such as DiMaggio were performing unevenly. After a year in the Merchant Marine, "King Kong" Keller hit .275 with 30 home runs, but also won the league's strikeout title with 101. Tommy Henrich was down to .251, and Phil Rizzuto batted .257, or what would be sixteen points beneath his ultimate lifetime average. Some good newcomers were on their way up, such as Raschi, Yogi Berra, and Bobby Brown, but they arrived only at the end of the season, and could not lift the Yankees out of third place behind Boston whose exceptionally solid hitting team featured Johnny Pesky, Dom DiMaggio, Pinky Higgins, Ted Williams, Rudy York, Bobby Doerr, and Wally Moses. Williams hit .342 in his first season since 1942.

DiMaggio was upset by McCarthy's departure. In his autobiography he says that at first the Yankees played all right though they did not match Boston's pace, which bothered them, as did McCarthy's resignation, which according to DiMaggio was caused by poor health. He does not discuss the fights between MacPhail and McCarthy, nor McCarthy's alleged drinking, though he does suggest the intensity of his feelings toward McCarthy by saying he "was like a father to most of us." At first DiMaggio batted well even while the Yankees were losing ground to the Red Sox. In the team's first 41 games he hit twenty home runs. Then he slumped, and hit sporadically for the rest of the year, adding only five more home runs to his total. His final batting average was poor for him, .290. Though he played in 132 games, he was either hurt or injured for most of the season. Just before the All-Star game, for which he was selected, he sprained his knee sliding into second base in an away game against the Philadelphia Athletics. What would become his famous heel injury began paining him in 1946, and he was forced to parcel out his efforts carefully over long stretches of constant playing or during doubleheaders. He explained to Bill Dickey that he was not loafing when he sometimes did not run out grounders with his old speed, because he was trying to conserve himself. The heel injury also affected his throwing though no one noticed that but him. So when he came back in 1946, he was a different player and a different person: older, more cautious, but still intense to win, trying to be more prudent in his relations with the press and public, his skills not so effortlessly demonstrated.

For the second time in his playing days the Yankees did not enter the World Series. In his autobiography he solaces himself with the observation that at least his home run total was four higher than it had been in 1942, that only five more hits would have lifted him into the .300 category, and that his runs batted in total was good enough for sixth in the league. Only a falsely dramatic account of his career would begin tugging at the bells tolling doom for him his first season back. If he had doubts that the very greatest must have when they realize they are no longer precisely on top, he never revealed them. If not the greatest, as *Time* suggested, he was still the great DiMaggio. *Sport* magazine, probably the country's preeminent generalized periodical on the subject during the 1940s and through much of the 1950s, featured him on the cover of their premier September, 1946, issue (an honor or sign of recognition they would continue for several years). He was still a celebrity, but not so often a hero in 1946.

Had DiMaggio's career concluded or trailed off significantly after 1946 it is certain that because of his past all-around proficiency, and particularly because of his streak, he would have remained a legend within baseball. It is doubtful however that he would have attained the greater mythic dimensions he ultimately achieved through his continued high caliber play coupled with his image as a wounded player who constantly came back and aided his team, despite recurrent injuries and, reportedly, incessant pain. Early in his career, before he played in a single major league game with the Yankees, he had twice demonstrated his proneness to injury and his ability to bounce back from it. Starting with the 1947 season and increasingly each year, he was frequently identified as a crippled player who even so, played with his entire body to win victory for his team. As Allie Reynolds, one of the stars of the Yankee's 1947 World Series championship team told Maury Allen, "He gave a thousand percent every game, day in, day out, for a lot of years. That takes a great deal out of a man."[48]

Reynolds came to the Yankees during the off-season in a trade that sent Joe Gordon to Cleveland. DiMaggio had in fact suggested that the Yankees ask for Reynolds, at that time a risky choice. Also new on the Yankees in 1947 was their manager Bucky Harris. DiMaggio missed the first four games of the season because Harris was afraid to rush him back into action while he was slowly recovering from an operation of January 7, 1947, to remove a three-inch bone spur from his left heel. The injury had been discovered when DiMaggio was given a physical shortly after signing his 1947 contract, which incidentally called for the same $43,750 he had received in 1942 and 1946. Dan Daniel's 1950 book contains both an X-ray photograph of the spur, which looks like a sharp scimitar jutting from the curve of DiMaggio's heel bone, and a picture of him fully dressed but with his left foot bare and bandaged. The heel, operated on by Dr. Jules Gordon, had not mended by March, and on the eleventh of that month Dr. Edward Hanrahan grafted a patch of DiMaggio's skin from his right leg over it, to speed his recovery. From 1947 on, the iconic newspaper and magazine photographs of DiMaggio emphasized his wounds more and more.

His once-fabled arm also troubled him badly in 1947 and went virtually dead. In his autobiography he notes that while in 1946 he threw out fifteen players in 1947 he had only two assists. He husbanded his throwing resources, and would make only two really solid throws from the outfield in pregame practice, to convince opposing teams that he still had power to spare.

In his first at-bat, after sitting out the opening games, he hit a home run. By June 16 *Time* reported exuberantly to the populace what local newspaper or *Sporting News* readers had been reading about all season, "The great Joseph Paul (Joe) DiMaggio, a man who had not been looking his best, was at last coming up to snuff." He was then the American League's leading hitter, at .361. The article compared DiMaggio with Johnny Mize, who would hit 51 home runs for the New York Giants that season. Though *Time* mentioned DiMaggio's age (32) it was silent about Mize's, who was actually born the year before DiMaggio. But DiMaggio was beginning to seem older than he was. Injuries contributed to his image as an aging player, but so did the role he assumed on the team more and more. To nearly all the other players, especially the younger and more recently arrived veterans, and even to the players who had performed with him before the war, DiMaggio was the "Big Guy," "The Yankee Clipper," the man they looked up to. While he was still seen as a loner during this time, in most players' minds he was the man who provided leadership or general guidance for them. Very rarely, as once when Yogi Berra dogged it and did not catch for both games of a crucial doubleheader, he would pointedly criticize. More often though, his advice was positive, or he would demonstrate by example.

In 1947 his special project was the struggling relief pitcher Joe Page. Known as the "Fireman," or more frequently as "The Gay Reliever" (a pun on the term for falsies [gay deceivers] focusing on Page's antic deviltries and definitely not on his sexual inclinations), Page roomed for a time with DiMaggio who had a fondness for a few players like Page; showboats and brawlers, heavy drinkers, talented scapegraces, his own opposites whose freedom from constraint he perhaps admired. He would tolerate though never condone their behavior if it appeared to limit their abilities. At first he tried to calm down and reassure the nervous, erratic Page of his talent. But as Page told Maury Allen, after he returned late and drunk to the room he and DiMaggio shared in Boston, he was castigated by DiMaggio and told he was destroying himself and hurting the team. After that espisode DiMaggio paid extra for a single room on the road, but he continued to befriend and support Page, who was grateful for DiMaggio's loyalty. The year turned out to be one of Page's best, and he saved or won many important games, e.g. allowing the Brooklyn Dodgers only one hit during the last five innings of the Yankees's final victory over them.

DiMaggio did not continue his early hitting pace, but finished the year at .315. His home run production was down to twenty, sixth in the league after Ted Williams's 32. His 97 runs batted in placed him second behind Williams's 114. Williams was also the batting champion with .343, and was first to DiMaggio's second in slugging average and total bases. Many still feel that Williams should have won the league's Most Valuable Player award, but for the third time the prize was given to DiMaggio. The strongest legitimate argument for that decision was the Yankees' pennant victory and Boston's third place finish. DiMaggio also made only one error in 141 games and was the league's leading fielder—weak arm and all—at .997. His 1947 performance demonstrated to the American people even more than his 1946 play had, that his performance was returning to normal. He provided yet another piece of the picture of "normalcy" that Joe Louis also had contributed to in 1946 by knocking out Billy Conn more rapidly and convincingly the second time than the first (in 1941), and Tami

Mauriello, one of a number of ersatz war-time claimants to the duration heavyweight title. Such victories were reassuring though, unlike DiMaggio, Louis's greatest days were all behind him.

Two events in the DiMaggio story, often retold by writers, occurred in 1947. One was silly, one was a heroic sports action. Early in the year DiMaggio took extra batting practice to help himself from a slump. The flamboyant, publicity-seeking MacPhail wanted to cut into this time for a picture-taking session, an interruption Ed Barrow would probably have sneered at. DiMaggio, together with five other players, refused and MacPhail punished the rebels with a celebrated $100.00 fine. On July 14, *Time*, ever supportive of management, attributed the Yankees' first place position partly to this action which it said "cleared the air . . . when club president Larry MacPhail fined six stubborn players (including DiMaggio) for refusing to cooperate with the Yankee promotion office." MacPhail later gave DiMaggio a chance to recoup his loss by awarding him the cash prize in a home run hitting contest, but DiMaggio reportedly told him to donate the money to charity. Gene Schoor (1956) claimed that from this time on DiMaggio was privately cool to MacPhail.

The second and more legendary event of the year came in the Yankees' sixth game in the World Series with Brooklyn. The Series had already seen one rare and thrilling moment when Floyd "Bill" Bevans almost threw a no-hitter in game four, only to watch, appalled, when with two out in the ninth inning, Cookie Lavagetto doubled home two men to win the game. DiMaggio, who hit only .231 in the seven games, won the fifth game for the Yankees, with a home run. The sixth game was frantic with a record 38 men used. In the sixth inning the Yankees were losing 8-5 with DiMaggio at bat and two men on base. DiMaggio hit the ball hard directly toward the 415 foot sign in left field. Everyone who writes about the World Series, the Yankees, or DiMaggio tries to recapture the splendor of Al Gionfriddo's last split-second leap, grab, and trap of the ball to rob DiMaggio of what would have been a game-tying home run, but it was one of those brave catches whose beauty is in its absolute unrecapturability. It was as John Drebinger wrote the next day, October 6, in the *New York Times*, "a breathtaking catch" that "stunned the proud Bombers and jarred even the usually imperturbable DiMaggio. Taking his position in centerfield with the start of the next inning, he was still walking inconsolably in circles, doubtless wondering whether he could believe in his senses." A number of players and writers have commented that it was one of the few times that DiMaggio showed anger on the field, kicking the second base bag as he trotted angrily out to his position, sending up swirls of dust. The game was televised, and I can still remember watching in horror, heartbroken with millions of other Yankee rooters, the incredible upflinging of the nondescript Gionfiddo's body, and his plucking of the tiny ball from the vast Yankee Stadium air. He was five feet, six inches tall, and after 1947 he would never play major league baseball again. John Drebinger referred to him as a "25-year-old gardener," but he has a place in baseball history because of that one moment.

Page starred the next day, and the great World Series was over. The Yankees defeated a Brooklyn team whose players' names roll off the tongue like an incantation of baseball magic, some of the boys of summer in Roger Kahn's book, evoking grass green memories of their now gone greatness, legends mingled with DiMaggio's own: Dixie Walker (not yet traded because, so they said, he hated Jackie Robinson's blackness); Jackie Robinson himself in his first of ten historic years; feisty Eddie Stanky; Pee Wee Reese; Spider Jorgensen; Gene Hermanski; Carl Furillo; Pistol Pete Reiser; Cookie ("Cookie! Cookie!" came the cries all over Ebbets Field when he came to bat) Lavagetto; Gil Hodges; and Ralph Branca, his heart two years away from being broken by Bobby Thomson's playoff victory swat.

DiMaggio had good reason to be satisfied with the season. He had not overwhelmed enemy pitching as he had in his early years, certainly not like the younger Ted Williams did, but he had targeted his abilities in the right direction, and his team had won. In his autobiography he recollected that Phil Rizzuto and Tommy Henrich were the only 1942 Yankees to play regularly against Brooklyn again in 1947. He had befriended Rizzuto his first spring training with the Yankees. Though Henrich told Maury Allen "everybody" knew that "Joe was kind of a cold guy" he also thought he was "the greatest ballplayer I ever saw" and "the most moral man I ever knew."[49] The old Yankees and the new, Reynolds and Page, recognized that if DiMaggio was not the league's most valuable player in 1947, he was close to it.

DiMaggio's private life at this time revolved around his son, when he could see him. Joe Jr. lived mainly with his mother or attended private school, but his father had visitation rights that enabled him to spend time with his son off season, and occasionally permitted the boy to watch him at spring training or during the actual season. Joe had continued to see his ex-wife Dorothy to work toward a reconciliation, until her marriage in 1946 to George Schubert, a stockbroker. Dorothy even helped Joe recollect some of his days of glory for Tom Meany who was writing Joe's autobiography. The first edition of *Lucky to Be a Yankee* is most flattering to Dorothy, but the later editions which incorporate his baseball experiences through 1950 remove some pleasant allusions to her. Otherwise, Joe seems to have established no deep relationships with women during these post-war years strong enough to draw the attention of writers. George Solotaire, one of Joe's best and most loyal Broadway friends, who after trying a number of vocations in attempts to make himself a feature of the city's life became best known as a very successful ticket broker, continued along with Toots Shor and a few of the older sportswriters to form a friendly male community in which DiMaggio could feel comfortable in New York. In San Francisco his own family occupied much of his time, though by 1948 he no longer took any active role in running the famous restaurant that still carried his name.

Many of the women he saw in New York he seems to have met through Solotaire, who was glad to locate attractive dates for him just as he would have been glad to get him tickets to a good show. The women were invariably attractive, young, and happy to be seen with the great DiMaggio, but there is no record of an enduring romance with any of them. Although for at least one-third of each year he was not playing baseball, biographic detail about these times is generally sparse, as though he went into hibernation between seasons. He was emotionally close to his son and clearly missed not sharing a common, constant life with him, though as a baseball star he could not have achieved this easily anyway. He was aging rapidly as an athlete and entering into a phase of his playing days in which his injuries increasingly affected him and this must have also made him anxious. He lived very fully in the life of his old family, but must have wondered what kind of a new family he would establish for himself, since a future with Dorothy was out of the question.

The Yankee management changed slightly in 1948 but this did not bother DiMaggio because the odd man out was Larry MacPhail. Dan Topping and Del Webb were now the chief owners and George Weiss was general manager. Like Ed Barrow, a tough, hard man to deal with, Weiss bullied players when possible. In his autobiography *Number One*, Billy Martin called him "a very serious, humorless man. He ran the Yankees like a Hitler." He also had contempt for most of the working press. "You can buy any of them with a steak," he once said.[50] Bucky Harris was again field manager. DiMaggio's salary took a great leap forward to around $70,000. According to Maury Allen, in April, 1947, Topping and Boston Red Sox owner Tom Yawkey had discussed and tentatively concluded a trade of Ted Williams for DiMaggio.[51] Though the deal made a crazy kind of sense—for the dimensions of each star's home field were better suited to the other player—it was never consummated. Now in 1948, DiMaggio, as always, seemed a solid fixture in center field, again a performer whose playing skills matched his reputation. A Yankee press release for opening day stressed DiMaggio's centrality to the team. In this silver anniversary season, which would begin with the presentation of World Series rings and watches at home plate by baseball Commissioner A. B. "Happy" Chandler. "Jolting Joe DiMaggio," the Yankees announced, "their brightest star, will linger to receive the Judge Landis Memorial Plaque, rewarding his selection by the Baseball Writer's Association of America as the Most Valuable Player in the American League." Another ceremony honoring Yankee announcer Mel Allen as baseball's "No. 1 broadcaster" followed, and then the Seventh Regiment Band played the national anthem as it had "at every Yankee Stadium opener since it was honored in 1923 by guest conductor

John Phillip Sousa.'' Miss Lucy Monroe, ''the Star Spangled Banner girl'' sang. To continue the festivities joining the old and the new and linking baseball to the heart of the American way of life, Governor Thomas Dewey of New York (in half a year he was to be humiliated by Harry Truman's upset presidential victory over him) would throw out the first ball before thousands of spectators, ''including Babe Ruth, the outstanding figure in Yankee Stadium quarter-century history.'' (Ruth would die August 16 of that year).

After such an auspicious start, the 1948 season was an anticlimax for the Yankees. Although engaged in a three-way battle for first place they finished third, behind Boston and Cleveland, who eventually defeated the Boston Braves 4-2 in the World Series. After the season was over, Harris was fired as manager, and Casey Stengel hired. DiMaggio had an excellent season, though it was physically costly. He played in 153 games (once singling as a pinch-hitter) and led the league with 39 home runs and 155 runs batted in. He batted .320 and while his slugging average was second to Ted Williams's, his total bases led the league. Among active players his career home run total was the highest in the league and, when he hit his 300th against Detroit late in the season, he became only the tenth player in major league history to achieve that mark.

1948 was also one of the years when DiMaggio played in pain much of the time. He had developed another bone spur, this time in his right foot, that would prove even more troublesome than the earlier spur in his left foot. Several sources report him saying that at times the pain felt like ''someone driving an ice pick into my heel.'' Various devices were installed in his equipment to alleviate the pain, and he even tried to change his way of running and walking, which usually pounded rather heavily on his heels. These makeshift nostrums only brought new pressures on other parts of his body which then became stiff and sore. But because the Yankees were in a struggle for first place, he remained in the lineup day after day. When his old friend sportswriter Jimmy Cannon caught him at his hotel walking down the stairs gingerly like an old man, he made Cannon agree not to print the news until after the season was over.[52] He began to sometimes seek reassurance from other Yankees about his ability. Peter Golenbeck reports him asking one of his teammates after a time at bat ''How . . . how . . . how did I lo-lo-look up there? Did I look okay?'' He also seemed, according to Golenbeck, to enjoy ''little pep talks'' before he hit. '' 'You've got to really bear down and knock in these runs,' [Billy] Johnson or [Johnny] Lindell would say to DiMaggio.''[53]

But he did not play tentatively and was the team's leader as much as ever. Eddie Lopat, a pitcher new to the Yankees in 1948, reported that after Yogi Berra begged off catching the second game of a difficult doubleheader, DiMaggio, who played both games and ''was totally out on his feet'' afterwards, ''flopped . . . down'' in the clubhouse and just sat and drank a beer until Berra started telling jokes in front of him. "You're 23 years old, and you can't catch a doubleheader? My ass," DiMaggio yelled. "You could have heard a pin drop in that clubhouse," Lopat said. "He chewed out his ass for twenty minutes. . . . After that, Yogi caught more games than any other catcher."[54]

Telling of another game around this time against Cleveland, Lopat also provided an insight into one of the many "intangibles" so many players and writers claim DiMaggio possessed. Pitching against the Cleveland shortstop Lou Boudreau in a close game with the winning runs on base, Lopat ptiched two balls to Boudreau. Lopat looked into the outfield and saw DiMaggio in dead center. Turning back to the batter, Lopat threw "a fast ball over the middle of the plate" that Boudreau whacked into left center where Lopat figured it would be good for a double or triple, but when he glanced back he saw DiMaggio positioned directly in front of it, catching the ball for the final out. Lopat asked DiMaggio why he had moved and DiMaggio said he figured with the count two and nothing Lopat could not afford to keep the ball away from Boudreau and would throw it where Boudreau could pull it if he connected.

One of the most revealing days in DiMaggio's career came in the season's final series with Boston at Fenway Park. By this time the Yankees were no longer in contention for the pennant, which would go to either Boston or Cleveland. Hurting badly, DiMaggio was told by Bucky Harris he did not have to play, but DiMaggio insisted because he felt fans would think he had voluntarily removed himself to give his brother Dom's team a better chance at victory. On the next-to-last day of the season, with his father in the stands rooting for Boston, DiMaggio made three hits including a home run, though the Red Sox won. On the last day he went four for five. His last hit bounced off the left field wall but all he could do was limp to first. Bucky Harris then removed him from the game, and as DiMaggio says in his autobiography, "I hobbled off the field on my bum gam." The Boston fans—who were always more appreciative toward DiMaggio than New York fans were to Williams—gave him a tremendous ovation: the wounded hero had triumphed in defeat. On October 4, *Time* magazine put DiMaggio on its cover again and celebrated his skill and his injuries. "The center-fielder of the New York Yankees had the worst charley horse he could remember. He wore a thick bandage over his left thigh (to support the strained muscles) and a second bandage around his middle to hold up the first one. Said Joseph Paul DiMaggio, more in simple fact than in complaint: 'I feel like a mummy.'" *Time*'s cover photograph of his face shows him a handsome man, unlike the homely kid he had been as a rookie. Though even in his early days his name had been associated with injury, now it was almost synonymous with achievement through enduring pain.

Events following the 1948 season, which brought him in some ways both his best and worst times as a player and a person, further reinforced and intensified this part of his image. His identity as a sports hero was strengthened by his triumphs over adversity. DiMaggio's actions following the 1948 season and through closing day for 1949 are sometimes puffed out of proportion by sportswriters and idolatrous fans. But if he is perceived as a craftsman or perhaps an artist who suffered the crippling of his skills through physical infirmity brought on partly by aging and partly by the reckless intensity with which he typically practiced his vocation, then the kind of attention he received is more understandable. A. E. Housman's lovely poem "To an Athlete Dying Young" suggests that athletes are symbols of human fate, that all stardom is temporary; perhaps it is right to revel in its occasional peak performances. By 1949 DiMaggio had become a symbol of athletic and therefore human greatness, a focus of popular attention whose burden or privilege it was to embody certain skills and virtues transcending sport. His comeback in 1949 struck even non-baseball fans as a meaningful human achievement and not just another athletic victory. His earlier greatness, his continued superiority to most players year in and year out, and particularly his unparalleled (and in the public mind anyway, unmatchable) hitting streak made his status as a baseball legend secure, though ultimately very different than it had been early in his career, both more human and more than human.

The physical problem that caused him so much bodily and emotional grief was another bone spur, in his right heel this time.[55] The heel had pained him since shortly after the start of the 1948 season, and on November 11 he entered the Johns Hopkins University hospital in Baltimore, where a week later Dr. George Bennett operated on it (as he had almost exactly a year previously operated on DiMaggio's throwing arm).[56] The success of the operation would not be known until DiMaggio tested his heel during spring training.

A less gnawing but as it turned out more long-lasting problem he experienced during the off season was the adjustment to the idea of Casey Stengel as his new manager. Stengel had been hired shortly after the World Series to replace Bucky Harris, who had not delivered the expected pennant to the Yankee management. DiMaggio was one of the first of the team to pose with Stengel, probably to symbolize Stengel's acceptance since Harris had been popular with most of the players and the press. In 1949 Stengel's image as a comic if not a clown was infinitely firmer than his status as a weirdly astute and perceptive handler of talent. In only one of his ten previous seasons as a manager had his teams won more than they had lost, and their highest finish was fifth. Stengel advocates might claim he guided mediocre teams to even better records than they otherwise would have achieved, but since his teams finished seventh five times, this interpretation would have been argued by many in 1949. DiMaggio, unlike Ruth, seem not to have possessed any clear and immediate desires to become a manager, but it appears that around the time Stengel was hired he would have liked to have been asked or consulted with. "In later years" George De Gregorio wrote, "he would confide to friends that he was never approached about it and that he thought it would be bad form for him openly to have sought the position." Joe McCarthy, the greatly respected coach of his early years, now managed the Boston Red Sox (from 1948 through the first 62 games of 1950). DiMaggio was comfortable with continuity, and as an older player with physical problems it was natural for him to feel some anxiety over what Stengel's regime might be like. The days were long gone when DiMaggio could relate to managers as father figures, and it is questionable whether he would ever have been emotionally attracted to a leader with Stengel's funny, undignified, yet strangely effective manner. On Stengel's side there was a matching anxiety, for he knew that the moody DiMaggio was a strong fixture on the team, an on-the-field leader if not one who ordinarily meddled in the everyday direction of the players, a very highly paid (in 1949 his salary was about $90,000) but aging star performer.

At first, both moved carefully into their relationship and its chemistry was unremarkable. Though according to Robert Creamer, Stengel was "uneasy in his relationship with DiMaggio during the three seasons Joe was under him as a player,"[57] he treated DiMaggio very gingerly, advising him for example to set his own pace during spring training. Certainly during the nerve-wracking but ultimately splendid 1949 battle for the pennant, the public was unaware that in some ways, Stengel and DiMaggio were a bit like two wary dogs sniffing each other before deciding how they were to respond. Stengel was especially gracious and after DiMaggio's great performance in Boston said in language amazingly direct for him, "He's the best I've ever had." Possibly, as Phil Rizzuto—no great supporter of Stengel—told Maury Allen, "Stengel was as much in awe of Joe DiMaggio . . . as any player on the team."[58]

The year 1949 itself progressed well enough. In February, the Italian-Americans, who had been so loyal to DiMaggio since his San Francisco Seals days, awarded him another honor, the *Unico National* calling him one of the "ten outstanding Italian-American men in the United States." The list demonstrated the breadth of Italian-American achievement and included John O. Pastore, then Governor of Rhode Island; Enrico Fermi, the atomic energy genius; and Frank Capra, one of the country's most important film directors. Not all of the names on the list were of lasting distinction—few remember today the popular Newark baritone Phil Brito, who was recognized for his significance as an entertainer and a social worker—but the announcement nonetheless indicated DiMaggio's continued ethnic popularity among a group who had only recently emerged from the particularly complicated trauma of a world war in which the country of their national origin had been America's enemy. That one of the leading players in the most American of professional games was of Italian descent was still important to the Italian-Americans.

DiMaggio vacationed in Mexico City before spring training, and an atypical picture in Dan Daniel's monograph shows him awkwardly but happily dancing in a nightclub there with an attractive young woman who was wearing a scanty costume. Not long after the picture was taken, DiMaggio reported to spring training at St. Petersburg, and soon bad things began happening to him, really bad things and not just minor annoyances. He was going to be going through one of the worst times of his adult life, not just as a ballplayer, but as a person, a time more painful probably than the protracted period of his first divorce.

With Stengel's endorsement he started training slowly and under his own direction, so he could discover how well his heel had recovered from the November operation on it. From the earliest training days in St. Petersburg "he was a very worried man," Arthur Daley reported, "strangely abrupt and almost surly."[9] He played to test his heel and also to satisfy the paying customers who came to watch him, but he played unhappily. During a tour of Texas, on April 10 he batted one for two in a game against the Class B Greenville Majors in a game the Yankees lost 4-3, and left limping after hitting in the third inning. He had also limped during the team's previous game at Beaumont. On April 11 against Dallas of the Texas League he batted zero for two and left the game early again, being replaced by Hank Bauer who had joined the Yankees the year before. DiMaggio was still visibly limping by this time. On April 12 the Yankees reported that DiMaggio would miss their opening game once more, and newspapers the following day conjectured whether he would ever play again. Following the Dallas game, on the suggestion of Johns Hopkins's Dr. George Bennett, DiMaggio had been taken to a well-known local orthopedic specialist, Dr. P. M. Girard. Bennett had been consulting with Dr. Sidney Gaynor, the Yankee physician, since the training camp period in St. Pettersburg. In Dallas, Dr. Girard recommended reinstatement of treatment by "injections and X-ray." DiMaggio was flown to Baltimore and early on the morning of April 13, he was admitted to Johns Hopkins for observation and the start of treatment. He was discharged April 14.

Some of the Yankees were shocked by DiMaggio's sudden departure. Jerry Coleman told Maury Allen that "it took the heart out of the ball club and made everybody grouchy." In Baltimore, DiMaggio was bitterly frustrated about his condition and became extremely angry at reporters who asked him the same questions over and over again, and who were invading the corridors of the hospital to penetrate his private feelings. Desperately anxious over his condition he wanted to be by himself; to him it seemed that the reporters were hounding him. From the reporters' standpoint he was the news they had to cover; to the object of their interest they might have seemed like buzzards circling around a staggering body. As a *Newsweek* reporter wrote on April 11 "he was still the man the Yankees must have," and if they were not to have him because of his heel, people would want to know. As if to question why DiMaggio was so testy now, the same article noted that before "he had never been the kind to baby himself. Last year, despite a bad heel, swollen knees, strained tendons, and a charley horse that bulged grotesquely in one thigh, he had played in 153 games and had led the league in homers and clutch-spot hitting."

During his stay at the hospital they buzzed around him like gnats. Gene Schoor (1956) reported that while DiMaggio was being wheeled to an operating room a photographer snapped his picture and Joe "screamed at the man." "Reporters Upset Ailing DiMaggio" the *Times* headlined April 15, quoting DiMaggio's answer when asked as he hobbled through the hospital lobby if he wanted to see the reporters, "You're damned right. . . . Don't you think you've gone far enough?"

According to *Time* on April 25, in a depressingly titled article that posed the same question that doubtless DiMaggio kept asking himself, "A Few Weeks or Forever?", when he finally limped from the hospital on crutches he "snapped at reporters: 'Leave me alone . . . you guys are driving me batty.' It was not like the usually soft-spoken DiMag, but the Yankee's center fielder had cause for being testy: it seemed possible he might never play again." A few days later (actually one day, on April 15), according to *Time,* DiMaggio tried to apologize for his outburst and claimed that he expected "to be back in the line-up this season . . . these things have been cured before, and I guess it's just a matter of time."[60] In his autobiography his apology is worded in a strangely un-DiMaggio-like idiom, more resembling that of Lady Brett in Hemingway's *The Sun Also Rises* than his own: "when a chap is sick with worry, he doesn't always think of the other fellow."

So he returned to his New York apartment and lived like an invalid, listening to the Yankee games on the radio or watching them on television and feeling both bored and tense. Sometimes he talked to old friends such as Toots Shor, but of course no one could cure his heel for him or enable him to play the one game he had so far demonstrated talent in, the one activity that lifted him from indolence and anonymity and gave him money and fame. When May warmed up both New York and the pennant race he still spent most of the time in his rooms, sometimes with his son, who he said in his autobiography, gave him somebody beside himself to think about. He read books sometimes and drank coffee and stayed up until three or four in the morning, unable to sleep.

He left New York once in early May to attend his father's funeral in San Francisco. Giuseppe DiMaggio had finally been able to pass his naturalization test April 9, 1945, so that he could become a citizen. He had tried earlier in December, 1944, but he was not strong enough in understanding written English, an inability caused by either nervousness or lack of practice, since he was clearly intelligent enough to master the rudiments of the American language. He was also illiterate in Italian. When he first failed the judge told him to "go home and study a little harder," which though he was in his seventies he did. Rosalie had passed in December, an achievement Giuseppe must have greeted with mixed feelings, considering his own failure. He always belonged to the tightly-knit Italian-American community, and though all his children became thoroughly integrated into American ways of life, in his day-to-day existence he was often immersed in an Italian social and linguistic context. He always spoke with a thick Italian accent and as late as eight months before his death, when he traveled east to watch Dominic and Joe in the final games of 1948, questions asked of him in English sometimes had to be translated into Italian so that he could answer them better. Tom told Maury Allen that it was just a story that Giuseppe DiMaggio vigorously objected to Joe's playing baseball—his argument was that Joe should get an education, that was the way to become a success in America. He did not know at first that baseball was a way for some to earn a very good living. When he saw that first Vince and then Joe would be rewarded for playing their American game he was very pleased with them. But he never lived in the American grain as his children did. It may even be that his difficulties passing the naturalization exam resulted from a resistance to do so, a reluctance quite natural to many immigrants who felt they could embrace dual loyalties, rarely a popular concept among American officials who determined immigration policies.

In stories about his most famous son, Giuseppe is usually portrayed as a gruff, hardworking man but slightly comic too, slipping into the life-with-Luigi stereotype popular among Americans even before the radio character presented it before national audiences. In this comic book characterization—one that dominates even more literate works such as Gene Schoor's books—he is a slightly befuddled figure. He was a man born into poverty, whose hard life in the new world demanded that he rise before dawn each day that he hoped the fish ran, so that he could place his family into a position where they might not have to scratch so hard to make a living as he forced himself to; who saw his son (several of his sons) rise to a rare level of material and social success for a game played a couple of hours in the afternoon spring and summer; who saw one son honored by grand institutions and important political figures. He was a figure that writers found easy to sentimentalize, but his gritty, complicated, pressure-filled life as an immigrant and father of nine children, as a worker in a highly competitive business, should dispel that image of him. The pictures *Life* selected for inclusion in their 1939 article about Joe are revealing about his father. In a group photograph he stands to one side as his wife stands at the other, both heavyset with gray hair, very solid looking parents, almost like columns containing the rest of the happy family (except Vince and "several peewee DiMaggios") between them. Already Giuseppe looks older than a typical American father with his old-fashioned, immigrant's hair cut. In another picture he sits, obviously posed, with Joe. Both are holding crabs, Giuseppe easily and Joe gingerly. Still another picture shows Giuseppe and Rosalie sitting stiffly in new chairs in the living room of the house their dutiful son has bought them.

As though the fact were too private for him to mention, DiMaggio's father's death on May 3 is unnoted in his autobiography.

Another occurence that is not mentioned in his autobiography or in most of the literature about him, that began while DiMaggio's heel was, he hoped, mending, was more bizarre. DiMaggio began receiving love notes from a woman he did not know. The notes were signed "Junior Standish" but Miss Standish, a Broadway dancer who did know DiMaggio, had not written them. Columnists also received letters from the false Junior Standish telling them about the imaginary romance. Since DiMaggio's love for her was only in the letter-writer's mind, and since he did not even know who she was or how to contact her, the woman's love remained unrequited. She threatened, in later notes she wrote during the summer, to kill herself if he remained aloof. Some publicty in the press enabled the police to track the writer down. During questioning the woman worked herself into a hysterical outburst and she had to be taken to the psychiatric ward of a Bronx hospital. Police concluded that she was imitating the actions of Ruth Ann Steinhagen, who earlier in the year had written a note coaxing the Philadelphia Phillies's first baseman, Eddie Waitkus, to her hotel room. She then blasted away with a rifle at Waitkus, whom she had never met before. He recovered from his bullet wounds, and the interlude was eventually memorialized by a similar sequence of events in Bernard Malamud's novel *The Natural*. To say the least, the false Junior Standish incident was unnerving to DiMaggio and definitely not a healthy distraction from his own problems.[61]

Several versions exist relating how DiMaggio's wound finally healed, and DiMaggio has narrated at least two somewhat different accounts himself, one far more magical than the other. In *Lucky to Be a Yankee* he says the heel simply got slowly better, that he felt its pain decrease and that by the end of May he was hardly limping at all and that when he felt ready for workouts he was suddenly "loose all over." He took morning batting practice at the stadium and by the middle of June felt fairly confident he could play again. Following a western swing, the Yankees returned home and he went to Stengel and told him he was ready to see how it felt playing again. On June 17 he performed unspectacularly against the Giants in an exhibition which suggested to him that though his timing was off, his heel was sound.

The other version of his recovery is more dramatic. In an article appearing under his name in *Life*, August 1, 1949, DiMaggio related the problems he had with his heel from the 1948 season, and his subsequent confrontation with the press in April, 1949. Emphasizing the pain in his heel which made it feel hot to him, he says "one morning I stepped out of bed, expecting the pain to shoot through the heel as usual. Nothing happened,'' however. "Now it was cool." Most writers have preferred this version to the more pedestrian narrative.

Peter Golenbeck says that on "a bright summer morning late in June, . . . in his room at the Edison Hotel in Manhattan, Joe DiMaggio rolled out of bed. When he gingerly lowered his right foot to the floor, the incessant, stabbing pain in the heel that had dogged him for the past couple of months, had miraculously vanished in the night." De Gregorio dates the miracle in mid-June. After chronicling several pages of DiMaggio's painful and soul-searching anguish, Gene Schoor (1956) juxtaposes a teary paragraph about Rosalie DiMaggio, a continent away, praying nightly for her family but especially "for her Joe—that he should get well and be happy again." Apparently her prayer does not fall upon deaf ears, for in the very next paragraph, Joe awakes "one morning feeling fine," his hot, painful heel now cool and well.

Newspaper accounts in the New York papers do not mention the efficacy of prayer. The *New York Times* on May 24 remarked that prior to the previous evening's game with the perennially last place St. Louis Browns, around 5:00 P.M., DiMaggio took batting practice and shagged flies, but noted also that his heel still hurt and burned. The following day (May 24) he felt physically sore and mentally unhappy and did not work out, nor did he practice on the 25th. On Tuesday, June 14, there was still "no news of the physical condition of Joe DiMaggio and his ailing heel," but, the *Times* stated, he would appear as Honorary Mayor of Mending Hearts Village, for the National Children's Cardiac Home that Sunday. The news on June 15 was that he took his turn at batting practice, but that "the condition of the Yankee Clipper's heel remains unchanged and he is far away from getting back into the line-up." A week later, however, on June 21, the Yankees announced that DiMaggio would enter a home run hitting contest prior to the charity game against the New York Giants on June 27. On the 22nd, the *Times* revealed that he had been participating in practice for a week "and has not complained about his heel. The signs have been most encouraging," though he was not expected to play in the benefit game. He shagged flies and fielded grounders following the June 25 game with Detroit, and "gave the impression" he might "be back in action before long." On the twenty-seventh, a sub-headline declared "DiMaggio May Play Soon," for Stengel had told reporters if DiMaggio still felt in good condition after the home run contest, he might start the game. On June 28 the *Times* printed the headline "DiMaggio Returns to Line-Up. Great Reception for DiMaggio," and published a photograph captioned "Yankee Clipper Takes His Turn At the Plate."

Miraculous or not, DiMaggio's recovery was stunning and completely authentic. Although he did not travel with the team, he flew to Boston where the Yankees were to play a particularly critical series beginning June

28 with the powerful Red Sox, who were in third place and who had won ten of their last eleven games. Some accounts suggest that he was not positive he was going to perform, but Robert Creamer in his recent book on Casey Stengel reports him saying "I knew I was going to play. I wasn't going to give that Boston ball park up." The Boston newspapers said he was going to appear, and *Newsweek* on July 11 noted a disclaimer he had issued to the press saying "I am returning for the first time since April 11 with the hope that the fans will appreciate my deficiencies in training and will not expect me to drive the ball out of the park every time I come up." In his *Life* article he claimed he "didn't expect to do much in the Boston series."

Considering the situation—his protracted injury, the closeness of the race—his three-day performance was the most shocking of his career. In the first game he singled his first time at bat and hit a home run his second time up, high over Ted Williams's head. In the fifth inning he broke up a double play by banging into the shortstop covering second, Vern Stephens. In the ninth inning, with the score 5-4 Yankees, he caught Ted Williams's long drive for the last out of the game.

The next day with the Yankees behind 7-1, DiMaggio hit his second home run of the series and the year, lifting the score to 7-4. Then later with the score tied 7-7, he hit his third home run, to win the game 9-7. The third day with the Yankees ahead narrowly, he hit another home run to clinch the win. Fans and writers were astounded. He hit five for eleven, a .455 batting average, with four home runs and nine runs batted in. After his first home run the Red Sox fans gave him a great ovation. Before game three, according to several reports, a small airplane with a banner fluttering behind it saying "The Great DiMaggio" circled the field.[62] Once again, only this time as an older and hurt player, DiMaggio had performed amazingly when special attention was focused intensely upon him. He had sustained a remarkably high level of brilliant, game winning play for the three-day series. That was what was so stunning. He never let up. He began at a high pitch and remained there. The fact almost could not be believed. It was—again—too much like a movie sequence. One almost expected inspirational music constantly climaxing in the background of his real exploits as day after day, the spectacular event (as sensational in the sports world as a compressed version of his 56-game hitting streak) unwound.

Nearly all the weekly magazines retold the event. *Life* featured him on the cover again August 1, calling him "a national hero" who had returned triumphantly "in perfect fairy-tale fashion" taking "his place in that select circle of athletes, like Babe Ruth and Jack Dempsey, who are not only admired but beloved." The nationally syndicated columnist Robert Ruark (a friend and imitator of Ernest Hemingway, in his literary work and lifestyle) declared he was the "first real sports colossus since the Dempsey-Jones-Ruth era." In *Lucky to Be a Yankee* DiMaggio said "it certainly was good to be back in harness."

Once in the daily lineup, he continued to hit well throughout the season. On July 12, in Brooklyn, he was one of a number of American League All-Stars who clubbed out an 11-7 victory over the Nationals, hitting a single and a double and batting in three runs. Lou Boudreau had asked him if he wanted to play while he was recuperating, and he agreed to, although All-Star games were not ordinarily where he performed best. The Yankees maintained their lead over the Red Sox while DiMaggio played, but he grew progressively weaker throughout the summer dropping fifteen pounds in weight, and with twelve games remaining had to leave the team with a viral infection he had contracted battling a form of pneumonia. The Yankee lead over Boston was two and one-half games. DiMaggio's illness was symptomatic of the Yankees' condition in 1949, for throughout the season one player after another was injured or became ill. Accurate statistics are not kept on the degree to which teams lose efficiency because of the physical disabilities of their players, and press descriptions are often the only sources for determining the apparent condition of a club. In 1949, after a number of players suffered injuries either during spring training or early in the season, the writers and sportscasters following the team began emphasizing the extent to which the Yankees were hurt. They possessed the image of a crippled body of athletes valiantly patching their lineup with whichever players were healthy on a given day, a brave but hurt crew fighting courageously to win in the Yankee tradition. DiMaggio was the outstanding symbol of this much praised effort that turned the Yankees into scrappy underdogs rather than the old all-conquering, smoothly performing victory machine they were usually thought to be. The role change was dramatically reported in the New York metropolitan newspapers, in national periodicals, and over the broadcasting media as well. Now their manager was Stengel, an inspired clown who pieced together the shakily performing mechanism each day with the parts available to him, not the silent, cool, efficient McCarthy with his powerhouse diesels.

With DiMaggio out, the Red Sox, who had been eight games behind after DiMaggio's June triumph, inched into first place by one game, with two games left with the Yankees in New York, where the newspapers were glum over the team's chances. Prior to the first game on October 1, the fans held a full hour Joe DiMaggio Day celebration before 69,551 paid spectators. The still sick and weakened star received a rainbow spectrum of gifts including a new Cadillac (which he reportedly gave to his mother), a television set, a bicycle for his son, many ties, and for some obscure reason, a supply of lima beans. The affair was an orgy of fan adulation communicated in the strange and yet understandable way spectators in America express what must be called their love or admiration for star performers (whose salaries ordinarily greatly exceed theirs). Presenting gifts—in this instance totaling almost $35,000 in value—is the way fans show their identification with, their love for heroes. The occasion is also the opportunity for male emotional behavior. Al Silverman reported that for the second public time in his career, DiMaggio cried (the first had been at Lou Gehrig's 1939 goodbye); the entire season had been exceptionally emotional for DiMaggio, the old "dead-pan," beginning with his angry outbursts at prying newsmen, the sadness at his father's death, the ecstasy of his three-game explosion earlier against Boston, and now this ritual where the fans wallowed in their regard for him and he let them see that he recognized and welcomed their worship. Even the day's entertainers, Phil Brito and Ethel Merman, were his Broadway friends, performers within his circle. In his thank-you speech he called his teammates "the gamest, fightingest bunch of guys that ever lived." And he concluded "I want to thank the Good Lord for making me a Yankee," imprinting God's influence upon the occasion. Of course the almost 70,000 fans cheered wildly as he walked off the field into the dugout with his mother (whom he knew was dying of cancer; photographs taken at the event reveal a sadly thinner woman than the plump mother he had known as a young man).

In his book on Casey Stengel, Maury Allen relates that in the dugout afterwards, DiMaggio told Stengel, "I'd like to try it." He wanted to play.

The Yankees won both games and thus on the last day of the season, the pennant. The Dodgers won their pennant on the last day also. DiMaggio hit a single and a double the first game and a triple in the second before pulling himself out in the ninth inning after Bobby Doerr tripled over his head and he realized he was simply not strong enough to play effectively. On October 3, a *New York Times* reporter wrote that "Joltin' Joe, a sick man these past three weeks, received a great ovation as he walked off the field." In his autobiography, DiMaggio stated that a statistician claimed the Yankees collected a total of 49 significant injuries during the season. Other writers reported various numbers such as 71 or 74. The number and extent of injuries became such a highly publicized feature of the season that the situation became almost comic: even Yankee trainer Gus Mauch's fractured rib, suffered when he walked into a parking meter, was noted. DiMaggio's hurts and his comeback permanently etched deeper lines in the hero's picture, and added shadows and depth to the legend's story.

He was too weak to perform well in the World Series, though the Yankee spirit seemed to maintain its pennant-winning momentum against Brooklyn, whom they defeated in five games. DiMaggio had only one hit until the last day, when he homered down the left field line into the lower deck. His World Series batting average was a pitiful .111. He had hit .346 during the regular season and was third on the team in runs batted in. No one claimed that he had frozen in the clutch. He concluded in his autobiography that other than missing the first part of the season and slumping in the Series, the year hadn't been "too bad."

The 1950 season was a less dramatically dispiriting year for DiMaggio and a less dramatically exciting one also. Though he suffered no crippling injuries in preseason or during the regular season, he rode a somewhat leveled-out rollercoaster of performance as the Yankees once more won the pennant and the World Series. Billy Martin and Whitey Ford first played for the Yankees in 1950; Mickey Mantle would not join them until the next year. DiMaggio was more and more the team's elderstatesman, an older figure distant to Ford and Mantle. His physical problems during the year seemed simply a nagging accumulation of all his old minor pains and the deterioration of body tone that accompanies aging. He ended the year hitting .301, but early in the season he slumped badly. His hitting lacked authority and consistency. More than ever he brooded and his relations with Casey Stengel were, on his part anyway, often very cool, especially at those times when Casey seemed most in command of the team and when DiMaggio was performing at his worst. It was a grueling season of attrition for DiMaggio, with a public wearing down of his skills. Still, through a spectacular last part of the season, he managed to finish at a level roughly equivalent to what was expected of him.

Realizing that he could not expect to play very much longer, DiMaggio began trying to prepare for the time when he would retire. He appeared on radio shows with Gene Schoor, aimed at children interested in sports, and then signed for a series of Saturday night broadcasts packaged by Jack Barry and Dan Enright featuring his answers to questions asked by children. DiMaggio was more at ease with this format than with regular sports reporting or interviewing. He admitted to the *Times*, February 16, 1950, he was "no crackerjack yet" on the radio, and the show was never very popular. Early in 1950 he once more had a period of closeness with his ex-wife Dorothy, but that ended disappointingly too and before long he was worrying whether Dorothy's third marriage might not be good for young Joe since it would present him with his third father.[63] As always, the Yankees featured him in their publicity about the team, but interestingly enough the first page of two on a preseason release from Yankee Stadium for general newspaper distribution, expended two-thirds of its space detailing how much money DiMaggio had earned in regular and World Series pay since 1936 ("mighty close to a half-million dollars"). The second page reprinted his regular, World Series, and All-Star batting statistics. The Yankee players still seemed to think he was worth his pay—$100,000. According to Dan Daniel's monograph, they responded overwhelmingly with his name when asked in a January, 1950, front office questionnaire to list their "baseball model" and the player "you most admire." But in May he was at bat thirteen consecutive times without hitting, and went ten games without an extra base hit. Except when he pulled a back muscle on May 14 there seemed no clear reason for his decline. At the end of May he was batting .243. As his slump continued his relations with Stengel deteriorated. Phil Rizzuto said that Stengel and DiMaggio "never got along." Actually, when DiMaggio played well there was at first no great friction between the two, though no close affinity either. In 1950, "DiMaggio's feeling for Stengel, never warm, turned decidedly colder" but only when his hitting faltered.[64] One action that particularly infuriated DiMaggio occurred July 4, when Stengel got him to try playing first base. Stengel used Dan Topping to make the suggestion to him not wanting to incur DiMaggio's wrath himself.[65] DiMaggio reluctantly went along with the experiment and made thirteen put-outs without self destructing, though he was stiff the next day when Stengel sent him back to center field because injuries to others now demanded that DiMaggio return to his familiar post. Stengel claimed plausibly enough that he played DiMaggio where he thought he was needed, that the switch enabled him to slot one of his many young outfielders (Bauer, Mapes, Woodling, or Jensen) into the lineup and hopefully add batting strength, and that if the move had been successful it could have prolonged DiMaggio's career. DiMaggio, as he often did, submitted to authority . . . silently. But he was sullen about the matter as though he had been asked to perform in dotted swiss pantaloons. Center field was his position. Stengel also tried Johnny Mize, a year older than DiMaggio, who hit 25 home runs in 90 games that year, at clean-up and dropped DiMaggio to fifth in the batting order. That was one of the ways Stengel managed, shuffling players around in the batting order, tinkering, trying one thing and then another, and during his career as a Yankee manager usually winning. The moves were hailed as an example of his genius, his two-platooning baseball's new look. He yanked players out and shoved players in, and often they hated it, but players with special talents got to perform when the time was right for their skills, and sat on the bench when Stengel felt they should. From DiMaggio's viewpoint, he had earned the right not to be treated in this fashion, and if anybody had, he had. He was struggling, but he had struggled before, when he was in poorer shape. He probably felt breaking from his slump was just a matter of time, and Stengel probably felt that it was DiMaggio's decline that was a matter of time. Another low point of DiMaggio's season and his relations with Stengel came when he was benched in August, not voluntarily and not because of injuries, but because he was hitting poorly and Stengel thought a rest might help him.

On August 18, DiMaggio returned to the lineup, and hit above .400 for the next eleven games, and .373 in September. It looked like Stengel was right, but so were the hated messengers and seers in Greek plays who told the haughty leaders unpleasant truths. DiMaggio performed inestimably better after he was sent to the bench, and that may have been what he needed, though it had never been in the past. But who could now guarantee that he could ever play again as he had in the past? Stengel himself, no brooder, seems not to have retained ill-feelings toward DiMaggio if he ever had them to begin with. In Maury Allen's biography of Stengel, the foxy manager spins a marvelous web of words to describe DiMaggio as a player, but also to lead the listener away from discovering what Stengel thought of him as a person: "Now wait a minute for crissakes," Stengel replied to Allen who wanted to know about DiMaggio the player. "You're going into too big a man. Maybe he woulda been an astronaut if he wanted. He could hit some balls off the moon and see if they'd carry. There were a lot of great ones and Ruth could pitch, too, but this fella is the best I had. . . . He started with a bang and never stopped." Did Stengel get along with him though? "They said I didn't like him, but every time I saw him, my wife Edna, would say hello to him and poke me and I would say hello."

Had DiMaggio played for Stengel earlier, their relationship might have been closer and warmer, and had DiMaggio played for Joe McCarthy now, he might not have admired him so much. But Stengel arrived too late in DiMaggio's season. Still, DiMaggio ended 1950 fifth in the league in total bases with 307, fifth in runs batted in with 122, third in home runs with 32, and first in slugging average with .585. But it had been another rough year, like 1946, and he must have suspected that the old high level of grace, consistency, and seeming ease would never be reached again. He had a good World Series against the Philadelphia Phillies' "Whiz Kids," with Richie Ashburn, Del Ennis, Robin Roberts, and Jim Konstanty, batting .308 as the Yankees swept through in four games. Phillies catcher Andy Seminick remembered "DiMaggio hitting a perfect pitch from Bob Miller. . . . even when Bob put the ball exactly where he wanted to put it."[66] More memorable was the home run he hit in the tenth inning of the second game to beat Philadelphia's best pitcher, Hall of Famer Robin Roberts. Roberts still remembers exactly what pitch he threw—as does DiMaggio—and exactly how he felt when DiMaggio cracked it into the stands.[67] Roberts had gotten DiMaggio to pop out four times and thought he could put him down this time too, but the pitch was just a fraction off, and DiMaggio was waiting for it. After the game some of the New York newspapers carried a quotation by DiMaggio saying it was the most important home run he had hit in his career. He repeated the claim in his autobiography, saying it was so significant because his year had been bad. In the last revised edition of *Lucky to Be a Yankee*, he admitted that before the 1951 season he was "just about stepping off the hill and going down the incline," and that he did not know how many years he had to offer as a player. He even discussed retiring with Dan Topping, but Topping persuaded him—it does not seem to have taken much effort—to sign another contract for 1951 after he assured DiMaggio he would not be taking "money under false pretenses."[68] For most great ballplayers, there is always one more year.

The level of acceptance that DiMaggio had reached by the end of the 1950 season, by fans and sportswriters, is best illustrated by two articles in widely distributed publications which also reveal some interesting sidelights on the kind of life he lived at this concluding stage of his career. The first was written by Gilbert Milstein, and appeared July 9 in the *New York Times Sunday Magazine*. The article points out that DiMaggio was then "currently afflicted with the worst slump of his twelve years in the major leagues" though he had "hit more home runs and batted in more runs so far this season than any other Yankee." DiMaggio had just gone hitless in eight attempts during a doubleheader, yet as Milstein wrote, he was "applauded with more vigor and greater warmth the last time he took his turn than he had been the first." DiMaggio's response to his difficulties at bat was to assume "an almost monastic silence." Of course the spectators at Yankee Stadium and the millions of others listening and watching radio and television were disappointed when he failed to hit either in ordinary or crucial situations, but they would not hound him or boo him.

The article also discusses his private life sketchily, noting that he shared a hotel suite with his friend George Solotaire, the ticket broker, that he ate frequently at Toots Shors except when he was slumping, that he read books such as *The Gay Bandit of the Border* by Tom Gill and *Silvertip's Chase* by Max Brand (both westerns), and that as an unidentified friend reported, "he's the sort of guy who's a dame guy and he isn't a dame guy, if you know what I mean." The analysis had a Damon Runyonesque-New York-*Guys and Dolls* twang to it, and probably suggests that DiMaggio liked attractive women well enough, but only as they fit at appropriate times into his man's world. They were good to take to dinners and shows and to please your friends with because they were lovely ladies, but you would not want to sit around with them talking about baseball at Toots's. Milstein also revealed such trivia as the facts that DiMaggio was paid $50,000 for his radio activities, that he had endorsed a cigarette ("say it ain't so, Joe"), and that he had compensated for that crime against children by recording an album of children's records called "Little Johnny Strikeout."

Another article is darker in its assessment of DiMaggio's role with the Yankees, which is odd since it appeared in *Sport* magazine in November, 1950, after DiMaggio's relatively successful season's end. It also includes incidental information about his private life, showing a picture of him with a woman named Peggy Deegan in a nightclub and with the caption, "Joe has become a fixture in New York's cafe society." The article focuses mainly on DiMaggio's decline, though it recognizes that the star had redeemed himself by the end of the year. "Harassed by physical difficulties and batting slumps, the Yankee Clipper was having a tough season. The experts started to write him off. But they buried him too soon." The piece is titled "What About DiMaggio Now?" and is attributed to no single writer; instead it is assigned to "the Editors of *Sport*." One cannot escape concluding that the editors wanted to talk straight in the column, but were disinclined to be identified by DiMaggio. They tell about his rough times but suggest he was lucky not to have been treated worse early in 1949 when he told the press they were driving him crazy. DiMaggio, they claimed, had in fact been protected for many years by the press who had not criticized him for such failings as making so few public appearances.

Making no bitter accusations themselves, the editors did mention that in August, Joe Trimble of the New York *Daily News* wrote that DiMaggio had given a "sophomore snub" to Casey Stengel. Though the editors did not mention it, the *News*, New York's most popular (or largest selling) newspaper, which featured trashy articles about grisly axe murders and plutocrat love nests as often as it could, had in the past printed other charges against DiMaggio that had gone otherwise unrecorded in the more conservative metropolitan press. Once in the late 1940s their sports editor Jimmy Powers had suggested that DiMaggio's Air Force enlistment was actuated by essentially non-patriotic reasons. The *News* typically praised DiMaggio too, but as the newspaper aiming most successfully at mass consumption, it often tried to drag down the famous and wealthy.

Sport's editors also quoted Ben Epstein who wrote for New York's other but somewhat less successfully sensational popular picture newspaper, the *Daily Mirror*. Epstein said DiMaggio "today sulks in the midst of probably his longest temperamental outburst as a standout athlete." Possibly he had been worshipped too much, "grown too big for his breeches." Having printed the charges of other writers, *Sport*'s editors themselves offered softer words of understanding about DiMaggio. That he was old and perhaps over-protected was not his fault. And it was not easy to be affable when you are relatively unsuccessful. But, they concluded on an upbeat note, patting on the back the man to whom they had just offered presumably corrective criticism, still "he's a champion." As was his custom, DiMaggio did not comment publicly about this analysis of his behavior.

During the off season DiMaggio often hinted or stated outright that 1951 would be his last season. Of course even he could not predict this absolutely, and had he returned in 1951 to his old, good form as he had late in 1950 he might not have retired. He was old but not nearly as old as some of the other great players when they retired, but in 1951 he did not have a good year, and it was his last as a player in organized baseball.

Certainly he and his country had changed a great deal since he had started with the Yankees as a rookie in 1936. Then the country was in an economic depression, which it left to enter World War II, the last of our wars to generate much patriotic fervor. In 1951 the country was in what seems now a moral depression. In 1950 a planned motion picture production of Longfellow's "Hiawatha" was shut down because Monogram studios feared its plot might appear to offer encouragement to communism; Senator Joseph McCarthy waved his infamous list of 205 members of the Communist Party who were supposedly employed by the State Department. In 1951 Ethel and Julius Rosenberg were sentenced to die in the electric chair for supposedly providing the Russians with atom bomb secrets, and the country was in the midst of the drab, cruel, puzzling war in Korea. General Douglas MacArthur would be hauled home for disobeying orders and receive the greatest public reception of any American hero for years, and the black educator, scholar, and civil rights champion W. E. B. Du Bois, born only three years after the end of the Civil War, would be handcuffed and finger-printed by Federal police on a charge of subversion that would later be thrown out of court because of its flimsiness.

Naturally DiMaggio's image had changed over his years of performance. Inevitably, his age (though he was not particularly old) was now emphasized instead of his youth, and his quietness and solitariness shaded now into indications of his weary loneliness rather than his innocent provinciality. Typical of the sentimental copy written about him is Mel Allen's reminiscence of his last years as a player. The "painfully shy" DiMaggio, "idol of millions . . . was an intensely lonely man. 'Everyone has a home and a family to go to' he once said to a writer after a game at the stadium. 'All I've got when I go back to my hotel tonight is an empty room and a box of fresh laundry on the bed.' "[69]

The family he would return to after the 1950 season's end was diminished June 18 by the death of Rosalie DiMaggio at age 72. Like her husband Giuseppe she had played a very traditional role in the story of DiMaggio's youth, providing him with warmth and stability and understanding when he did not want to join the crew of his father's boat. She seemed to side with him and to protect him while he decided what he was going to do with his life. He always spoke of her as a good son should, honored her with a new home, and probably more important to her, praised her homemaking and loved her cooking. None of the women he was seen dating were the least bit like her. They all belonged to a different world, seeming perfectly in place in nightclubs and on dance floors but not in the kitchen where she reigned. In pictures she never looks like a modern American woman. During her last years cancer thinned her formerly thick body, but never, not even in the modern rooms her son provided for her, would she look stylish. She was as her obituary in *Newsweek* stated, an "Italian immigrant woman whose convincing arguments with her fisherman husband carried the day and won the right for three of her sons (Joe, Dom, and Vince) to become baseball players, thus establishing baseball's greatest family dynasty." In photographs she always seemed a lady in plain, dark clothes often with her hair in a bun, an old-fashioned woman. She was like a good mother in a movie about immigrants and their rise to success, only she was real.

By 1951 most of the old Yankees, Dickey, Keller, Henrich, Page, were gone. The new Yankees featured younger players such as Berra, Whitey Ford, Gil McDougald, and Mickey Mantle. Ford had joined the team in 1950 and his locker was near DiMaggio's. He "couldn't believe it" when he first saw DiMaggio. "I just stared at the man for about a week. He'd say hello and things like that, but I think I would've fainted if he's said more than that to me." Mantle's first year with the Yankees was 1951. He said that though "DiMag was my hero . . . he couldn't talk to me because I wouldn't even look at him—although he was always nice and polite to me."[70]

Of the new Yankees, DiMaggio was closest to Billy Martin, who like DiMaggio was (part) Italian, from the San Francisco area, and had grown up aware that many of the Anglo kids were far better off socially and economically. Unlike DiMaggio, he was a carouser and scapegrace which may be what Dimaggio liked about him. Martin's story of his childhood shows it to have been filled with violence, and his family life was often unsettled. His parents were very different from DiMaggio's, with changing fathers and a mother who "never took shit from anybody" and once ripped the dress off a teacher of Billy's who was giving her, so Billy claimed, "a hard time." Martin describes DiMaggio as mainly a loner, but one who took the fresh rookie out to dinner often, and made him feel welcome. DiMaggio seemed unperturbed by Martin's brashness. In a way the two were like a king and his jester, but DiMaggio never made Billy feel like a clown, even when Martin pulled some silly trick like asking DiMaggio to autograph a baseball using a pen that squirted disappearing ink. Once in 1951 when DiMaggio hit a home run to the opposite field he told Martin it was a "piss home run," and Martin says he knew 1951 would be his hero's last year. Ironically, while filming a Buitoni TV commercial for DiMaggio in 1952, Martin would crack two bones in his ankle and miss the first part of the season.[71]

That DiMaggio would take the time to befriend the rookie Martin suggests the admirable side of his behavior as team leader, since for most of 1951 he played poorly and was depressed. He quarreled with Stengel publicly and then the two made up in the press, but as long as he was playing far below his normal level of ability he would be unhappy with himself and unhappy with Stengel who needed a well-functioning DiMaggio in the battle with Cleveland and Boston. Their most publicized squabble that often bitter year started in a series with the Red Sox. On July 7 both teams were behind Cleveland by one game. After the first inning the Yanks were so badly battered that Stengel decided to make some changes in the Yankee lineup, either in a desperate move to salvage the game with new players, or, as newsmen were later told, to rest "a few of his frayed veterans" because the game was beyond winning.[72] Billy Martin replaced Phil Rizzuto at shortstop, Gil McDougald replaced Jerry Coleman at second, and as Boston was preparing to bat in the bottom half of the second inning, Jackie Jensen ran out to center field and replaced DiMaggio, who had the night before in another (6-2) loss to Boston stranded six men while he was at bat. Stengel later claimed that removing DiMaggio in full view of the fans was a mistake caused by confusion in the dugout, and that anyway, Jensen had merely told DiMaggio if he wanted to take the rest of the day off he could. If this were so, Jensen would have looked like a fool and DiMaggio obdurate, had DiMaggio declined to leave, for Jensen would have had to lope back into the dugout with his glove to sit down again. So Stengel's story seems odd.

The Yankees did not win, and slipped behind one game. In the New York papers of July 9, reporting events of the eighth, Stengel declared how surprised he was to learn in the Boston papers that he was again feuding with DiMaggio. Casey claimed he was ignorant of any disagreements over the replacement the day before, and related his explanation that Jensen had only been offering DiMaggio a chance to take it easy if he wished it. He also said troublemaking Boston reporters had blown out of proportion a "surly" response DiMaggio had given a reporter during the heat of the moment when asked if injuries accounted for his removal. John Drebinger of the *New York Times* wrote "what the scribe didn't realize was that this had been DiMaggio's mood for a long time. In fact, he rarely talks to his teammates or manager, let alone anyone remotely associated with the press. On a recent train ride following a night game in Philadelphia, DiMaggio, in the Yank's special diner, sat by himself at a table set for four. It's a queer set-up, but almost everyone traveling with the Bombers is leaving the Clipper severely alone." Some of the details in Drebinger's account are themselves open to question. DiMaggio later claimed he was sitting by himself because he was waiting for some teammates he had agreed to save places for, but the mood the article describes does recapture the atmosphere of unpleasantness the season sometimes possessed for DiMaggio.

There were some good days, as in August when his timely hits won at least three important games. On September 16 against the second place Indians, when he was batting fifth after Yogi Berra, with the Yankees holding a slim 3-1 lead in the fifth inning, Cleveland decided to walk Berra to get at DiMaggio and put runners on first and second. He had the satisfaction of cracking a double deep into left-center, scoring two runs and putting the game out of reach. But those days were few. He commented upon the congratulations he received after such a game by saying "now when I get a hit . . . they send me telegrams."[3] His final .263 batting average was better than that of many of the league's outfielders, but it was the lowest among those who played those positions for the Yankees with any regularity: Woodling (.281), Bauer (.296), Jensen (.298), and Joe Collins usually a first baseman but with some outfield play, .286). Even Mickey Mantle, who did not play the whole year but was returned to the minors for further seasoning, hit .267. The Yankees ultimately won rather handily, five games in front of Cleveland and eleven games in front of Boston, and in the final months, DiMaggio especially made contributions to the team's increasing lead, but he could not kid himself that he was playing well, nor that he was the key performer on the squad. Unlike 1936 and so many years afterward, he did not make the difference in any way that could be measured. So it became a season of lasts: he hit the last home run of his regular game career on September 28, against Boston.

His last World Series was against the same team the Yankees had played in his first, the Giants. After the series, which the Yankees won 4-2, a cruel scouting analysis by Andy High, a scout for the narrowly defeated Dodgers, was published October 22 in *Life* magazine, noting the weaknesses of DiMaggio (and the strengths and deficiencies of the other Yankees also). DiMaggio, it said, could "not stop quickly and throw hard" and "you can take the extra base on him. . . . He can't run and he won't bunt. . . . his reflexes are very slow and he can't pull a good fast ball at all." To the extent that the cruel observations were accurate—they seem somewhat overstated, as though angry that DiMaggio was no longer what he once was—they told DiMaggio nothing he did not know about himself. Years later Jimmy Cannon remembered him "apprais[ing] himself with a cruel knowledge" and once "when despair seized him . . . griev[ing] about his vanishing gifts" after hitting "flabby pop flies" in batting practice. He had turned to Cannon and said "the old boy can't be that bad." Ordinarily he was not, but he was not great. *Life*, which had previously in two notable articles (one supposedly written by DiMaggio himself) burbled his triumphs throughout the nation, perfectly demonstrated, by publishing High's notes, the public exposure that athletes who fail or who are deemed inadequate are subject to, a public humiliation most Americans whose skills or levels of acheivement decline with years do not have to face. But then these people never receive the cheers and adulation either.

High's scouting report was published after the Series but was slipped to the Giants before its start. It appeared prophetic during the first three games, when DiMaggio went hitless. In the fourth game, however, with the Yankees one game down, DiMaggio starred, singling and hitting a home run off Sal "the Barber" Maglie. Willie Mays, who claimed that he patterned his batting style after DiMaggio's (this seems doubtful though it is a sign of his regard for his fellow center fielder's reputation), said of his idol, "I only saw him play once. . . . in the 1951 World Series. . . . They said he wasn't the DiMaggio of old. That didn't keep him from breaking open the World Series against us."[74] In the fifth game which the Yankees won 13-1 he drove in three runs, and by the time the Series was over he had raised his batting average to .261. In his last time at bat he doubled and stood on second base a long time while the fans cheered. Probably many thought that was the last time he would be on base in an official game.

According to newspaper accounts he hit his last home run as an active employee of the Yankees on November 16, in Tokyo, during a two-month tour of Japan that had begun October 15. Although Dan Topping apparently offered him his old salary to play another year, he declined, and in a news conference held at the Yankee offices in the Squibb Tower, 745 Fifth Avenue, he announced his retirement. In an editorial on December 12 the *New York Times* recalled his link to the success of the Yankees and compared him once more to Babe Ruth, for though not as powerful a hitter,

DiMaggio's 56-game hitting streak would probably last as long as Ruth's record 60 home runs in a season. The editorial further stated that, DiMaggio combined "proficiency and exquisite grace" in demonstrating the "art of playing center field." The *Times* also reiterated what had already become a standard comment about DiMaggio, that beyond his quantifiable attainments, he possessed "something that no baseball averages can measure." Graciously ignoring his moods and sulks, they characterized him as "modest to the point of self-effacement. . . . at the same time a greatly feared competitor and an athlete of exemplary sportsmanship." His resignation shared the front pages of the metropolitan newspapers with dull news of Attorney General J. Howard McGrath "vigorously defend[ing] the administration of his office today," possibilities of a truce in Korea (the war would grind bloodily on until July, 1953), and disputes in Iran unsettling the Mossadegh government that few Americans knew about even after its leader was assassinated with support from the C.I.A.

The newspapers and national magazines related his retirement address and showed pictures of him that look as though he was crying. Like *Newsweek* for December 24, some pointed out that his thirteen-year career had been much shorter than that of some of the other baseball superstars such as Ty Cobb (24 years), Babe Ruth (22 years), or Tris Speaker (22 years). But then he had been hampered by injuries, his Air Force stint, and night baseball. His statistics were reprinted, and the *Times* related that his "Decision to Retire Saddens Japanese." Most of the quotations from DiMaggio were terse and predictable. Why was he quitting? "I no longer have it." What about his future in baseball? "I never wanted to be a manager and I never will."

The retirement ceremony is one of baseball's stereotyped rituals, but one that is a part of only the superior or particularly memorable player's career. DiMaggio's farewell was unusual in the extraordinary attention it received nationally. His fame as a player accounts partly for its broad communication in the media, but so also did, again, the fact that his exploits centered in New York, yet his roots were across the continent in San Francisco. Radio and television stations naturally reported the event, and the Columbia Broadcasting System's Dallas Townsend presented a special program the evening of December 11, encapsulating the event, relating DiMaggio's history, bestowing praise upon him spoken by Dan Topping and Casey Stengel, and incorporating an interview with DiMaggio himself. He said he was not certain of his future but that he had received several offers from inside and outside the Yankee organization, and that he would always remain close to baseball (it was expected that he would stay with the Yankees as a radio or television broadcaster). The ritual suggested the high esteem in which he was held, and that though he was dead as a player he would live again as an announcer or in some capacity with the team to which he gave all honor. He would live also in the hearts of his fans, and one old fan (CBS reporter Lou Cioffi) and one young fan (an eleven-year-old sandlot player cub scout from San Francisco) attested to the strength of his legend, particularly among Italian-Americans.

DiMaggio's farewell speech, read originally at the news conference by Yankee public relations director Arthur Red Patterson, compares favorably with Lou Gehrig's, though naturally it lacks the tragic poignance of Gehrig's short goodbye. A "real pro," DiMaggio speaks as an amateur in it, one who played lovingly for a pleasure now gone. CBS later presented him reading his words in a strong but occasionally stumbling manner, sounding like what he was, a professional baseball player who often dropped final "g's" in "ing" words, and not anything like a polished announcer, which he would only become two decades later in his commercials.

According to Townsend, DiMaggio was "outwardly unruffled, inwardly perhaps, sad and regretful" as he read his speech. "I said last spring, I thought this would be my last year. I only wish I coulda been a, or had a better year, but even if I had hit .350, this would have been my last year for me. You all know I've had more than my share of physical injuries and setbacks during my career. In recent years these have been too frequent to laugh off. When baseball is no longer fun, it's no longer a game, and so, I've played my last game."

"Since coming to New York, I've made a lot of friends and picked up a lot of advisors, but I would like to make one point clear; no one has influenced me in making this decision. It has been my problem, and my decision to make. I feel that I have reached a stage, where I can no longer produce for my ball club, my manager, my teammates, and my fans the sort of baseball their loyalty to me deserves. In closing, I would like to say I feel I have been unusually privileged to play all my major league baseball for the New York Yankees. But it has been an even greater privilege to be able to play baseball at all. It has added much to my life. What I will remember most in days to come will be the great loyalty of the fans. They have been very good to me."

In the off season DiMaggio now lived with his sister Marie DiMaggio Kron, a widow, in the house he had bought for his parents when they were alive. He came east again in the spring to begin his pre- and post-game interview show for the Yankees, a job he held while the team won another pennant and World Series. With DiMaggio, the Yankees won nine World Series and ten pennants in thirteen years. Phil Rizzuto, the last of the pre-World War II Yankees to remain with the team said "it just wasn't the same ball club without Joe. . . . His leadership was essential."[76] But without him they won ten pennants and six World Series during the next twelve years. The broadcasting never gave him much satisfaction and so he tried it only one year. Each show made him nervous, and though at the end he was more competent than he had been at the start, the work was not a source of satisfaction for him. He was always anxious that he would look bad, and insisted that as much as possible of what he was going to say be written on cue or "idiot" cards so he could read his lines. Unsurprisingly, the show lacked spontaneity, and anyway, DiMaggio was so much greater than most of the players he interviewed that his conversations often seemed silly: why should he be asking Irv Noren or Bob Kuzava questions?

It would be incorrect to portray him as a forgotten man after his retirement, however. The "Yankee Sketch Book" for 1952, commemorating the team's 50th season in the American League, was dedicated to Ruth, Gehrig, and DiMaggio. The dedication page contained three pictures of Ruth, two of Gehrig, and three of DiMaggio. Ruth and DiMaggio were top vote getters on a Yankee dream team with 48 members. More significantly, the September 1 issue of *Life* featured Ernest Hemingway's novella, *The Old Man and the Sea*, which contained several key references to DiMaggio in it. Perhaps the single most publicized literary event of the year (along with the September 8 issuance of a hardcover edition by Scribner's), the book was the first successful long work, since the 1940 *For Whom the Bell Tolls*, for America's best known major writer and constituted a comeback for Hemingway, who so often conceived of his artistic activities in athletic metaphors. DiMaggio's name was not merely alluded to in the generally well-received story of victory through endurance, pain, and seeming defeat, but was clearly woven into the book's texture very carefully and became enwrapped with the Hemingway myth over the years.

In San Francisco, DiMaggio had plenty of time now to chat with friends and relax. While not fabulously wealthy he had enough income to live comfortably, and to choose among offers that promised him more money. Never ambitious except in baseball, he selected positions that did not demand too much of his time or energy, and interrupted his life the least. He hung around his old restaurant often, late in the mornings especially, talking to friends he liked and making himself inaccesible to nearly everyone else. He felt no desire to bathe in the ocean of his fans' adulation for him. His good times and his bad times were scaled down now. He was disappointed when in the first election for which he was eligible (1953) he was not voted into the Baseball Hall of Fame, but he knew he would enter soon enough anyway. The *Sporting News* for February 4, 1953, printed a cartoon of DiMaggio and Bill Terry (fourteen years with the Giants, lifetime batting average .341) who was also turned down saying "It wasn't our year after all." DiMaggio was eighth on the list of nominees, polling 117 votes while 198 were needed for entry. Among the reasons the *Sporting News* suggested were responsible for his rejection were anti-Yankee hostility and the pressure New York writers exerted on his behalf, which was perhaps resented by nonmetropolitan writers. Being the Yankee darling of the local press could also be a liability. But DiMaggio would be elected two years later anyway, and Terry, who retired in 1936, would have only a one year wait. Other honors arrived steadily. June 5, 1953, he was at the White House along with Joe Louis and Rocky Marciano, attending a luncheon with President Eisenhower given for forty-three outstanding sports figures just before the annual Congressional baseball game for charity. Most of the news about DiMaggio was good, but small apples compared to what was happening in sports and the world outside sports in America. On June 12, he became the West Coast vice-president in charge of public relations for the Buitoni Corporation, a company specializing in Italian foods such as spaghetti and macaroni ("*Buitoni sono buoni* means it's clearly understood, that Buitoni is so good, yes Buitoni is *so* good," their jingle sang). They had sponsored some of his television shows and respected him, and he became a stockholder in their company. That news did not compare with Enos "Country" Slaughter's fielding and batting heroics a month later on July 14, as the National League All-Stars defeated the American League 5-1.

Since DiMaggio was perhaps consciously nonpolicital, it would be farfetched to think he was aware of the American ironies observable in the chance juxtaposition of events shortly following Eisenhower's smiling recognition of his contributions to American society: Julius and Ethel Rosenberg were executed for espionage against the United States June 19, 1953, Eisenhower steadfastly refusing to pardon them. In DiMaggio's life that year, his brother Michael's sudden and violent death was naturally a much more terrible event.

DiMaggio was in San Francisco with Marilyn Monroe when the shocking news that Michael had drowned in a fishing accident reached him.[77] The two were together because Monroe had persuaded Joe to rescue her from the anxiety she was experiencing making *River of No Return* for Otto Preminger in Banff, Canada, in the summer of 1953. Though he hated the phoniness of the movie world he had flown there because Marilyn seemed to need him. She was unhappy with the film and furthermore had injured a leg ligament during the preparations for a raft scene with her co-star Robert Mitchum (Mitchum said she twisted her ankle trying to walk the way Preminger had said she should)[78] and distrusted the local doctor Preminger produced for her. Sick of the local scene, she called for DiMaggio and welcomed her deliverance even though they had previously quarreled over when and if she would marry him and if she did, how her movie career would be affected by her new role as DiMaggio's wife. In San Francisco, the pair reversed the positions they had played after the Hollywood star's flight, and Monroe had the rare opportunity of supporting the emotionally bruised DiMaggio. Both were for the moment off guard, DiMaggio because he was distraught and needed Monroe's consolation and she because she was attempting from her own frail reserves to minister to him. They ended by agreeing to marry.

The two had met in the spring of 1952, and before the end of the year DiMaggio was serious enough about her to take her to San Francisco to meet his brothers and sisters for the first time. Their relationship was periodically intense, their lives often mutually abrasive, and yet they often seemed to satisfy each other as no others did. Much of the time they spent together appears to have been filled with boredom or anger, though at crucial periods (generally not when they were married) Monroe sought DiMaggio for love or help, and it is clear by the depth of his attachment to her that in being where she wanted him, he was fulfilling a sharp need in himself also. But they could never live together for long, for they wished to live completely different lives.

Following the course of their relationship is both difficult and easy, rather like pursuing the track of some marvelous animals traversing the ground trampled afterwards by hosts of adventurers and entreprenuers who sought their path. The landscape of their story is littered with what Norman Mailer labelled "factoids . . . creations which are not so much lies as a product to manipulate emotion in the Silent Majority. . . . The most mysterious property of a factoid is that it is believed by the people who put together the factoid printed next to it.''[79] But while study of the life of each must ultimately focus upon the mutual enhancement their intersecting myths provided, so that the distinction between facts and factoids becomes almost unnecessary to ascertain, it is also important to plot the real terrain upon which their often fantasized stories are based.

During spring training, 1952, Gus Zernial, a power hitter for the Philadelphia Athletics, had his picture taken with Marilyn Monroe as a publicity stunt. At the time Monroe was more famous for her nude calendar photograph than for the few solid films she had appeared in (together with some B-minus programmers) such as *The Asphalt Jungle, All About Eve*, and *Clash by Night*. When the photographs were published, DiMaggio, temporarily at the Athletics camp, joked with Zernial about them and found out from him the name of the press agent, David Marsh, who had arranged for the photograph session. Later back in Hollywood, DiMaggio contacted Marsh and asked him about Monroe, and Marsh, undoubtedly dreaming of all the publicity angles he was being offered, arranged for a dinner date between Monroe and DiMaggio. Monroe arrived very late and exhibited no particular attraction to DiMaggio, talking mostly about her film being shot then, *Monkey Business*, a comedy with Cary Grant. Not until Mickey Rooney showed up did her interest in DiMaggio increase. She had made a racing picture called *Fireball* several years before with Rooney, a known if not always shining star, and his obvious worship of DiMaggio (and ignoring of her) impressed her. When she later got up to leave, saying she had an early call for her next day's shooting, DiMaggio offered to take her home in a cab. She answered she had her own car and offered to take him home instead. In the car he suggested they drive around a bit and they did. Some later reports say she felt exceptionally happy driving with him, but if she was, her feelings did not cause her to answer his repeated requests over the next days for another evening together. After a week of being turned down, DiMaggio finally received a call from Monroe asking him if he would like to take her to dinner and he of course agreed.[80] After that they began seeing each other more frequently and more seriously.

Marilyn Monroe had been making pictures since 1947 and by the time she began seeing DiMaggio had appeared in about fifteen films (not counting *Scudda Ho, Scudda Hay!* from which she was edited out except for a brief indistinguishable appearance with another girl in a distant canoe). While popular (or notorious because of her nude calendar photograph), she was not yet an established star. Directors seemed not to know exactly what to do with her talents and needed great patience with her. She herself was highly uncertain about her own abilities although she possessed a tremendous drive to become a star, sadly coupled with an exceptionally shaky sense of self. She was far from a good actress as that term is ordinarily defined—she lacked professional range and depth—but she developed an extraordinarily strong presence on screen, and she could play comic and in time melodramatic scenes well. In *River of No Return* Preminger seemed determined to change her portrayal from that of a dance hall tart who wiggles her crotch at surprisingly restrained gold miners during the film's opening scenes, to something she clearly was not—a hardy outdoorswoman. He mocked her sexy swagger and Robert Mitchum asked aloud how he could kiss her when she kept undulating her mouth so. Her performance was undistinguished. She performed far better when directors could unleash those qualities she seemed naturally to possess in abundance—her playful sexuality or her honest uncerebral melancholy. When she met DiMaggio she was perhaps a star but a newly arrived one in a very slippery business where stardom is nebulous. When DiMaggio visited her on the set of *Monkey Business* and pictures of Monroe, DiMaggio, and Cary Grant were taken, the subsequent newspaper photographs had Monroe cut from them.

When the two went out in public they were invariably noticed and often bothered by outsiders, and cooed over in the press because of their fame. Sometimes they "visited friends" or "spent evenings at Marilyn's apartment, where DiMaggio watched television," according to Edwin Hoyt. As long as DiMaggio was courtly and reassuring and Monroe beautiful and charming, their romance developed. Sometimes DiMaggio offered her advice (e.g. she should stop playing primarily sexy roles) that she seriously considered though did not always follow, and at first she welcomed his counsel. At other times he showed sharp disdain for her vocation and the people involved in it, and that brought trouble. When she was making *Gentlemen Prefer Blondes*, one of her best films, she kept him and a photographer waiting while she primped, preparing herself for publicity shots Twentieth-Century Fox had requested and DiMaggio agreed to. Her delaying tactics manifested her neurotic insecurity. No patient psychologist, DiMaggio became infuriated and canceled the session he thought a lot of nonsense anyway. He argued with Monroe in her dressing room and she seemed chastened when they came out, but her behavior was typical and compulsive. Late in 1953 they had bitter words again when DiMaggio said he would not attend the premiere of another of Marilyn's pictures, *How To Marry a Millionaire*. He could not understand why the event was so important to her. Later he called her from New York and apologized, but she was unforgiving over the telephone.

Calm and reassuring about Marilyn's insecurities and crises, when something really went wrong DiMaggio was at his best, as when he thoughtfully wired flowers when she had an appendectomy. Compared to many of the men she had known in her life, particularly in Hollywood, he was an honest, helpful, respectful person, attentive to her, and neither sexually nor commercially exploitive. DiMaggio and his family way of life must have seemed very restful to Monroe at times. Once she said the people she met were always trying to take a chunk out of her. DiMaggio never gave her this feeling. He did not like her desperate pursuit of Hollywood stardom and that bothered her, but it also presented her with a very peaceful domestic fantasy she could dream about, something for her future, maybe.

On January 14, 1954, during a time she was having trouble with her studio because of her refusal to accept certain roles she did not consider suitable, Marilyn Monroe married Joe DiMaggio in San Francisco before a small group of family and friends of Joe's in the private chambers of Municipal Court Judge Charles S. Perry. Reno Barsocchini, a one-time bartender at DiMaggio's restaurant, was best man. Less than a year later, he would help DiMaggio pile his gear into a car when Joe moved out from the apartment he shared with Monroe. If they had dreamed of privacy for their wedding day they did not achieve it. More than a hundred gawkers, fans, and reporters created a publicity circus around them after the ceremony, which *Time* for January 25 said capped a "Storybook Romance." The *Los Angeles Times* declared it "could only happen here in America. . . . Both of them . . . had to fight their way to fame and fortune and to each other: one in a birthday suit, as a foundling, and later as a calendar girl; the other in a . . . baseball suit." Incredibly enough the garish and consciously cute reporting about the event did not dim its magnitude or turn the popular rite into a joke. What could easily have become cartooned into the grotesque coupling of a woman always perilously close to being considered a lubricious bimbo and her enthralled, ex-athlete hero made captive by lust (an American version of Marlene

Dietrich making Emil Jannings cackle like a chicken in *The Blue Angel*) was not.

Escaping the crowd in San Francisco, Joe drove his bride to Pasa Robles, California. He stopped at the Clifton Motel and asked its owner, Ernie Sharpe, for a room with a television set in it. That was where the DiMaggios spent their honeymoon night, just like the average American couple. After several weeks in Palm Springs the couple stayed briefly in San Francisco. Marilyn appreciated the closeness of what remained of the DiMaggio clan, and she would retain a warm relationship with Joe's son even after her divorce and until her death. One of her last telephone calls was apparently to him. Usually she enjoyed San Francisco itself though she and DiMaggio would have some unhappy times there too. In Robin Moore and Gene Schoor's book Joe tells his sister Marie, "Don't keep her [Marilyn] out of the kitchen if she wants to get up a meal once in a while. . . . I think it would be good for her." Whether or not he ever said these exact words, the idea behind them would not have seemed strange to him, and suggests one of the reasons for their arguments. The image of Marilyn Monroe preparing his meals as a matter of custom did not seem bizarre to him. Apparently, again according to Moore and Schoor, the idea of Marilyn Monroe acting like an ordinary wife did seem bizarre to DiMaggio's former wife Dorothy. She still retained custody of Joe Jr., and supposedly said she did not "want to see my son in the company of that woman."

Still early in the winter of 1954 DiMaggio and Monroe departed San Francisco for a good-will tour of Japan. The trip was hectic and concluded probably the happiest married time of their life together. Stopping briefly in Hawaii, the two were met by a screaming crowd at the airport, just the kind of almost-out-of-control pack that DiMaggio, nearly always gracious and appreciative of spectators constrained in the stands, abhorred. Marilyn's business was, however, to attract if not incite mobs, and she rather enjoyed their press and near touch. In Japan, DiMaggio received the special welcome appropriate to the high regard in which he was held by Japanese baseball fans as he toured the country with Lefty O'Doul giving baseball clinics. Marilyn had agreed, apparently happily, for it would bring her exactly the kind of publicity she felt her career required, to entertain American troops still stationed in Korea after the July 27, 1953, armistice. DiMaggio did not look forward to her departure and subsequent appearances before masses of howling soldiers but did not prevent her from going. Her reception was tumultuous and greatly reported on, a real publicity coup. The soldiers and sailors greeted Monroe's swooping helicopter as though it contained a goddess from the sea, a very fleshy goddess they could scream for with harmless frenzy and adoration, because she was beautiful and unattainable, and at the same time projected that quality that seemed to declare she would be happily available for some good, impermanent, sexual fun. She wore low-cut, tightly fitting clothes made inestimably more provocative by her full body which she, innocently enough it seemed, loved flaunting before them not as a tease, but as a sensuous woman who loved being adored by men. According to at least one report, she once made her entrance before the First Marine Division stationed north of Seoul by hanging out of a helicopter flying over her audience while two soldiers held her feet.[81]

She returned exhilarated, exultant, and sick to her sullen husband in Tokyo. He gave her antibiotics and helped nurse her from the slight case of pneumonia she had contracted during her triumphant tour of the bases. An often repeated anecdote tells of Monroe supposedly explaining to him her feelings of passionate excitement, saying he had never heard such cheering, and he is supposed to have replied simply but with crushing matter-of-factness, yes, he had.

Back in America, in April, they lived in San Francisco for a time but soon moved to the Los Angeles area to be closer to her work. In both places they quarreled about her career, the extent to which each felt she should devote herself to it, and the character portrayals most suitable for her. DiMaggio possessed a very open contempt for Hollywood. Marilyn's friend Sidney Skolsky said that he "had a very simple idea about Hollywood: ignore the publicity and get the money while it lasted. . . . He had no use for most of the Hollywood people he knew."[82] He resented the way other Hollywood people pushed her around and manipulated her, and he did not like her in the sexy dumb broad roles he thought she most frequently played. On the set of *There's No Business Like Show Business* he yelled at her that her stardom was produced by the people around her and could be taken away as quickly as it had been fabricated. Her co-star, Ethel Merman, was from Broadway, and Broadway (like San Francisco) he could understand. On Broadway you fashioned your own talent. It was not constructed, superimposed upon you. He supported her in the demands she made upon the studio and took care of her when she was sick or imagined she was, but he did not respect the world in which she sought recognition, viewing it as carnivorous and phony. Doubtless they had good times in that brief period during which they were married and lived together, but clearly they were not building any future with each other. Joe had a great deal of time on his hands, but that did not make him seem unhappy. He enjoyed a few rounds of golf, watching television, eating a good meal at home. Marilyn's appetite for success was still unsatisfied and growing. She truly seemed to like the Hollywood parties Joe first hated and then declined to attend, and she thought they were good for her career. Her dresser Lena Pepitone reported her saying "I had always been nothing, a nobody. Then I had the chance to be somebody. I couldn't give it up, just when things were looking good for me. Not just to be a housewife, even Joe's housewife."

DiMaggio told his old friend reporter Jimmy Cannon that living with Marilyn in Hollywood was "dull. . . . She works like a dog. . . . When she's in a picture, she's up at five o'clock in the morning and she doesn't get through until around seven. Then we eat dinner, watch a little television and go to sleep.'' That was how America's golden couple spent their time together. Cannon asked DiMaggio ''Is she a good cook?'' It was obviously a question DiMaggio did not consider strange. ''While she's working . . . she's usually too tired. But she broils a hell of a steak. We're both meat people. We like our steaks.'' In some ways, he still lived in his father's male world.

When Marilyn prepared to travel to New York City to shoot exterior scenes for what turned into one of her best pictures, *The Seven Year Itch*, she told Joe she was taking along her drama coach Natasha Lytess for support, one of the many figures in her life upon whom she developed a dependency. Often these people would give her conflicting advice about her acting (she needed more discipline; she needed more to be herself; she needed more training; she needed to be more natural) and further undermine her fragile sense of adequacy. Lytess resented DiMaggio's male role in what she considered her charge's life, and DiMaggio naturally felt highly uncomfortable with Lytess's grasp upon his wife. He said either he or Lytess would go with Marilyn but not both. Marilyn apparently deemed Lytess crucial to her well-being as an actress, and said she was still going to ask her. So DiMaggio drove Monroe to the airport but would not fly with her to New York. Later the same month, September, he joined her in the city and while he was there Marilyn was filmed in the most famous scene from *The Seven Year Itch*. Planted with her legs apart above a subway grate, her flimsy skirt billowing high above her bare thighs, a delighted Marilyn at her juiciest stands helpless to prevent the subway's hot summer air (actually electric fans underneath) from washing up over her skin. The crowd on Lexington Avenue went wild as gust after gust shot between Marilyn's legs, and the sequence either as finally recorded in the film or in the even more popular still photos remains one of the most iconic posters of her playful exuberant sexuality. To DiMaggio, who may have been in the crowd watching the filming and was most certainly in the city while the filming was going on, the picture and the fuss it caused was only another manifestation of the brazenly erotic postures his wife was manipulated into assuming by her Hollywood bosses. Before they were married Joe had been offended by photographs taken of Marilyn in Atlantic City, New Jersey, in an extremely low-cut dress she had worn in *Niagara*. While her sex appeal was of course one of the qualities that most attracted him, his idea of woman's behavior was very traditional and he did not appreciate her flaunting in public the very sexuality that attracted him, particularly when it was connected with a commercial enterprise such as movie making. As Lois Weber Smith remarked in Maury Allen's biography, DiMaggio was ambivalent about Monroe's attractions. ''He wanted her for all the reasons any other man would want her. . . . but didn't want her to be like that for any other man.''

After arguing with Marilyn in their hotel room, Joe angrily returned to their Beverly Hills home. Clearly Marilyn was determined to pursue her career in films and would not change her way of life. Clearly he could not endure it any longer. In early October, 1954, divorce papers were brought to the apartment and Marilyn signed them. Before the first week of the month had ended, the two agreed to separate and Joe cleared his golf clubs and two suitcases from their house.

Newspapers and national magazines naturally treated the breakup as a noteworthy public event. *Newsweek* for October 18 showed Monroe in a car with a handkerchief at her mouth, presumably grief-stricken, and told much of the couple's story through headlines coarsely transfiguring the sad event into a media extravaganza: "WHY WAS DIMAG BENCHED?" "JOE MUST GO." "JOE FANNED ON JEALOUSY." "NIGHTS WERE DULL AT JOE AND MARILYN'S." The *Reporter* for October 21 pompously intoned "we like the way Joe DiMaggio has behaved in his week of crisis. Unlike our statesmen in the face of events of similar magnitude, Joe has kept a stiff upper lip. . . ." John Lardner in *Newsweek*, December 13, 1954, focused on the print uproar about the divorce in a satiric essay on "Public Love," in which everyone feels they can play "a hand."

While the marriage of Joe DiMaggio and Marilyn Monroe could be understood as the merging of two cultural fantasies, their divorce seems solidly explicable as a breakdown between two people who really were not meant to be married to each other. Their divorce was granted on October 27, 1954 and was accompanied by a standard litany of public accusations, Monroe's half of the truth about what went wrong: DiMaggio would not speak to her for days at a time; he would not allow certain of her visitors in their house; he was cool and indifferent to her. As a newspaper might have phrased it, Joe did not get a turn at bat.

DiMaggio's relationship with Marilyn Monroe during this period most resembles a melodrama. While the word tragic has been used often to describe the affair's end in Monroe's suicide, pathetic might be more technically accurate. At times, after they were divorced and after Monroe was also divorced from Arthur Miller, when DiMaggio often comforted Monroe and they loved each other again, their affair contained quiet pastoral elements. But in November, 1954, immediately after the divorce, an event occurred that can only be called slapstick comedy, as though the Marx brothers and Raymond Chandler had perhaps written a frantic new version of something like *Guys and Dolls*. Two versions of the scenario exist.

One story was told by a private detective named Phillip Irwin before a California state legislative committee inquiring into the "operation of private detective agencies and their relationships with scandal magazines.'' Irwin stated that on November 5, 1954, he called his employer Barney Ruditsky, a former New York City policeman, to tell him he had observed Marilyn Monroe's car at an apartment building not her residence, in the evening. Irwin was interested in this fact apparently because he was hired by Ruditsky who had been in turn (possibly) hired by DiMaggio to get information on Monroe's private life, perhaps of an incriminating nature. This was just a week after Monroe's interlocutory (tentative) divorce had been granted. Ruditsky and Irwin, according to Irwin, summoned other men including Joe DiMaggio and Frank Sinatra (a friend of both DiMaggio's and Monroe's). Eventually some of these men—as reported in *Confidential Magazine* for September, 1955—kicked in the door where they had been told Monroe was secluded, flashing lights into the befuddled eyes of a woman named Florence Kotz. Marilyn Monroe was nowhere to be seen. Actually, the Keystone crew had blundered one floor too low, for Monroe was a flight above with a good friend of hers, Sheila Stewart.

Sinatra claimed before the same investigating committee that he was parked in his car a half-block away from the apartment house being visited by Monroe when the men, who included DiMaggio, "left him to obtain divorce evidence against the blonde actress." Shortly afterward, the men returned muttering something about "the wrong door." And that, Sinatra said, was all he knew about the business. The inquiring committee could not resolve these two stories, and as the *New York Times* on March 2, 1957, stated, "took pains to file in evidence material bearing on possible perjury charges in connection with conflicting accounts of Frank Sinatra's role in the Marilyn Monroe–Joe DiMaggio divorce case." Interestingly enough, DiMaggio's role was never further investigated by the commission. No charges were ever filed on the case. A year later, however, the *New York Times* on September 11, 1958, reported that "a $200,000 so-called 'wrong-door' suit filed against Frank Sinatra, the actor, and Joe DiMaggio" by Florence Kotz Ross was dropped because it had been privately settled for $7,500. The foolish action of a daffy night, whatever actually happened during it, took three years to smooth over if not disentangle outside of court. Back in November, 1954, DiMaggio rebounded once more into Marilyn Monroe's life almost immediately after the silly and abortive espionage job he was linked to ended. While his ex-wife recuperated in the Cedars of Lebanon hospital after treatment for a gynecological condition that supposedly made childbearing impossible for her, he visited her daily. During the following years until her suicide, he would frequently comfort or aid her during crises. He was steady and reliable in his love for her, but she could not live in the unfulfilling way he wanted her to, nor could he straighten out her life as she felt compelled to lead it nor finally, could he enable her to endure living.

She had apparently met the playwright Arthur Miller in 1950 and began seeing him again in the spring of 1954, when she was still married to DiMaggio. After her November hospitalization Marilyn Monroe was in the company of many men, and DiMaggio also began dating other women, but until her romance with Miller became serious the two often sought each other out and enjoyed each other's company for short periods of time. June 1, 1955, Marilyn's birthday, DiMaggio attended the premiere of *The Seven Year Itch* with her at Loew's State Theater in New York City. Afterwards they attended a party at Toots Shor's but reportedly had an argument and Marilyn left alone. Shor's was still DiMaggio's turf and in later interviews Toots Shor would depict him at this time as a lonely man, but DiMaggio seems to have been as active, socially and otherwise, as he wanted. Certainly, as he aged, DiMaggio experienced some of the same feelings of personal dissatisfaction possessed by men and women passing from a time of significant productivity to a quieter, more off-stage, less active way of life. He had just retired in 1951, and concluded a hectic marriage in 1954. Doubtless his feelings were intensified by the knowledge that slightly over forty, his period of high and active greatness was gone. But it would be wrong to sentimentalize him into the stereotype of the forgotten hero, the resourceless ex-athlete doomed to an empty daily existence. Toots Shor's, while not the Yankee Stadium during a World Series game, was hardly pale oblivion. DiMaggio had jobs, he had a social life, he had personal responsibilities, and while the offers he received were not always the ones he desired most, he did not have to accept any that dissatisfied him.

Late in the summer of 1955 he traveled to Italy where he was known and respected, though not a national hero. A translation of his book on baseball had been published there in 1952 with an introduction identifying him as probably baseball's most popular figure. One night the ex-dropout from San Francisco seems to have enjoyed particularly was spent at a barn dance held in Venice for the Venice Film Festival, where the *New York Times* for September 5 reported giddily "Margaret Truman whirled in a square dance, Joe DiMaggio executed a rumba, and a Russian delegation drank vodka."

As he had done occasionally during his playing days though without much ostentation, he devoted some time to charitable activities. He was the 1956-57 chairman of the National Paraplegic Foundation, an organization originally formed as the Paralyzed Veterans of America, whose function was to collect and distribute funds for research on spinal injuries. He replaced his old friend sportswriter Bill Corum as chairman.

Marilyn Monroe reentered his life in 1960. Her 1956 marriage to Arthur Miller lasted until that year, and though it had been longer than her marriage to DiMaggio it had not been much more successful. Monroe had of course the same unsatisfiable emotional needs; Miller's writer's world was as separate to him as DiMaggio's athlete's world. Monroe was locked out while Miller in his study tried to compose great and meaningful plays, and though most versions of their story show that Miller also worshipped Monroe (sometimes), finally, he too could not give her the care she required. Probably no one could. Monroe had made some good pictures after her divorce from DiMaggio, and had attempted to take greater control over her professional life. She was for most critics appropriately vulnerable and charming in *Bus Stop* (1956), and even *The Prince and the Show-girl* (1957) in which she co-starred with director Laurence Olivier was not the flop many predicted it inevitably had to be, for she was sweet and cleanly sexy in the film—a showgirl fit for a fairytale prince. But the movie was not a popular success and wore her out emotionally just as she wore out nearly everybody connected with it. Her neurosis was tiresome to others, her compulsive lateness, caused by her abject insecurity, maddening. Still, had she been healthier emotionally, she could have considered the risky film a triumph in that it had not been made badly, and because Olivier had not dominated her on the screen. In her next movie, *Some Like It Hot* (1959), she was only one of a number of accomplished farceurs including Joe E. Brown, Tony Curtis, and Jack Lemmon, and with them she was terrifically funny and gorgeous (even if as Tony Curtis cruelly remarked, kissing her was like kissing Hitler). The film was a great comedy, and its greatness partly resulted from an excellent performance coaxed from her by Billy Wilder, but obviously within her to elicit. *Let's Make Love* (1960) with Yves Montand was a dull flop. She had an affair with Montand, who several commentators have noted resembles DiMaggio, but that ended disappointingly for her as she should have known it would, when he returned safely to his wife Simone Signoret.

In the summer of 1960 she was making *The Misfits*, a movie that has always carried with it a thick aura of sorrow and depression. The film is difficult to see knowing that at the time of or shortly after its release two of its stars, Clark Gable and Montgomery Clift, were dead, Monroe's marriage with Miller was over, and within a year Monroe would commit suicide. Arthur Miller clearly wrote his script for it with Monroe in mind, and his next work using her nature as its basis would be the harrowing *After the Fall*, a drama about one woman's disintegration and one man's rehabilitation after failure.

As *The Mistfits* was being filmed in 1960 Monroe was suffering (and the crew along with her) through one of her periods of feeling extreme inadequacy and fear, and moreover she was taking a great many pills to move her as though she were a truck being pushed through the day, to wake her up and to put her to sleep and to smooth her nerves made ragged by other pills. Sometimes she was sick and Miller would visit her, though these visits would not aid her to get better. Often they argued with each other, or Monroe and John Huston, the film's director argued, or Miller and Huston argued. Marilyn got along well with Clark Gable and Montgomery Clift, and was especially cheered when DiMaggio visited her. "He came! He came!" Monroe's dresser and confidante Lena Pepitone remembered Monroe telling her. "Lena, he looked so good. When you get sick, you see who really cares." Pepitone also reports that after her brief hospitalization during shooting, Marilyn left Los Angeles and visited DiMaggio in San Francisco before returning to location in Reno.

On September 12, 1960, Monroe took the first legal steps to obtain a divorce from Miller. She would not complete another picture and often lived in New York City, continuing her lessons at the Actors' Studio with its founder Lee Strasberg, another of her dependency figures. She continued to see DiMaggio sporadically both before and after her Mexican divorce was finally official on January 20, 1961. As Pepitone points out, DiMaggio would stay with her and lift her spirits, particularly when she was depressed, as over Christmas, 1960, when both her fond friends, Clark Gable and Arthur Miller's father, died. His visits, Monroe told Pepitone, were to be kept secret since she said DiMaggio did not want any publicity—none at all, "Zero." Pepitone commented, "He really did inspire confidence and nobody needed it more than Marilyn." In her apartment on East 57th Street she pasted a full-length picture of DiMaggio inside her closet and according to Pepitone looked at it almost daily in ritual fashion.

In March, 1961, DiMaggio returned for the first time since his retirement to the Yankee spring training camp. Richard Schaap reported in the March 20 *Newsweek* that everyone was delighted he was back. Ralph Houk was the team's manager and DiMaggio was to be a special unpaid assistant to him. Schaap reported that DiMaggio looked good with graying hair and tanned face, and that he still weighed what he did during his playing days, 195 pounds. He had returned after ten years, he said, "because I was asked for the first time." In *Dynasty* Peter Golenbeck states that Dan Topping had in 1954 "asked DiMaggio to return to the club as a coach, hang around for a couple of years, and replace Casey Stengel when he stepped down," but DiMaggio has never corroborated or acknowledged this. He has demonstrated ambivalence about the matter. Publicly, he has always claimed that he was not interested in managing, but at the same time has indicated his disappointment that the Yankees never really offered him a suitable position other than broadcaster.

DiMaggio, on leave from his job as a good-will ambassador for the V. H. Monette Company, a food purveyor to military commissaries, seemed the same quiet person to Schaap he had always been, only more completely at ease. But a telephone call from Marilyn Monroe burst into his apparent tranquility. Depressed about her divorce, the deaths of Clift and Gable, and the unsteady status of her career, but most of all from the amorphous dread that periodically and reasonlessly overwhelmed her, she had committed herself to the Payne Whitney Psychiatric Clinic in New York City. She found the place unbearable and called DiMaggio for support and for help in getting her out. He flew to New York immediately and presumably was responsible for her discharge and transferral to the Columbia-Presbyterian Medical Center. She found her new quarters far more congenial than her old, which she described to Lena Pepitone as a prison with bars and padded cells where she was about to be straitjacketed. When she left the more congenial Columbia Center she joined DiMaggio at the Yankee camp in Fort Lauderdale. She was, she said, "always . . . able to count on Joe," whom she referred to as her "ex-ex," "as a friend after that first bitterness of our parting faded."[83] He had aided her during her depression just as he had helped her the previous year when she had to be rushed to the Polyclinic Hospital in New York for yet another of her operations, one to remove her gall bladder. In Florida, as Joe offered pointers to the Yankees on how to bat better, Marilyn posed happily in inevitable publicity photographs, taking her turn at the plate, and for a time the two lived together again pleasantly. Taking care of Marilyn Monroe was a little bit like the equivalent in life of his 56-game hitting streak, something he would have had to do every day no matter how he felt, something that would have demanded tight attention and control. But of course life is more complicated than baseball, and there were far more elements that could get out of hand for DiMaggio and Monroe than there had been when he set his famous record. Lena Pepitone said when she asked DiMaggio why he did not marry Monroe again, he answered he still loved her and would do anything for her but that the two together "just didn't work." If only she'd forget her career they could be happy, but otherwise. . . . Pepitone says DiMaggio clutched his stomach "indicating a terrible pain."

DiMaggio's relationship with Monroe continued off and on until she died from an overdose of barbiturates the evening of August 4, 1962. Sometimes they saw and enjoyed each other and sometimes they quarreled over her movie work or DiMaggio's attitude toward it or about the conduct of her private life, for example when she was having an affair with a married man. The time was generally one of emotional decline for Monroe, and increasing conflict between her and her studio, Twentieth-Century Fox. She demanded more control over her career, greater respect for her talent, and a fairer share of the profits the studio made from her. They wanted more reliability from her, more obedience, and more professionalism than she often demonstrated in her working behavior. Assigned the starring role in what could have been either another dead-end piece of schlock or something she might have helped transform into a lovely, funny comedy, *Something's Got To Give*, she rebelled by her usual strategy of slowing down production through excruciating and expensive delaying tactics. She appeared on the set far fewer than half its first month of shooting days. Her actions were both compulsive and willful but in some ways justifiable, viewed from the perspective of an actress with a major talent she was not permitted to direct. Like most stars she was still a commodity the studio used primarily in its own interests and not hers. However, even to the extent that she was right in refusing to cooperate with the company that owned her and wanted to force her to perform in ways she felt it not in her best interests to do, she was not in charge of herself when she did not do their work. She was breaking down as she had often broken down before. If she was doing the right thing she was doing it in large part through confusion.

In June she reported ill on the set again, and Nunnally Johnson, the movie's original writer and a competent director called DiMaggio in London and asked him if he would fly to Los Angeles to help Marilyn meet her obligations and to support her. DiMaggio said he would telephone her but that he was really in no position to aid her as she needed. It would be no good for him, he said, to go to Hollywood again. In June the studio suspended Monroe and sued her for $750,000. After the debacle Fox had experienced in the titanically overbudget disaster *Cleopatra,* starring Elizabeth Taylor, they were determined not to let another of their entertainment dreadnoughts sink without retaliation.

Her death by probable suicide was a sensational event unrivalled by anything in her life, and accompanied, as anyone but an alien from a far galaxy would know, by endless commentary and speculation to this day. She became more of a cultural symbol than ever before, and like most symbols a changing sign for each interpreter. But whatever she represented, DiMaggio came to stand during her funeral and afterward for an element of decency and even nobility in her life and death. The teller of DiMaggio's story must note the macabre truth that DiMaggio's totally unselfconscious performance during this sad time added to his image one more very important manifestation of his greatness of character. His image gained by her death.

Hearing of her death he canceled an appearance he was supposed to make in a charity baseball game in San Francisco and traveled immediately to Los Angeles. Though so many had wanted a piece of her while alive, apparently there was no one to take charge of her dead, and so DiMaggio did. Seeing Hollywood still as her enemy and now as her killer, he arranged for a very simple funeral ceremony that excluded and angered many of Monroe's celebrity acquaintances, such as members of Frank Sinatra's Rat Pack and President Kennedy's sister Patricia. Only a few intimates, who DiMaggio considered Monroe's friends and her closest staff served as mourners. In the afterglow of remorse that so many commentators felt following her death, DiMaggio shone again as a hero of integrity and order. A range of reporters, from her earthy dresser Lena Pepitone to the distinguished critic Edward Wagenknecht, noted DiMaggio's dignified presence. Somewhat sentimentally, Pepitone remarked, "He had always come through for her, and he came through again in the end, when for all her fame, she had no one else who would take care of her burial." The more restrained Wagenknecht remarked that "thanks to the good taste of Marilyn's former husband Joe DiMaggio, she was interred with simple, quiet dignity in the presence of only a few close friends.''[84] Norman Mailer, often wildly wrong and whackily speculative about Monroe wrote a kind of elegy about her death concluding: ''Let us take our estimate of her worth by the grief on Joe DiMaggio's face the day of that dread funeral in Westwood west of Hollywood.'' And truly the picture of DiMaggio crying at the ceremony showed no dead pan, but a face twisted by loss. His courtly lover's gesture of having roses placed several times weekly at her crypt, which he stopped only in 1982, giving no reason for the discontinuance (possibly it was because necrophiles kept stealing the roses), became an act perhaps made tritely romantic by the publicity that has been shoveled onto it, but was surely intended as a sincere sign of love and grief. He was sincere too about the snub he gave Robert F. Kennedy three years after her funeral at a special day for Mickey Mantle at Yankee Stadium because he considered Kennedy part of the crew of beautiful people who in Hollywood and elsewhere ruined her.

The conclusion to his relationship with Monroe brought DiMaggio the last great flood of attention comparable to what he received periodically during his playing days, but since that time there have been lesser waves keeping him in view of the American public to an extent unusual among retired athletes. Mostly, however, he has lived comfortably at a self-determined pace. He was given a special birthday dinner to commemorate his fiftieth year on November 19, 1964, in San Francisco. President Johnson sent him a congratulatory telegram and more than a thousand guests at the Sheraton Palace hotel cheered when he cut into a seven-foot wide birthday cake with the number five crowning it. He also received a Chevrolet Impala, a gold-plated Louisville Slugger baseball bat, and an award from the local Police Athletic League.

Gay Talese described him around the time of spring training in an article appearing in the July, 1966, *Esquire*. The tone Talese seems to have selected for the article is melancholy, with constant playbacks to former days of DiMaggio's hitting glory or to his turbulent time with Marilyn Monroe, whose ghost haunts the view of DiMaggio that Talese offers, even more than his rousing days of baseball greatness. Talese quotes Billy Wilder as saying he saw a ''look of death'' in DiMaggio's eyes when Wilder supposedly spotted him in the crowd viewing the ballooning skirt scene of *The Seven Year Itch*. Talese also described DiMaggio coldly and angrily refusing to see an unnamed man from New York City who had come to San Francisco to interview him on some vague unstated matter of sociological research. The narrative here is doubtlessly correct. Otherwise DiMaggio seems unexcited and at loose ends, though his day is actually fairly full, spent partly working for Continental Television, playing golf (a relaxation he later would have to cut down on because of recurrent pain from his baseball injuries), and attending a boondocks banquet with friends including Lefty O'Doul. DiMaggio looks at pretty women and meets one in a bar, but Talese shows him most at home with men. With the Yankees, DiMaggio is persuaded to take batting practice after Mickey Mantle and Roger Maris are through. He chokes up on the bat as he had never done as a player, and hits a couple of balls solidly, but finally hurts his hand on a bad connection and stops. He stays at the best room of the Yankee Clipper Motel. Talese does not mention that this is DiMaggio's motel, and somehow—the fact would have fit perfectly into the narrative as Talese designed it—misses the detail that it was from the Yankee Clipper that Marilyn Monroe had summoned DiMaggio to get her out of the Payne Whitney Clinic four years before.

On September 21, 1967, DiMaggio, along with television master of ceremonies and New York *Daily News* reporter Ed Sullivan and the great Chicago Bears quarterback Sid Luckman, testified for the defense in the trial of Louis Wolfson, the industrialist and stock speculator. Wolfson was charged with violating the Federal Securities Act of 1933 by selling unregistered shares of Continental stock. The *New York Times* reported September 22 that DiMaggio stated on the witness stand that he held Wolfson in high regard and called his "reputation for honesty 'excellent.'" More pleasant news came on October 22 when Charles "Charlie" Finley announced that DiMaggio had been hired as an executive vice-president for the Oakland (formerly Kansas City) Athletics, consulting on player personal community relations and other front office operations. DiMaggio was also to assist the A's recently hired manager, Bob Kennedy, by coaching. His job with Oakland was perhaps the one he would have liked with the Yankees but was never offered. In some ways it seemed better since it was closer to his home, but it never worked out and after several seasons of diminishing involvement he withdrew from the affiliation.

The biggest news about DiMaggio in 1967 was not anything he did, but a song in which his name was an important if somewhat cryptic allusion. One of the most popular films of the 1960s was *The Graduate* starring Dustin Hoffman and directed by Mike Nichols. Like Hemingway's *The Old Man and the Sea*, it was a work that aspired to be art, but it also became in short time a popular cultural event with social significance that will be examined in greater detail later. The movie seemed to crystallize midway through the 1960s much of the distinctive flavor of the decade, particularly the search of the period's youth for standards acceptable to them in an indifferent or corrupt world dominated by the outmoded and disdained values of their parents' generation. In one of the movie's most memorable songs, Paul Simon's "Mrs. Robinson," still recognized not only for its music but for its youthful complaint, DiMaggio's name is used several times as a lament for lost innocence and true greatness, something good to believe in that was no longer apparently part of the American grain. Played over and over again, the song floated DiMaggio's worth before audiences some of whom could remember firsthand his days of inspired performance, and some of whom became familiar with his virtues through the song itself—thus he linked the disparate generations.

The decade's end brought him new awards and renewed recognition. On May 19, 1969, along with Rocky Marciano, golf's Gene Sarazan, and a stand-in for Vince Lombardi, he was honored at the Americans of Italian Descent Salute held in Madison Square Garden. On July 21 as part of the celebration commemorating baseball's centennial, he was selected as the sport's "Greatest Living Player," along with Babe Ruth who was honored as the "Greatest Player Ever," John McGraw as the "Greatest Manager Ever," and Casey Stengel, termed "Greatest Living Manager." DiMaggio was also a member of the "Greatest Players Ever" team determined "by the votes of the baseball writers and broadcasters throughout the country from single-team nominations voted upon by fans in each city." The value of this honor was very high, though endlessly arguable, since so many factors irrespective of ability affected the final decision. Since all four of the highest awards went to New York personalities it is clear that the disproportionate attention given New York performers by the media was an aid to selection. However, the selection was still significant even though most of those who voted had never seen all the players and managers they voted for in action, since many voters would have been relying upon the reputations of the nominees, and since all the eventual winners would have to be considered as at least worthy and legitimate contenders.

The 1970s were similarly good to DiMaggio in terms of the public attention he continued to receive and the comfortable life he appeared to live. If he experienced few intense times of excitement (though at old-timers reunion games or at benefits his name was usually announced last and to the wildest applause) there were no events that brought him, as Monroe's death had, crushing despair. In 1972 he was disappointed that his hoped-for realliance with the Yankees did not materialize but over the years that link had become tenuous anyway. As is frequently the situation in abortive business deals, the reasons DiMaggio was finally not able to participate in Yankee ownership are not clear. Michael Burke, president of the organization at the time, undoubtedly irritated DiMaggio by claiming in the newspapers that "he wants to come back with us. We'd like to have him if we can work something out," for DiMaggio never publicly placed himself in the position of seeking anything from his old team. DiMaggio said that some associates contacted him about forming an organization and buying into the club, but that after a time he was no longer consulted on the deal.[85]

Reunification with the Yankees would have kept his name more constantly before the fans, but he accomplished this anyway in a novel fashion and one that through his later years, enabled him to live in greater financial security and maintain his image. In the chain of events that has kept DiMaggio's name and talents before the public to an extent possibly unparalleled by any athlete of his time, his television appearances as a commercial spokesman are artificial but at the same time important in solidifying his persona as a dignified, reliable, and (something new) congenial human being. The advertising agencies and commercial enterprises who capitalized on and augmented his fame were of course manipulating both him and the television audience to increase business profits. But it is also clear that DiMaggio was very conscious of his image and the ways he would allow it to be used, and he managed not to violate his already established myth by involving himself in patently crass or demeaning activities.

Although athletes had for many years associated themselves with various commercial products, they did so usually only briefly and at the height of their fame—not over an extended period of time, nor long after their playing days had finished. Further, DiMaggio was one of the first star athletes to become an institutional spokesman, whose image was recruited by the dominant popular medium of the day, television (appearing also in newspaper, magazine, and radio advertisements) so that he would become identified with the institution and it would become identified with him: there would develop a blending of selected attributes of each, and a commerically successful relationship between the man and the institution would be inaugurated. DiMaggio, with his roots in old-time baseball, became one of the first athlete-stars of the post-industrial society. In 1972 he was the spokesman for the Bowery Savings Bank, a New York based financial house that called itself the nation's largest. He was hired to capture and retain a designated target audience of mature men and women, people with strong family ties, who knew the value of and practiced saving. He represented skill, reliability, willingness to help, dignity, trust-worthiness—and charm and affluence. Later he became the national media spokesman for Mr. Coffee, the coffee-making machine, and this further extended his fame and displayed his now well-developed talent as a smooth, effective announcer. He never seemed a salesman and was never glib nor slick. With Mr. Coffee for example he seemed a very male friend simply enjoying coffee, not an actor hawking it. When he began making commercials he was quite reticent about his participation and at first exhibited some of the awkwardness he displayed in the 1950s in his pre- and post-game shows. But after a relatively brief time he found his new role easier to fulfill, and in some ways even satisfying as he participated more in the processes of production. He remained selective and mentioned in an excellent interview with Thomas Boswell of the *Washington Post*, September 1, 1983, that he had turned down offers from such concerns as Grecian Formula hair preparation and Polident Denture Cream because he neither tinted his hair nor wore false teeth, but probably also because he considered the products inappropriate for him to be identified with. Unlike some other athletes who have incorporated themselves and hired consultants to market their names, faces, feet, and sometimes pelvises,

DiMaggio has appeared to remain essentially disconnected from advertising though clearly he engages in it. He never seems to be selling a product for the money it brings him. Thus, his legendary quality remains undisturbed though he is obviously engaging in a very mundane and materialistic activity.

While journalists were appalled by Muhammad Ali's thick-tongued shill for a bug killer, they seemed pleased or at the very worst respectfully amused by DiMaggio's television salesmanship. And they recollected with pleasure his rookie skills and yet how much he had grown as a person from his apprenticeship days. Arthur Daley in the *New York Times*, May 13, 1973, "marveled at the graceful way he accepted the plaudits" he received at a $100.00 a plate dinner of the Multiple Sclerosis Society at which he was guest of honor. It seemed ages ago to Daley that DiMaggio had been shy and resentful over invasions of his privacy, as when he had been jostled by a crowd at some earlier All-Star game and asked Daley to take him into his cab and rescue him. Very rarely in newspapers or magazines were DiMaggio's old rough edges, his sulks and fierce desire for privacy, mentioned during these later years. "Reminiscence," by Schuyler Bishop in the September 1, 1983, *Sports Illustrated* told a story (written almost more as fiction than as an article) implying that when Bishop was twelve DiMaggio had acted rudely by failing to return after half time to the seat Bishop's father had so graciously given him to that year's Army-Navy game, had failed even to tell the father and his hero-worshipping son that he was leaving.

Ordinarily, the news published about DiMaggio's life these years reflected his status as a greatly respected sports hero who had become a greatly respected man. While it is not difficult to find reporters who will talk about sitting next to a silent DiMaggio at some affair, such information is hardly newsworthy and is usually accompanied by a shrug and some verbal variant of "that's just the way he is sometimes." DiMaggio would never become Mr. Affable to all. He always carried with him an element of potential reserve. When he appears at baseball shows, gatherings of people who buy and sell often expensive baseball trivia such as baseball cards, he may tire of signing autographs and become cold as ice to those around him. With DiMaggio there are always limits.

But these limits also help define him and prevent him from blurring into some other softer image which would be untrue to his nature. Among modern heroes he is a king, usually a good king, but never a Prince Hal. In his day-to-day behavior he surely behaves imperfectly. But outnumbering stories such as Bishops' are complimentary remembrances such as the time Robert Lipsyte recalls in *Sportsworld* that DiMaggio went out of his way to provide him with a jacket on a cold day of practice, or the morning Robin Roberts related when in a crowded hotel cafeteria, DiMaggio insisted that Roberts's son share his breakfast table, producing as much delight in the boy as he had disillusion in Bishop.[86] It could be claimed that in these three situations, DiMaggio acted well toward the famous and inconsiderately toward ordinary people, but it is also probable that if he could be rude to Robert Kennedy, he could be rude to anybody.

More typically the press reported awards he received and good-will appearances, or sought his comments on various events relating to baseball. On January 27, 1974, for example, the "Casey Stengel-You-Could-Look-It-Up Award" for hitting streaks that he was given by the New York baseball writers gained attention in the metropolitan area, as did his remarks in February, 1975, when he revisited Japan for the first time in almost two decades. He worked for a week as batting coach for the Lotte Orions and graciously remarked that there was no "appreciable difference" anymore between the Japanese and American players, and five more years might bring a meaningful World Series. On October 1 the same year, he was one of many athletes eulogizing Casey Stengel, who had just died. He laid aside their old differences and said his old manager was "wonderful, he understood his players and he knew what to do with the talent he had."[87] In 1976 President Ford named him as one of 21 Americans receiving a Medal of Freedom, along with "Lady Bird" (Mrs. Claudia) Johnson, the ex-President's widow, and Nelson Rockefeller. On February 7, 1979, the New York Board of Trade honored him for his contributions to New York City, Senator Jacob Javits declaring that DiMaggio was "synonymous with what's great about New York." Every so often newspaper news would reveal the hero's feet slightly speckled with clay. A June 6, 1980, article in the *New York Times* tells how DiMaggio had lost a suit before the San Francisco Board of Permit Appeals, seeking to make Mr. Jeffrey Hsia, a neighbor, do something about the extension he constructed on his house in the "fashionable Marina district," which DiMaggio claimed spoiled his view. DiMaggio treated his defeat philosophically. "You win some, you lose some. I really wanted a hearing and I finally got one. At least I wasn't shut out." This kind of article was an exception, however, and was more than offset by numerous items recollecting various events in DiMaggio's baseball career, particularly around the time in July and August, 1978, when Pete Rose was battling through his 44-game hitting streak. Most of these articles accepted the point developed in Melvin Durslag's Arpil 18, 1981, *T. V. Guide* essay on "Why Hasn't DiMaggio's 56-Game Streak Been Broken?"

David Voigt was correct in pointing out in *American Baseball in a Changing Society* that while DiMaggio still earned money twenty years after his retirement as a player "modeling for a New York bank," he "never surpassed Babe Ruth's reputation." However, DiMaggio's status as a culture hero was more firm by the late 1970s and early 1980s than it was at the time he stopped actively participating in sport, for beyond his image as a superb performer with distinctly admirable characteristics as a player on the field, he had acquired added fame for representing selected elements of good in the American character. He came to represent something special in American life, in large part because of the decency and nobility he was perceived as displaying in his relationship with Marilyn Monroe. Moreover, his image was kept fresh before the public through his role as a television spokesman, and through the cascade of print appearances in books, magazine articles, and newspaper notes that dealt with aspects of his playing and non-playing career. And as he was a dominant symbol of courage and triumph over pain in 1954 in one of the best known novels by one of the most popular and seriously thought-of American novelists, and a hero of vanished decency in one of the most popular songs in one of the most popular films of the 1960s, so in the later decades he has frequently been used by other writers for artistic purposes in a symbolic fashion, because his name is so well-known and his life and image are so rich in possibilities for interpreting America. The ill-fated 1981 play *The Amazin' Casey Stengel, or Can't Anybody Here Speak This Game*, the film version of E. L. Doctorow's *The Book of Daniel* (*Daniel*, in which the title character is instructed in the decadence of the ruling class by being taught how DiMaggio is a tool of the exploiters), the most recent film remake of Raymond Chandler's *Farewell My Lovely*, and Nicholas Roeg's film *Insignificance* are just a few of the entertainments in which DiMaggio provided a point of reference. Almost always, when Marilyn Monroe's story is retold in fact or fiction, he is featured as part of her legend. So unlike the hero in Housman's poem "To An Athlete Dying Young," he is not one of those whose "name died before the man."

Now in his seventies, DiMaggio told Thomas Boswell he still has "to work for a living," but what he clearly meant was that he worked to keep active and not that he needed to make money in order to survive or even to survive comfortably. He seems satisfied neither remaining at his home in San Francisco, nor in traveling non-stop about the country making public appearances or shooting commercials, so he divides his time between home and the road. He told Boswell he made fourteen trips to New York City alone, in 1982. If this rhythm of movement followed by withdrawal, of quick trips surrounding himself with strangers followed by quiet times secluded with old friends, suggests the fragmented existence of a man not quite content to do whatever he is doing for long, it also shows a full life, scaled down from but similar to his old days of stardom and privacy, of road trips with the Yankees and off season returns to his family and to wherever the crowds were not. He is still connected to baseball but not very closely except through his reputation as a player, which seems as strong as ever. He is listed each year in the American League's *Red Book* as one of the directors of the Baltimore Orioles, whose Chairman of the Board and President, Edward Bennett Williams, is his friend and legal advisor. Sometimes he appears at big league games. Boswell's article was accompanied by a picture showing him throwing out the first pitch, opening Seattle's 1978 season.

When he makes public appearances he avoids excessive publicity. In the Tampa Bay area during the January, 1984, Super Bowl week for a celebrity-businessman golf tournament sponsored by the Warner-Lambert Company, he played golf quietly but remained, according to the one local sports commentator who discovered his presence, "aloof but not forbidding. . . . looking older than on his TV commercials, looking a little stooped, yet with a curiously regal quality, like one of those exiled kings . . . on the French Riviera, waiting for a call that he knows will never come again."[88] The remarks are typical in that they emphasize Dimaggio's unique grandeur, but also turn him somewhat sentimentally into a symbol of past and irreclaimable greatness.

It will never be possible to turn DiMaggio into King Lear. Unlike Ruth and Cobb, bitterness is not a strong part of his life after reigning as the top player for baseball's top team during the last years before that kingdom, in 1953, began shifting its territories for the first time in half a century and then began expanding beyond easy focus; the last years before players (especially the best players) began traveling from one team to another and from one allegiance to another. Unlike a star performer such as Red Grange, he is not forgotten. Grange, undeniably one of football's greatest heroes who along with Bill Tilden, Babe Ruth, and Jack Dempsey were legends during the golden 1920s was still living in relative obscurity in a small town in Florida in the early 1980s. Who but sports fans knew his name?

DiMaggio's exploits on the playing field were considerable, and without them he would never have become a legend. But the exploits themselves were only the foundation of the story ending with him becoming an American myth, a culture hero whose significance as part of the American scene extended much farther than the playing fields on which he starred. Certainly his abilities were high. At his best he hit well and was especially tough in pressure situations. He fielded gracefully and expertly, and possessed a strong and accurate throwing arm. He was a skilled base-runner. His record of hitting in 56 consecutive games is one of the greatest achievements in modern baseball, and even if surpassed (as were Ruth's records of 60 home runs in one season and 714 over a lifetime), will be remembered as one of baseball's most treasured accomplishments. He was known as a team player in the best American tradition, a performer who took upon himself the burden of leadership for the most successful team in the history of baseball. Moreover, he became known as a player not simply blessed with natural skills, but one who despite injuries could triumph over pain and come back and perform spectacularly.

Much was expected of him as Babe Ruth's successor and so great attention was focused on him from his major league start, and he more than fulfilled the hoped-for expectations of writers and fans alike, in what was then the biggest and most culturally powerful city in the nation. He was a special hero to America's Italian-Americans, a people emerging strongly into social and political acceptance during the early years of his stardom, a time of particular crisis in the ethnic community because of Benito Mussolini's controversiality as a world figure. The community needed heroes who would be acceptable to all Italian-Americans, and respected by Americans generally. Embodying as he did so many desired characteristics of the American hero—emerging from a large, somewhat poor immigrant family, exemplifying the American success story—DiMaggio was never just an ethnic favorite, but provided a symbol of admired achievement for many Americans.

Some of the measures of his greatness as a player are observable, quantifiable; others are not. But he has been consistently praised for both his tangible and intangible skills. Reports about him by writers have been overwhelmingly positive. While from time to time less admirable qualities in his nature have been mentioned, these have been treated as the exception. At various periods, such as when he was holding out for more money during his early years as a Yankee, sportswriters have been critical of him, but the major writers for the major print media have always minimized his personal deficiencies, his gracelessness as an interviewee for example, and have often turned what might be seen in others as defects, into virtues: he was not merely some sulky isolato, he was simply shy, a young kid feeling his way around or an older veteran seeking privacy. He was nearly always well treated even before his greatly celebrated hitting streak had been written about in *Life*. He was declared not only a great player but a quintessential American, a local hero who could also represent the finest qualities of national character. In time, partly because of his athletic exploits and partly because of the dimensions his image had come to achieve in the public consciousness, writers and filmmakers whose domains extended far beyond the sports page came to use DiMaggio as a symbol representing various good qualities that in him somehow withstood the rot of Western life in the second half of the twentieth century. After baseball stardom, his life seemed to resemble, at least on its surface, a story about the after-play years of a decent ex-athletic champion. Though his interlude with Marilyn Monroe contained periods of dreary boredom and bitter acrimony and even, with the bungled Frank Sinatra caper, absurd ludicrousness, it has come to present about DiMaggio more than anything else, in its most frequent and popular retellings, his pain and courage, his hatred of corruption, and his loving grief. And so the episode, whatever its reality in factual detail, had fit as gracefully into his legend as baseballs slipped into his waiting mitt when he played center field so expertly.

Throughout his reported career, DiMaggio has seemed to remain constant and yet he has constantly changed. It is as though some magic conveyor were awaiting his step when he began playing with the Yankees, to transport him to greatness if only he would not fall off, as do most pretenders to heroism. The management of his team, the fans, the writers, the Italian-American public, Americans at large during the Depression, were waiting to cheer him on if he succeeded, and he succeeded beautifully. And so he moved along on the conveyor (which in reality only his rare skill would permit him to do) often smoothly, sometimes with a lurch or a bump. At the end of the ride he got off the conveyor (it would be an escalator, of course) and in many ways was the same person that got on—shy, private, sulky, taking charge as long as his body allowed him to, trying his hardest, displaying amazing skills until the end. But he would also be changed. The very limited kid from San Francisco would be known as an exceptionally natty dresser. The rookie who did not know what a "quote" was, had become somebody Ernest Hemingway felt a poor, victimized fisherman would think about during his ordeal with loneliness, pain, and defeat; someone who might understand the trial the fisherman was undergoing. Somehow he remained almost pure, and played the game the way it should be played, for all of us, and stopped when he should.

Perhaps more surprisingly, having stepped off one escalator when he retired, DiMaggio stepped on another shortly after. He has lived a life in public view beyond his playing days that has brought him continued recognition, and during it he has continued to remain the same and also to evolve. He is still, after Marilyn Monroe, and being sung about (like old heroes of legend were) in one of the sixties' most memorable and culturally revealing songs, considered a man of reliability and quiet strength. With even more rough edges rubbed away during the development of his image, he has become a great and handsome gentleman, a hero of old wars in repose but not in disrepair. He is solid as the bank he represents. He seems to be what most Americans would aspire to be when they age: nice looking, healthy, financially secure, respected. He goes where he wants to and leaves when he feels like it. The high school dropout, whom we are told his father thought was a lazy bum, looks like a millionaire and on May 27, 1983, was awarded an honorary Doctor of Humanities degree by Holy Cross College. According to the headline accompanying Thomas Boswell's article in the *Washington Post*, "At last, DiMaggio feels comfortable in public." He seems to decide, however, who his public will be, and to resent intrusions from those who are not part of it, or who want to get close to him. And he still seems to be a solitary man.

NOTES

1. I have pieced together the most probable version of Joe DiMaggio's parents' early years by comparing details given in the biographical sources discussed later and by verifying details—when possible—with Vince DiMaggio and Marie Dimaggio (Kron).

2. Dates kindly provided by Marie DiMaggio (Kron), unpublished letter to Jack B. Moore, 21 August 1984.

3. In order to eliminate excessive or obtrusive documentation, I have attempted whenever possible to indicate sources within my text, and use footnotes only where an intelligent reader would have difficulty locating references. Reynolds wrote two early articles on DiMaggio. This excerpt is from "The Frisco Kid," *Collier's*, 13 June 1936, p. 22.

4. According to most accounts, e.g. Maury Allen's *Where Have You Gone, Joe DiMaggio?: The Story of America's Last Hero* (New York: E. P. Dutton & Co., 1975), neither Vince, Joe, nor Dominic speaks with an accent, and Vince has stated (interview with Jack B. Moore, 25 June 1984) that Tom did not.

5. Unless stated otherwise, ellipses are mine.

6. In an article appearing under DiMaggio's name, but actually written by Carl Lundquist ("I'll Always Remember the Man by the Fence," *Parade*, 11 September 1955, p. 2) yet another version of the discovery story is related. In this version, Hennessy says "don't you realize that you can get bloodshot eyes looking through a knothole like that?," and tells DiMaggio "you don't know it but I've been watching you play Sundays on the sand lot." In "Meeting Joe DiMaggio," *Washington Post*, 7 August 1984, William Gildea writes that Henessy said to Graham "I want you to meet the greatest 'lamb' I have ever recommended." Vince DiMaggio stated his disclaimer in an unpublished letter to Jack B. Moore, 12 October 1984.

7. An undated clipping in Vince DiMaggio's scrapbook, dealing with his 1932 season with Tucson, tells of "'Babe Ruth' Demaggio" singing "*O Solo Mio*" at the ballpark. In the same scrapbook a newspaper photograph of Joe hitting in his 49th consecutive game (1933) calls him Joe "DeMaggio." Another undated article from a local newspaper in the 1933 season, states "Vince insists it is Di and Joe persists in his De." Mrs. Vincent DiMaggio in an interview with me, 25 June 1984, explained that her sister-in-law Frances wanted to Americanize the name by spelling it the way it should have been pronounced—DeMaggio (Dee Maggio), not DiMaggio (Die Maggio).

8. Jocko Conlon and Robert Creamer, *Jocko* (New York: J.B. Lippincott Company, 1951), p. 41.

9. Undated item in Vince DiMaggio's scrapbook dealing with his minor league years.

10. Edward Grant Barrow with James M. Kahn, *My Fifty Years in Baseball* (New York: Coward McCann, 1967), pp. 174-75.

11. Dave Anderson, "The DiMaggio Years," in *The Four Fabulous Eras of Baseball's Most Famous Team* (New York: Random House, 1980), p. 63.

12. Barrow, p. 155.

13. *Daily News,* 4 March, 11 March 1936.

14. Barrow, pp. 173, 177.

15. Jimmy Cannon, "The Joe DiMaggio I Remember," in *Sport Magazine's All-Time All Stars,* edited by Tom Meany (New York: Atheneum, 1977), p. 154; originally in *Sport Magazine*, September, 1956.

16. Jack Mann, *The Decline and Fall of the New York Yankees* (New York: Simon & Schuster, 1967), p. 149.

17. The frequently quoted remark is remembered in, for example, Red Smith's

New York *Herald Tribune* column for 8 February 1979, "Mr. New York, Mr. Bowery and. . . ."

18. David Q. Voigt, *American Baseball, From Gentleman's Sport to the Commissioner System* (Norman: University of Oklahoma Press, 1966), p. 214.

19. Mann, p. 146.

20. John Durant, *Highlights of the World Series* (New York: Hastings House Publishers, 1971), p. 89.

21. The files are at Yankee Stadium. Mostly they consist of newspaper clippings about DiMaggio and publicity releases prepared by Yankee staff.

22. David Q. Voigt, *American Baseball, From the Commissioners to Continental Expansion* (Norman: University of Oklahoma Press, 1970), pp. 195-96.

23. Quoted in Donald Honig, *Baseball When the Grass Was Real* (New York: Coward, McCann & Geoghegan, 1975), p. 34.

24. Honig, p. 224.

25. Anderson, "The DiMaggio Years," p. 70.

26. Cannon, p. 155.

27. Anderson, "The DiMaggio Years", p. 62.

28. George DeGregorio, *Joe DiMaggio, An Informal Biography* (New York: Stein and Day, 1981), p. 70.

29. Larry Merchant, *Ringside Seat at the Circus* (New York: Holt, Rinehart and Winston, 1976), p. 11.

30. Ibid.

31. Ellipses are Powers'.

32. Reported in Gene Schoor, *Joe DiMaggio, The Yankee Clipper* (New York: Julian Messner, 1956), p. 122.

33. Al Silverman, *Joe DiMaggio, The Golden Year, 1941* (Englewood Cliffs, N.J.: Prentice-Hall, 1969), p. 101.

34. Durant, p. 72; John Devaney and Burt Goldblatt, *The World Series, A Complete Pictorial History* (Chicago: Rand McNally and Company, 1972), p. 161.

35. Devaney and Goldblatt, p. 161.

36. DeGregorio, p. 75.

37. Silverman, pp. 97-98.

38. Robin Moore and Gene Schoor, *Marilyn & Joe DiMaggio* (New York: Manor Books, Inc., 1976), p. 47.

39. Joe DiMaggio, *Lucky to Be a Yankee* (New York: Rudolph Field, 1946), p. 83.

40. Melvin Dubofsky, *We Shall Be All* (New York: Quadrangle, 1969), pp. 423-24.

41. De Gregorio, pp. 88-89.

42. Silverman, p. 172; Anderson, p. 77. John Holway, in "The Pitcher Who Stopped Joe DiMaggio's Streak," *Baseball Digest*, March 1963, half-seriously noted that DiMaggio was "stopped 11 games into his streak by a sore-armed left-hander" named Jimmy Halperin pitching for the Class-B Norfolk team.

43. Silverman, p. 178 and passim. The ellipses are Silverman's.

44. Anderson, p. 82.

45. DeGregorio, pp. 129-37 is virtually alone in writing about these events.

46. Ibid., p. 129.

47. Allen, *Where Have You Gone, Joe DiMaggio?*, p. 81.

48. Ibid., p. 101.

49. Ibid., p. 68.

50. Maury Allen, *You Could Look it Up: The Life of Casey Stengel* (New York: *Time* Books, 1979), p. 8.

51. Allen, *Where Have You Gone, Joe DiMaggio?*, p. 89. See also Dave Anderson, "Those Sundry Yankee-Red Sox Deals," *New York Times,* 18 December 1980.

52. Schoor, *Joe DiMaggio, The Yankee Clipper*, p. 160.

53. Peter Golenbeck, *Dynasty, The New York Yankees 1949-1964* (Englewood Cliffs, N.J.: Prentice-Hall, 1975), p. 76. Ellipses are DiMaggio's as reported by Golenbeck.

54. Ibid., p. 90. The Lopat story that follows is also told here, and in Allen, *Where Have You Gone, Joe DiMaggio?*, pp. 98-99.

55. The story told by Dr. Sidney Gaynor in Allen's biography of DiMaggio is confusing on the sequence of DiMaggio's heel injuries. It is informative, however, in condemning Larry MacPhail for sending DiMaggio to a doctor who was no specialist, but a friend of MacPhail's. This doctor allegedly mishandled the operation on DiMaggio's left heel.

56. De Gregorio, p. 94 and passim, is the best book for information on DiMaggio's right heel injury.

57. Robert W. Creamer, *Stengel, His Life and Times* (New York: Simon & Schuster, 1984), p. 14.

58. Both quotations are in Allen, *Where Have You Gone, Joe DiMaggio?*, p. 17 and p. 12, respectively.

59. *New York Times*, 14 April, 1949.

60. Ellipsis is *Time*'s.

61. De Gregorio tells this story, pp. 200-201.

62. Golenbeck, p. 16; Anderson, p. 91.

63. Golenbeck, p. 37.

64. Ibid., p. 51; Creamer, p. 238.

65. Golenbeck, p. 60. Sportswriter Shirley Povich's column, circulated nationally the day following the game, reported DiMaggio saying he was "all set . . . if someone will show me where first is in this park." DiMaggio joked for the benefit of photographers and writers prior to the game, and according to Povich made several fine plays, but was generally awkward and ill at ease. The injury to Hank Bauer which necessitated DiMaggio's return to center field extricated the Yankees, Povich said, "from an embarrassment that threatened appalling proportions." It seemed as though the sun had been shifted from its central position in the solar system.

66. Devaney and Goldblatt, p. 211.

67. Interview with Robin Roberts, 23 January 1983.

68. Golenbeck, p. 31.

69. Mel Allen with Frank Graham, Jr., *It Takes Heart* (New York: Harper & Brothers, 1959), pp. 35-36.

70. Joseph Durso, Whitey Ford, and Mickey Mantle, *Whitey and Mickey* (New York: Viking Press, 1977), pp. 21-22.

71. Billy Martin and Peter Golenbeck, *Number 1* (New York: Dell, 1980), pp. 48, 152-53, 159.

72. See, for example, *New York Times*, 8 July 1951.

73. Golenbeck, p. 61.

74. Willie Mays, as told to Charles Einstein, *Born to Play Ball* (New York: G.P. Putnam's Sons, 1955), p. 54.

75. Personal transcript of audiotapes, Michigan State University archives.

76. Allen, *You Could Look It Up,* p. 160.

77. The two sources I relied on most frequently for general details about Marilyn Monroe and her relationship with DiMaggio were Fred Lawrence Guiles, *Norma Jean* (New York: McGraw-Hill, 1969), and Edwin Palmer Hoyt, *Marilyn, the Tragic Venus* (New York: Duell, Sloan & Pearce, 1965).

78. Alvin H. Marill, *Robert Mitchum on the Screen* (New York: A.S. Barnes, 1978), p. 33.

79. See Norman Mailer, *Marilyn* (New York: Grosset & Dunlap, 1981), pp. 8, 63.

80. Moore and Schoor's account of their first meeting is relatively full if somewhat gushingly narrated.

81. Again, Moore and Schoor offer an appropriately sensationalized account of Monroe's trip.

82. Hoyt, p. 109.

83. Alan Levy's "A Good Long Look at Myself," *Redbook*, August 1962, is very helpful on this sequence.

84. Lena Pepitone, *Marilyn Monroe Confidential* (New York: Simon & Schuster, 1979), p. 249; Edward Wagenknecht, *Marilyn Monroe: A Composite View* (New York: Chilton Book Company, 1969), p. 164.

85. See *New York Times*, 19 February 1972.

86. See my interview with Robin Roberts.

87. See reports in *New York Times*, 28 January 1974; 15 February 1974; 1 October 1974.

88. Jacquin Sanders, of the St. Petersburg *Times*.

2

A HERO'S WORLD

I would like to isolate and briefly discuss certain elements of DiMaggio's story in order to make them more meaningful to my analysis of how he came to represent the figure into which he has evolved. I wish in some instances to step beyond DiMaggio's immediate life to spotlight some of the historical terrain in which it is located, to place his life in an illuminating historical perspective. Some of my remarks will be speculative though grounded in reality.

THE ITALIAN CONNECTION

From the outset of his career, Joe DiMaggio was identified as an Italian-American. His story and the story of his family reflect much of the history of Italians in America. His popularity, and thus one of the sources of his legend, is highly understandable in historical terms.

Joe's father Giuseppe was part of the flood of Italian immigrants inundating America from 1880 until shortly after World War I. In 1924, legislation drastically reduced the number of new Americans entering the United States from all but a few countries.[1] A long list of unfavorable conditions in Italy made the journey to the newer and more prosperous land tempting, despite its uncertainties, insecurities, and the wrench such a drastic and problematic move would demand of many young Italian men, their wives, and families. During the period when Giuseppe DiMaggio was born and grew up, there were periodic famines in Italy, a constant struggle by the peasantry to eke out a living from depleted soil, and frequent workers' disturbances (a particularly bad one the winter of 1893-94 just prior to the inglorious war with Ethiopia) which all contributed to a very low standard of living compared to what American workers generally attained. While in 1902 a common Sicilian laborer received about twenty-five cents a day for twelve hours of work, his American counterpart averaged about $1.50 to $2.50 a day.[2] Italian workers could listen to or read the letters from compatriots in America who claimed to be on easy street. While they might not know that "except for Portugal, no country in Europe had a lower consumption of meat per inhabitant"[3] they would know when they and their families were hungry. And Italian laborers did not see any political force in their lives that seemed capable of changing the situation. Living in poor housing, in increasingly debasing conditions, they would also see little relief from the compulsory military service that all had to contend with. In addition, as was true all over Europe, the rising birth rate meant even more competition for seemingly fewer jobs. In Sicily, many of these pressures brought on riots (*Fasci Siciliani*), from 1892 to 1894, that demonstrated the times' unrest.

It has been estimated that depressed "social, political, and economic conditions encouraged the flight of 8.5 million Italians prior to the first world war."[4] Some were urged by nebulous, but nonetheless, strong feelings of idealism to travel across the ocean to America, or were prompted to escape from the strong parental authority so prevalent in Italy and probably so unwanted or even resented by many young men and women. Clearly, a significant demographic movement took place in the period with repercussions for both Italy and America. Giuseppe DiMaggio, his wife Rosa, and their first-born daughter Nellie were part of the movement of what are often called "new immigrants;" people who entered the United States after or around 1880, who tended to be from southern or eastern Europe (often Russian Jews, Slavs, or Italians) who were frequently perceived as being different than earlier immigrants from northern or western Europe and Great Britain. In the industrialized, urbanized America that the new land was increasingly becoming in the years after 1880, the new immigrants often met more organized resistance from already established Americans than many of the earlier immigrants had experienced. Labor unions, for example, and representatives of the old, genteel, ruling families of New England, together with a variety of other individuals and groups, began to agitate on the basis of their nativist perceptions against what they regarded as the influx of potentially damaging and dangerous newcomers, who were often associated "with the ever-growing slums, poverty, government corruption, and class conflicts which pervaded the nation."[5]

Giuseppe DiMaggio was a Sicilian, an Italian from the south. The prosperity and progress Italy achieved in the years of industrialization after Camillo Benso Cavour did not reach the south, for the "fruits" of advancement did not usually fall to "the peasants of the *Mezzogiorno* (the South)." For them the glorious revolution displacing the monarchy had been "a *rivoluzione mancata* (lost revolution)." Just as the Sicilians had been joked about and treated as far less than first-class Italians in Italy, "even in America" they "were ostracized by other Italians, who believed them to be of non-Italian and even savage origins." Northern Italy possessed a higher standard of living than the south, and a far greater accumulation of wealth. Andrew Rolle offers statistics indicating that from 1899 to 1910, three times as many northern Italians received professional training than Italians from the south, and that the literacy rate in the north was about 88 percent while in the south it was less than 50 percent.[6] No wonder Joe DiMaggio's father had trouble with the written sections of his American naturalization test. The great eighteen century German writer Johann Wolfgang von Goethe stated the matter succinctly: "After Rome you enter Africa," a remark disparaging Africa of course, but intended openly to ridicule the Italian south, of which Sicily was a prime part. In America, as in Italy, Sicilians who strove to succeed carried a special burden, and partly for that reason, tended to band together.

Giuseppe DiMaggio is an interesting example of the new immigrant who faced a not entirely welcoming nation upon his arrival in the United States. He was one of the many Italian *braccianti* (laborers) who sought a better life in the new world. Like most, he would succeed financially and socially, but not without facing hardships and prejudices. That he and so many of his children would triumph over these made his story especially palatable to Americans seeking corroboration of the American success myth and the so-called melting pot myth, which deeply flawed as it may be in terms of its historical validity, is still very compelling as myth.

Italian, Southern Italian, Sicilian, Giuseppe DiMaggio can be viewed even more narrowly as an immigrant from Isola delle Femmine; a small island northwest of Palermo, on the Golfo di Carini, where he had grown up and where his father and grandfather before him had scraped out a living as fishermen. The population of this tiny island fishing port was 1,352 around the middle of the nineteenth century, and climbed to 1,927 in 1891 as the island shared, in its small way, the population increase throughout Italy during those years. By 1901, however, the island's population had dropped to 1,002, and the major cause of the decrease seems to have been emigration to the United States.[7] Either the fishing gave out in the region those years or other economic conditions made life less bearable than usual for the mostly poor citizens of the region. In leaving the island as he did, by family tradition because he had received a letter with words of hope in it from America, Joe DiMaggio's father was doing nothing his compatriots would have found unusual. In his award-winning study *From Italy to San Francisco*, Dino Cinel says that "by late 1898 almost all the fishermen" had left the island and settled "in Calfiornia. . . . By 1903, 3,000 people had migrated to" the region "from Isola delle Femmine."[8] Giuseppe was participating in a "chain immigration," whereby one member of a family would write back to another still in the homeland with either the promise of a specific job or clear hopes of obtaining one.

More than 70 percent of these immigrants settled in eastern states. In 1900, New York City alone housed some 145,433 of the nation's approximately 484,207 Italian immigrants. The west attracted a minority of the new people, partly because it was more expensive to reach, partly because people went to where others of similar background were, to the relative security of fairly large immigrant enclaves. Of the minority who traveled to California in 1901, well over sixty percent were northern Italians. A popular phrase of the late nineteenth century said that "America beckons, but Americans repel." However, "Despite their initial sufferings, the [Italian] immigrants found freedom in America's west rather than rigidity, openness rather than closed privilege."[9] There was discrimination to fight, but not as much as Italians in the eastern cities faced, and certainly not as much as Orientals experienced in California. Perhaps it was because more of the poorer Italians had to remain east, perhaps it was because though large, the number of Italian immigrants was not overwelming and threatening, perhaps it was because so many Californians were not native Americans (almost 40 percent of the population in San Francisco in 1900 was foreign-born), perhaps the Spanish influence helped soften prejudice against the new Mediterranean-based immigrants. At any rate, the Italian compatriots of Giuseppe DiMaggio found life in California, while hard, less harsh than their countrymen experienced it in the crowded eastern urban centers.

A source of resistance to Sicilians such as Giuseppe, was the entrenched northern Italians already in the San Francisco area. California was a favorite with some Italians because they were less discriminated against there than elsewhere in America, and because parts of it—the mountains and warm valleys—reminded them of Italy. Often, occupations that had been pursued in the native land could be practiced in California also. Fishing was one of these occupations. Ordinarily, Giuseppe could have looked forward to working as a fisherman when he came to San Francisco, but he could not, because the Genoese who had controlled the industry since the 1880s would not permit the latecomers to enter their very profitable business. "By 1898 almost all the fishermen from Isola had left the city and settled in the coal mining town of Black Diamond, later called Pittsburg,"[10] near Collinsville where Giuseppe located so he could work, but not at his fisherman's trade.

In time, the Sicilians came to dominate the fishing industry and Giuseppe could again practice his vocation. Throughout this time of transition, neither the northern nor southern Italians necessarily thought of themselves strongly as Americans. The Sicilians particularly, as is true of many ethnic or regional groups whose identity is determined partly by pressures exerted upon them from the outside, who feel discriminated against (as the Sicilians often did even in their homeland), sometimes resisted assimilation into whatever they considered to be mainstream America. Men like Giuseppe, who worked hard to build up his family and its place in the community, did not always seek to shed those social patterns and practices that would signal their transformation into Americans. Such persons would naturally have wanted to succeed in the new world, and in fact, fought strongly to achieve success. But they would be ambivalent about shedding the vestments or core of what was most Italian about them—certain social arrangements such as their family patterns, or their language. Their children's aims, of course, might be different, but would always be influenced by parental lessons.

Much of the early publicity about Joe DiMaggio during his apprenticeship years called attention to the fact that he was a member of a large Italian family. This was an appealing aspect of his story that made him a more attractive performer and ultimately a hero in the public's eyes. It supported the traditional American emphasis on a large, close, and affectionate family produced by strong and loving parents. Even during the Depression when children were an expensive and complicating element to add to a struggling marriage, the dream of the large family remained a reassuring fantasy in American life, though in reality the average family size was dwindling. Giuseppe, like so many other Italians as soon as they "had enough money to bring their wives to the United States" did so, to reestablish "the home . . . as the hub of Italian life."[11] Marriage to an Italian woman in America would not have been easy, since prior to the first world war, about 80 Italian men came to America for every twenty Italian women. A possible result of the imbalance—along with intermarriage with non-Italian women—was a shift that occurred among other ethnic groups in America as well: women, as a relatively rare entity, assumed even more influence in the home than they had in the old world. Though typically, and the DiMaggio family was no exception, Italian households were "mother centered and father dominated,"[12] an Italian mother such as Mrs. DiMaggio might have had greater authority in the home than she would have had in Italy: her defense of Vince's and Joe's wishes to break away from the fishing life, displacing family goals by personal ambition, perhaps counted for more in America than it would have in Isola della Femmine. In that sense, Rosalie represents among other things, part of the process of Americanization which would also become an attractive element in the myth of DiMaggio's success.

As Joe grew up, the life of his family continued to reflect how extensively the DiMaggios duplicated basic patterns in Italian and Sicilian immigrant history, and show why he was such a particular favorite of Italian and American fans. When shortly after Joe's birth the family moved to the crowded house on Taylor Street, they were at once demonstrating their advance in America, and further entrenching themselves in what has often been described as an ethnically "self-contained community." After a time Giuseppe would reach one of the great goals of the fishing Sicilians, who by then had ended Genoese domination of the industry: he would own his own boat, named after his wife. But the family still lived in the tight quarters Joe always remembered (which were similar to those in which other Sicilians who wanted to move upward economically lived), "homes and tenements" consisting usually of "two or three rooms which accommodated four to six persons. . . . Enterprising Italian immigrants had coined an expression which noted that the smaller the room a man lived in the larger his bank account would be."[13]

By the time Joe DiMaggio began his professional baseball career, the Italians in America had gone through their most intense period of social struggle. Immigration slowed down considerably in the 1920s, and by 1930 the Italian immigrants in California were replaced by the Mexicans as the most numerous foreign-born group in the state. Throughout America, the 1930s were in part a period of consolidation and of demonstration of attainments for Italian-Americans, for proofs of their success socially, economically, and politically as an ethnic component within the country, and as a people integrated into the American way of life. Furthermore, in Depression America, particularly since large-scale immigration no longer existed, Americans were receptive to ethnic heroes, men and women who (now that swarms of foreigners no longer "threatened" cherished native ideals) made up the great multiethnic team symbolizing the American spirit that could eventually draw the country from its economic morass.

When DiMaggio began his career, the mayors of the two cities that housed his teams were of Italian descent. In San Francisco, Mayor Angelo Rossi (1931-44) must have been unusually pleased to honor the Seals' hitting star for his 61-game streak, just as in New York City Fiorello La Guardia (1934-45) was particularly proud to be in the stands when DiMaggio broke Willie Keeler's streak. Americans in general wanted heroes for the same reasons they had always wanted them, to declare the superiority of American achievements and to embody what Americans like to think are American virtues and standards. During the Depression, Americans had a special predilection for strong, self-assured, unbraggartly, even unassuming kinds of men such as Joe Louis. These were the fellows who appeared, like Gary Cooper would later, to have greatness thrust upon them, who struck back because someone had struck at them first, tight-lipped performers who did not flaunt flamboyant individualism but who were exceptional individuals nonetheless. Italian-Americans also needed heroes to help erase old sterotypes engrained in nativist thinking about them, images popular in hundreds of books, movies, and other manifestations of popular lore. In the popular media, Italians, often specifically labelled Sicilians, were frequently viewed as knife-wielding, rat-like criminals, or when docile, comical creatures who gestured wildly with their hands.

As a symbol of Italian success in America, DiMaggio was an almost perfect hero for projecting a strong, positive view of the Italian-American. Strong, shy, from a hard-working family, he played the game most popular and most visible in America at that time, a sport that had provided the country with many of its athletic heroes, as had prize-fighting. Baseball, however, was a much cleaner sport than boxing, and represented the purity and innocence of America's community heritage while boxing was a bloody paradigm of survival-of-the-fittest notions, or suggested backroom deals leading to tank jobs, battered ears, crushed skulls, stammering speech, and shuffling steps. Baseball was not a murderous sport. It was supposed to be as clean as its white lines and green fields. Italians participated in it at the big league level in increasing numbers. Statistics in Steven Reiss's *Touching Base* indicate that while in the years 1901-1906 the percentage of Italian-American players was negligible, in 1920 it was two percent and by 1941 had reached eight percent.

The 1930s provided a number of gifted Italian-American baseball players and prizefighters. The popular Tony Canzoneri was featherweight champion in 1928, and lightweight champion 1930-33 and 1935-36.[14] But neither Canzoneri nor any other Italian fighter of the decade was a national hero in the sense that DiMaggio or Joe Louis were. Unfortunately the best known Italian fighter of the period was Primo Carnera, whose career as a hero contrasts interestingly with DiMaggio's. Carnera came to America in the aftermath of the Tunney-Dempsey years when a collection of generally mediocre heavyweights—either with negligible talents or who like Max Baer never fulfilled the potential their native abilities promised—competed for the most important title in boxing, both financially and in its mythopoeic significance.

A tremendously strong-looking, exceptionally large (even for a heavyweight) fighter, Carnera fought the likes of Jack Sharkey and various other competent but often washed-up boxers, and showed mainly a stout heart coupled with incredible clumsiness and, when fights were honest, meek power that seemed comically disproportionate to his enormous size: a man-mountain producing a mouse of punching strength. When he first arrived in America his size and musculature induced awe and torrents of copy from sportswriters, some of whom were supposedly, it later developed, rewarded by Carnera's backers for the hype they ground out like sawdust-filled sausages. At the height of his career after a whirlwind campaign featuring, it was later alleged, more tank dives than any Olympic pool ever produced, Carnera was manipulated in 1933 into a title fight with the enigmatic Jack Sharkey. For much of the fight, Sharkey eluded Carnera's ponderous but usually ineffectual punches which whooshed through the air like large falling timbers made of balsa wood. But he finally succumbed to what was generously termed a "phantom punch" invisible to most human eyes. Carnera was briefly champion then, until in 1934 Max Baer nearly killed him in a clearly unfixed fight.

While Carnera may have raised the hopes of Italian-Americans seeking a powerful symbol of their success (Rocky Marciano remembered bonfires in

Brockton's Italian community when Carnera beat Sharkey), eventually he became a comic figure of inability not unlike Mussolini in that he promised so much and delivered so little and ended his career so ingloriously. After World War II he returned to America and became a very successful and liked wrestler, when wrestling was a gymnastic entertainment though not a sport. Increasingly an embarrassment, Carnera's boxing career became a clown act prior to DiMaggio's starring performance, and like the protagonist of *I Pagliacci* he was ultimately that most pathetic of creatures, an unhappy clown. In the spring of 1936 while DiMaggio was startling onlookers at his first Yankee spring training, Carnera was preparing for yet another Madison Square Garden fight. On March 3 the New York *World Telegram* told its readers about the great size of DiMaggio's bat: "DiMaggio Swings Big Man [sic] Club." The next day it printed news of "Da Preem" and his upcoming fight against Izzy Gastanage, together with a standard caricature of the homely Carnera who is called "the squad of Mussolini's Infantry that will mobilize" Friday night. Two weeks later, DiMaggio was still reported whacking the ball and fielding with grace, while the March 17 *World Telegram* told sadly of Carnera who had been "still a valuable side of beef" before his most recent fight, when a "three-round knockout by Leroy Haynes hurl[ed him] into pugilistic oblivion." After this devastating defeat, the paper declared, Carnera was left forgotten in the ring "by all but [a] process server" who sought him to collect old debts. When DiMaggio flopped briefly in the 1936 All-Star game, sportswriter Dan Parker compared him to Carnera, an analogy DiMaggio remembered.[15]

Carnera's failure as a hero was particularly disheartening for Italians who were seeking a figure of strength to represent them in the sports world. When DiMaggio entered the major leagues in 1936, the international figure who in modern times had most forcefully stood for the power and authority that had been for so long lacking in the Italian image, Benito Mussolini, was undergoing sharp attacks in the press and in America. Mussolini's status in both America and the Italian community, was undergoing a change that would eventually turn him from a man whom many Americans and Italian-Americans viewed as a potential savior, to a hated enemy and betrayer.

Today it is not easy to remember the very strong and positive perception of Mussolini in America during the 1920s and early 1930s. He has emerged from the cartooning of popular history as either the strutting, pompous buffoon (played by Jack Oakie) of Charlie Chaplin's *The Great Dictator,* or as the horribly mangled corpse strung upside down for display by partisans in the final phase of World War II. But he once was a world leader, looked to from the political right as a model commander of his people, an imaginative, disciplined man who could supply solutions to the worldwide depression and social chaos that seemed to be eroding the western civilization of his day.

In *Mussolini and Fascism, the View from America*, John P. Diggins has skillfully examined Mussolini's reputation in America. President Roosevelt himself had to keep in mind Mussolini's popularity among Italian-Americans, and it is clear that many non-Italians found him a popular leader. Diggins concludes that "whatever Mussolini's repuation is today, from the time of the March on Rome to the beginning of the Ethiopian War he was an esteemed figure."[16] In 1934, it was not simply Italian-Americans who were singing Cole Porter's song that said "You're the tops—you're Musso-li-ni." Mussolini was especially attractive to Italians in America not just because he seemed to present workable solutions to the complicated social, political, and economic issues of the troubled times, but because he embodied virtues of strength and courage that in nativist stereotypes, had been so long denied them. He was a respected man and a figure of power, whether he was liked or not. He was no creature of inferiority.

At precisely the time DiMaggio was emerging as a sports hero, Mussolini was engaging in two adventures that increased his disrepute among detractors, and caused him to lose some support among his adherents. The Italian attack upon Ethiopia and the formalizing of the Italo-German axis that eventually brought Mussolini under Hitler's domination brought about a clear shift in many attitudes toward the Italian leader, making him not nearly as attractive a figure to support or admire, for both Italian-Americans and non-Italians. While Diggins points out that "until the summer of 1940 there was no question that Italian-Americans in general were solidly behind Mussolini,"[17] he was increasingly a figure they would have been defensive about. Mussolini's aims and practices, his megalomania, seemed less and less consonant with democratic ideals. Furthermore, his proclamation that Italians were still Italian, no matter what country they resided in, could only make many Americans (unfairly enough, as World War II history clearly showed) question the allegiance of Italian-Americans.

Joe DiMaggio presented no problems of divisiveness to his Italian-American fans. He stood for all of Italy in America, and all Italian-Americans could cheer for him. While superficially he could be compared with Mussolini, who was also an Italian success story (sometimes called "Italy's Horatio Alger" because his birth was lowly), DiMaggio was completely apolitical and, moreover, played the most American of sports. He possessed an image of power, but power totally unrelated to cruelty or cunning. Though in "an age hungry for heroes, Mussolini was also written up as a hero of sport."[18] DiMaggio was a true sports hero, graceful and efficient, the master of his game, with no bluster about him. He was no ersatz sportsman, no pop-off, he never seemed to pose, and could almost never be caught in postures of absurdity or ill-grace. He was tall and muscular, not, after all the muscle-flexing was finished, stumpy and a bit plump, as was Mussolini. In nearly all ways, DiMaggio was a much safer and more ingratiating hero for Italian-Americans than Mussolini.

From the start of his major league career, DiMaggio's exploits on the sports pages contrasted brightly with the darker, historically weightier but far more troublesome news about Mussolini appearing in American newspapers and magazines. Many of the same papers that printed the Associated Press wire news on March 9, 1936, that in St. Petersburg "regular infield practice would take place and an outfield shaped up probably with Joe DiMaggio in center," showed pictures the next day of Hitler and Mussolini, "Two Dictators," shaking hands, "War or Peace in their Hands." In the New York *World Telegram* March 18, Joe Williams's sports column was headlined "Another Italian Problem/Yankees Face Real One/DiMaggio Part of It." Williams wrote with silly facetiousness alluding to a historically tragic event: "Mr. Joseph McCarthy of the Yankees extended the hand of sympathy to Emperor Haile Selassie of Ethiopia today. It seems the Italians are causing him some concern, too." McCarthy's problem was whether DiMaggio could hit to center and right field. In the *Collier*'s feature article for June 13, 1936, leading journalist Quentin Reynolds (a liberal and no lover of Italy's leader) wrote that the DiMaggio family was large enough to satisfy even Mussolini, who desired the most fit of his country's citizens to produce more and more babies for the good of the nation. *Time* featured DiMaggio on its July 13 cover and contained a highly complimentary article about him. In the same issue, *Time* reported Haile Selassie's famous speech at the League of Nations seeking help for his powerless nation against the Italian onslaught. In its next issue, July 20, *Time* placed Mussolini on its cover. Throughout the decade, side-by-side features juxtaposed DiMaggio's clean successes with Mussolini's dubious achievements. *Life* for May 1, 1939, placed DiMaggio on its cover with a long article praising DiMaggio, mentioning specifically his Italian ancestry. The lead item in "The Week's Events" section reported Mussolini's attack on tiny Albania, ridiculing the war as "a cheap and easy victory" and a "simple rape." Mussolini's Italian soldiers were mocked: "some went on by tank, some by lorry, the fastest by cycle."

Though some Italian-Americans, especially those in the political left, had opposed Mussolini throughout the 1920s and 1930s, most supported him whole-heartedly until he began to be tightly drawn into Hitler's circle in 1936. Even so, general support for him did not dissipate until the start of the next decade. Non-political families such as the DiMaggios thought well of him not because of his fascism, but because he appeared to be restoring order in Italy, and perhaps more significantly, because he was the image and instigator of Italy's assumption to world power for the first time in centuries:[19] for a time he was viewed by Italian-Americans as a standard-bearer of their hard won respect and achievement. By the mid-1930s however, while still supported by many non-Italian-Americans, Mussolini had become a tainted hero outside the immigrant community and a frequently questioned figure within. As a culturally symbolic event, the

1935 Joe Louis-Primo Carnera heavyweight fight was a debacle for the Italians, since Carnera, shoved unfairly into the role of Mussolini's surrogate against the Son of Ethiopia, Louis, was easily crushed.

DiMaggio was so safe a symbol of Italian success that he, at least in a small way, blunted the anti-Italian sentiment that formed in America during the first year of the war. Motivated by fears that an Italian fascist fifth column might attempt sabotage to hinder America's war effort, the government began acting in January, 1942, to reclassify the country's 600,000 Italian-American aliens, a move which shocked and dismayed the overwhelmingly loyal and strongly pro-American group.[20] For a time, the movements of these non-citizens were impeded. Donna Gumina reports that some of the North Beach Italians "who had fished for decades were now ordered to fish only from those boats in which the captain or 50 percent of the crew were American citizens."[21] In San Francisco, some areas were restricted, and though Giuseppe DiMaggio could still visit with his cronies, as a non-citizen there were territories around the wharf presumably containing critical installations he and other aliens were not permitted near, to live, to work, or even to visit. His son Vincent has said that he accepted this,[22] but the limitation spurred his and Rosalie's efforts to finally obtain citizenship in the country where they had lived and worked for almost half a century. Suspicions of Italian-American disloyalty were not nearly as sharp as those that led to the notoriously racist response against Japanese-Americans: Italian-American political power also helped deflect the zeal of government spy-hunters. The DiMaggio family played its part, as this bizarre exchange at the "2nd Session Hearings Before the Select [House] Committee Investigating National Defense Migration" reveals. "Chairman [John Tolan]: Tell us about the DiMaggios. Tell us about the DiMaggio's father." [Attorney Chauncey] Tramulto: Neither of the DiMaggio seniors is a citizen. They have reared nine children, five boys and four girls, eight of whom were born in the United States, and the other one is a naturalized citizen. Three of the boys are outstanding persons in the sports world. Joe, who is with the Yankees, was the leading hitter for both the American and National Leagues during the years 1939 and 1940. His younger brother, Dominic, is with the Boston Red Sox, and his older brother Vincent is with the Pittsburg team of the National League. . . . to evacuate the senior DiMaggios would, in view of the splendid family they have reared and their unquestioned loyalty, present, I am sure you will agree with me, a serious situation."[23] The DiMaggios were relieved when on October 12, 1942, President Roosevelt officially stated that the order declaring Italians in America enemy aliens had been rescinded.

The final link in DiMaggio's Italian connection that needs demonstration and some analysis is the remarkable extent of his popularity as an ethnic hero.

In his definitive study of *American Baseball*, David Voigt quotes from an

article in the *Literary Digest* for July 2, 1932, titled "How Tony Gives a
Latin Tone to Our National Game," which somewhat patronizingly
declares that Italian-Americans "take to baseball quicker than they take to
spaghetti."[24] In the 1930s baseball did particularly appear to offer an
opportunity for Italian-Americans to validate both the melting pot myth
and the American dream of success. Even before Joe began his dramatic
baseball career, his older brother Vince tapped the residual enthusiasm on
the West Coast that awaited Italian ballplayers. Referred to in newspapers
as the "Walloping Wop," Vince was also written about in 1932 as the son
of a fisherman born poor in Sicily.[25] Other newspaper articles about him
stressed what sports stories later would state about Joe, that he was but one
of a contingent of Italian-American big leaguers. One item from 1932 in
Vince DiMaggio's scrapbook lists Ping Bodie (born Francesco Stefano
Pezzolo), Tony Lazzeri, Frank Crosetti, Babe Pinelli, Art Garibaldi,
George Puccinelli, and Dolf Camilli as San Franciscoans who either had
played in the majors or would eventually play there (all did, if only briefly
like Garibaldi). Any San Francisco Italian who played a decent game of
baseball was certain of special support from the Italian fans. Even as a
minor leaguer, Joe's fame spread quickly to Italian-Americans outside the
bay and California area, and a year before his major-league career began,
the Boston equivalent of *Il Progresso* printed a tiny item indicating that
"the New York Yankees today purchased Joe DeMagio [sic] from the San
Francisco Seals."[26]

Gene Schoor reported (1956) that shortly after DiMaggio's successful
debut at Yankee Stadium, "a newly formed DiMaggio fan club" hung an
"Italian flag . . . over the railing" to honor him. In *It Takes Heart*, Mel
Allen claimed that in DiMaggio's first season, "for the first time the large
Italian populations in the cities that made up the American league took an
interest in baseball. They flocked to the Yankee Stadium and other
ballparks, carrying big banners and Italian flags which they unfolded and
waved whenever their hero performed the spectacular—as he often did."
Martin Appel and Burt Goldblatt estimated (improbably enough) that
23,000 Italian-Americans "waved flags at DiMaggio's debut."[27] Allen says
that one Italian-American poet scribbled "DiMaggio's tripple/Aroused da
pipple." In 1941, Clarke Robinson employed both DiMaggio's popularity
with Italian fans and the melting pot myth to produce a very explicit plea
for what would soon become wartime solidarity. If you travel to Yankee
Stadium, he said, or any place in America the "Yanks" play (clearly
alluding to the nationalistic implications of the team's name) you will
probably sit next to some "young Italian-Americans" who are "with their
fathers who probably never saw a ball game before in their lives." They are
there to "Looka d' Dimagg makka d' hit." Robinson draws a star-spangled
moral: "In a world beset by misquided and ambitious dictators it is
refreshing to find that the exploits of one lone lad, in a sport known for its

cleanness and ethics, can chase gore and slaughter off the front pages of the newspapers and lead those who came from the land of his ancestors on to appreciate achievements that their sons can accomplish in America. Defend it? You bet we will and we'll have many a World Series as Hitler strikes out.''

Although it is possible that writers may have recollected more flags waving or more Italian-Americans at DiMaggio's earliest games than were actually there, hard evidence does indicate that he was an exceptionally popular symbol for the relatively recently accepted ethnic group. Less than a month after DiMaggio appeared as a player in Yankee Stadium, May 23, 1936, an amusing letter to the sports editor of the *New York Times* suggests the place he had quickly found among Italian-Americans. Joseph Pappiano of Connecticut wrote "there's a tavern here, in the heart of the large Italian section, and when the boys gather around at night they ask one another, 'How did Peppino do today!' Who's Peppino? Why, Giuseppe Paolo DiMaggio, of course. Any Italian named Giuseppe is called Peppino by everyone who knows him. Peppino will make the Yanks forget the Bambino,'' whose nickname, but not parentage, was Italian. On the CBS special nationwide broadcast discussing DiMaggio's career on the day he retired, radio reporter Lou Cioffi spoke about how "especially important to Italian kids" DiMaggio had been when he was growing up in New York in the mid-1930s, for DiMaggio proved they could rise to the top. In 1941 a group of older Italian-Americans formed a "Davedi" club whose acronym symbolized their respect for three great Italians, Dante, Verdi, and DiMaggio.[28]

The honors given him by Italian-American groups such as the Unico National in 1949 are one sign of his strength as a symbol of the accepted and integrated Italian-American. Non-Italians also respect and recognize his achievements in embodying and symbolizing immigrant success and fusion with the American mainstream. He has become reassuring proof that though the American streets were not paved with gold (indeed as the immigrant joke has it the streets were not paved at all and had to be constructed by Italians) application to your task could bring wealth and acceptance. As Allison Danzig and Joe Reichler discuss Americanization in their *History of Baseball*, when the second-generation American establishes a career in a sport such as baseball, "the true meaning of America as the land of opportunity and equality comes home to their fellow-patriates. Joe DiMaggio becomes a national sports idol, reaps a fortune and provides comforts for his family they never dreamed of, and each naturalized Italian in his community feels a little closer to America and more a part of America." Richard Lipsky in *How We Play the Game: Why Sports Dominate the American Life,* similarly uses DiMaggio to symbolize the success and integration many Americans feel are attainable by immigrants through participation in sports (irrespective of historical validation of the idea). He cites the evidence given by Martin Ralbovsky that because of DiMaggio, baseball cut into the separate world of Italian-Americans. "Whenever Joe DiMaggio came to bat, life would come to a grinding halt . . . on Goose Hill [in Schenectady, New York]: Italian men would yell out to their noisy families, 'Hey a Joe Dee Maj ess up, now—a shed-op, or I whip-a you ess.'" Luciano Iorizzo pointed out that DiMaggio along with Frank Sinatra has come to represent "a glamorized, positive image of Italian-Americans, one which replaced the glamorized, negative image of the Italians during the Capone era. . . . Capone was held up as a pariah. DiMaggio, however, became the epitome of the honest self-made man."[29] DiMaggio, Iorizzo notes, arrived at a crucial time for Italian-Americans, "when Washington and Italy were on a collision course." His background was thoroughly Italian, but his person and the worlds he moved in—Yankee Stadium, Toots Shor's Broadway, Marilyn Monroe's fantasyland—were All-American. As Andrew Rolle has suggested, to his parents and many of his fellow Italian-Americans, DiMaggio could remain a "non-intellectual celebrity," one of the good children with some schooling but not a great deal of formal education who "remained big-hearted, generous, and relatively unchanged boys."[30] But to others outside that community, he could be a hero precisely because of the changes he represented in his progress through life.

THE STREAK

Several important elements of DiMaggio's 56-game hitting streak have already been discussed, including the streak's fortunate duration: long enough to generate considerable media and spectator attention, yet concentrated enough to sustain tension and intense focus; its susceptibility to later formulaic retellings; its similarity in outline (forced or inherent) to a number of well-known legendary or literary quest and trial stories, for example the waste land pattern (DiMaggio becomes the ailing leader [he was slumping] of a decayed dominion [the Yankees were not in first place] whose marvelous powers [his batting ability] ultimately revivify the land [head the Yankees toward the pennant] through his prowess).

As Dave Anderson pointed out, the hitting streak also "shaped" DiMaggio's mythic figure, demanding the qualities DiMaggio increasingly became known for, consistency, reliability, being a team player whose efforts brought team and not simply personal victories; who could produce at critical moments under great pressure. He achieved something absolutely unique, establishing a record that, like Babe Ruth's home run total or Roger Bannister's four-minute mile, will never lose lustre.

Finally, much has been written about the event showing a perception of it as what Anderson termed "a sociological phenomenon." Certainly the hitting streak was one of the biggest stories of the year and achieved an importance in the general culture that went beyond the sports pages. A contemporary account in *Time* for July 14, 1941, suggests both its specific and extended interest among sporting Americans and Americans at large. "In 102 years of baseball, few feats have caused such nationwide to-do. Ever since it became apparent that the big Italian from San Francisco's Fisherman's Wharf was approaching a record that eluded Ty Cobb, Babe Ruth, Lou Gehrig and other great batsmen, Big Joe's hits have been the biggest news in U. S. sport. Radio programs were interrupted for DiMaggio bulletins."

Another claim that is difficult to substantiate, but that may be true, is the idea that as Bob Broeg states in *Superstars of Baseball*, "At a time when war was raging over Europe and when America was only a sneak-attack away from involvement, daily bulletins of DiMaggio's streak were sports pages' good news equivalent—or contrast, rather—of the news page disaster overseas." Silverman's 1969 chronicle often balances the terrible events of the year against the continuing efforts of DiMaggio to break and then maintain the hitting streak record. In 1950, Dan Daniel set the tone for many later narratives linking DiMaggio's achievements inside baseball with the outside disorder and violence that was beginning to hold dominion over the world. "It came before World War II" he wrote of the streak, "when fans could give plenty of attention to baseball. They were glad to do so, to divert their minds from the ominous rumblings from overseas and the talk of preparations everywhere for trouble, which finally broke out explosively with the sneak-bombing of Pearl Harbor, December 7, 1941." Clarke Robinson's earlier October, 1941, article noted that DiMaggio's exploits had "chase[d] gore and slaughter off the front pages" and would act as a call to arms against foreign tyranny. In the same September 29, 1941, issue in which *Life* published the painting by Edward Lanning commemorating DiMaggio's record-tying hit, companion articles were titled "Ships Carrying a Trickle of Arms to Britian," "Angry Orators Make Fifth Avenue Nightly Forum on War," and "General Pershing Reminds Americans Their Army Can Be Great." Given the usual function of sporting events to act as opportunities for escape from pressures of daily life, with the press supplying descriptions or just the scores of multitudinous contests to satisfy or delight the reader, it seems plausible that DiMaggio's streak was particularly welcome during an otherwise distressing year.

Whether or not the event dramatized to Americans that individual and team effort working together could eventually bring victory to the side of decency, even when times looked most bleak, is arguable. Michael Seidel hypothesized in the May 16, 1982, *New York Times* that DiMaggio and Charles Lindbergh represented in those trouble-filled spring and summer days when London was being bombed by the Luftwaffe, "the two most prominent emblems of American heroism." The baseball player "day after day kindled a sense of almost epic accomplishment that in its way countered the tentative position we were taking in regard to active participation in the war. Lindbergh represented the darker mood of the day, the traditional wariness of the American character.'' How aware most or even any Americans of the day were of the historical balancing act the two were performing is problematic. No doubt DiMaggio's exploits could be profitably compared to those of other public figures of the time, President Roosevelt himself, for example, whose course between non-involvement and commitment in England and France's struggles pleased few, and brought feelings that he was performing inadequately to many. DiMaggio's greatly publicized activities were of an inestimably lower order, of course, though the amount of public energy that became absorbed in his unique and centrifugal effort was disproportionately great. Today, the streak still evokes strong responses. DiMaggio is asked about it in interviews, and it is often referred to when other sporting streaks are being discussed.[31] It has become the streak to which all others are compared for relative significance, a touchstone record, an infinitely retellable event.

Concerning the streak, DiMaggio is outspoken, considering how rarely he comments on other aspects of his game. A *T.V. Guide* article for April 18, 1981, by Melvin Durslag, showed DiMaggio's zealousness regarding his accomplishment and also demonstrated the continuing interest in his phenomenal performance. Answering the question posed by Durslag, why ''in this age of super youth and super science, have heroes not ground Joe's record to powder,'' DiMaggio challenges the idea that he played under conditions facilitating his streak and suggests that today's ballplayers actually should have an easier time hitting. Durslag concludes ''in connection with the record's longevity, every probability may have been explored except one—no batter in the last four decades has been good enough to hit with DiMaggio's consistency.'' The streak is graced with a rare vitality, a freshness that perhaps only exceptional performances that have become part of a culture's identity possess. It is a record few want to see broken. Along with Joe Louis's victory over Max Schmeling and Jesse Owens's triumph at the 1936 Olympics, DiMaggio's 56-game streak seems to tell Americans something about their past, and about their past heroes, that they do not want forgotten. The streak appears to teach lessons that should always be current in American society, such as the fact (or myth) that individual Americans—particularly those who stem from humble and minority origins—can triumph over practically any opposition. Whether the lesson is true or not is arguable, but not the events the lesson is based upon.

OTHER SPORTS PERFORMERS

DiMaggio's special popularity as a player and after, and his particular image, have also been affected by the other baseball figures with whom he has come into contact. Touted as the successor to the country's best known and perhaps greatest player, he was early afforded a spotlight at least equal to his talent. His relationships with two managers who were themselves baseball legends helped shape both his career and his myth just as interlocking stories about the immortals who became constellations provide a web of characters who shine together in the same sky and shed light upon each other in the imagination if not in reality. But relative worth apart, players do exist in context with each other. DiMaggio played with Gehrig and not with Ruth, and that has affected his career and his image. Ruth played with Walter Johnson, Tris Speaker, and Ty Cobb, and he is fixed in their world, not Stan Musial's. Individual players help shape (as do their managers and owners) the era in which they participate, and thereby influence each others' stature. It will be instructive to briefly look at the life and image of at least one player who belonged to DiMaggio's baseball world—just as seen from another perspective, DiMaggio belonged to his.

Throughout many of their playing days, DiMaggio and Ted Williams were compared and contrasted with each other. In some ways, Williams's performance was superior to DiMaggio's. Clearly he was a better batter. Though it might be endlessly debatable who hit better in clutch situations, Williams's lifetime batting average of .344 was much higher than DiMaggio's .325, his home run total of 521 in nineteen years greatly outdistanced DiMaggio's 361 for thirteen seasons. (John Thorn and Pete Palmer in *The Hidden Game of Baseball* (1984) calculate through sophisticated computerized estimations that had DiMaggio played in Fenway Park, and Williams in Yankee Stadium, DiMaggio would have out-hit Williams .340 to .328, and hit 417 home runs to Williams's 497). Williams was also a superior player longer than DiMaggio. In his nineteen seasons with two periods of baseball inactivity, 1943-45 and 1952-53, Williams dipped below .300 only once (in 1959 when he hit .254) and in his final year hit .316.

Williams's career has been filled with incident. He was badly injured twice (in 1950 with a broken elbow and 1954 with a broken shoulder) and came back to play; he holds innumerable records and was the last player to hit .400 (.406 in 1941); he twice performed meritoriously in the armed forces, the second time in Korea when at age 35 he flew 39 missions with the Third Marine Wing, was often under fire and hit by flak, and finally became so ill with pneumonia and other infections he was finally released.

Despite his undeniable and in modern times unequalled batting skills (as late as 1957 he hit .388 and though sick in September and incapable of daily play, pinch-hit four successive home runs), his dramatic career (like the hero of a movie he even hit a home run his last time at the plate) and fascinating life story—well told in *My Turn at Bat* with the help of John Underwood—Williams never became quite the culture hero that DiMaggio developed into.[32] He has had his own troubadours, the man-of-letters John Updike, for example, whose widely reprinted l'envoi to Williams, "Hub Fans Bid Kid Adieu," is unmatched artistically by any piece in the DiMaggio canon. But he has not endured in precisely the same way that

DiMaggio has or rather, he has endured in a different fashion, befitting his evolved image.

A number of differences distinguish Williams from DiMaggio and make him less accessible as a public hero, a popular, cultural symbol. As a player, he is not usually considered as proficient an all-around performer, his fielding and base-running being deemed not nearly as well-developed as his hitting. He is by reputation not known particularly as a team player. This may be more a matter of image than performance.[33] It is difficult to perceive a player who hit as consistently well as Williams not being of great benefit to his team. However, throughout his career, as the title of his autobiography suggests, he has been thought of chiefly as an individual batting star. He is not associated with winning teams (he was in only one World Series, in 1946 against St. Louis: Boston lost and he hit .200), and his Boston teammates while often excellent performers (such as Dom DiMaggio) have generally lacked the national exposure and glamour of DiMaggio's Yankee colleagues. This partly stems from Boston's second-rank status as a communications and entertainment center compared to New York.

Further, Williams did not enjoy the almost constant adulation of the important New York-based press. This may have resulted from Williams's aloofness, or from what often appeared his open antagonism toward the writers: stories were always circulating about obscene gestures he directed to them, or his spitting at them. It may also be, for reasons beyond the scope of this investigation, that Boston sportswriters as a group are not the same as New York writers. Updike selected for his essay a representative story by a Boston sportswriter that begins "Williams' career, in contrast [to Babe Ruth's], has been a series of failures except for his averages." Updike also points out that some of the antagonism directed toward Williams results from Williams's own nature. His famous remark "All I want out of life is that when I walk down the street folks will say 'There goes the greatest hitter who ever lived'" would if typically narcissistic disqualify him for the roles into which Ernest Hemingway or Paul Simon cast DiMaggio. But Williams's life story also reveals he was born into a milieu publicists or myth-makers would have problems transforming into cause for adoration. *My Turn at Bat* might have provided Theodore Dreiser opportunity to present the story of a socially victimized, sensitive young man emerging from emotionally deprived beginnings, but would not offer much to anyone wishing to present a reassuring true-life success myth. As he tells his story in *My Turn at Bat*, Williams seems totally cut off from his Mexican-French (on his mother's side) Welsh-English (on his father's) ancestry.

In place of the warm, loving family presented throughout DiMaggio's story, Williams's life as related in his exceptionally honest autobiography offers a mother who was a religious zealot, an embarassment to her young son whom she occasionally dragged along on her Salvation Army forays into the sin-filled city of San Diego, a woman Williams describes as "narrow-minded," who kept a dirty house. She seems like a character from *An American Tragedy*. Williams's father was away from home most of the time and after twenty years finally left his wife, something Williams says he probably also would have done. He was by his own admission never very close to his father, and often in his autobiography writes of sad, yearning, but understandable relationships with father substitutes who supplied him with at least some of the love and guidance his real father was apparently incapable of providing. Williams's recollections are also filled with seemingly random violence. He mentions one young friend with whom he played a losing game of marbles and then adds "right after the war he was in Mexico City and crashed his plane off the end of the runway, killing himself and one of his children." Williams's and Underwood's book seems aimed at a more sophisticated audience than *Lucky to Be a Yankee* and that affects the treatment of the material Williams provided. DiMaggio has yet to be depicted in as harsh a light as Williams apparently allowed in *My Turn at Bat*. The two players are presented by writers with similar flaws of surliness, but DiMaggio's is ordinarily seen as a response given only in despair whereas Williams's is viewed as more constant, a behavior interwoven through his character. One of the prickly Williams nicknames is after all "The Splendid Splinter," and he was legendary for supposedly never tipping his hat to the fans. Updike suggests this manifests a god-like quality in Williams, but if so, he was a distant god who appealed to a very special kind of worshipper. His intellectuality also distanced him. While both DiMaggio and Williams were naturally gifted athletes, Williams has frequently been presented (and portrays himself in his autobiography) as a student of baseball, particularly of hitting. Part of the attitude Richard Hofstadter so convincingly documented in *Anti-Intellectualism in America*, is shown in the bemusement fans express toward athletes who appear to them also as intellectuals, and their general preference for more natural, less studious heroes such as DiMaggio, the comic book reader. On the basis of the known details of the lives of each, DiMaggio would seem the likelier candidate for enshrinement in the hearts of his countrymen. His life seems planned—and has clearly been shaped by writers—so that he might become, in Dan Daniel's words, "an embodiment of the Great American Success Story, and without getting his head turned a bit," or as Gene Schoor wrote a "Horatio Alger hero come to life" who "won his way to fortune and into the hearts of the American people."[34]

MARILYN MONROE

Although the history and some of the implications of Joe DiMaggio's relationship with Marilyn Monroe have already been briefly investigated, some important elements of their connection remain to be looked at. He was viewed, in the years following Monroe's funeral, far more as a lonely, even tragic figure than ever before. The dignity he developed after his apprenticeship years became magnified, and more somber tones became intensified in his character, at least as the public has imagined him. Now he is viewed not only as a great sports hero embodying the American success myth, but a great man who emerged enobled from a terrible trial.

DiMaggio would not be precisely the same fixture in American life that he has evolved into, had it not been for his romance with Monroe and had she not died before her potential was realized. Whatever Monroe symbolizes, she represents it frozen in death, her talent undecayed by age, and DiMaggio is unalterably locked into her story. Her life has been turned into an exemplary fable proving many things to many commentators and she is thereby a culture hero (or victim) in her own right, but for whatever purpose her career is dredged up in the public consciousness or by cultural historians, DiMaggio must play almost as central a position in it as he did for the Yankees. Though he could not rescue her from death, he did by all accounts endow her death with a final dignity her life often lacked. Ironically her death gave new life to his story, and changed its shape for as long as his story will be told.

Monroe is a much more complicated and international symbol than DiMaggio, and has compelled or inspired a literature far more sophisticated in its cultural analysis. Their relationship, bereft of DiMaggio's role as supporter in her life and mourner at her death, has most often been viewed as a freakish occurrence eliciting at first great popular approval but finally becoming the occasion for a few esoteric analyses: the public seems more comfortable with Dimaggio at Monroe's graveside than in her bed. With the tact and grace of a heat-seeking rocket, Robin Moore and Gene Schoor in *Marilyn & Joe DiMaggio* struck deeply into the steaming, tacky heartland of American tastelessness in writing about their romance, calling it "an American Tragedy," declaring that "it was the spotlight which was to prove the serpent in The Garden of Eden Marilyn and Joe had intended for themselves, a garden of innocence, bliss, joy," and terming DiMaggio grotesquely enough "baseball's greatest lover."[35]

Norman Mailer's equally fevered though more profound imagination raced through the same material, hacking about like a frantic but occasionally dazzling swordsman, sometimes in the same sentence or paragraph, calling DiMaggio a "retired hero of early high purpose too early fulfilled . . . a legend without purpose," claiming it was "natural" for him "to look for a love where he can serve." Whether Mailer is correct or not, he subjects DiMaggio to a scrutiny he had never received before, weird and sex-obsessed, but intelligent even when loony. Seeing DiMaggio carnally and humanly as no other writer either would permit himself to see him or as no other writer was permitted to see him, Mailer looks both sharply and fantastically at the sexual link between Marilyn and Joe that was perhaps always the unstated joke underneath the public's smiling glee at their coupling and the faintly suppressed titters at their divorce. "The lack of complete commitment to the marriage" Mailer guesses "creates a lack of finality in the separation. It is as if they cannot excise what was never finished, and the conclusion returns that they were locked like sweethearts, egotistic, narcissistic, petulant, pained, unwillingly attracted, and finally together for sex."[36]

Typically, commentators have stressed their differences. His family was affectionate, close, and traditional; she seemed in Hoyt's words "the product of no home at all,"[37] her parents promiscuous, unstable. He was from colorful, warm, ethnically rich San Francisco; she from lower middle-class Los Angeles with its crowded bungalows, dark, packed rooms, boring cult churches advertised by dull neon signs. He was sustained and nourished within his immigrant family; she was recurrently cut adrift from hers, dropped upon foster parents, and she claimed without a shred of geneological evidence, James Monroe, our fifth president, as an ancestor. She was neurotically insecure, he seemed a statue of certitude; she constantly sought advice and guidance and was a veritable leper of insecurity, he possessed solid and untarnishable accomplishments and only rarely appeared bothered by self-doubts; he was a natural hero (though Spud Chandler wondered if he had not had his jutting teeth fixed),[38] she though possessing renowned natural attractions, starred in the movies and that meant having been fabricated by make-up technicians, dress designers, film photographers, and god only knew what kinds of wizard mechanics to create a marketable structure of gorgeous but strategically designed flesh; he stood for old-fashioned virtues, she seemed to promise raw and unpunished sex; she was constantly in debt, he saved the pennies he earned during the Depression and bought his parents a home with his baseball money. She was weak and lacked self-control, he was strong and disciplined. As is often the case with stars who promise sexual fantasies, it is her possibilities that excite far more than her accomplishments. The reverse is true of DiMaggio: though a great player, he has attained an amazing cultural stature considering his recorded achievements. Finally, Monroe is viewed as a victim. Diana Trilling said she "was a tragedy of civilization."[39] DiMaggio is a triumph of success that seemed simply to envelop him, to settle about him without him seeking it. Monroe died for success.

It is also important to recognize the similarities between the two, which are not strange, since athletic heroes and entertainment stars possess much in common, particularly when the stars are known primarily as beautiful women. The careers of both are fragile, often brief, and quickly ended.

The greatest talent in each was usually perceived as the result of natural expression, in DiMaggio's instance his athletic ability, and for Monroe, her natural (though apparently deeply buried) instinct for projecting sex, innocence, and vulnerability. The literature about Monroe underscores constantly that she was a market commodity for her employers, an owned property. The same was true of DiMaggio who could either play for the team that had purchased his contract, or not at all. DiMaggio like Monroe had contract squabbles, and sat out part of the time he was to have been working for his employers. These disputes however seem not to have been as destructive to him as Marilyn Monroe's disputes were to her. DiMaggio's owners were as tough-minded as Monroe's studio bosses, but in the boy's world of baseball, these owners are often presented as stern father figures, rough, tough, but caring—not like blooksucking, boorish, sexually demanding Hollywood moguls.

Mailer pointed out that DiMaggio was "in fact, even more used to the center of attention than she is, and probably has as much absorption in his own body."[40] In his often revealed need for privacy, and in the anger he flashed particularly toward the end of his career when he seemed super-sensitive to probing from the outside, DiMaggio showed he knew the feeling Monroe so intensely described: "everybody is always tugging at you." She said once, "They'd all like sort of a chunk from you. They kind of like to take pieces out of you."[41]

But ultimately DiMaggio triumphed in his American life, and Monroe lost. It is his success that is so often celebrated, and her failure that is dissected. Through his life the greatness of America is projected, in hers the hardness and cruelty. One of the recurrent jokes about DiMaggio and Monroe tells of someone—Joe himself or a sportswriter—being asked if the marriage was a good one. The answer is "it's better than rooming with Joe Page." Yet the romance which seened so absurd at the start, was clearly no joke after all.

A FOLK/ART HERO

Alan Courtney's song "Joe . . . Joe . . . DiMaggio" written during DiMaggio's hit streak in 1941 is one of the earliest examples of a creative work employing DiMaggio as a cultural symbol. The song had one life as a popular novelty number, and a longer afterlife as phrases from it would be sung years later around neighborhoods when it was no longer played on the radio, by those who found its simple messages particularly appealing. Thus it has become in some ways a folk song modified and its life extended by people who knew little of its origin as a recording created by a specific songwriter at a specific time.

Examined either as a folk or commercial song the piece seems distinctly deficient, but it was very popular for a time and long remembered by many fans (some of whom like Dave Anderson and Al Silverman later became writers),[42] particularly for its catchy refrain sung by a chorus declaring their desire for DiMaggio to join their team. It tapped the public's adulation for DiMaggio, not simply for his streak but for his performance generally.

Passed down to later fans long after his streak had ended, it helped determine his image for them. In its longest, standard version (reprinted by Anderson) its first stanza emphasizes that DiMaggio comes through in the clutch. When his team needs a hit DiMaggio whacks a home run and is awarded the traditional prize for this blow, a supply of "Wheaties," whose popular slogan, "the Breakfast of champions," was familiar to most Americans.

The second stanza alludes specifically to Dimaggio's consecutive game hitting streak and the excitement it has caused among fans but declares also that the Jolter is still an ordinary person and not some strange sideshow attraction: while he is an inspirational hero he is yet a natural performer (and therefore not the "machine" some sportswriters had dubbed him). Stanza three sings about his breaking Keeler's record of 44 consecutive games and announces the new, 56-game standard he has set. Stanza four declares the national scope of his popularity, reinforcing the idea that he is not simply a local hero, and suggests that he has added a glorious element to baseball lacking before his unparalleled achievement. Stanza five predicts his fabulous future as though his enshrinement in baseball's Hall of Fame were now pre-ordained, and offers the oracular prognostication that his fans will tell their children about his greatness, which is attributed to solid, steady performance. Stanza six introduces what in older, starker ballads was often a deadly or shadowy element in the course of the hero's life, mentioning unnamed villains who whispered softly about stopping DiMaggio, as though there were something mordantly terminal in his snapped streak. Constantly separating these individual stanzas in its first, recorded version was the group chant that spotlighted one of DiMaggio's chief virtues as an American hero of the 1930s and 1940s, that he was a team player anyone in the entire country would want on their side.

Because of his special popularity, DiMaggio has often been used by various kinds of creative writers as a recognized point of reference. Many of these allusions seem almost accidental and added little to his image. For example, in Rodgers and Hammerstein's smash 1949 musical *South Pacific*, Bloody Mary's skin is described as being "tender as DiMaggio's glove," actually an enigmatic reference since it could either mean that her skin was as rough as most ballplayers' mitts, or that her skin was truly tender since DiMaggio's reputation as a skilled, graceful outfielder would have endowed him with an especially soft glove. But there is nothing random nor enigmatic about the use of DiMaggio's name in Ernest Hemingway's *The Old Man and the Sea*. As Leverett Smith points out in what is probably the best, extended analysis of how DiMaggio functions in the novella, the baseball player was used carefully and extensively for thematic reinforcement throughout the story.[43] According to Smith, DiMaggio's image was set for Hemingway by the qualities of character DiMaggio himself emphasized in his autobiography, and by DiMaggio's known exploits, primarily as exemplified in his remarkable comeback achieved over pain in 1949. Two elements of DiMaggio's character particularly qualified him as a representative hero for Hemingway and Hemingway's peasant fisherman protagonist, Santiago: first, DiMaggio's special gifts were God-given. He was naturally, inherently skilled—born to his profession, ordained for it. Second, his life embodied a constant struggle with adversity. Moreover (though Smith does not precisely make this point) much of the adversity DiMaggio faced stemmed from within him. The famous burn was self-inflicted, and the first ligament tear resulted from DiMaggio's own awkwardness leaving a conveyance on the way to his sister's. That Santiago goes out too far in attempting to catch the gigantic fish he cannot bring back whole to home port, results from his own desires, and in no way stems from a condition imposed upon him from outside the self.

For Smith, the "central question Hemingway dealt with in *The Old Man and the Sea* is how one plays the game, the same question that interested sportswriters when they talked of DiMaggio." The answer to the question is provided in the book's fable and DiMaggio's public story: one plays with dignity, does not succumb to one's wounds, one perseveres with endurance and demonstrates skill win or lose. One does not complain. Finally, the game—baseball, fishing, life—is engaged in with love, because that is what you wish to do, the way you express yourself, and not simply for gain even when play turns to work and the amateur (the lover) becomes a professional.

In many of his allusions to DiMaggio, Santiago shows his identification with the Yankee star. DiMaggio's father was also a poor fisherman, and DiMaggio played with pain (the bone spur that DiMaggio overcame in 1949 is mentioned in the novella several times). Often Santiago uses DiMaggio as a measure of his own efforts: would DiMaggio have stayed as long as he with the great fish? Would he have liked the way Santiago hit a shark in the brain? "Think of the great DiMaggio." Think that the game can be won, that the loser can turn winner. The Yankee star is the model of behavior for Santiago, who thinks to himself during his ordeal at sea that he "must be worthy of the great DiMaggio."

In a number of ways, Santiago's comparison of himself to DiMaggio presents an ironic commentary on several of Hemingway's themes in the book and endows Santiago with greater poignance of character. Santiago is clearly one of life's losers. His fishless streak is the opposite of DiMaggio's hit streak (as the book's narration begins "He was an old man who fished alone in a skiff in the Gulf Stream and he had gone eighty-four days now without taking a fish"). From the time DiMaggio started playing baseball, he was successful and did not know economic want. He was from the start associated with his large family, while Santiago is alone except for the boy who leaves his own family periodically to join him. These contrasts bestow upon humble Santiago a sad dignity and play a subtle joke on DiMaggio for through Santiago's partly self-induced and self-lacerating trial, this socially insignificant fisherman seems greater than the important, outside world's hero. Santiago is attacked by the real sharks of his world, his cruel predators, his fate. His combat is juxtaposed with the distant DiMaggio's. And it is the real human, DiMaggio, who comes to seem unreal, or possibly diminished as though seen through a wrong-ended telescope. His exploits on the sporting field seem child's play next to Santiago's deadly adventure. DiMaggio in the book lives mainly in Santiago's fairytale vision of his life, while Santiago lives in his own world made vital, it seems, by his sweet, strong, almost saintly, and very ordinary self. Ultimately of course, Hemingway created both Santiago and the DiMaggio of the novel. In the book Santiago through his thoughts creates DiMaggio in such a fashion that both ennobles the performer and decreases his heroic stature.[44] But through Hemingway's artistry, (as through Monroe's fame), DiMaggio was lifted out of baseball into the culture at large—an international culture, considering Hemingway's influence upon foreign writers, his stature among international critics, and his popularity among international audiences.

Other contemporary writers have also used references to DiMaggio in some integral fashion in their works, and have thereby extended his image's cultural significance. In *The Great American Novel* Philip Roth employs DiMaggio as a touchstone, a great player whom lesser heroes attempt to surpass, thinking they are better than he. In Roth's "Patriot League," however, players tend to slide into disaster. One of these is Roland Agni, "in '43 a kid of eighteen tapering like the V for Victory from his broad shoulders and well muscled arms down to ankles as elegantly turned as Betty Grable's . . . and in his own baby-blue eyes destined to be the most spectacular rookie since Joltin' Joe. One difference: the Yankee Clipper, aside from being four years older than Agni when he entered the majors, had also played a few seasons down in the minors." Agni starts out well and is able to write his father "I am leading the league in batting in my rookie year! There's been nobody like me since Joe DiMaggio, and he was twenty two!"

The league's leading hitter in his rookie season, Agni is told he may become "even greater than the great Joe D." but he will not: for he is killed after only one sparkling, crazy season. In Roth's ingenious parody-fable about twentieth century America and its once favorite professional sport, Agni as his name suggests symbolizes some sort of sacrificial victim and not an American success story. Except for his batting skills he seems the opposite of DiMaggio. The only son of a non-immigrant father, Agni brashly declares "I got the greatest physique of any boy my age in America." Told he is "*not* God's gift to the world" he replies, "But I am—to the baseball world that's just exactly what I am." His father arranges for him to sign with the worst team in the league, the Ruppert

Mundys, because they are the only organization who seem uninterested in the boy, just to teach him a lesson, and for the same reason (totally unlike DiMaggio's father) agrees to pay for his son's room and board. In the book's wildly reflexive and ambiguous conclusion, Agni is possibly assassinated as perhaps part of a communist plot to infiltrate baseball and destroy America. The book also includes among its varied attractions a lengthy fake report of a deep sea fishing expedition with a gifted but contentious great American novelist named Ernest Hemingway.

Roth's novel presents a fully realized shadow league complete with beautifully named players such as the Mundy's Frenchy Astarte, Hothead Ptah, Bobo Buchis, and Applejack Terminus. Though lacking the manic intensity and private madness that pervades Robert Coover's *The Universal Baseball Association, Inc.*, the book is still satirically rich in its portrayal of the national fame. Unlike *The Old Man and the Sea, The Great American Novel* presents a world of artifice, cunningly but clearly fashioned by Roth, a book whose texture though often revealing about baseball, seems clearly peopled with creatures of its author's invention. Roth's creativity is stunning and he knows baseball as his random historical allusions to the game in this novel and his ode to the joys of that "delicious DiMaggio sensation" playing center field in the earlier (1969) *Portnoy's Complaint* demonstrate. Curiously, as DiMaggio appeared unreal in Hemingway's novel, a product of Santiago's fantasies, in Roth's book he seems an allusion to something real beyond the crafted comic fable the book becomes. *The Great American Novel* openly declares itself a work of fiction, and DiMaggio's presence in it by the reality of his achievements and the strength of his unfabricated history reaffirms the book's novelistic texture. In a small way DiMaggio provides a normative point of comparison against which the follies of Roth's characters play. By using him technically in this manner, Roth reaffirms in a small way DiMaggio's greatness, and the strength of his image.

DiMaggio's greatness and strong image were also reaffirmed in Paul Simon's song "Mrs. Robinson," an amazingly compressed and intellectually complex lyric which in its haunting performance by Simon and Art Garfunkel far surpasses the earlier DiMaggio song "Joe . . . Joe . . . DiMaggio" by the distance DiMaggio surpassed the abilities of most players he performed with. Written more than a decade after his retirement, the song operated on an almost esoteric level in addition to being a popular hit, and thus appealed to people who were not particularly interested in baseball, those who were much younger than the fans who had supported DiMaggio during his playing days, mass audiences, and to the intellectuals who might have read about DiMaggio in Hemingway's book.

In the film *The Graduate*, Mrs. Robinson is a hard, sexy, well-educated but morally tasteless older woman who helps educate the recently graduated, wistfully lustful Dustin Hoffman into the ways of the adult world, by seducing him. Mrs. Robinson is a calculating, unpleasant woman who seems to want pleasure from her young lover without really giving anything of her heart in return: the boy is a nice piece of meat to a hungry carnivore. Hoffman comes eventually to love Mrs. Robinson's fresh young daughter, played by Katherine Ross with the pristine and warm innocence of a blossoming young woman awaiting good, clean, beautiful 1960s flower child sex. This twists the slightly unwholesome affair between Hoffman and his older, clutching bedmate into something even more repugnant and incestuous. The movie is quite cynical in presenting the viciousness of the adult world surrounding Hoffman, which he and Ross eventually flee from like Huck Finn lighting out for the territories (where will he find them though?) with a perhaps more nubile Becky Thatcher.

DiMaggio is not actually mentioned in the sound track, but only in the earlier, fuller version of the song which presents Mrs. Robinson as a sick person in a morally empty, depersonalized, wasted society. He is featured in only four lines of the lyric but they are four crucial, exceptionally memorable lines frequently alluded to by writers and the general public into whose domain the song's phrases seem to have entered. Maury Allen used the DiMaggio sequence's opening question as the title for his 1975 book *Where Have You Gone, Joe DiMaggio?* The softly sung but psychologically jolting answer is that the Jolter is simply no longer here. He has vanished. The haunting lyric does not say precisely why DiMaggio is sought but his absence is grievous, not just to sad Mrs. Robinson but to the America of the 1960s, a lonely land. The earlier song about DiMaggio was like a cheer and assumed his vital presence; "Mrs. Robinson" is a dirge lamenting his departure.

Asked by Larry Merchant if the verses were "a plaintive wail for youth, when jockos made voyeurs of us all and baseball was boss?" Simon answered, "It means . . . whatever you want it to."

"I wrote that line," he claimed, "and didn't know what I was writing. . . . But as soon as I said the line I said to myself that is a great line, that line touches me. It has a nice touch of nostalgia to it. It's interesting. It could be interpreted in many ways.

"It has something to do with heroes. People who are all good and no bad in them at all. That's the way I always saw Joe DiMaggio. . . . For years I wouldn't read the back page of the [New York] *Post* when they lost. The Yankees had great players, players you could like. They gave me a sense of superiority."[45]

In the context of other images in the song, the lines about DiMaggio suggest he will not return. He is a creation of fantasy or of a particular time of life, childhood, when heroes are pure and good and always win. Like God and Jesus, also mentioned in the song, DiMaggio belongs to a world that Mrs. Robinson is locked out from. They are all, for her, vanished.

DiMaggio occupies much the same place in the song "Mrs. Robinson" that he did in *The Old Man and the Sea*, as a secular hero with religious overtones. Santiago implies this not only by the intense fervor with which he recollects DiMaggio at moments of crisis and invokes his name as though it were that of a saint, but also by placing him in a specifically religious context: "San Pedro [St. Peter] was a fisherman as was the father of the great DiMaggio." Santiago thinks of him as one in whom belief, faith, can be placed. He belongs to the child's pure world of morality where the good win if they play the game steadfastly enough. This is the same world DiMaggio inhabited in Paul Simon's mind. Simon admitted he would not permit himself to read about the Yankees losing. His sense of superiority, achieved in part through identifying with DiMaggio, demanded that the good win, the right triumph. The wounded hero would come back as DiMaggio did. For Mrs. Robinson probably there will be no comeback unless she returns to a state of innocent grace which seems impossible, for that is not the way of her world. Santiago came back to port but with his great fish destroyed, and in the next to last incident in the book the fish is no longer even recognized for the great animal it is. Hemingway himself came back with *The Old Man and the Sea*, a book which renewed for a time his general popularity and helped bring him the greatest literary prize of his life, but still he eventually sank into crazy depression and killed himself as his father had.

Far more Americans probably became familiar with Paul Simon's song or with the film *The Graduate* with which it is linked, than read Hemingway's novel. But in each work the image of DiMaggio is employed as a potentially redeeming figure, a hero who represents the best virtues of a civilization, a distant figure who will probably never appear close again, in the societies presented in either the song or book. Neither of these two works in which DiMaggio is employed as a symbol of integrity strikes sounds of unmuted triumph. "Mrs. Robinson" with its ironically jaunty melody is more a blithe dirge for lost worlds and even *The Old Man and the Sea* which at first was often hailed as a paean to the inner victories humans can win when their connections to the natural universe are reacknowledged, appears upon closer analysis now a sad elegy to small, rare triumphs in a brutal (sharks devour the great marlin) or indifferent (dumb tourists think the marlin's spinal remains are those of a shark) time. The one clear image the disparate works share is that of the dignity and grace, perhaps no longer attainable, of DiMaggio who in the works found his greatness as a cultural symbol reaffirmed and extended.

Alan Courtney's strictly Tin Pan Alley tune, Paul Simon's unsimple song, and Ernest Hemingway's rich novella appeared in three separate decades and were aimed at audiences of widely different levels of intellectual sophistication. In superficial and deep ways these creative works aimed at connecting with DiMaggio's power-laden and meaningful image, and each in turn enhanced DiMaggio's reputation among a variety of

American and (in the instance of "Mrs. Robinson" and *The Old Man and the Sea*) foreign audiences. In 1941 he was shown to a people hanging between an economic depression and a war, as a hero of great promise. In 1952's victorious and prosperous nation he was presented as a completely fulfilled hero, and in 1965's divided, self-tortured land he represented a heroism now vanished from the land. In the process of becoming a folk hero he was always wanted "on our side" though to judge from these three sightings of his figure anyway, he grew with his courage, honor, and strength increasingly distant from the games we play.

NOTES

1. I am indebted to a number of scholars for the general information and many specific details in this discussion of DiMaggio's Italian background. The sources I found particularly helpful were: Dino Cinel, *From Italy to San Francisco* (Palo Alto, Calif.: Stanford University Press, 1984); Deanna Paoli Gumina, *The Italians of San Francisco, 1850-1930* (New York: Center for Migration Studies, 1978); Luciano Iorizzo and Salvatore Mondello, *The Italian Americans* (Boston: Twayne Publishers, 1980); Andrew F. Rolle, *The Immigrant Upraised* (Norman: University of Oklahoma Press, 1968), and *The Italian Americans* (New York: The Free Press, 1980).

2. Rolle, *The Italian Americans*, pp. 3, 7.

3. Rolle, *The Immigrant Upraised*, p. 21.

4. Rolle, *The Italian Americans*, p. 2.

5. Iorizzo and Mondello, p. 63. The standard, and brilliant analysis of nativism is John Higham, *Strangers in the Land, Patterns of American Nativism 1860-1925* (New York: Atheneum, 1967).

6. Iorizzo and Mondello, pp. 3-4; Rolle, *The Immigrant Upraised*, p. 99.

7. *Istituto centrale di statistica . . . dal 1861 al 1951* (Rome, 1960).

8. Cinel, p. 226.

9. Rolle, *The Immigrant Upraised*, p. 336.

10. Cinel, pp. 218-221.

11. Iorizzo and Mondello, p. 92.

12. Rolle, *The Italian Americans*, p. 113.

13. Gumina, pp. 33, 25.

14. Steven Reiss in "Race and Ethnicity in American Baseball, 1900-1919," *Journal of Ethnic Studies* 4 (Winter, 1974): 47, passim, notes other Italian-American champions, including Pete Herman (featherweight, 1917), Young Corbett (a.k.a. Ralph Giordano, welterweight, 1933), Bat Battalino (featherweight, 1928-1932), and Joe Dundee (Sam Lazzaro, welterweight, 1927). According to Reiss, Italian-American titleholders dominated 1920-1935.

15. DiMaggio, *Lucky to Be a Yankee*, p. 22.

16. John P. Diggins, *Mussolini and Fascism: The View from America* (Princeton: Princeton University Press, 1972), p. 57.

17. Diggins, p. 349.

18. Diggins, p. 61.

19. Interview with Vince DiMaggio.

20. Diggins, p. 339.

21. Gumina, p. 199.

22. Interview with Vince DiMaggio, June 25, 1984.

23. Diggins, p. 400.

24. David Q. Voigt, *American Baseball, From the Commissoners to Continental Expansion* (Norman: University of Oklahoma Press, 1966), p. 219.

25. Vince DiMaggio, scrapbook, unpaged and often without dates, in the possession of Vince DiMaggio.

26. Reported by Red Smith, *New York Times*, 8 February 1935.

27. Martin Appel and Burt Goldblatt, *Baseball's Best* (New York: McGraw-Hill, 1977), p. 51.

28. Al Silverman, *Joe DiMaggio: The Golden Year, 1941* (Englewood Cliffs, N. J., 1969), p. 188.

29. Iorizzo and Mondello, pp. 275-76.

30. Rolle, *The Immigrant Upraised,* pp. 323-24.

31. See for example the controversy starting 23 January 1984, in *Sports Illustrated*, over the comparable significance of hockey star Wayne Gretzky's scoring streak and DiMaggio's hitting streak. DiMaggio himself was reported saying Gretzky was lucky he never had to worry about a mid-game washout.

32. Most details about Williams's life are taken from his autobiography as told to John Underwood, *My Turn at Bat* (New York: Simon & Schuster, 1969).

33. In Tom Meany, *The Yankee Story* (New York: E.P. Dutton, 1960), p. 139, the author tells a typical story no doubt unfairly contrasting the two. Both DiMaggio and Williams faced similar situations in a Boston-New York game, with runners on first and third and a 3-2 count. Williams takes a ball just out of the strike zone not to his liking, while DiMaggio reaches for an outside pitch and singles to right, scoring a run. "It was the difference between an individual star and a star team player," DiMaggio's friend Meany comments.

34. Dan Daniel, "Joe DiMaggio, My Friend—The Yankee Clipper," in *Sporting News Year Book* (St. Louis: Sporting News, 1950), p. 24; Gene Schoor, *The Thrilling Story of Joe DiMaggio* (New York: Frederick Fell, 1950), p. 14.

35. Robin Moore and Gene Schoor, *Marilyn & Joe DiMaggio* (New York: Manor Books, 1976), pp. 2, 3, 214.

36. Norman Mailer, *Marilyn* (New York: Grosset & Dunlap, 1981), pp. 96, 97.

37. Edwin Palmer Hoyt, *Marilyn, The Tragic Venus* (New York: Duell, Sloan & Pearce, 1965), p. 134.

38. Interview with Spud Chandler, 6 May 1983.

39. Diana Trilling, in Edward Wagenknecht, ed., *Marilyn Monroe: A Composite View* (New York: Chilton, 1969), p. 141.

40. Mailer, p. 100.

41. Richard Merryman, in Wagenknecht, p. 10.

42. Both reprint the song.

43. Leverett Smith, *The American Dream and the National Game* (Bowling Green, Ohio: Popular Press, 1975), pp. 84-100.

44. The many books and articles on Hemingway and *The Old Man and the Sea* frequently discuss DiMaggio's appearance in the work. See, for example, Sam H. Baskett, "The Great Santiago: Opium, Vocation, and Dream in *The Old Man and the Sea,*" *Fitzgerald-Hemingway Annual* 1976: 230-44; George Montiero,

"Santiago, DiMaggio, and Hemingway: The Ageing Professionals in *The Old Man and the Sea,*" *Fitzgerald-Hemingway Annual* 1975: pp. 273-80. The latter article contains a good bibliography. The Hemingway-DiMaggio connection is interesting. They attended the Ray Robinson-Carmin Basilio fight together, 23 September 1957. Hemingway's definition of courage as "grace under pressure" has often been applied to DiMaggio, for example in De Gregorio when he described DiMaggio's performance in his 1949 comeback, p. 197. See also Christian K. Messenger, *Sport and the Spirit of Play in American Fiction* (New York: Columbia University Press, 1981), pp. 293-96.

45. Larry Merchant, *Ringside Seat at the Circus*, (New York: Holt, Rinehart and Winston, 1976), p. 12.

LITERATURE ABOUT JOE DIMAGGIO

So far I have discussed many of the print sources of Joe DiMaggio's story when they had some contribution to make in establishing the details of his life or myth. I will now examine selected books and articles along with a few other miscellaneous popular print items that played a part in determining or reflecting what the public knew about DiMaggio as his image as a popular hero and cultural symbol evolved. My purpose is to indicate the contributions these works made to the establishment of his narrative, his story, rather than to focus on his life as I have done up to this point.

One of the first writers to set DiMaggio before a national auudience, even before he entered the major leagues, was Quentin Reynolds, one of the country's best known journalists. In the mid-1930s he was a feature writer for *Collier's*, then one of the country's top magazines in terms of distribution and almost as popular as its chief competition, *The Saturday Evening Post*. Reynolds only occasionally wrote sports articles for *Collier's*. During World War II he became a leading war correspondent and wrote a best-selling account of England's fight for survival. He was respected by his readership and by other journalists for his smooth writing and for his knowledge of current events. He was an experienced journalist with a wide readership extending far beyond the sports pages.

He wrote for the September 7, 1935, issue of *Collier's* an article about minor leaguers who were potential major league stars. The first player discussed and the player whose picture dominated the article's two-page spread was the Seals's Joe DiMaggio, who was according to his manager and Reynolds's friend Lefty O'Doul, "About to Shine." O'Doul bet Reynolds "that within two years every baseball fan in the country will have heard of DiMaggio," whom Reynolds admits had been previously unknown to him. Emphasizing DiMaggio's throwing ability ("the best arm" O'Doul had ever seen) and his 1933 record-breaking hitting streak, the article does not mention that he was destined for the Yankees. DiMaggio's Italian ancestry and identification with San Francisco are stressed: Reynolds claims that "ever since Ping Bodie of Telegraph Hill hit the big leagues it has been the ambition of all San Francisco Italian youngsters to be ball players." However, Joe's Americanization is also suggested: he "started playing ball as soon as he heard of the game and he heard of it before he heard of marbles or bocchie, which is a great pastime among Italians in that section."

The size of DiMaggio's family is not alluded to, but his "crab fisherman" father and ballplaying brother Vince, who first "brought his kid brother to [the Seals's] camp," are mentioned. He is characterized as "Dead Pan Joe," though the accompanying photograph shows him smiling while spearing what looks suspiciously like a planted baseball in his upthrust mitt, and is compared to the Yankees' Bob Meusel who also had "ice-water in his veins." Reynolds refers to DiMaggio's injured leg but only to insist that he is now "sound again and . . . [b]etter . . . than all right," and reports that the Yankee scout Joe Devine considers him the West Coast's best prospect. Ty Cobb thinks "he's going to be a big-league sensation some day." Beyond predicting greatness for DiMaggio, then, the article introduces a number of future elements of his story, including his San Francisco and Italian background, his impassivity or coolness of character, and his triumph over injury, to audiences who had not yet seen DiMaggio play.

Reynolds alludes sarcastically to Mussolini in the article, though he does not directly compare DiMaggio with him. Lefty O'Doul had bet Reynolds that DiMaggio would shortly be a star. The sportswriter Sid Mercer tells Reynolds if he gives O'Doul good enough odds he will "bet you that Germany won the war" and "that Mussolini discovered the North Pole." Thus the unassuming DiMaggio is by faint implication compared to the braggartly Mussolini.

The article might have been cause for bestowing the title of baseball prophet of the century upon Reynolds, for picking this "pearl out of the minor-league oyster bed." Unfortunately, the other mollusks his article dredges up are Ted Duay, Harvey Green, Steve Messner, Albert Milnar, Ward Cross, Manuel Onis, Howard Mills, John Hassett, Frankie Hawkins, Gene Lillard, Joe Holden, Hal Kelleher, and Lyn Watkins, a generally lustreless string of artificial pearls more suggestive of bargain jewelry counters than Van Cleef and Arpels. Milnar's lifetime batting average over a decade in the big leagues was .203. Lillard pitched two years in the majors and emerged with a 1-2 record, Kelleher pitched four years and achieved the same percentage with a 2-4 record. Hassett hit a more than respectable .292 after seven years with three big league teams including New York, for whom he hit .333 in the 1942 World Series. Manuel Onis's record was best of all. He hit 1.000, in his only major league at bat, with the Brooklyn Dodgers in

1935. Concerning the others, *The Baseball Encyclopedia* maintains a clam-like silence.

Reynolds followed up his first *Collier's* article with another on June 13, 1936, "The Frisco Kid," focusing on DiMaggio alone. With a light, half-comic touch that his readers enjoyed, Reynolds (who had by this time met his subject) developed more fully several of the salient elements of DiMaggio's life first mentioned the year before, and added a few new details, some of which were wrong or misleading but which did not disturb DiMaggio's basic image. Again Reynolds identifies him as a popular Italian-American and once more alludes to Mussolini satirically. Depicting DiMaggio as a member of a large and not wealthy Italian family, Reynolds names all Joe's brothers and sisters for whom his poor father had to provide food, confirmation suits, and (for the girls) "hair ribbons and pretties," and then asks "and how's that for a family, Signor Mussolini?" Characterizing DiMaggio in more detail than in his first article, Reynolds portrays him as a simple, "nice-looking twenty-two year old youngster" whose seeming flaws turn out to conceal virtues. That he cuts out clippings of himself at night is not conceit, Reynolds declares, just thoughtfulness in providing his "kid sister back home in San Francisco" with reports that give her "a big kick" when she pastes them in the scrapbook she keeps. Still a "Dead Pan Joe," he is merely following the orders of his former mentor Lefty O'Doul who warned him never to clown around. He'll talk baseball "all day" but prefers listening, and reminds Reynolds of another 1930s athlete just beginning to become an American hero, "another Dead Pan Joe—Joe Louis." That the New Deal Democrat Reynolds would link these two ethnic stars is particularly revealing, since both sport stars would become symbols of America during the Depression and war years.

Thus, early in DiMaggio's career he was already being written about nationally as a pleasant, quiet, reserved young man of exceptional baseball skills, who came from a poor, large, Italian-American family. Adding depth to this all-Italian-American image Reynolds again notes that DiMaggio overcame the damage to his leg in 1934 and that though "the victim of a rather odd but painful accident" during spring training he later collected three hits his first day of major-league play. Reynolds was one of the first national writers to tell what would become the legendary story about DiMaggio's joining the Seals, setting down for *Collier's* readers the star-is-born monologue delivered by Spike Hennessy to DiMaggio as the eighteen-year-old kid peered at his brother Vince through that knothole at Seals' field: "Listen kid . . . I'll get you into the ball park. . . . in fact, I'll fix it so you can work out mornings with the team." In similar style Reynolds prints manager Ike Caveney's momentous line of 1933, "Go up there, DiMaggio."

One statement by Reynolds which misdirected a few writers was that DiMaggio "didn't know whether he wanted to play baseball or be a fisherman." He claims that "Brother Tom . . . strictly the Head Man in the family now. . . ." settled that dilemma by ordering his younger brother to stay in school. This would accord with both the American work ethic and democratic educational ideal; in reality, however, DiMaggio of course neither wanted to fish as his father had, nor did he remain in school. Reynolds informed his readership that DiMaggio was "more concerned about getting out there in the bay with his father's fishing boat" than with playing baseball. When his school coach Ed White told him if he put his mind to it he "might be good enough to play for the Seals sometime," DiMaggio murmured (according to Reynolds) "*Sei mutto da leggare*," or in Reynolds's translation, "you should be put in a straitjacket, you're that crazy." Now, Reynolds states, "there are those who insist that he will eventually develop into the greatest right-hand hitter since Rogers Hornsby." He had played his first major-league game little over a month before on May 3.

Just one month after Reynolds's article, *Time* published on July 13 an unsigned piece on DiMaggio and featured him on its cover. The article reiterated that DiMaggio was a player of exceptionally high skills from a big Italian-American family in San Francisco, a humble and responsible lad who was "the American League's most sensational recruit since Ty Cobb." The ballyhoo surrounding DiMaggio's appearance with the Yankees according to *Time* set him up for a quick downfall, but "far from achieving the collapse which his billing led sophisticated baseball addicts to expect, Rookie DiMaggio proceeded to make the notices seem inadequate," for example by batting .400 his first month and being named the Associated Press "hero of the day" seven times.

Time also reprinted the story about DiMaggio's discovery by Spike Hennessy at the famous knothole, correctly adding that he received his big chance at the start of the 1933 season, when the Seals were short an experienced outfielder because brother Vince had badly hurt his shoulder and was unavailable for duty. *Time* also noted his tendency to injure himself, citing both the bad leg and burned ankle he had to overcome. His principal virtue according to the article was "his ability to make timely hits." DiMaggio was considered already perhaps the finest clutch hitter on his team. Although Lou Gehrig was hitting .398, according to the article "rival pitchers consider DiMaggio more likely to break up a game." *Time* did not reckon that DiMaggio was equal to Babe Ruth in power but claimed he was "already almost as much a hero as Ruth used to be. The clubhouse boy who sorts the Yankees' fan mail estimates DiMaggio's to be as large as Ruth's. Most of it comes from Italian well-wishers," the boy said, although how he knew this is unstated.

Time also reported DiMaggio's seeming behavior flaws only to turn them into popularly endearing characteristics. "When New York sportswriters first encountered DiMaggio, they mistook for exaggerated evidences of self-assurance his promises to make good which, it became apparent even before he had time to fulfill them were actually the entirely defensive protestations of a naturally diffident youth [twenty-two years old, actually] who had never before been more than 200 miles from home." *Time* further noted to DiMaggio's advantage that "like many young brothers in large Italian families, young DiMaggio is characterized by a solemn, almost embarrassing humility which is exceedingly useful because it causes his elders and superiors to take paternal interest in him."

Even more pointedly than Reynolds's article, the *Time* cover story roots nice boy DiMaggio in his Italian-American family, stating that he used to help support it by selling newspapers (his life imagined already as a typical poor boy makes a good movie scenario) and that he sends almost his entire salary home so his folks can live in comfort. Though a star Yankee in New York, DiMaggio still has close ties to parents and siblings. Marie gave him a signet ring when he left for training in faraway Florida, and maintains his scrapbooks. Older brother Tom almost got him put back on the fishing boats when he advised Joe to hold out for a piece of the purchase price the Seals received for him. That family story ended happily however; Joe received his extra money and did not have to return to the boats. The anecdote underscored the article's unstated theme, which was that DiMaggio was a great success in all ways, on the field and off. He had become a star, he was still a good boy, and with the extra money he got from the Seals, according to *Time*, he bought his brother Mike a fishing boat. After he was sold to the Yankees, at a celebration in his honor he was too frightened to say a word of the prepared speech of thanks the team's trainer had written for him and drilled him on. Now, *Time* remarked "he has since become an accomplished radio speaker." Ben Franklin's rise had been faltering, compared to DiMaggio's.

Before his second season in the majors, DiMaggio was written about in books intended for children and for readers primarily looking for entertaining, light stories about various sports stars of the day. In *Famous American Athletes of Today* (Fifth Series) his virtues were extolled by Harold Kaese alongside those of baseball's Dizzy Dean and Gabby Hartnett, track's Jesse Owens, and boxing's Jimmy Braddock. All the articles in the popular volume are adulatory, and often treat their subjects as exemplary heroes whose lives provided inspiration and guidance to youngsters. This follows a familiar pattern in American sportswriting which has tended to separate an athlete's game exploits from his basic character praising the one while often ignoring the other, or modifying the athlete's real behavior to conform to his playing identity. The article on Braddock, for example, without going into his nature very deeply at all, presents him simply as a Depression hero who after a promising start and precipitous decline "started" in 1934 "the most remarkable comeback in pugilism" culminating with his heavyweight title defeat of Max Baer, a vastly more glamorous opponent, characterized usually by later writers as a fighter of great skills which he misused by behaving like a "madcap" or "playboy." Reduced to stevedoring as a result of his early, botched fight career, Braddock eventually "left the dull, drab, sheep-run life of the slums and dock walloping and went forward to the golden, glittering life of a world champion." The moral-political lesson his achievement as a plucky, hard-working Irish-American lad triumphing over Baer, who "disported himself during 1934 in a giddy whirl of night-life," must have been obvious even to readers untrained in allegory. Unfortunately the Cinderella Man, as writers termed him, was defeated in his first defense of the title against Joe Louis June 23, 1937, the same year *Famous American Athletes* lauded him, and Louis would inherit most of his Depression fame (though Braddock was reputed to have a contract guaranteeing him a percentage of Louis's profits for about ten years.)

In Kaese's article, DiMaggio is depicted as an all-around star of the greatest magnitude who in his first major-league year "batted so powerfully, fielded so steadily, threw so accurately, and ran the bases so speedily, that the New York Yankees won the American League pennant." The "fuzzy-cheeked youngster" was "the key man, the spark-plug." Kaese at the time was a sportswriter for the *Boston Evening Transcript* so he could not be accused of puffing a local hero. He supplies quotations from Joe Cronin and Joe McCarthy to corroborate his claim that DiMaggio was the Yankees' winning difference, reporting Cronin's words that "any one of four other teams in the league" would have won with him, and McCarthy's pre-season remark that "we are depending on DiMaggio to take up the slack and win the pennant for us." Like several later sources, Kaese repeated *Time*'s opinion that DiMaggio's entrance into major-league play "was the most brilliant since the debut of Tyrus Raymond Cobb in 1905" without checking to see that Cobb hit only .240 that year, the very lowest in his career.

DiMaggio's Italian-American and San Franciscan background are mentioned along with his large family. Kaese gets closer to the truth about DiMaggio as a prospective fisherman than Reynolds had, stating that while Joe worked on his father's boat from time to time, he was never part of its fishing crew. Against the grain of tradition that hard work coupled with education brought success, DiMaggio is described as having been bored by school and worked only one day in his life. "I joined an orange juice company, but after peeling oranges—and the skin of my fingers—for eight hours, I resigned." It was not DiMaggio's adherence to the work ethic for which he was held up to readers. Instead, the key to his success is determined by Kaese to be his behavior. "How Joe DiMaggio came through with flying colors so gloriously . . . is probably answered in one word, disposition." DiMaggio was "one of the least emotional athletes ever to play in the American League." His "nerves carry ice water." His "even temperament was DiMaggio's greatest asset as he met adversity.'' He is a ''dead-pan'' with no nerves and ''about as much'' color as ''a bucket full of white wash.'' Though he lacks Cobb's ''explosive brilliancy'' and Babe Ruth's ''boyish bent for trouble,'' DiMaggio possessed ''a complete mastery of baseball'' that Kaese says may enable him to excel either player. While ''many athletes become famous because of their personalities as well as their abilities'' DiMaggio should become famous by virtue of ability alone. This would make him an ''extraordinary'' player indeed.

Kaese's account was one of the most detailed to appear in popular nationally distributed print so far. It contains statistics from DiMaggio's semi-professional days, and supplies a story that, though not as picturesque as Reynolds's knothole tale, generally coincides with one that Vince DiMaggio related, that Vince suggested Joe play the final few days of the 1932 season for the Seals. Kaese adds that in 1933 Joe edged Vince from his job, a story that frequently was accepted by later writers and by some of DiMaggio's first year teammates. Vince stated that Joe took his job only as any acceptable outfielder might have, for his arm was so sore he could not play, and he was ripe for replacement; there was no struggle nor competition between the two, as traditionally there is in fairy tales between younger and older brothers. For its time, Kaese's article was highly informative and relatively accurate. The only truly bad mistake Kaese makes in his narrative is to call his subject ''Joseph Thomas DiMaggio.'' Worse, the layout of the book was designed so that at the top of alternate pages the name of the hero of that section was printed in large letters easily seen by readers while flipping through the book. So on page after page the name ''Joseph Thomas DiMaggio'' is printed like a mocking echo that must have infuriated Kaese who clearly took pains of his own in compiling the narrative.

By the start of the 1939 season, the predictions of writers such as Reynolds and Kaese seemed to have come true. In its first issue (May 1) after the opening week of play, *Life*, perhaps the most read or most looked at magazine in the country, called DiMaggio in its lengthy cover story about him ''baseball's No. 1 contemporary player.'' The article by Noel F. Busch accompanying the picture story provides a sometimes curiously written commentary on the eight-page picture spread *Life* presented on the young but already dominating player, mainly furthering the image of DiMaggio as a performer of almost unparalleled skills who exemplified—but with a bizarre twist Busch provided—the American success story. He is once more strongly characterized as the cherished idol of fellow Italian-Americans (in the same issue Mussolini's son-in-law Count Ciano is depicted assuring Albanian citizens that the Italian take-over of their tiny country was only ''to bring order and progress'') who brought huge flags to unfurl during Yankee games. But, DiMaggio is almost but not quite mocked by Busch as a lazy guy who just happened to possess great athletic abilities enabling him to play supremely well and thus profitably employ that ''muscular lethargy'' of "good athletes . . . which enables them, when called upon for reflex action, to furnish it with an explosive violence garnered from doing nothing at most other times.''

Though the article contains praise of DiMaggio's game-winning talents, offering many examples of his hitting and fielding skills, Busch consistently patronizes his subject and comes close to depicting him as an anti-hero. Though several of the pictures surrounding the article show DiMaggio in less than heroic poses, they are more traditionally complimentary of him. It is as though for one audience (the kind that only looks at photographs) *Life* decided to offer standard, worshipful fare; for more literate readers they provided intellectually snappier and presumably wittier matter. The article's first sentence confronts the reader with a verbal picture of DiMaggio entirely at odds with the handsome, smiling, pleasant hero shown in a full head shot on *Life's* cover. Busch describes contrarily enough, DiMaggio as he appeared opening day three years previously: "a tall, thin, Italian youth equipped with slick black hair, shoe-button eyes, squirrel teeth and a receding chin.'' The cover photo shows a very changed person with naturally damp-looking hair brushed back neatly but not slickly underneath his baseball cap, bright eyes, a smiling mouth with good, strong, fairly even teeth, and almost a square jaw—a friendly, well-fed but far from fat face. Busch's depiction of the rookie DiMaggio coupled with the cover photo represents an aspect of DiMaggio's success: his physical appearance seemed modified, and over the years he would become more and more handsome as he aged gracefully and succeeded as a person even more. At the same time, it introduces an element of satire in Busch's portrait that he maintains to his conclusion.

Following the curiously derogatory opening paragraph, Busch praises DiMaggio for more than justifying the high price paid for him (given incorrectly as $50,000) and proving he was an even better player than early expectations—so often misleading—promised. Because of his powerful bat, clutch hitting, and all-around ability, "experts are agreed that DiMaggio is entitled to more of the credit'' for the Yankees' predominance "than any other single member of the club.'' Thus he is declared the key component of a winning team, a position of eminence Busch emphasizes he has achieved while laboring "under severe handicaps,'' a series of injuries and his 1938 holdout for more money, which Busch calls a "strike. . . . not due entirely to avarice. Another factor was his brother Tom, vice-President of San Francisco's energetic Fisherman's Union.'' Tom had to learn that baseball was run along "fascist'' and not democratic lines, and that his brother was not entitled to a greater percentage "of the money he brought to the box office.''

Busch's clownish tone describing the holdout cynically accepts the rightness of baseball's monopolistic grip on its players and suggests the futility of attempts to change the system in a capitalistic society. The "strike was a failure." Players are rivals and there is no chance for solidarity among them, therefore when they act individually as DiMaggio did, and apparently as they are trained to act, they will always be defeated. DiMaggio learned that fans favor management in most cases especially those like his, for "a young man in his third term of a major-league competition should be satisfied with $25,000 a year."

The knothole story of Joe's discovery is once more related, but Busch uses his ethnic background as another excuse to satirize the work ethic and success myth elements so frequently stressed in DiMaggio narratives. DiMaggio, Busch states with a verbal straight face, was lucky he was born to his Italian family and was in character diffident. "Italians, bad at war, are well-suited for milder competitions, and the number of top-notch Italian . . . baseball players is out of all proportion to the population." Doubly fortunate, DiMaggio was "lazy, rebellious, and endowed with a weak stomach" while his other brothers and sisters were "docile" and obedient. Joe refused to fish because it made him sick and "driven to idleness" he began to play baseball with the other kids around the block. "Joe DiMaggio's rise in baseball is a testimonial to the value of general shiftlessness." His Americanization is also viewed comically and in terms of blatant ethnic stereotyping. "Although he learned Italian first, Joe, now 24, speaks English without an accent and is otherwise well adapted to most U.S. mores. Instead of olive oil or smelly bear grease he keeps his hair slick with water. He never reeks of garlic and prefers chicken chow mein to spaghetti."

While the article treats DiMaggio as an authentic baseball star, perhaps the best contemporary player of all, it makes fun of him as a person. His "sudden transformation from a penniless newsboy to a national celebrity" is shown based on solid athletic achievement, but Busch is constantly smug and patronizing about DiMaggio off the field, a young man who "has never worried his employers by an unbecoming interest in literature or the arts, nor does he wear himself down by unreasonable asceticism. In laziness, DiMaggio is still a paragon." Busch says he is happy only on the field or at home and the article concludes late in the morning in the house DiMaggio bought his parents, as Rosalie DiMaggio upon a signal from Joe—the raising of the Venetian blinds in his bedroom across the courtyard from her kitchen—starts making his favorite breakfast, an "omelet flavored with onions and potatoes. . . . He sits down in the kitchen comfortably and eats it."

The article is exceptional in the literature about DiMaggio. While not precisely debunking him, it presents him comically and unheroically. The piece is rarely quoted by other writers except to deride it. Why Busch took the stance he did—why *Life* printed the piece as it stands—is difficult to fathom. The photographs which the text accompanied, probably the focal point for most *Life* browsers, presents a far more traditional view of the

Yankee hero. The first picture is a portrait of the DiMaggio clan, a large, happy brood at home, flanked by proud parents and packed with sons, daughters, and grandchildren. Subsequent photographs depict him as a child, and then as a conquering hero paraded through the streets of San Francisco following the 1936 World Series victory. One five-picture sequence shows the family's first small, drab house in San Francisco, the "handsome house" DiMaggio bought his parents "when he grew rich and famous," his mother and father (a bit forlorn) at the new home, and two shots of his famous restaurant which cost, *Life* materialistically points out, $100,000. Twelve smaller pictures of a batting sequence are ribboned across the top of two consecutive pages, while twelve showing his skill in center field stretch across the bottom. He is shown listening to a cash register, tasting spaghetti, surrounded by starlets while being groomed for a movie scene, pretending to play a ukulele poolside with more young women, hauling up a dead fish, handling (gingerly) a crab with his father—all standard "casual" celebrity shots very mildly parodying such pictures and at the same time providing interested fans with informal views of their star at play. One photograph shows him with fellow champ Joe Louis. The caption says like Louis, "DiMaggio is lazy, shy and inarticulate." Another depicts him at training camp in St. Peterburg signing authographs for kids: "Like other celebrities, DiMaggio sometimes cynically signs a pseudonym." One odd view shows a trouserless DiMaggio from the back, his shoulders slumped, and reveals that "Sliding Pads Are Worn Under DiMaggio's Pants."

Together, the article and photographs present a star of "sensational" exploits on the field, but an ordinary person off. Slanted to maintain the interest of sophisticated readers, the article while not iconoclastic exactly, offers a distinctly tongue-in-cheek portrait of the young star whose acheivements sportswriters sometimes treated as though they were the labors of Hercules. It is easy to develop an exaggerated view of sports heroes if you see them only within the boundaries of their own insulated and hysteria-filled activity. Busch's article is in some ways refreshing, nearly a put-on, except that sometimes its humor (with allusions to Italians as bad fighters and smelling of garlic) seems, today anyway, questionable. At any rate, his view of DiMaggio has not lingered long among other later writers, and is not even mentioned in the standard *Reader's Guide to Periodical Literature*.

In 1941 DiMaggio's reputation which had since 1939 leveled out at a very high point, soared higher as he pursued and overcame the consecutive hitting record. This achievement placed him on a special plateau and forever established him as a baseball star of unique achievements. *Time's* story for July 13 in now typical fashion rehearsed his poor and Italian immigrant background to contrast him with what he had become. As the son of a fisherman he was perhaps "shy and inarticulate. He may have been once, but he had plenty of poise this day. He is a good-looking chap, with black curly hair, sparkling eyes, and a rather long nose which gives him a sort of Cyrano de Bergerac profile.'' Though at bat he still had his old ''dead pan'' he had loosened up in private, particularly when he roomed with Lefty ''Goofy'' Gomez. *Time* reported the pair once would ''drop paper bags full of water out of hotel windows, but this doesn't happen any more.'' Another anecdote demonstrating his fondness for the comic book ''Superman'' implied his continuing non-intellectualism as did his stated preference for pulp westerns. But he did not read much anyway, since it hurt his eyes, *Time* related. His coolness as a hero is exemplified by the story told of his meeting with Ed Barrow when still a rookie and Barrow warned him about the attention he was about to receive. DiMaggio responded, ''Don't worry, Mr. Barrow . . . I never get excited.'' DiMaggio is clearly presented in the article as he would be frequently throughout his career, a spectacularly gifted but unassuming player not given to trumpeting his achievements. He is quoted saying he did not think much about breaking Willie Keeler's record until he got ''within three games of it,'' and concerning the adulation he received he said ''I like to be popular, who doesn't? But I don't pay much attenion to the fans. While I give them all I have, and I hope I can make good for them, primarily I am out there playing ball for the club—and for myself,'' for ''this is the way I make my living.''

Clarke Robinson's article in *World Digest* for October, 1941, has already been discussed because of its strong presentation of DiMaggio as a symbol of America on the eve of World War II. One of a series of ''Silhouettes of Celebrities,'' the piece ironically preceded the December issue's ''Silhouette'' of Admiral Harold R. Stark, who would be removed soon from his position as Chief of Naval Operations of the Navy in the aftermath of the American disaster at Pearl Harbor. With the excitement caused by DiMaggio's streak still dominating the description of DiMaggio, he is introduced to readers as ''the biggest thing in baseball today,'' a player liked by all who freely gives his autograph to ''urchins'' and is ''idolized by his fellow Italian-Americans.'' Very brief mention is given to his wife Dorothy, who was pregnant at the time the article was written. This fact, along with the unimportant information that his favorite foods were shrimp cocktail and steak, seems to be included because it humanizes DiMaggio, because all these details make him even more of a typical ''Joe.'' Like other Americans transformed into a national symbol during times of crisis, he was portrayed as both common and extraordinary, one of the people and yet exceptional, therefore fit to respresent the American spirit: ''Since boyhood he's always been an open air young man doing the manly things that youngsters like.'' Though Robinson does not refer to that year's popular song, it is clear he views DiMaggio as someone all Americans would like ''on our side.''

The 1941 *Current Biography* entry for him was also written following his batting streak. Since the publication regarded itself as a research guide, its depiction of DiMaggio is particularly interesting. The article's first two paragraphs focus on the slump he was in prior to his hit streak, whose achievement is then noted. Thus the article emphasizes his ability to come back after experiencing bad times. Then his life is outlined with occasional errors in fact: he was born in Martinez the youngest of nine children. His Italian father was a fisherman and so were two older brothers. Joe DiMaggio sold newspapers "to help support his family" (something which may have been true in desire but not in fact) which was poor: "his father, with nine children to support, couldn't afford any extras." Lefty O'Doul, it is claimed, first let him practice with the Seals in 1932. In 1933 as soon as he was switched from shortstop to the outfield "from the very first day . . . he covered . . . [it] like a tent." The article portrays him as a naturaly gifted player and not one who had to work hard to achieve his considerable greatness. He was the "greatest player the Coast League had ever produced," and (quoting but not attributing *Time*) "the American League's most sensational recruit since Ty Cobb."

DiMaggio's knee and foot injuries are described, and his holdout in 1938 (in the article mistakenly stated to be 1937) is called his only mistake so far. What seemed at first his brashness, resulted from his youth, for he is "essentially" a "modest fellow with a sense of family responsibility typical of his Sicilian-American upbringing." His popularity among Italian-Americans is tremendous: "30,000 San Francisans tried to crowd into the Cathedral of St. Peter and Paul on the occasion of his marriage to lovely Dorothy Arnold, an actress." Thus fact and fancy are mixed in this standard biographical source which leaves mainly the impression of DiMaggio's natural skill, and how far he had come from his early days as a poor Italian lad. After all, "Joe has been praised by Taub (haberdasher to America's famous athletes) as a smooth dresser."

The 1951 *Current Biography* entry on DiMaggio was written after his retirement. It refines the 1941 picture, and adds details to portray an athlete who has fulfilled his early promise as a performer but also as a human being. The famous streak is mentioned of course but new space is given his comeback against bone spurs and Boston in 1949 and specifically notes his history of "playing when in pain from illness or injuries." The account is more sober, emphasizing his solid achievements but placing these in a new context: "known for years for his powerful hitting, graceful fielding, and silent, dean-pan proficiency," he was also famous "for having overcome a series of physical mishaps."

The review of his life and career as a player is more free from error. His newspaper route is alluded to but no claims are made that he helped support his family by it. Lefty O'Doul is called his guide but not his discoverer. A few more details are supplied suggesting how he also grew up while playing baseball: "the shy youth began to imitate the better-dressed, more sociable teammates" and also "received the guidance of Seals' manager Lefty O'Doul." The ugly duckling turns into a swan partly through his own powers of observation, then, and partly through his apprenticeship to wise mentors. The article implies that while still primarily a "natural" baseball player, DiMaggio worked at becoming socially skilled and capable of writing, with the help of Tom Meany and Marion Simon, the instructional book, *Baseball for Everyone* (1948). When he was booed for holding out he said, "It got so I couldn't sleep at night." Aloof in the locker room, mild-spoken, "never speaking ill about other players," the DiMaggio presented in *Current Biography's* 1951 review of his life is a person of considerable growth, one who had not merely lived through a greater number of experiences since the 1941 biography, but whose character had been enriched by the life he led. Now he was divorced but had his own son. He is "a theatergoer and . . . there are flecks of gray in Joe DiMaggio's curly black hair." He describes himself as "shy, sensitive, and restless." He has changed and not just aged.

Lucky to Be a Yankee (1946) was the first book devoted entirely to telling the highlights of DiMaggio's life and career. Although nothing in its introductory material indicates that it is anything but an autobiography written by DiMaggio himself and thus possessing the authority and insight of a first-hand revelation, it was actually composed by Tom Meany. Much of the information Meany relates could have come only from DiMaggio who oversaw the book's writing and collaborated with Meany on its constitution. Though in a specific sense DiMaggio did not create the book word-by-word, he ultimately controlled its general outlines and thus shaped it both by the information he provided and the themes whose expression he permitted (or prohibited). Therefore I shall examine the book as though DiMaggio wrote it, although technically speaking he did not, though much of the book's content results from Meany's craft and not DiMaggio's.

Lucky to Be a Yankee stands in a long tradition of autobiographical works written in America by famous men or women intended to supply basic factual information about their subjects, to satisfy public curiosity about an interesting life, but also to explain to audiences how the well-known persons became the important people they are. Benjamin Franklin's so-called *Autobiography* is a well-known book in this genre. Such books typically not only deal with certain critical events in the lives of their heroes that are thought particularly significant and revealing, but also omit other events which do not correspond with the image of self that the subject wishes to present to his or her audience. Often, the autobiographical writers are aware that they are offering themselves as models of achievement and character to their readers. Also the autobiographies must frequently create ways to defend themselves from the appearance of excessive egotism in writing so much about the self, even while parading before the reader a series of experiences establishing the subject's importance. American autobiographies also often contain some unconscious or explicit awareness of the subject's identity as an American, which until very recently, since America was a country largely made up of people from other countries or whose parents were from other countries, was not an element of identity that could be taken for granted. This last concern may be primary and overt or it may be submerged as in DiMaggio's book, whose very title, relating as it does to the national pastime and employing a national nickname, could easily be interpreted in light of his parents' immigrant status as *Lucky to Be an American.*

Even before the book's autobiographical narrative commences, its preliminary text places DiMaggio in a context that affects his forthcoming presentation of self. In the fullest version, James A. Farley introduces the reader to the book. Farley was himself a well-known power in New York and Democratic political circles, and from 1933 until 1940 he was Postmaster General of the United States. A sport enthusiast and part of the very traditional male world of Broadway celebrities DiMaggio often socialized with, Farley represents the outside, great world beyond sports that has recognized DiMaggio's exploits. DiMaggio's story, Farley emphasizes, "could have happened only in America, the story of Joe, the son of immigrant parents, of a boyhood which was far from luxurious, and his rise to national eminence on the strength of his baseball ability." Through baseball "the DiMaggios were able to forge ahead." DiMaggio presents a classic American success tale.

In a foreword, Grantland Rice, perhaps the best known sportswriter of his time, treats DiMaggio more narrowly as a player, one of a special breed demonstrating "perfection." DiMaggio has often been termed a perfect player and sometimes, particularly during his early years, a model of mechanical perfection (Harold Kaese in 1937 referred to him as "a mechanically perfect batting machine"). In a literal sense, no human performer is perfect: Babe Ruth strikes out, Jack Johnson misses a jab. What Rice refers to is a skill raised to such a degree that at times it presents the illusion of perfection: "Joe DiMaggio possesses that magic gift of perfection in his swing at the plate." Rice further distinguishes DiMaggio's greatness as an athlete (Farley focused upon his social significance) by noting his "effortless ease" that no other athlete quite possesses, underscoring one of the autobiography's recurring themes, the naturalness of DiMaggio's skill. "If ever an athlete was meant for a sport, DiMaggio was meant for baseball." Rice's attitude here helps explain why DiMaggio's story can safely be used as a model for American youth despite his early refusal to work hard as young Americans should: he was special, he was only naturally following a higher destiny that did not want him to follow the standard path to success. In drifting into baseball, he was obeying some force that had singled him out for his special fate, one that brought him great fame but also great pain and many days of toil. So in the end, he worked hard anyway.

Finally the full version of the book contains "Acknowledgements" presumably by its autobiographic author, dedicating the book to "Baseball, the great American game," to the fans, to the "sports writers who have always given me a 'break,'" and to all the ballplayers in both leagues, "a clean bunch of fellows and all grand sports." Here can be seen the world the book will illustrate and the audience for whom it is intended. Clearly this is to be a nice book about a clean sport written about and performed by decent people. It will give offense to few if any, and will present an innocent, sanitized view of the game either for children, or for adults who view baseball and sports as embodying the best in American life. Like Franklin's far more cynical and yet equally manipulative work, it offers the public a scrubbed and idealized version of reality. The book presents a pastoral version of baseball and DiMaggio's life, which is perhaps appropriate because baseball more than any other American sport is seen as re-creating a pastoral mode of life with its big grassy spaces and slow pace. It is the most old-fashioned of our team sports.

The basically prewar (dealing with events prior to DiMaggio's return to play in 1946) version of the book begins with a story of failure, though at a high level, in the All-Star game of 1936 when DiMaggio flopped. In this fashion DiMaggio indicates both the skill he exhibited even as a rookie, and his modesty, for he presents himself in a failing performance. He can afford to do this because for him failing was atypical, but still he demonstrates the humility that is one of the chief character traits he displays in *Lucky to Be a Yankee*. As a good moralist, he draws lessons from his poor play: "that anything can happen in any one ball game," and "that things are hardest, just when they look easiest." He learns the dangers of "overconfidence." He often tempers tales of triumph with cautionary reminders of his flawed skill. After he hits a triple his very first time at bat with San Francisco, he plays shortstop and either heaves the ball "over his first baseman's head or into the dirt." Cheered for throwing out a runner to win a game against Detroit his first season with the Yankees, he admits his toss was not good because it travelled to Bill Dickey on the fly rather than on one bounce as it should have, so it could be handled more easily or cut off if desired. At other times his lack of egotism is demonstrated by the humble interpretation he gives events. He admits that after four weeks with the Yankees he needed a police escort to get into the Stadium but claims this was partly because "the fans knew all about the others and I was virtually a newcomer." In most instances the modesty or humility seems real and not assumed.

Chapter 1 (in the prewar version) is titled self-derisively "The Old Horse Laugh" and Chapter 2 is "The Old Horse Lot." Here he returns briefly to his childhood. The book is not long and the individual chapters are never extensive—there are seventeen of them totaling 180 pages of narrative. The book's language is unpretentious and natural, almost in the vernacular, with few metaphors and nothing young boys might call flowery. It is quite effective in conveying DiMaggio's seemingly uncomplicated, even-tempered nature. In Chapter 2, the language is particularly appropriate for conveying the story of DiMaggio's earliest years when he was just another boy growing up in a big, poor, Italian family. Baseball was his only game because since he did not like to work fishing, he had to occupy his time somehow, playing on no "fancy cut out diamonds, with green grass and all the trimmings." He and his chums commandeered in time-honored boys' fashion an old lot used to park milk wagons (when they were still drawn by horses, thus plunging the reader back to a much earlier, seemingly simpler world), with rocks for bases, an oar for a bat, and a ball held together by tape. Most of the boys played without gloves because they were too poor. In this world a young boy might very well be discovered while peering through a knothole.

Fans and fiction readers alike enjoy stories about lowly beginnings, but what most want more is the march toward success together with demonstrations of greatness. DiMaggio begins satisfying this craving in Chapter 3, "With the Seals." But his story of success here and elsewhere in the book is never an unalloyed tale of triumph, for success (what kids often desire from narratives of heroes is a pornography of pure success they would probably soon be surfeited with) extended and unabated is traditionally a prelude to disaster: it is suspect. DiMaggio uses success to introduce three themes. First, he insists that his skill at least in "hitting is a God-Given gift," not an ability that can be acquired by diligent practice. He respects techniques that can add to a player's ability, and offers a few toward the conclusion of his story, but he states flatly that he knows he is a professional "because at the age of 18 I had a natural gift for hitting and for no other reason whatsoever." Thus at once he advances his greatness, and disclaims credit for it.

An example of his great hitting—the 61-game streak for the Seals— presents another lesson that success taught him, "the tremendous factor team spirit is in baseball." Throughout the book the teams he played for are seen as families to which he belonged, peopled with parental figures (coaches) and siblings (fellow-players). The Yankees were so good in 1938 because they "were happy about playing together. Everybody was interested in the welfare of everybody else." What pleased him most his rookie years "was the rapidity with which I had been accepted as one of the family." For DiMaggio "the Yankees were more than just a bunch of stars. They were a team in all that the term implies." The celebration the team gives him for hitting 56 straight was "the greatest thrill I've ever had in baseball. . . . It's nice to know that the guys you work for think you're a regular guy, too." Though outside reports indicate that friction existed on Yankee teams from time to time throughout DiMaggio's career, and that sometimes he was less than a popular figure with all his teammates (when he held out in 1938, for example, and again when he retreated into himself during slumps in the 1950s), this cozy, boy's view of familial camaraderie remains constant in the autobiography.

Finally, in Chapter 3, the reader learns DiMaggio's successes are often attended by bad luck particularly in the form of painful injuries. Though much of DiMaggio's life and career is omitted from the book the major injuries are detailed in expressive language. The pain of the knee injury he received in 1934 "was terrific, like a whole set of aching teeth in my knee." It sounded like "four sharp cracks" and made him fall "as though I had been shot." In supplying information about his injuries DiMaggio was recording part of his history but also adhering to the image of the wounded hero he possessed even prior to his comebacks from injury in the late 1940s. He conformed to the model of the victorious comeback hero that people have traditionally admired, but also supplied a special attractiveness to young American boys growing up the years he played, who themselves often found masochistic delight in their play portraying soldiers, cowboys, or Indians who were invariably and often spectacularly wounded in play. Rare was the boy who did not possess a repertoire of dying gestures or who did not relish staggering crazily from a bullet slug in the gut that did not quite prevent him from performing some disabled act of valor. Socialized to learn to accept and even appreciate pain, boys were later expected to wage games or fight wars wounded, and DiMaggio was the sort of maimed star who would appeal to their sense that men played with pain.

DiMaggio, however, is no warrior manqué in *Lucky to Be a Yankee*. Clearly he likes to win and plays hard to achieve that goal, but in no way does he foreshadow the winning-is-everything, viciously competitive spirit of Vince Lombardi. There is rather something courtly in his attitude toward competing—the good player does his best, but performs with a gracious and even noble spirit. He reports that in the last days of the 1935 season with the Seals, when he is fighting for the batting leadership with Ox Eckhardt, the official scorer gave him a hit on a ball that fell before a stumbling center fielder who otherwise would have caught it. "I didn't want any base hits of that type" he says and went to the official scorer after the game "to demand that he change the hit to an error." Later, with the Yankees, he states his admiration for Joe McCarthy emphasizing that "he stresses dignity." Describing Ernie Lombardi's "snooze" in the 1939 World Series, he courteously explains "In justice to Lombardi . . . I believe he was momentarily stunned when Keller ran into him." His behavior as he describes it is nearly always gentlemanly. He describes his confrontation with Whitlow Wyatt in the 1941 World Series as the result of communications garbled in "the heat and tension of the game." Wyatt and he "never got within twenty paces of each other" during the incident, and afterwards he says "there were, of course, no hard feelings. Wyatt came over to our dressing room after the game to congratulate us" and even wished the

Yankees a pleasant winter. He is one of the "clean bunch of fellows and all grand sports" with which DiMaggio peoples his major leagues.

Launched into the great world of the "Big Apple" in Chapter 4, DiMaggio continues his growth as he is able to see "America for the first time." He finds happy camaraderie among the Yankees and is even "treated . . . swell" by his "friends" the sportswriters. There is in fact no one in the entire book who is sharply criticized, no antagonisms that are rehashed. He gives the impression that baseball is inhabited by exceptionally pleasant and helpful people, all of whom respect each other. "That First Season" described in Chapter 5 becomes after his burned foot heals a season of triumph culminating in a World Series victory, only the first of many for one of the game's great winners. He concludes this episode of victory over adversity with the happy recollection that his mother watched him and the Yankees win and became "hysterical with joy." Her own social progress (in part advanced by his) is symbolized by the thrilling surprise she felt seeing the Statue of Liberty for the second time in 34 years—the first being when she had entered the country a poor immigrant from Palermo. The episode of 1936 ends with DiMaggio heading on the train back to his home in San Francisco, a trip he will almost invariably make in the following years after riotous New York wins. He "had had a good season, a group of wonderful fellows as teammates," and lots of stories to tell the old gang. Like a good fabulist, he does not have to underscore his point here: the big city star was still one of the boys back at his old home, where he still belonged. Winning had not gone to his head.

Nor would it in 1937 with the "happy" Yankees, a team with great players but "no big shots in the disparaging sense of the term." The "whammie" on him brings a sore arm and tonsillitis and once more prevents him from playing opening day, but once he breaks into the lineup all is well again. With new stars such as Tommy Henrich and old reliables like Lefy Gomez and Red Ruffing, the Yankees win their league by thirteen games and DiMaggio for a brief time challenged Babe Ruth's home run record. The Giants fall again, in five games, in the World Series and after "a great season" all DiMaggio "wanted was to get home and rest." He had again experienced all a kid could hope for: some adversity and pain to triumph over, the friendship of a good and happy crew, enough stardom and victory to satisfy the most gluttonous success seeker, and at the end of the long delightful tiring day, sweet home to return to from the great world beyond.

Home meant family and in *Lucky to Be a Yankee* DiMaggio often recollects with pleasure his mother, father, sisters, and particularly his brothers, while recounting his progress toward greatness. Rosalie and Giuseppe are not portrayed in full detail, but they are always mentioned warmly throughout the text. Joe's desire not to fish, and his decision to quit school are not dramatized with nearly the schmaltzy intensity that other authors, such as Gene Schoor, employ to dramatize these events. A paragraph in the prewar version stating that though his father finally believed that fishing made him sick he concluded his son "was a kid who never would amount to anything, anyway," was dropped from the later 1949 and 1951 editions. In another paragraph Joe says he was not "particularly happy during my two years at Galileo High, through no fault of the school" (this is a no-blame book) but that if he could live the years over again (are you listening boys and girls?) he'd have stuck with school longer, thus proving his "mother's judgment on the subject of education was correct"—she wanted him to continue—"as it was in most all other matters." When, late in the book DiMaggio travels "Along Memory Lane," over a page is devoted to his pop, a "Santa Claus" who proudly prepared meals for special vistors to the DiMaggio restaurant in San Francisco, and avidly scanned the newspaper box scores each morning during baseball season to see how his three sons performed.

DiMaggio's brothers Vincent and Dominic complete the picture of close family unity the book very comfortingly provides. Vince's role in preparing the way for Joe's decision to make baseball his career is suggested though not fully developed. DiMaggio recalls thinking as a teen-ager that since "Vince was making good in a big way" and could "get dough for playing ball," he could too. And it is while trying to see Vince through the knothole in the Seals's fence that Joe is so magically plucked from sandlot ball by Spike Hennessy. In DiMaggio's version, incidentally, no sign of strong parental resistance to his decision to become a professional appears. As DiMaggio relates his own story, from time to time he will note the added pleasure he received knowing his brothers were also doing well in baseball, and is open in his continuing admiration for the skills of both; Dom, he thinks, is the "best defensive outfielder I've ever seen." Joe seems totally without jealousy when he writes that "Pop's pride and joy was Dom, the smallest and youngest of us." So the book very definitely locates DiMaggio in his parents' family even years after he had established for a time his own family of wife and child. The book is dedicated "to little Joe" and he tells one anecdote about his wife Dorothy helping him break a slump. The 1951 version however cuts a reference to "Dorothy . . . the best catch I ever made in my life" which first appeared in the original text and was retained in 1949. DiMaggio's marriage is only referred to fleetingly and his mother and father occupy his thoughts and his life more than his wife, which seems appropriate for the boy's world the book presents. In this almost shadowless world there is no room for DiMaggio's divorce or his father's death, which are both unmentioned though teammate Lou Gehrig's passing is mourned.

Rich in anecdotes about the background to great events in DiMaggio's playing career and very earnest in the traditional morality it urges implicitly or explicitly throughout its narrative, but thin in developing any of the personal or professional conflicts that might have vexed him, much of *Lucky to Be a Yankee* is devoted to stories about other players. Many of the photographs show not DiMaggio but star performers such as Tris Speaker, Babe Ruth, and Ty Cobb, older greats in whose company their pictures here suggest DiMaggio belongs. Dom DiMaggio is also depicted, as is the 1937 Yankee team and Red Ruffing. Another photograph recaptures thirteen members of the DiMaggio clan when Joe played for San Francisco and Vince for Hollywood in 1933. As a group, the pictures demonstrate DiMaggio's skills, link him to the tradition of older stars, root him in his family, and closely identify him with all the good fellows he played with, particularly with the Yankees he contributed so much to as a team player.

One chapter tells about the noble Lou Gehrig, and another concerns "The Gay Cabellero" Lefty Gomez. These sequences balance each other and provide human perspectives generally lacking in DiMaggio's self-related narrative. The passage on Gehrig is somber in portraying his gradual physical deterioration and death in what should have been his prime. Gomez is Gehrig's and DiMaggio's antithesis, "El Goofo," possessing all the comic sense and color DiMaggio lacked. The chapter "All Stars Aren't Yankees" tells pleasant anecdotes about fine fellows like Bob Feller, Ted Williams, and Jimmy Foxx. Career shadows such as Foxx's drinking problem are naturally not mentioned.

The sections of *Lucky to Be a Yankee* written after its original publication continue the themes of the earlier version. DiMaggio is still a team player for whom "hits can't mean much to a ball player unless they mean a lot to his ball club." He is still proud about his family (including son Joe) and after a victorious season heads for his San Francisco home again. The pain of playing increases but his comeback (including the famous one in 1949) are more triumphant. There are still no bad guys in the game, and what in reality was his barely stifled rage at being taken from the lineup by Casey Stengel is laundered into "Stengel asked me to take a little rest." The fans are still swell and not just the Yankee fans; at the end of the season when he plays in Boston not feeling his best, the Boston fans cheer him with an affection that particularly delights him. The book becomes more reflective, has less to say about spectacular exploits and more to tell about enduring wounds. A major controversy described in the prewar edition was his holdout in 1938, an episode which clearly bothered him for he discussed it twice. In the later edition he mentions his 1949 flap with the press who had been hounding him to learn the extent of his injury. Both disputes are offered in highly sanitized versions that ignore the bitterness Dimaggio originally felt for management and the press. Both pre- and post-war editions of his autobiography smooth some rough edges from DiMaggio's career. The chapters added concerning the 1949-50 seasons contain their moments of joyful triumph, particularly the new Chapter 2 called "Good to the Last Drop" which tells of 1949; but more than the previous segments they speak of an aging hero of diminished abilities who knows he "would be foolish not to admit that I was just about stepping off the hill and going down the incline," who "was a young fellow once upon a time" that "somebody had to move over on the bench to make room for." None of the new material is placed at the end of the book however. It is all added to its first half, so that a kid or fan wanting immersion in a kid's world could read *after* he had learned about Joe in the 1950 season about his "hitting in 56 straight" in 1941 and about all the other good guys like Gehrig and Gomez. The reader of later editions would find out that Joe McCarthy's career with the Yankees ended in 1946. The reader would not be told that McCarthy was apparently drinking too much and that his departure was accompanied by behind the scenes turbulence among Yankee management that continued several seasons and found its public expression in the swirl of managers the team experienced before management settled on Casey Stengel. The reader would learn no more about DiMaggio's own war years in the later editions than the scant few references provided originally. They were for DiMaggio drab years apparently of unheroic events. Along with bad things like divorces and his father's death, such news was banished or hidden in DiMaggio's public recollections.

In *Lucky to Be a Yankee*, DiMaggio like Huckleberry Finn's Mark Twain, told the truth mainly, but of an entirely different kind of world from the rapacious and egocentric land Twain described. DiMaggio's world is one of great personal achievement won through natural and inimitable gifts, a world of good parents and children, of families who stay together, where nice guys finish first—and second and third and fourth. DiMaggio describes himself in as low-key fashion as possible, considering the nature of his career. He stresses that he is a decent fellow who behaves decently among other decent fellows, who loves his mother and father, who does not give up even when hurt, who plays for team and not for self. He is very convincing in his autobiography, and seems a likeable fellow worthy of emulation. He understates his greatness while in the act of portraying it, and manifests a likable humility that becomes ingrained as one of his major characteristics as a victorious hero.

In his fine book *The American Dream and the National Game,* Leverett Smith estimates that DiMaggio's autobiography was intended for an audience of fourteen-year-olds. In fact there is little in the book that identifies it particularly as written for juveniles when one takes into account that its information and delivery are similar to what had been written about DiMaggio on sports pages and in national magazines, for a decade previous to its publication. Its tunnel vision focusing upon certain of DiMaggio's baseball exploits and highly selected aspects of his private life presents nothing strikingly different though the book is far more detailed than any prior single item had been. Its persistently moral tone also found its counterpart in earlier newspaper and periodical literature. DiMaggio's (or

Meany's) language and his attitudes toward baseball and his life in it would not have made adult readers of sports literature feel they were intruding upon a child's book. DiMaggio's autobiography may have presaged later texts intended and marketed strictly for juveniles, but it was not one of them.

A few comic book versions of DiMaggio's life offer better models for stories intended strictly for young audiences. A brief sequence about DiMaggio written at the peak of the first half of his career, before he entered military service, appeared as part of a longer "authorized story of the UNBEATABLE YANKS" appearing in the July, 1942, issue of *Trail Blazers* comic. This issue also featured stories on three other successful entertainment figures, the nineteenth century magician Robert Houdin, announcer (then for the Brooklyn Dodgers) Red Barber, and radio star Fred Allen. The portion featuring DiMaggio is only five panels long and the drawings of him do not in the least resemble him: most of the players drawn in the article look alike. In one panel a scout (so labeled) looks interested in DiMaggio but his sight line leads directly to DiMaggio's knee and the scout thinks "Great hitter but I'm afraid of his leg." In the next panel a large, seated figure with "Yankees" written across his chest picks up a toy sized doll marked "DiMaggio" and grins broadly at it. Captions note that the Yankees took a chance and bought DiMaggio for five players and $25,000 which they did not pay until the end of his last minor league season, which the comic states is 1936, and adds that the Yankees won their gamble. The third panel shows DiMaggio jumping up and down like a spoiled brat, yelling for $25,000. A caption adds he "is quieter now." The fourth panel shows his restaurant, very crudely drawn, and says he operates it in San Francisco though he "remained in New York the past winter." The largest panel shows DiMaggio completing his swing and dominates half the one-page sequence. DiMaggio is but one of several Yankee players depicted in what is essentially a story in praise of the tightly organized, ostensibly well-paying and eminently successful Yankee organization. Lou Gehrig receives more space and is depicted more positively and more nobly. The most distinctive characteristics of the section on DiMaggio are the poorness of its drawing and the lack of unity in its unheroic presentation of him.

A later story about DiMaggio appearing in the May, 1948, issue of *True Comics* is far longer and incorporates more aspects of the DiMaggio myth as it existed at that time. "The Story of Joe DiMaggio, America's Greatest Baseball Player" is the comic book's lead item. Its cover depicts a recognizable Jolter blasting a home run, to judge from the facial expressions of the catcher, umpire, and fans who form the illustration's background. The story draws its information about "The Yankee Clipper" from some of the earlier magazine articles but mainly from *Lucky to Be a Yankee*. It begins incorrectly, however, in Martinez, California, where Joe's father bawls out his callow son for playing baseball, for "wearing out shoes and pants when you should be helping me fish,'' and accuses him of being "lazy." "A few months later" when Joe announces at the family dinner table that he has a job selling newspapers, his father derisively says that is just the job for him: "All you've got to do is stand and yell." Vince suggests he try out with the Seals, but Joe—eating spaghetti—claims he is "not good enough." Found outside the knothole looking in at the Seals, he is hired by them and "learned there was more to baseball than just hitting the ball": a picture shows him throwing far beyond the first baseman's reach. The ensuing pages essentially follow DiMaggio's story as he presented it in his autobiography, depicting his 61-game Seals streak (including the praise Tom Sheehan gave him for hitting his best pitch); his knee injury and subsequent purchase by the Yankees; the friendly welcome given him by his new teammates; his 1936 preseason ankle injury; his unpopular 1938 holdout; his batting streak when brother Dom supposedly robbed him of a hit; and the party his teammates gave him for hitting in 56 consecutive games. An error in the story whose source was not DiMaggio's book is the statement that he played his first major league game in May, 1935. *True* adds a patriotic panel not based upon DiMaggio's autobiography showing DiMaggio saluting Joe McCarthy and saying "I've come to say good-bye. Uncle Sam needs me," to which McCarthy stoutly replies, "Fight to win like you always did on the diamond, Joe." DiMaggio spared his readers such false heroics. The caption to a final picture of Joe catching a fly, running out a hit, and gripping a bat, briefly relates his career since the war, his return "to even greater heights" in 1947 (it does not mention the relatively unsuccessful 1946 season) and his third Most Valuable Player award.

Even more than *Lucky to Be a Yankee* had, *True Comics* presents DiMaggio in a magical, self-enclosed world in which his rise to success seems even more like a fairy tale. The story's first words misrepresent fact but place DiMaggio in a simple, ethical context young readers could identify with. He is "the boy who wanted to sell newspapers," and thus a rightminded young lad. The very next panel however shows him not on the street corner holding a newspaper but standing at bat while his father clenches his fist and shouts at him that he should be helping him fish. In the next panel the father is dangerously close to DiMaggio with both fists upraised almost as though he were going to pound his skinny son on the chest. The father's body is drawn in an aggressive posture to emphasize his anger, while DiMaggio stands slack and slump-shouldered as few good batters but many a teen-aged boy did. Unlike his picture on the magazine's cover he does not look like DiMaggio as he ages through the succeeding panels. This results from poor art work more than conscious editorial design, but also perhaps enabled the story's readers to more easily place themselves in his position.

"A few months later" DiMaggio is shown in his family's dining room together with Vince, Dom, and Papa DiMaggio. Joe's mother is absent, and in the drastically restricted comic book depiction of his life only one woman from his personal life appears, the sister he visits when he injures his leg ligaments. Joe enters (to his left a large crucifix hangs on the wall: his household is religious, a point made and then not underscored further) and announces he has a job selling papers. His father uses this as an opportunity to insult him for his uselessness. Brother Vince rescues him by saying "Stop teasing him, Pop," and suggests that since he has a job with the Seals, Joe should try out too. The story is only four panels long at this point and while the first two panels showed Joe playing baseball the game was among kids and highly informal so in terms of the sequence of events the magazine has offered, Vince's suggestion is highly unrealistic. If the story is viewed as a fantasy children would enjoy placing themselves in (the mean, unbelieving father, the good, indolent son who really does have special talents) the narrative's omission of background makes sense; like the artwork itself, only the few salient surface details are illustrated. Event is uncontaminated by preparation just as panel drawings contain only essential details. Caught looking through the Seals's knothole, Joe is whisked to an office, told by an un-named man that his play had been observed, and marched toward the dugout saying "what a break!"

Almost five pages of panels illustrate Joe's childhood life and his play with the Seals. On the team he is drawn still as a spindly youth, bodiless under his unattractive uniform. Slightly over three pages show him performing with the Yankees at which time his body becomes bigger and stronger. Many an adolescent fan could have dreamed of achieving similar progress, of disproving ominous parental predictions, of overcoming awkwardness and the occasional bad luck that finally seemed the only force capable of hindering DiMaggio from becoming a star.

The comic books offered a greatly compressed and simplified view of DiMaggio and his life, by design a two-dimensional reduction of his story. In the *Trial Blazers* narrative he is shown as a one-time crybaby who somehow learns not to complain and thereby to fit in better with his team and win even greater financial rewards. The penultimate panel shows him yelping for more money, but then explains that he no longer behaves in this fashion, while the final panel depicts his restaurant. The implication is that not complaining is profitable. In his autobiography, DiMaggio takes almost five pages to discuss the holdout issue and finally, grudgingly concludes that since "the fan pays the freight. . . . He has just as much right to boo as he has to cheer. . . . I took it, but I didn't like it." The point is not that the comic books lack space to discuss nuances of interpretation but that the nuances are not desired in their formula. In the *True Comics* story, DiMaggio's apprenticeship years on the San Francisco sandlots are not illustrated because while his discovery is significant his preparation is not, because young readers are interested in becoming stars but not really in the training stardom usually demands, and because after all, how does one prepare to become Joe DiMaggio? The hero's life is miraculous.

Even more stripped down in iconographic content are the baseball cards on which DiMaggio has appeared. Some of these are valuable to collectors not so much because of DiMaggio's talent or popularity, but because of their relative rarity. The 1939 "Play Ball" card is fairly expensive, bringing a price of about $125.00 in the early 1980s. Issued by GUM, Inc., the series originally included about 250 "leading baseball players." DiMaggio's photograph is not complimentary, showing a thin-faced, buck-toothed star whom the text nonetheless calls "the greatest outfielder in baseball today." Among DiMaggio's listed accomplishments are his .398 batting average for San Francisco in 1935, his American League home run championship in 1937 and the fact that he was the leading vote getter in the 1938 All-Star game. His hitting is emphasized. His present-day and very inexpensive "SUPERSTAR" card reveals him as an older player, fuller faced, studying the hitter at bat while kneeling on deck. The card's point of view identifies him as a past hero, "The Yankee Clipper . . . one of the greatest outfielders of all time. Voted the Greatest Living Ball Player in 1969." Seen as a giant among stars, "he held baseball's vastest turf, Yankee Stadium's centerfield, in the palm of his hand during his years with the Yankees." His .398 and .346 rookie year batting averages are supplied, and the card adds that "his lifetime average .325 was despite injuries and time out for the service during the war." Here DiMaggio is seen from a distance as larger than life and yet, though the card's inscription is considerably shorter than the "Play Ball" printed message, more human: reference to his injuries and service years adds some depth to his portrayal which in the "Play Ball" card was primarily a statistical outline. The "SUPERSTAR" card also shows how time smooths out unwanted edges in the picture of heroes, claiming "he was an automatic Hall of Famer in 1955" while glossing over his failure to achieve appointment in 1953 and 1954, the first two years he was eligible. Cards and comic books, while offering interesting partial portraits of DiMaggio at different stages of his career, and circulated widely, could only present highly selected angles of his image. After the war years, lengthier recitals of his accomplishments proliferated in articles and books.

Baseball for Everyone (1948) was intended for children and teen-age boys (the book shows no awareness that girls might like to play baseball too), and was supposedly written by DiMaggio, though he acknowledges in the book's introduction the "cooperation" of Tom Meany and Marion Simon. Some of the information the book contains seems to stem directly from DiMaggio's experiences, though again, the shaping and some of the detail was doubtless provided by Meany and Simon and some data possibly originated with the "many authorities" the book's dust jacket blurb claims that "DiMaggio consulted." Some of the writing is rather clinical and surely was not articulated by DiMaggio: "A National Recreation Association survey shows that in 1946, the most recent year for which figures are available, 1,153 cities reported the operation of 4,323 municipal baseball diamonds." Yet even stray advertisements today still maintain the pretense that the book is DiMaggio's.

The book offers sound enough but not startling advice: "The leg on which the slide is made must be relaxed"; "Hold the bat loosely and as the pitcher delivers get the bat parallel to the ground." Sometimes the advice is not so much technical as admonitory. "If a boy sincerely believes that he has a chance to become a professional ballplayer, he should not haggle too much about a bonus." Though DiMaggio admits he had been a holdout, he exculpates himself by declaring his case is different because he was a professional and already a regular, and the youngster would just be trying to get his foot in the door (ignoring that he haggled with the Seals over a percentage of his sale price to the Yankees that he felt entitled to). Generally he shows good sense in his attitudes towards children's sports. He feels that the regular diamond, for example, is too big for kids to play on, straining their small, undeveloped arms and teaching them bad habits. The catcher might learn (like Harry Dunning of the 1938 and 1939 New York Giants against whom he played in the World Series) to take an extra step throwing to second base.

Some of the book's charm resides in the stray information DiMaggio provides his young audience about his own early years when, he admits ruefully, he was called a "Dead Pan." He was about ten when he first started playing, he says, and when he was a boy he and his friends would "buy spikes in a sporting goods store and have the neighborhood cobbler attach them to a pair of ordinary street shoes." Emphasizing neither his Italian nor his large family background, he uses his own experience sometimes in a way that would have been reassuring to young boys hungry for encouraging words in their dreams of greatness. He quotes Joe McCarthy who said if a player has the skill plus the determination, "he'll make the majors, no matter what the odds may be." Sweet music to boys who bounced balls off stoops, shagged flies with their friends, took endless turns at bat and swung hard and never missed by much, really. Generally, the book is as low-key as DiMaggio himself seemed, at worst harmless and at best offering some sound instruction emphasizing playing well rather than winning at any cost. Today, it seems old-fashioned. Several years after its American publication it was translated into Italian as *Baseball* (undated but probably 1952) even though as its preface states (in Italian) that "to speak of baseball to an Italian is like speaking of soccer to an American."[1] DiMaggio is called "one of the greatest baseball players (he has just retired from 'active service') and still retains his popularity—is probably the most popular player in the United States."

Jack Sher's lengthy article in the September, 1949, *Sport* is clearly an adult view of DiMaggio as a great but aging player whose surface image is misleading. "DiMag: The Man Behind the Poker Face" is not so much an exposé as it is an attempt to look hard at the reality of DiMaggio's life. The essay concludes not by debunking DiMaggio's heroic attainments but by placing them in the context of a very human existence containing real shadows that do not disappear as easily as the setbacks in comic book drawings.

Sher knew DiMaggio and many of his Broadway friends directly, but his view of him seems relatively objective and not the standard, glorified view many of the early articles presented. Either Sher wrote naturally with greater sophistication than the earlier journalists who had told DiMaggio's story or he was simply participating in a newer kind of sports journalism that practiced greater realism in its portrayals of sports heroes. Much of his information seems to come directly from DiMaggio's autobiography which he says he has read, especially details relating to DiMaggio's childhood and first years as a professional. So he once more relates that Joe came from a poor but good immigrant family, that he was discovered looking through the knothole, that Tom Sheehan stopped in the game he was pitching against the Seals to congratulate DiMaggio on hitting his best pitch. Sometimes Sher personalizes his, by then, generally available information by adding that he reported it as it was presented in DiMaggio's autobiography and "as he told it to me." Sometimes he adds interesting details to the known account, noting that DiMaggio remembered his family's poverty in particular terms of not having enough money to see the film *All Quiet on the Western Front*. Sher is openly DiMaggio's advocate but he is aware also that the best of DiMaggio's career was over and that DiMaggio was entering a new stage in life for him, that he was making what pop sociologists would later term a "passage."

Sher's picture of DiMaggio in 1949 is a portrait of a hero but. . . . There is an undercurrent of uneasiness about DiMaggio's stardom in the article. Sher calls him "the most beautiful performer of our era," yet seems bothered that "he has never been glorified to the degree of other diamond greats," a remark that seems strange in retrospect. For Sher, DiMaggio's problem is that he is no longer the almost constantly gifted player he once seemed. He is aging. The injuries that he endured and came back from, were coming back upon him. He was at that moment in his career when an athlete "realizes that he is no longer able to do, wholly and completely, the things that have set him apart and above all other competitors." He sees DiMaggio as a success story, relating that when he was a Seals rookie and asked for a quote by a newspaperman, he did not know what a quote was: now, in Toots Shor's words, everyone knew "the kid *attained* class." But when Sher ranks DiMaggio with the very greatest players such as Ty Cobb, he justifies his rating by claiming "no ball player can be completely judged by what is found in the record books," a rationale supporters of DiMaggio tended to offer after his post-war career but not often advanced during his first seven years in the majors. Sher offers DiMaggio's injuries and wartime hiatus as reasons for the statistical decline.

Sher recognizes that DiMaggio has mellowed since his rookie days. He "has a gentle, warm quality that men who are wholly masculine always have." He no longer is characterized as a comic book reader, for Sher says he reads authors such as C. S. Forester and according to DiMaggio himself "books that make a comment on our times, such as *The Naked and the Dead*" and Roger Butterfield's *The American Past*, a good pictorial history of the United States. But beneath his poker face DiMaggio the great team player was "an incredibly lonely man." This is a new way of viewing DiMaggio who, while perceived as a loner previously, was not usually depicted as lonely. "When he's not playing baseball" Sher says, "the roof seems to have fallen in." Sher adds to the image of DiMaggio the idea that outside his now waning life in baseball, there existed an emptiness in his life. This is a commonplace in hero's narratives (Tennyson's "Ulysses" languishing at home after wondrous wandering, or Grant without a Civil War, even when President). Echoes of this theme would be heard later particularly in the accounts of DiMaggio's after life by Gene Schoor, Maury Allen, and Gay Talese. Sher wrote toward the end of DiMaggio's career but while he was still active, so he had fresh in his mind pictures of the star's sensational 1949 achievements even while observing how his body was giving out. He concludes that DiMaggio was still "the guy who made the hard ones look easy," but his article proves he knew soon the easy ones would be hard—and that would be difficult for DiMaggio's fans, harder still for DiMaggio, now a hero with limited horizons.

Dan Daniel's very long article—monograph really—prefacing the 1950 *Sporting News* baseball annual, is a much breezier but still very good journalistic introduction to DiMaggio's life lacking Sher's thoughtfulness but still providing one of the most sensible overviews of DiMaggio's career by a writer who knew and admired him but did not view him with awe or sentimentality. Daniel was a prototype pre-World War II sportswriter, a much respected working journalist at his best writing for the sports pages with enough wit and accuracy to make his daily reports enjoyable as well as informative. He had no pretensions to greatness as a writer, and his style is not as facile as Meany's, but neither is it intrusive. Once his jaunty sportswriter's idiom is accepted (sportswriters are "aces," DiMaggio is "The Jolter," "Giuseppe," "Josephus," home runs are round trippers and four baggers that are belted, swatted, and crashed) he can be read with a simple pleasure if not delight. Where he is wrong, he is clearly in the wrong, and usually because his good heart would not permit him to be accurate, for example when he links Ruth, Gehrig, and DiMaggio together as "humble." Ruth certainly was not. Daniel had the advantage of knowing DiMaggio over the years, of having DiMaggio's confidence in him as a fair man and one of the sportsmen along Broadway whose company Joe so greatly enjoyed. He was a good newsman who seems to have checked what facts he could without performing like a professional researcher.

Daniel's greatest success in "Joe DiMaggio" (subtitled "My Friend—The Yankee Clipper)" is to present a sensible view of DiMaggio, his family, early years, and status with the Yankees. For example he is the first journalist, certainly in a book or periodical, to write of Giuseppe DiMaggio Sr.'s war record with the Italian Army in Abyssinia. He is reasonable about home conflicts, saying that Joe's father feared the boy would be lazy (common among parents) and that Joe's seeming diffidence hid his wait to find something he really wanted to do. Concerning Joe's start in professional baseball, Daniel is similarly sensible. He says "Spike Hennessy, who scouted the sandlots for Owner Charley Graham's San Francisco Seals of the Coast League, had known and helped Vince DiMaggio. After seeing Joe in a few sandlot games, Spike took him to the boss and eventually wangled him into a workout with the Seals." This may not make great myth, but it possess authenticity. He is however aware of the mythic dimensions of DiMaggio's story, pointedly remarking that he embodied "The Great American Success Story," but his awareness is without pomp or pretense. Though more articulate than DiMaggio, he probably perceived the world in much the same way, without heroic vision but with the eyes of somebody real in ordinary society. He does not make DiMaggio into something he is not, nor present baseball as a sacred game. He reports on the squabbles preceding Joe McCarthy's departure in 1946. His appraisal of DiMaggio is unsentimental. His language lacks aesthetic grace, but it does not bloat DiMaggio's image through straining for higher effects. His statement explaining what the American dream represented in DiMaggio's life in 1936 is in its way perfect: "he was to get aboard the gravy train at last, to taste the glory and acclaim that America lavishes so bountifully on its sports heroes." Beyond providing fresh, first-hand, information about DiMaggio's family background and his professional life, Daniel's greatest accomplishment is to present DiMaggio as a great player and good person but not as a national legend, nor as a tragic hero. It is a limited view by a limited writer, one of the last of DiMaggio's older contemporaries to write at length about him from the vantage point of having seen him closely and off the pedestal. It is a refreshing, informative, if circumscribed view.

The pictures accompanying Daniel's article are also well chosen, and show DiMaggio in a variety of situations; swinging for big hits; joking with fellow servicemen; his "cool, steady gaze, which puts fear into the hearts of opposing moundsmen"; with Col. Ruppert; with his family in San Francisco (the old *Life* photo); jubilantly showing his chest muscles in 1936; eating his wedding cake; signing autographs; dancing with a barely dressed "night club" performer in Mexico City. Even his famous bad heel is presented in X-ray and under bandages. The photographs, like the text, make DiMaggio real, like snapshots from a family album.

In the same year that Daniel's piece appeared (1950), Gene Schoor published the first of his books on DiMaggio, an account that traverses much of the familiar territory Daniel also recorded, but written in a more excited style and with a greater sense of inspirational glee than Daniel was able or cared to project. The work is based partly upon the essential facts of DiMaggio's life as they were recorded in his autobiography, and upon research in older articles that is difficult to follow precisely, because like Daniel, Schoor credits no secondary sources. Sometimes Schoor's unquestioning acceptance of DiMaggio's book perpetuates errors while seeming to corroborate fact. He tells how Dom DiMaggio robbed Joe of a hit just before he broke Keeler's consecutive hit record, repeating Joe's (or writer Tom Meany's) mistake. Sometimes Schoor's attributions are slightly misleading. When in Schoor's book DiMaggio relates the story of the celebration the Yankee players threw for him after his 56-game streak was over, Schoor introduces the narrative with "As Joe tells it," and then places most of DiMaggio's phrases in quotation marks. In Schoor's text it looks as though DiMaggio had related this to Schoor, but what Schoor appears to have done is modify simply and silently DiMaggio's story as it appeared in the autobiography. The practice, which Schoor apparently employed in later books on DiMaggio, would not have bothered his readers though it provides some problems for the historian.

Schoor's talent, not yet fully developed here, was his conscious sensitivity to the fact that in writing about DiMaggio he was dealing with a legend, so that even in this basic and brief study (not much more than an introduction to a collection of photographs) he begins to register the dimensions of DiMaggio's myth. Schoor begins a process he will develop more fully in his subsequent treatments of DiMaggio's life: he takes the various elements and episodes in DiMaggio's life that proved most popularly appealing to his public, and focuses consistently and in increasingly dramatic detail upon them. In Schoor's works, DiMaggio comes more and more to resemble the image that large numbers of his fans thought him or wanted him to be. And—not so much here but in his two other longer books on DiMaggio—he dramatizes that image, recording scenes showing that image in action. The more Schoor writes about DiMaggio, the more his life resembles a motion picture about an archetypal popular hero, what used to be called a "biopic."

Schoor accurately spots nearly all the themes running through DiMaggio's life story as it has become generally (if sometimes unrealistically) known. In his retelling he may sentimentalize and sensationalize the themes somewhat—fairly enough the title *The Thrilling Story of Joe DiMaggio* announces that his is not to be a subtle, academic analysis—and writes with an appropriately campy flair. Others might state that boys in America dreamed of playing baseball, but Schoor says "There's something about the horsehide-covered ball that holds the promise of glory for every American kid, and it is men like Joe DiMaggio who keep that promise alive." On DiMaggio's ability to play with pain he writes, "It was that same fighting spirit which pulled him out of the hospital, following a seige of that debilitating virus pneumonia, [and] get out on the field for the last eleven games of a torrid season to beat out the Red sox for the League flag. The flesh was weak and the legs were wobbly, but that will to win which spells Joe DiMaggio sent the Yankees" to the World Series. DiMaggio's reaction to these events? " 'I'm lucky to be a Yankee,' says the Clipper in his humble manner."

The interesting photographs which Schoor's text introduces document the portrayal of DiMaggio as a star performer who is also an extremely nice and almost saintly person: Joe's mom "fondly looks at a picture of her son as she tunes in the ball game"; "The kids of the National Children's Cardiac Home in Miami present Joe with a scroll"; "Little Joe sits on the bat rack and takes in the scene at Yankee batting practice"; Joe with his family leaving for the Yankee camp in 1936; with Ty Cobb after a World Series; in the batting cage—"Ask a big leaguer how he does it and the Clipper will tell you it's work, work, and more work"; with Jim Braddock and Joe Louis; "S/Sgt. DiMaggio is the typical G.I. Joe, as he disembarks from a Navy transport at Hawaii"; "America's top star always lends a hand in the typical American Way. DiMag takes time out to chat with a polio victim in Jersey City's Medical Center after launching Sister Kenny Polio Fund Drive"; giving batting tips to a one-armed boy; with Joe Louis and Gene Schoor on the radio.

Schoor invents nothing new in his verbal and visual picture of DiMaggio, but he assembled most of the features of DiMaggio's image that were popular with the American audience, and refines the shape of the image to project DiMaggio's heroic dimensions more clearly. A few of his details may be wrong or misleading—for example he states DiMaggio was born November 29, 1914 (not November 25)—but there is no doubt that beginning with this *Thrilling Story*, he was presenting a clear and compelling reflection of what DiMaggio had come to mean to America. Most writers portrayed DiMaggio as a nice guy, but like a combination public relations director and cheerleader, Schoor provided touching documentation.

"He's Hero No. 1 to all the kids in New York, from Pelham Bay to the Bowery. He's Hero No. 1 for kids all over the country. They elected him Honorary Mayor of Mending Heart, Florida, the National Children's Cardiac Home. . . . if anyone deserves a place in the hearts of the kids of the country, it's Joe." Schoor's account is an enthusiastic hagiography. His DiMaggio sells papers to help the family, endures paternal resistance to play baseball, overcomes frequent injuries, plays always for the good of the team, practices hard, performs with "flawless precision" like "a highly calibrated machine" but unlike a machine helps his fellow players like Charlie Keller and Joe Page with good advice. He even gets "visibly angry" when asked what he thought of "Negroes" like Jackie Robinson playing in the big leagues. "What difference does a man's color make?" he broadmindedly replies. "All that matters is—can the guy play ball."

What does not conform to DiMaggio's lovely image is generally omitted from Schoor's story. His parents and siblings and child are mentioned but not his ex-wife, as though his son were born through parthenogenesis. His sulks are ignored. His holdout in 1938 is noted but miraculously no one emerges badly in the paragraph discussing it, neither DiMaggio, management, nor the fans. When Schoor takes DiMaggio down from one pedestal, the "Horatio Alger hero comes to life," who has "won his way to fortune and into the hearts of the American people," he is placed on another pedestal. He "doesn't shove his weight around" and hires no publicists. "In his personal life, Joe is the average American citizen. He likes to fish and hunt" and "talk with the old gang" back at the San Francisco docks. He's Mr. Wonderful.

Schoor ballooned his version of DiMaggio's story into two additional books, *The Yankee Clipper* (1956) and *Joe DiMaggio, A Biography* (1980), which seem like two editions of the same work, the latter narrative expanding and updating the earlier but retaining much of its content. The overall picture of DiMaggio that emerges from all three works does not change radically. Particularized dialogues between many of the individuals whose names are often mentioned throughout the literature on DiMaggio constitute a major feature of the longer book(s). Many of the interludes in DiMaggio's life are turned into dramatically conceived scenes reminiscent of Hollywood biographies about poor kids growing up in teeming cities and making their way to stardom (or ultimate disaster as criminals): *Rhapsody in Blue, Pride of the Yankees*, and seemingly numberless Jimmy Cagney and John Garfield films provide analogs for the presentation of DiMaggio's early years. Many of Schoor's scenes, such as the squabbles over Joe's alleged laziness between his mother (kind and understanding) and father (angry and frustrated) invite casting games. Sarah Allgood would be too Irish for Joe's mother. Maybe Rosemary de Camp? Buela Bondi? Morris Carnovsky, though Jewish, could handle Giuseppe's role, or even better Lee J. Cobb who anticipated Schoor's Giuseppe in his portrayal of Joe Bonaparte's papa in *Golden Boy*.

The game is not pointless for it demonstrates how devotedly Schoor has packaged the DiMaggio story into an immediately recognizable picture portraying not exactly real life, but the reflection of real life many Americans are familiar with, through popular media formulation. The seeming ease with which he accomplishes this trick, sticking mainly to the actual outlines of DiMaggio's life while embellishing some of the details, demonstrates how perfect a candidate for popular mythologizing DiMaggio was.

The book is highly successful in dramatizing the DiMaggio myth. A case could be made (but probably should not be) that its frequently bad writing is appropriate since it is the verbal equivalent of the vulgarized form of the myth that Schoor presents, just as *Rhapsody in Blue* and *Pride of the Yankees* vulgarized their subjects. The book contains cliches ("A hush fell over the giant stadium. You could hear a pin drop in the stands") and turgidly lush descriptions ("The fog rolled in silently off the bay, wet and cool, a dirty gray blanket that settled swiftly in thick folds over the city, dimming the street lamps to a feeble flow") that seem like products of an automatic writing machine programmed to communicate in the idiom of bad movies, bad sports columns, and parodies of Dashiell Hammett.

As history, the work has clear deficiencies. Its dramatizations and descriptions made it in 1956 the most substantial third person picture of DiMaggio's life, and even its 1980 version which had to compete with other biographies of similar length seems in extensive detail a definitive if gushy account. However, readers who compare the two editions (or books) might question the authenticity of both presentations in certain particulars.

Some of Schoor's revisions correct his old mistakes. In 1956 he still wrote that DiMaggio was born November 29, 1914, but in 1980 he corrects this to November 25. In 1980 he also no longer describes as he did in 1956 Dom DiMaggio's phantom catch of the ball Joe never hit him during his streak. Twice in 1980, Schoor corrects errors he made in 1956 about Dom's age. Sometimes he adds details perhaps because greater research had provided him with more information, or perhaps simply to add verisimilitude. In 1956 he wrote that DiMaggio was reading a comic book the day he started his 56-game streak, in 1980 Schoor writes he was reading *Superman*, possibly as a presage of what DiMaggio was shortly to prove himself. Sometimes he adds humanizing details, for example in 1980 pointing out that DiMaggio's wife was pregnant during the hitting streak. In 1980 he also adds Sher's 1949 story about DiMaggio not knowing what a "quote" was. Some trivial changes are difficult to evaluate since no sources are supplied. In 1956 the crowd at DiMaggio's first minor league game is reported singing to a record of the national anthem; in 1980 they are described as silent. The "Army chow" that disagreed with DiMaggio's stomach in the 1956 version becomes "Army food" in 1980. Some modifications detract from the 1980 version's historical value since they remove factual material. In the 1956 version Schoor related that while DiMaggio waited in 1949 for his heel to grow less painful his father died, and DiMaggio traveled back to San Francisco for the funeral. In 1980 this detail is omitted, though why is unclear, unless Schoor thought it would jar his readers. But this is doubtful since he mentions that at the end of the 1949 season, Rosalie DiMaggio herself had cancer, and Giuseppe's death is alluded to once, when Rosalie is praying.

Some textual changes are particularly perplexing. Much of the book is dialogue and it is not always possible to tell what Schoor has reconstructed from reports the principals involved have told him (especially since he gives no sources, primary or secondary); what he wrote figuring that this was what it must have sounded like; and what he invented for his own literary purposes. Spike Hennessy's summation to Charley Graham about DiMaggio's prospects appears in two separate versions in 1956 and 1980 which match each other generally, but are verbally quite different. Either one seems plausible. Were he writing a novel this rewriting would be acceptable, but both the 1956 and 1980 texts are presumably biographies.

He also changes descriptions of actions for seemingly no reason at all—at least he provides no biographer's reasons—and this practice lends an arbitrariness to much of his incidental information. In 1956 he describes DiMaggio sitting on the edge of a pier overlooking San Francisco Bay by writing, "He just sat without thinking." In 1980 Schoor says, "He just sat thinking." Either DiMaggio was thinking as he sat or he wasn't. Is the reader to assume that between the writing of the 1956 volume and the 1980, Schoor somehow discovered that DiMaggio was in fact thinking as he sat? In the 1956 book at the conclusion to Chapter 5, prior to Joe's tryout, Vince and Joe discuss Joe's sandlot career and Vince's pleasure at being paid to play. Joe wonders out loud if that kind of career offers a good deal or not, "But in his heart" he knows "for the first time in his life, what he wanted." Then he falls exhausted asleep and later Papa DiMaggio passes his room and mutters as he watches his son, "That's a funny boy. . . . I don't know what's gonna be with him." It is a touching scene appearing in print nowhere else and one wonders how Schoor knew about it since Joe's father had been dead many years before Schoor's book appeared. In 1980 the sequence is shifted from its original location. Instead, at the end of the following chapter, and now after the tryout, Vince says Joe is going to play shortstop tomorrow, and Joe becomes very excited. In bed later that night Joe fantasizes being the hero and the goat next day. Then he falls "into an exhausted sleep," the same sleep Schoor had him in 1956 falling into months before. And Papa DiMaggio in his quaint accent wonders again, what's gonna be with his funny boy? Who told Schoor he had been wrong in 1956—or is the entire scene spurious?

In 1956 Schoor printed what was supposedly a newspaperman's report during DiMaggio's first spring training with the Seals. It says he is "tall, gawky, inclined to be rather surly," but also "He's the best-looking hitter seen this spring." In 1980 the report says "He's tall, stringy, sullen, and tough to interview. . . . He is the most sullen player I've ever seen." The story's tone has become much harsher. What did the reporter really write? In 1956 Schoor wrote that when DiMaggio heard the fans' jeers in 1938 after his holdout, a Philadelphia Athletics third baseman turned to him and said "They're sure on you, DiMag. . . . What's eating 'em?" In 1980 Schoor writes that the player said "They're sure on you, DiMag. . . . I guess it's because you're holding out for more money?" Why did it take the player 24 years to become more knowledgeable? In 1956 Schoor writes that Bill Essick, the Yankee scout, called Charley Graham to discuss DiMaggio's future. In 1980 he writes that Essick called Ed Barrow, though Essick gives the same report he had given Graham in the 1956 version. Ed Barrow is assigned words in 1980 mainly spoken by Essick in a conversation with Graham related in 1956. Finally in the 1980 version Essick calls Barrow to tell him to buy DiMaggio, and Barrow calls Graham to stipulate the conditions of the deal. But then when Graham calls DiMaggio to tell him the good news, he asks Essick—last heard from in the sequence calling Barrow—how soon DiMaggio is to report for his physical. The grinning Essick says tell DiMaggio to start packing. But how did Essick get to Graham's office after speaking to Barrow on the telephone? The lines of the story, telephone and narrative, seem tangled. The deal was less confusing in 1956.

Whatever may be the factual validity of Schoor's treatment of individual episodes in DiMaggio's life, whether or not the revisions he made in his biography reveal capriciousness or care toward reproducing the life faithfully, he seems on target in presenting the mythic image DiMaggio has achieved. The individual parts of the story, most of which in their general outlines conform to the known facts of DiMaggio's life, collectively add up to the figure of Joe DiMaggio depicted most frequently in the mass media. Schoor is complete in proceeding scene by scene through DiMaggio's known career, showing the early years with his big, affectionate family; the momentous discovery ("Someday, Charley, that kid's going to break a few records around this league. Or my name's not Ike Caveney") of DiMaggio's skill after the knothole incident; stardom in San Francisco; the silent trip with Lazzeri and Crosetti to the Yankee training camp; the injury jinx; all the big and little stories told to fit precisely into the myth. DiMaggio's comebacks are epic, his achievements as a human being and a player heroic.

Some parts of the story are related in much greater detail than others that in a rounded historical account would seem just as significant. It is appropriate that Schoor reproduces a picture of Joe's family life in as lengthy a fashion as he does, though DiMaggio's parents seem stereotypes, particularly DiMaggio's father who is at first the story's misguided heavy, like a dense father in teen-ager films: "I'm telling you, Rosa. That boy's never gonna be no good. Never." According to Vince DiMaggio, Giuseppe was not opposed to the idea of Joe's playing professional baseball, as Schoor here depicts him. Before Joe ever signed a contract, Vince had shown his father the money baseball could bring. The chapter on Marilyn Monroe is curiously bland. Schoor writes about the rich relationship Monroe and DiMaggio intermittently maintained after their marriage in one brief two-sentence paragraph which euphemistically buries Monroe's suicide in the phrase "tragic death."

Occasionally, as when he portrays Rosalie DiMaggio praying beside her bed in San Francisco for her Joe who walks fitfully through a New York apartment agonizing over the wounded heel he feels may end his career, the book appears to manipulate events to produce cloying sentimentality. Sometimes details seem contrived to fit the demands of story-telling. Before Joe plays his first Seals game, Schoor portrays a scene where Ike Caveney comically, dramatically, and anxiously asks Vince DiMaggio if his brother can really play. "Is he any good? Don't kid me, Vince" he shouts. But the Seals had full scouting reports on Joe at the time, and Caveney may even have seen him play. The scene would probably be funny and effective in a film, but seems contrived. Still, there is perhaps no clearer full-length picture of the DiMaggio image than Schoor's. It represents nearly all the component elements of DiMaggio's legend, and offers a generally accurate overview of his career. As a popular biography its craft is better than that of the wretched, filmed *Babe Ruth Story* with William Bendix, but not as powerful as *Pride of the Yankees*, the Lou Gehrig story in which Gary Cooper so successfully combined his quiet, rock-stable rightness with Gehrig's tale of a second-class hero and first-class victim.

There is a tendency to treat sports heroes ultimately as somehow victims, perhaps because that is so often their fate. Both Babe Ruth and Lou Gehrig are strongly remembered in their final incarnations saying goodbye, the playful, greedy, priapic Ruth hoarse with cancer, and Gehrig's dying voice echoing hollowly around Yankee Stadium repeating how fortunate he had been. Schoor is one of the first writers to identify the element of sadness in DiMaggio's once bright rookie's story. Though Schoor's book thoroughly details the full news and excitement of DiMaggio's life as a baseball star, he concludes both his 1956 and 1980 versions of DiMaggio's story with the same chapter showing Joe in 1955 sitting around at Toots Shors' (actually long gone in 1980) talking to writers and agents the day he was elected to the Hall of Fame. One of the agents suggests to Joe that he make some profitable personal appearances but DiMaggio scornfully replies "I'm a former ballplayer, not a circus freak." After Joe leaves—early—one of the writers says "there . . . goes one of the greatest players in the history of baseball." Another writer comments, "and one of the greatest guys." Schoor himself adds the last words in the book, the final image of DiMaggio, "And one of the loneliest men in the world." It is as though DiMaggio had left the spotlight to walk into darkness offstage: no matter how great the adulation of him remains, how friendly and fulfilled he seems in public appearances, there is in his image now an area of inviolate sadness, a part of himself he will not let others touch. Schoor shows that DiMaggio also embodies a counter-myth, that the American dream when achieved may bring success but not necessarily happiness.

Schoor was not the only writer to present multiple studies of DiMaggio around the time of his retirement in 1951, when books and articles increasingly portrayed DiMaggio as a fully developed part of the American scene, and as a star whose active career had run its course. The DiMaggio story had been developing exploit by exploit, article by article, story by story over the years. Now was the time for his image to be transmitted back in a full if not final form to the public who had participated as spectators in its development and to others for whom DiMaggio was a legend from the past.

Tom Meany, who had already collaborated on DiMaggio's autobiography, wrote a pamphlet titled *Joseph Paul DiMaggio, The Yankee Clipper* as part of an "All-Star" series of short monographs about sports figures in 1950-51. Though rambling and impressionistic, the work profits from Meany's extended, first-hand relationship with DiMaggio. Noting the success DiMaggio has achieved in his "rags-to-riches" career, Meany illustrates DiMaggio's progress by reporting that even while DiMaggio sat in his hotel room relating experiences to him, a bell hop knocked to announce that the Broadway and film actress Tallulah Bankhead was returning DiMaggio's automatic record palyer: truly he had traveled a long way from North Beach. Meany emphasizes Joe's comebacks rather than his bright promise and triumphs although these are documented. His DiMaggio is a player of proven if not unparalleled greatness, whose popularity he says "ironically enough . . . stems from his injuries, or rather from the spectacular comebacks he has made after them. Every time Joe has been floored by the jinx he has come up fighting." Meany also remarks that "Joe's personal life has been as tangled as his baseball playing has been smooth," a side of DiMaggio unrevealed in his autobiography.

Meany also referred to DiMaggio's "entangled marital status" in an exceptionally frank magazine article written for *Collier's* in 1952 titled "Joe DiMaggio As I Knew Him." This short piece perhaps more than any other of similar length presents DiMaggio as a real person. Meany contends that DiMaggio is "one of the most misunderstood" ballplayers of all time. "He leaves active baseball almost as much an enigma to the fans as he was in 1936." DiMaggio's recollections delivered to Meany range over some of the high points of his life and legend. Andy High's notorious scouting report ultimately published in *Life*, that so devastatingly spotlighted DiMaggio's weakness, played no role in his retirement, DiMaggio says, claiming "scouting reports don't bother me." DiMaggio states he knew in Phoenix during spring training for 1951 that the season might be his last. He was only surprised that the year turned out so badly. "I really thought I could make my last year a good one. I had a bad one instead. I guess the reflexes just weren't there any more." Concerning the famous story of the sinister taxi-cab driver's prediction that his hit streak was going to be snapped, DiMaggio says "I paid no attention" to it. When after the game Lefty Gomez cursed the "dirty so-and-so" who had "jinxed him," DiMaggio thought he meant Ken Keltner or one of the Cleveland pitchers. Contrary to the image that Schoor and others would in a few years popularize,

DiMaggio felt he was generally not a loner, and lists Frank Crosetti, Gomez, Joe Page, and Billy Martin among his particular friends. He also disagrees with the stories about him eating alone and sulking his last years with the Yankees, and shows he is upset over tales of his alleged feud with Casey Stengel. He tells Meany that his famous salary dispute with Ruppert in 1938 was not nearly as acrimonious as the confrontation with Barrow in 1942, when according to DiMaggio he was first offered a $2,500 cut in salary, and Barrow insinuated he was "lucky to be playing ball" at all considering the war. "I don't think anything ever burned me up as much as that did." Meany himself reveals that he helped Joe write his autobiography and instructional book, aided with the former by Joe's ex-wife with whom he was attempting in 1946 to reconcile. By 1947 Dorothy had remarried and Joe was "pretty lonely then."

Meany also comments on Joe's 1952 anxieties about being a baseball announcer and suggests DiMaggio's perfectionism was part of the difficulties, noting that Joe preferred "filmed programs" where directors could "edit out mistakes." The illustration accompanying the article places handsome and smiling DiMaggio in the center of other drawings of him hitting, running, fielding, and running bases. The article's final sequence represents DiMaggio's social success: Joe adjusts his suspenders "so that his trouser cuffs hang evenly. Adolphe Menjou," the dapper actor whose mode of correct dress made him fabled as a paragon of high class conservative fashion, "couldn't have been more meticulous."

Meany also stressed DiMaggio's attainment of "class" while rehearsing once again his famous baseball exploits in one section of *The Yankee Story* (1960), contrasting the difficulties DiMaggio experienced privately while publicly becoming a quick sensation. "While baseball came easily to DiMaggio, the ability to handle the responsibilities of stardom did not. . . . he had a horror of autograph seekers which approached claustrophobia" and his "tangled marital affairs contributed greatly to his moodiness." For a long while according to Meany he seemed comfortable only with a small band of friends and as late as 1957 when Meany visited him was still somewhat shy and reticent, though greatly improved in social skills. "Fame came too quickly for DiMaggio," Meany concludes, "and he was a long time developing a personality to cope with it." Meany's assessment, coming as it did from one who had worked closely and in a friendly fashion with DiMaggio over the years, seems particularly honest in showing DiMaggio as he really was and not as fashioned for hero-worship. The magnitude of DiMaggio's off-the-field growth, uneven as it was, is enhanced by the frank view Meany offers of him. As Meany's writings show, the man whose cuffs hung so neatly was built upon the boy who never finished high school. Being able to dress himself as handsomely as Menjou perhaps made DiMaggio better able to act surely, but possibly also disguised his social insecurity. DiMaggio's style revealed and concealed the man within.

Yankee announcer Mel Allen avoided penetrating DiMaggio's public image in his chapter on DiMaggio in *It Takes Heart* (1959). He limited himself to demonstrating DiMaggio's skill, thoughtfulness, and courage. In one anectdote Allen relates, DiMaggio displays his gentlemanly professionalism in the 1950 World Series, when New York beat Philadelphia in four straight games. After Granny Hanner booted an easy grounder in the third game, DiMaggio, on second base, consoles him. "Don't worry about it, Granny,' he said gently . . . it happens to the best of them." Allen concludes, "As one of nine men, DiMaggio is the best player that ever lived."

Even though the post-DiMaggio Yankee years were among the team's most successful, and new great players like Mickey Mantle and Whitey Ford performed in the tradition of the all-time superstars—which meant extraordinary media focus followed their winning exploits—DiMaggio continued to be written about often in the daily and periodical press and in books. Some of these items more concerned his role in Marilyn Monroe's life than his baseball prowess, but still kept his name before the public in a positive fashion enriching his story as a baseball player.

Some of the best writing about him was still evoked by his hit streak. Like his sensational 1949 comeback this was an intensely dramatic fact about which ample and very specific documentation existed. His career statistics while impressive were not as towering as those of the very greatest of players, such as Cobb, Ruth, and Speaker, to whom he was compared in ability, but no player could match the excellence he displayed in the streak. Writers could tout DiMaggio's mastery of intangibles, but more and more they were addressing audiences whose memories of his play were dim or non-existent. The streak was verifiable. It possessed an undeniable authority in the constant battle between the ancients and the moderns (any current generation of stars against previous generations) that is waged throughout sports literature.

Dave Anderson's "The Longest Hitting Streak in History" appeared July 17, 1961, in *Sports Illustrated* and was later revised as part of "The DiMaggio Years" section of *The Yankees* (1980). Anderson stressed that the streak was an unparalleled sports achievement for DiMaggio and a unique experience for baseball fans mainly because of "the relentless day-by-day pressure of the last few weeks of the streak." Anderson also recognized that when DiMaggio ultimately became a symbol of heroism whose significance extended beyond sports, it had been in large part "the hitting streak" that "shaped that symbol." Many of the components of the streak's narrative recited in later retellings like espisodes in an epic are mentioned in Anderson's swiftly paced and compressed account. The slump the streak broke for both DiMaggio and the Yankees; the time it was first noticed and the subsequent buildup of national excitement around it (with DiMaggio relatively solid and without much noticeable nervousness); vignettes such as Bob Muncrief's refusal to walk him or the loss of his favored bat; the great smash he hit between Yankee-killer Johnny Babich's legs; the streak's famous termination presaged by the prophetic cabbie—all are presented as details each adding its own spice to the story. Moreover, Anderson recognizes that the event was "a sociological phenomenon" and places it in the historic context of the world-wide drama building during that "strangely smoldering summer," when President Roosevelt spoke to national audiences of the coming "national emergency" and William L. Shirer's *Berlin Diary* was a best-seller.

One of the silly details Anderson includes to add quirky verisimilitude to his picture of what 1941 was like in America, is the popularity of the novelty tune "Hut-Sut Rawlson on the Rillerah." Al Silverman also features the song, perhaps as a symbol of something that like the streak is ultimately unexplainable, in *Joe DiMaggio, The Golden Year, 1941* (1969), one of the best books on DiMaggio.

Silverman presents information not just about the streak, but about DiMaggio's life and career. Though exasperatingly enough to the historian he provides no listing of his sources, he clearly performed considerable research preparing for the book, checking contemporary newspapers and magazines for fresh and accurate information, and undertaking interviews with a range of DiMaggio's teammates and opposing players. Far less sentimental and portentously dramatic than Schoor, Silverman presents the star as a performer of triumphant physical skills, a good man and a great athlete but no demi-god. One way Silverman achieves this tempered portrait is by including the comments of many of DiMaggio's contemporaries, both players and sportswriters, who viewed him as a player of exceptional abilities but also as a real-life fellow mortal and not some fabulous image projected on the national movie screen. The book's major structural flaw is perhaps forced upon it by the "Golden Year" series of which it was a part, for its development is not chronological. Instead, chapters on segments of the streak are alternated with chapters about DiMaggio's childhood and years of play, so that it is somewhat difficult to follow his evolution. Otherwise, Silverman's book is one of the best portraying DiMaggio realistically with freshness and insight.

A foreword by Murray Olderman indicates the complexity of DiMaggio's image, positing two popular views of him, the glamorous superstar and the noble recluse, and suggests that counter-images lay beneath the surfaces of each of these pictures, the "sullen, aloof man" whose personality came alive only on the field and its opposite, an "amazingly effusive" and often genial "source of news for writers." Silverman's text focuses on what is best and most likable about DiMaggio mainly by presenting details of his playing career with just enough personal background to suggest that he emerged a good and successful man from his immigrant family. There is some talk of his "fall from epic grace" at the end of his streak, and early in the book he is called "the once and future king of" a Yankee dynasty. The book's final sentence terms him a "noble American folk hero" whose actions "will be remembered and talked about and passed on from father to son for as long as they play this game of ours called baseball." But generally the narrative supplies a straightforward exposition of details and anecdotes.

Silverman sees the streak as the adventure which enabled DiMaggio to enter "the hearts of his countrymen" at an especially tense and uncertainty-filled time. Demanding skill, luck, an iron will, and the capacity to endure pressure, the streak captivated a nation hungry for escape as had few other athletic achievements in the country's history, because it evolved slowly but very steadily, containing no breathing spaces during which attention upon it could relax or falter. Day after day greater attention was given it, and the nature of the attention became more intense. Occasionally Silverman's details are questionable or call for some corroboration, such as the claim that it was common for radio programs to be interrupted to relate the ongoing progress of the streak, or that during 1936 after Yankee games were over police radios in San Francisco broadcast a summary of DiMaggio's activities that day. Far more frequently Silverman's facts are accurate and arrived at not through memory or hearsay but by slogging through contemporary newspaper accounts or checking and cross-checking with participants in the events of the streak or DiMaggio's career. Thus he corrects the story that Dom robbed Joe of a hit the day he broke Willie Keeler's record, though curiously does not note that DiMaggio himself remembered the event this way.

Not only is Silverman the fullest source for information about the streak, but his alternate chapters provide good and often new information about other aspects of DiMaggio's life and playing days. The section on DiMaggio's youth was perhaps the most lively and plausible retelling to that time. Nearly always in narrating the familiar outlines of DiMaggio's first, spectacular years of ascendency as a baseball star, Silverman is able to insert revealing new data, or an interesting slant that vitalizes the perspective on his famous subject. He refers to a column DiMaggio or more likely his ghostwriter conducted in 1936 in the New York *World Telegram and Sun*, that ended when the season finished, with DiMaggio's charming claim that the Yankees in their entire history since 1903 had "never before had a young ballplayer who was so determined to make good as your friend Joe DiMaggio." While other writers often noted how carefully DiMaggio considered the picture of him given to young children—claiming he refused to pose with a cigarette for example—Silverman recalls an advertisement that claimed "Win Or Lose—Joe DiMaggio, Kirby Higbe & Millions of Fans Agree—'There's Nothing Like a Camel.'" The cigarette company announced that "more than a symbol of American League power at bat . . . DeMaggio is power itself. Game after game, for 56 consecutive games, he came through with at least one hit. And day after day, he chooses Camel cigarettes—because, in his own words, 'They're Milder'". Silverman lets

DiMaggio himself voice his outrage at what he considered the "insult" of Ed Barrow's proposal to cut his 1942 salary. To underscore the theme of DiMaggio's rise in American life, he repeats relief pitcher Johnny Murphy's simple remark, "When I see Joe now . . . I tell him what great strides he made in his personal life. . . . He's an interesting man to be around now." Silverman's own language is unpretentious and effective, though without art. He does not strain after effect but usually employs a relatively simple and clear prose style. Only occasionally does he err badly, as when he writes that in 1938 when DiMaggio sought significantly more money "Barrow literally blew him out of the office."

Silverman uses what he terms "Stop-Action, 1941" sections to report what was happening in the world beyond DiMaggio's streak in 1941, to suggest the context in which DiMaggio's greatly popular act was occurring. Thus the streak is studied both in isolation, and as part of the history of its day. The "Stop-Action" sequences are similar to John Dos Passos's "Newsreel" chapters in his trilogy U.S.A., employing songs, newspaper headlines, and news briefs to communicate impressionistically the spirit of the day. One subject the items often return to is the developing World War, which Silverman directly relates to the baseball story his book tells, for example by mentioning player insecurity over the continued fate of the game, when draft registration was a fact of their lives. Some historic analogs seem strictly coincidental: DiMaggio's feat took place the same year James Joyce died, Virginia Woolf committed suicide, and Ava Gardner and Mickey Rooney wed. Others are more relevant. The special ceremonies commemorating "I Am An American" day, May 18, are viewed as rituals of national declaration and resolve at a time of growing crisis, into which DiMaggio's concurrent exploits fit with particular appropriateness. In Central Park that day, Mayor La Guardia decreed a celebration at which Eddie Cantor (a Jew), Bill "Bojangles" Robinson (a black), and Kate Smith (a quintessential WASP) starred. At Yankee Stadium, the Italian-American DiMaggio made three hits and knocked in one run.

Silverman calls DiMaggio rightly enough a "symbol of the time." He adds that "life was uncomplicated and understandable in 1941, and that was the way Joe DiMaggio played baseball." In this he seems correct only in the last half of his statement. DiMaggio was one of those rare athletes who for a time provided a sustained, simple, gloriously enjoyable event to contemplate. For a briefer time the American 1980 Olympic hockey team achieved the same burningly intense escape of national joy. But the era in which DiMaggio added flavor and relief was neither uncomplicated nor particularly understandable, except in the broadest historic terms. At the end of an economic depression and the beginning of a war, America in 1941 was as complex and mysterious a country as it ever had been or would be. What Silverman shows is that DiMaggio provided an excitement, a spark that brightened the lives of many who were then beleaguered with their own ordinary fearsome pressures, as people are when any hero sends up a flare signalling greatness, making them wonder what the equivalent to a 56 consecutive game hitting streak would be in their lives.

In the last few pages of his book Silverman briefly describes the agonies and triumphs of DiMaggio's last seasons in baseball. While he deals with the off-the-field youth of DiMaggio, he includes very little information about his life after retirement. Similarly, he devotes an entire brief chapter to recollections of what was occurring in America December 7, 1941, when the Japanese attacked Pearl Harbor, focusing mainly on DiMaggio and several of his teammates, while he compresses Joe's war service into one quotation that expresses quite clearly the impact of the war on him. "I thought it would never end," DiMaggio says. "Those years never seemed to move at all." Though he seems interested in the childhood out of which the legendary hero developed. Silverman seems unconcerned with the course of DiMaggio's life after his playing days, beyond simply noting he was "a hero in an Ernest Hemingway novel and a hero in a best-selling song, 'Mrs. Robinson,' that grooves for a new and different generation." He avoids discussion of Marilyn Monroe completely, almost as though that episode would muddle the clear image of the hero he presents throughout most of his book.

Though the picture of DiMaggio that emerges from Silverman's book is a strong and real one of him as a player, it is a partial portrait of him as a man. Even more partial a view is presented in Ann Finlayson's *Three Power Hitters* (1970), a book typical of those on DiMaggio clearly intended for children. Sometimes recycling comments from earlier sources (once again DiMaggio is claimed to have been the "greatest rookie since Ty Cobb") her dramatic technique often resembles Schoor's. In one early scene DiMaggio while still a Seals player is telephoned late at night by his "boss" that since "Babe Ruth is too old to play another season" the Yankees "need a new young hitter to step into his shoes." The shocked rookie replies "the Yankees have bought me?" as though his sale were a total surprise. Mama and Papa DiMaggio quarrel over whether or not son Joe is a lazy baseball bum, and Rosalie waves her finger at Giuseppe and scolds him as though participating in a situation comedy. DiMaggio amply demonstrates his mother's faith in him by performing all the familiar exploits, and Finlayson notes for her young readers that "often the highest praise showered on" her exemplary hero "has been for his workmanship. He did not make scenes or cause trouble or demand the spotlight." One of his great rewards was that "nobody admired him more than his own teammates." Clearly he was a model youth, quite worthy of emulation.

Presenting his life in geater detail and for a broader audience, Bob Broeg similarly portrayed him as a classic American success story in *Super Stars of Baseball* (1971). Broeg emphasizes the hard conditions of DiMaggio family life where "the family lived in close quarters" with the boys and girls in two separate rooms but "spilling out into the living room and dining room" when Papa DiMaggio left for work at 4 A.M. Yet "the poor foreign-born fisherman's son" grew up into "the game's No. 1 living player," a man "who seemed aloof, yet one who married the most glamorous motion-picture actress of the generation," and who reigned as "the living symbol of the game's first century." Broeg accentuates DiMaggio's triumphs in baseball and in life. The DiMaggio he depicts has grown in wisdom through suffering. His great comeback over pain made the 1949 three-game series with Boston for him "the most satisfying of my life and . . . taught me about faith and people." He is an American who has arrived at great heights splendidly through his skills, certainly not a lonely, bitter man.

DiMaggio's injuries are stressed in nearly all the accounts written about him after his retirement, not to depict him as a victim, a player cut off in his prime like Lou Gehrig, but to underscore his indominability and fortitude. The injuries thus became a positive part of his image, distinguishing him from some of the athletes with whom he was often compared at the start of his career, such as Cobb or Ruth. Thus in the 1949 edition of Robert Shoe-maker's *The Best in Baseball* his story was included in a chapter titled "After the Babe: Gehrig and DiMaggio" while in the 1974 edition of the same book Gehrig remains "After the Babe" but DiMaggio is placed in his own chapter, "Yankee Clipper." Both editions note that he was a "cool, efficient operator" who "appeared to be somewhat aloof from fans and players alike" and "machine-like in his perfection," but the 1974 text adds that "injuries plagued DiMaggio in his later years. At one time his throwing arm was so sore that he could make only one good peg a day from the outfield." The injuries humanized him and proved finally that he was not a machine: machines break down and get fixed, but they don't feel pain or come back.

In the years following his retirement, the testimony of other ball players also became increasingly important in establishing DiMaggio's abilities, because fewer observers had seen him perform and perhaps because his statistics did not quite match those of the highest rank of all-time stars, such as Ruth, Gehrig, Speaker, Wagner, and Cobb. Throughout the 1960s and 1970s fellow baseball players continued to be reported among his greatest admirers. Though from time to time newspaper accounts during his career alleged that some of his teammates were grumbling about him, for example during his 1938 holdout, specific players were customarily not named voicing alleged criticisms. The great Yankee pitcher Spud Chandler's reminiscences told to Donald Honig in his nostalgic *Baseball When the Grass Was Real* (1976) several decades after Chandler retired, are as much a panegyric as anything written by his literary image makers. "Of course we had Joe DiMaggio," Chandler says explaining the Yankees' success, "and that was a ball club in itself. For all-around ability and everyday play, DiMaggio was the greatest player I ever saw. . . . The most complete ballplayer I ever saw. And he was a great team man, very loyal to the ball club; he gave his best, he never caused any trouble, he never got into any arguments.'' For Chandler as for so many writers, DiMaggio was an exemplary hero.

For Robin Moore and Gene Schoor, co-authors of *Marilyn & Joe DiMaggio* (1976), DiMaggio was a romantic (almost an epic) lover. All the other books about DiMaggio had virtually omitted Marilyn Monroe from his life. Moore and Schoor rectified this lack with a vengeance. Their hot-breathed approach was well illustrated by the picture of Marilyn and Joe kissing on the book's paperback edition cover and in the blurb accompanying the picture: ''It was an impossible love story. They were married for less than a year, but they were in love 'til the day she died.'' Partly a biography of Marilyn Monroe, partly a review of DiMaggio's life and athletic greatness (following the story line of Schoor's 1956 treatment) the book achieved heights of enraptured prose unfound elsewhere in the literature about DiMaggio, though the inventiveness displayed in describing several scenes would be familiar to readers of Schoor's earlier work on the famous athlete, here metamorphosed into ''baseball's great lover,'' sadly playing now in an ''American tragedy.''

Certainly the Monroe episode was an important part of DiMaggio's life, and their unhappy marriage has become an event filled with cultural implications for many writers. Moore and Schoor perform the helpful service of trivializing aspects of the relationship, though this may not have been their goal. That Monroe was not particularly impressed by DiMaggio on their first (prearranged) date until Mickey Rooney came to their table and began fawning over him restores a salutary banality to their romance. When they depict the New York City crowd screaming ''Higher! Higher!'' as hot air blew up between Marilyn's legs during the famous filming of *The Seven Year Itch* revealing Marilyn's ''ruffled white nylon panties'' and bare legs, the level of their prose nicely parallels the level of unromantic, unpleasant sexuality the mob's shouts revealed. The disgust they show DiMaggio feeling upon observing this scene doubtless recaptures his feelings about what he considered Monroe's shameless public eroticism. There is some doubt that he was actually in attendance, however, as they describe him. Since they give no sources for their depiction, it is difficult to conclude how accurate that part of their re-creation is. While their account may be perfectly factual, their language seems more appropriate to a lurid detective novel or romance, for example when it describes an evening in San Francisco when Joe was absent and ''Marilyn had a great urge to move into the mysterious shroud which covered the waterfront. The fog comes frequently to San Francisco''—true enough!—''and Marilyn had been sensuously drawn to it before. This particular night, she could not resist its siren call.'' That Moore and Schoor wallow so often in this kind of musky verbiage does not improve the idea of their reliability.

Moore and Schoor are in the tradition of many books mainly about Marilyn Monroe written during the 1960s and 1970s that include sections on DiMaggio. It is difficult and here unnecessary to trace the tangled lines of descent of these books particularly since most contain essentially the same view of him as a great baseball star and a man of honor; a successful man with a sure sense of himself; a man who has experienced suffering. They display DiMaggio in action however not as a baseball player but as a man in an exciting and ultimately destructive and failed sexual relationship, and this of course was foreign territory to the books viewing him as an athlete. Some of the Monroe books seem calculated to satisfy if not glut the voyeuristic readers' appetite for signs of DiMaggio's lust and thus to demonstrate his defectiveness. But his continuing affair with Monroe was part of his record and therefore something absolutely necessary to write about when he is being dealt with as a culturally or historically significant person. Scenes such as the one Moore and Schoor refer to after *The Seven Year Itch* incident, when "people in the adjacent rooms at the Hotel Regis reported that they heard shouting in the DiMaggio suite, scuffling, then hysterical weeping," if they can be authenticated, probably must be included in detailed accounts of the DiMaggio story. Perhaps it is even necessary to repeat Monroe's leering innuendoes about DiMaggio's great sexual prowess (he and Frank Sinatra, she said, had something in common, and it was not that they were Italian) reported in Lena Pepitone's 1979 dresser's-eye view of the actress, for the insight they provide on Monroe if not on DiMaggio.

Norman Mailer's flights of speculation first published in 1973 concerning what the couple's life together—so romanticized and trivialized and glossily distorted in newspapers and magazines—was like in all its sad post-coital boredom, may illuminate a cranny of the American scene untraversed by romantic fiction or standard situation comedy views of American love. For observers interested mainly in DiMaggio's figure on the national scene, what is perhaps most interesting about how the matter of Marilyn Monroe has been processed and assimilated into the DiMaggio story is that mainly what does not conform to the accepted image of DiMaggio has been rejected for inclusion in his myth. What resides in the DiMaggio myth after the stories of his years with Monroe have been told and retold, is not that he was a great lover who bedded America's creamy and luscious sex queen, but that he experienced pain in his relationship with a doomed and lovely woman that he gallantly tried to save, and that he behaved nobly at her funeral. For him it was another comeback triumph (after the dismally failed marriage) that demonstrated his heroic integrity and selflessness.

The literature about his experience with Monroe demonstrates the scars the affair left on his image. That these would be viewed as scars of honor and not of folly or human frailty (for Monroe was seen as the frail one, not DiMaggio) shows the power his image possessed. Gay Talese's July, 1966,

Esquire article is a mournful account of the twilight of this scarred god now forced to live as an aging human. The illustration introducing Talese's story is a dreadful, nightmare companion to other cover representations of the hero that appeared when he was living times of triumph: in it, an unidentifiable black-suited man swings his bat in empty Yankee Stadium. Titled "'Joe' said Marilyn Monroe, just back from Korea, 'you never heard such cheering.' 'Yes I have,' Joe DiMaggio answered," and subtitled "The Silent Season of a Hero," the eligiac piece begins with a quotation from *The Old Man and the Sea* stating that Santiago would like to take the great DiMaggio fishing because he "would understand." In the context of Hemingway's novella DiMaggio's understanding is related to his having once been poor, but in the article it is clear his understanding stems from having mastered the pain of his experience with Monroe. The pain brings knowledge but not, as Talese describes his life, happiness. Vince, the article suggests, may be happier. DiMaggio's San Francisco upbringing and years of baseball glory are described, as are parts of his life with Monroe and his present daily occupations. His baseball past is viewed as a glorious time, his life with Monroe dreary. Marilyn is shown "running hysterically, crying as she ran, along the road away from the pier" in San Francisco. Billy Wilder is reported saying "I shall never forget the look of death on Joe's face" when he saw the crowd surrounding Monroe's leggy exhibition over the subway grating in New York City. In Japan when DiMaggio saw Monroe after her success with the screaming troops in Korea and she told him he had never heard such cheering, he said (glum and angry) yes he had. The lost love embittered him. He snubbed Robert Kennedy at a Yankee celebration in New York because he thought he was part of the beautiful crowd responsible for her death.

Now in San Francisco as Talese describes him, he seems restless, prowling about with nothing really important or satisfying for him to do. He plays golf, attends with Lefty O'Doul a farmer-filled banquet where the local candidate for sheriff distributes campaign leaflets at the door: "How did we get sucked into this?" DiMaggio asks O'Doul out of the side of his mouth. He coldly isolates himself from an interviewer waiting for him in Tom's restaurant but from somewhere in or near the premises telephones him and shouts "You are invading my rights. . . . get your lawyer." He ogles a pretty lady filing her nails at a gas station, and later in a bar apparently picks up another woman. The crowds still love him, but who or what does he love? What is there for him to do? What is there in his life to replace the illusion of love with Monroe or the real cheering of the old crowds when he was being praised for what he did and not for what fans had been told he had done? Certainly Talese does not show that the great DiMaggio would understand all this.

Peter Golenbeck in *Dynasty, The New York Yankees 1949-1964* (1975), also wrote about a scarred DiMaggio and included in his section on "The

Early Years" the same anecdote about Monroe and DiMaggio in Japan that Talese told. Similarly, his picture of DiMaggio is really several pictures, the phenomenal baseball star (particularly in the prewar years) and the moody, reclusive celebrity; the once shy rookie who did not know what a quote was, and a sulky player always who bore "a self-imposed cross" of perfectionism and responsibility for the team, so that "every game he played became an intense, bitter personal struggle." Golenbeck's DiMaggio is a man surrounded by "mystery and mystique." Not only will DiMaggio apparently give him no interview (and the book's strength is the almost one hundred other interviews Golenbeck gathered for it) but when he asks Joe's brother Tom for a few words concerning Joe's childhood Tom looks at him "disdainfully" and leaves the room in which Golenbeck remained "mouth open."

But this new realism about DiMaggio did not destroy the older, less disquieting image so often portrayed in the popular media. There is no sullen dissatisfaction in James Stewart-Gordon's August 1976, *Readers' Digest* "Most Unforgettable Character" article which talks briefly of the dignity given Monroe's funeral by DiMaggio's control over it, while ignoring all the grittier aspects of their marriage. Retelling many of the old stories of DiMaggio's childhood and brilliant career ("radio news reporters interrupted the war news of Hitler's invasion of Russia to announce that Joe DiMaggio had broken the world's record by batting safely in 42 [*sic*] consecutive games") Stewart-Gordon concludes with an appraisal whose tone if not literary style reflects the view of DiMaggio presented so dramatically by Gene Schoor. "But what has set him apart" he asserts "are his personal characteristics of graciousness, the bearing of a Venetian Doge and a genuine modesty. No one knows how many sick kids, hospitals, and old-time ballplayers Joe has visited and helped—because he refuses to talk about it." This is essentially the same DiMaggio Michael Gorkin presents in his March, 1979, article in *50 Plus* (the 50 stands for years). Written for older readers, the story's prose and pictures emphasize DiMaggio's contentment and success as a 64-year old American. On the magazine's cover and in the pictures inside he looks absolutely great. Other photographs from his past show him with his big Italian-American family, at bat, with Joe Jr., and in a San Francisco motorcade after his first year in the majors. His growing up is briefly retold; that his father once called him "lagnuso (lazy)" but ultimately "became a fan like everyone else" is pointed out. "He's never forgotten," Gorkin adds, "that he was a fisherman's son—and he's remained proud, but humble, all his life." Now DiMaggio exemplifies the idea that "not all old athletes fade away." His work with the Bowery Savings Bank has brought him increased fame among the kids who never got to see him play, and money too. Both the bank and the Mr. Coffee people "acknowledge that profits have jumped considerably in the six years since Joe DiMaggio has been working for them." No longer bothered by attention, according to Gorkin, DiMaggio had a fine past (one picture shows him pleasantly with Marilyn Monroe) and an equally good present. His outward appearance reaffirms and symbolizes his success and inner fulfillment. He looks "as athletic as ever, but with a sad smile playing across his tanned face. He had just been asked what it had been like to be an American hero at the age of 36 and then have to retire." Now he is a representative senior citizen, who was once a rookie. "Speaking frankly," DiMaggio answers, "for a guy whose only real talent was on the ballfield, I've made out fine." And as a senior citizen, he appears as successful as he had been a rookie. "I've now become an expert on retirement." The picture is not all glowing. He admits that while he never thought of himself after retiring as a "fallen hero," as some others did, "all he felt at the time was simply like an old ballplayer out of a job. I didn't know what to do with my life." While still deeply disappointed that his marriage to Marilyn Monroe did not work out, he clearly is depicted as having made the successful adjustments his new second life after baseball stardom demanded. So he is twice a success story. His new life is far from perfect—women constitute "one area where there has been relatively little fun" Gorkin clinically observes, and though DiMaggio considers himself lucky to have achieved a second career in the business world, he says he still wouldn't mind managing if the right deal came along. Still he has shown continued emotional growth as he has aged gracefully. Now he is a "warm, even outgoing, public personality," Gorkin claims. He still embodies the old integrity, however: he only works for products he believes in. Though he admits because of baseball his back is a wreck, his life is obviously, as revealed in the article, not. He is described at the article's conclusion as smiling. It might not be a smile of joy but it suggests at least satisfaction with his life.

It should be obvious that while a great deal of scattered information about DiMaggio has been published, he has never been portrayed in the depth and complexity a fully dimensional biography of him would demand. Further, there has been little serious attempt to resolve the sometimes conflicting testimony in reports about him: he is reticent, he is expansive; he is a team player, he is sulky; he is gracious, he is petty; he praises Casey Stengel, he abominated him; he is bitter, he is satisfied. One could conclude: of course—he is human. But his intricate humanity has never throughout his career been subject to the kind of scouting that a well-known writer or a leading politician might have received. His public image as it has evolved has controlled the literature about him. He has grown and changed over the years, matured in the public's eye as Babe Ruth never did, but then, from the first years of his stardom a strong element of his image has been that he was developing, from a rookie standout to a team leader, from a gawky kid to a classy dresser. He was becoming increasingly a figure of responsibility demanding respect.

The best book incorporating DiMaggio's many sides, accommodating both his myth and many details of his reality, is Maury Allen's *Where Have You Gone, Joe DiMaggio? The Story of America's Last Hero* (1975). Allen is an admitted fan of DiMaggio's, and at times the people he interviews on DiMaggio sound more as though they were talking about a monument than a man, but the portrait assembled includes so many comments about the "last hero" that he emerges as a highly detailed figure of many moods and attitudes and not just heroic temperament and behavior.

One of the book's greatest strengths is that it is based mainly on oral history interviews with a spectrum of men (and one woman) who knew DiMaggio from various vantage points throughout his life, in addition to some secondary print sources which Allen at least acknowledges at the start of his text even if he does not cite them throughout his narrative. By using the words of DiMaggio's teammates, employers, opponents, associates, and friends, Allen is able to endow nearly all the standard claims about DiMaggio with what seems documented substantiation. His completeness and naturalness as a ball player is confirmed by his manager Joe McCarthy, teammate Bobby Brown, and Cleveland Indians catcher Jim Hegan. His perfectionism is underscored by Eddit Lopat and Billy Martin, the "thousand per cent" he gave that placed so much pressure on him is noted by Allie Reynolds. All the praise given DiMaggio over the years seems verified in seemingly authoritative fashion here, not merely by claims but by illustrative stories. Even the most extreme adulation is made to appear valid. Joe McCarthy declares, "He never made a mental mistake. He never missed a sign; he never threw the ball to the wrong base." Hank Greenberg, his rival and along with McCarthy a respected member of the Hall of Fame, recounts a time he was surprised to see DiMaggio make a mistake, but the accompanying story he tells suggests the error could only have been committed by an athlete whose skill enabled him to enter higher realms of play: DiMaggio shocks Greenberg by catching an extremely long ball hit by him, and then forgets to pick off a runner who has strayed far from first because he never dreamed the catch could be made. Other familiar themes declaring DiMaggio's special value—that he played while in great pain, that he was actually often underrated because he did things so easily, that he was a team leader who made the difference between victory and defeat for so many Yankee teams, that he never realized how great a star he was, are all advanced and accompanied usually by stories told by people who were there watching him play, who seemingly know what they are talking about.

The book is organized in roughly chronological fashion. Though some of the interviews contain reflections about a variety of periods in DiMaggio's life, generally the vignettes are arranged stretching in order from his early years to his most recent. Often Allen is able to illuminate or bring freshly to life familiar sequences in DiMaggio's story, by presenting information through an apparently authentic voice. Thus DiMaggio's family background is discussed by Tom DiMaggio, who points out that tales of his father's resistance to baseball overstate the issue, but that Giuseppe

DiMaggio did fear Joe would not receive an education that would enable him to advance in life. A boyhood chum of DiMaggio's, Frank Venezia, tells of growing up with Joe, whose parents he recollects as "hermits" into whose house no one ever got invited. He further states that Joe and he were shocked when they went to high school and saw kids there so much better dressed than they.

Lefty Gomez talks about Joe as a rookie with the open warmth and affection his stories suggest Joe also felt for him, and relates the improbable sight of DiMaggio playing on his nose as though it were a banjo—surely a rare glimpse of the apprentice hero. Ken Keltner explains how it felt to participate in Joe's streak, and the Yankee team doctor Sidney Gaynor produces an insider's clinical explanation of Joe's fabled wounds, the heel, knee, and shoulder injuries that limited his career while providing it with a special grandeur. On a more gossipy level, Phil Rizzuto presents information on "The Trouble with Stengel," as one of the chapters containing Rizzuto's revelations is termed. Rizzuto is openly critical of Stengel and claims that DiMaggio shared his feelings. Jerry Coleman says "I really think Casey hated him." An especially well constructed section about "The Last Season" includes pictures of DiMaggio's frustrations and anxieties from the perspectives of Rizzuto, Coleman, Gene Woodling, Gil McDougald, Hank Bauer, and Eddie Lopat. The story their combined words tell is sad but not sentimental. As a perfectionist who hated to see himself in situations where he might seem inadequate, the final years posed a problem for DiMaggio solvable only by retirement. Coleman tells of a particularly poignant episode in "The Trouble with Stengel" when DiMaggio was robbed of a hit with men on bases. Terribly disappointed he returned to the dugout and kicked a bag he thought was empty, that was actually filled with baseballs that went rolling over the field. "His face got red but we all turned away and nobody moved. . . . I bet if you ask a dozen guys on the bench if they remember that day today they'd say they never heard ot it. Nobody would want to remember anything that embarrassed DiMaggio."

But a problem with the book is the same problem with much oral history. To what extent are the words of Allen's informants reliable? To what extent have they been guided even unconsciously by the nature of Allen's questions and his stated mission? One must also ask if Allen received information he decided not to include in his picture, that another writer might find important? How were the interviews edited? Sometimes it would seem a relief to read that somewhere in the major leagues, even on DiMaggio's team, existed a player who thought DiMaggio a mean bastard, and had a verifying story to back up his opinions, not because it is thrilling to see popular heroes disparaged, but because so sharp an opposing view would provide needed contrast to the nearly always reverent (though sometimes briefly critical) attitudes toward DiMaggio.

Ballplayers who are asked to publicly comment on their colleagues are often very guarded in their responses. Even when people reveal what they think, their information may reflect only their attitude and not reality. Tom DiMaggio claimed that his father was disturbed about Joe's education, but apparently none of the older DiMaggio boys completed high school, and Tom and Mike directly entered the fishing business with their father's approval. Education presumably was a way of getting clear from poverty, but according to Vince DiMaggio, by the time Joe was ready to play, Giuseppe, Sr., had been shown that baseball was a way to advance and make money. The point is not that Allen prints erroneous information in retelling Tom's opinions, but that other opinions on the same sequence might reveal other versions of the truth. One first-hand account is better than none at all, but cannot always be relied upon, and there is always the problem that not only do informants frequently tell interviewers what they think they want to hear, they often are not certain of the facts of their utterances themselves. Uncorroborated oral history places the interviewer at the mercy of his or her respondents unless their remarks can in some way be checked. In *Where Have You Gone, Joe DiMaggio?*, Phil Rizzuto tells about his first major-league tryout, when he was sixteen. He says he was hit on the back by a pitch, causing Casey Stengel to tell him to leave and "go get a shoebox, kid, you're too small anyway." The same story also appeared in Allen's book on Casey Stengel. In *The Scooter, The Phil Rizzuto Story* by Gene Schoor (1982), it is Giant's coach Frank Snyder who tells Rizzuto "What makes you think you can play ball? Go home and get yourself a shoeshine box." Which first-hand Rizzuto version is correct? Finally, sometimes remarks that might appear factual to the casual reader are only inauthoritative opinions. Allen provides no guidance here: all opinions seem equal. For example, what is the ultimate import of Toots Shor's evaluation of DiMaggio as "very decent, very strong, good morals, good family instincts"? What qualifies Shor as a judge of "family instincts"? Or is the remark just more show-biz gush like "Zsa-Zsa's truly a very beautiful person"? At least when "Old Reliable" Tommy Henrich says DiMaggio "was the most moral man I ever knew. He couldn't do anything cheap; he wouldn't do anything that would hurt his name or hurt the Yankees," the reader can appreciate Henrich's sporting frame of reference and judge his comment's significance accordingly.

   Though the book mainly validates DiMaggio's status as a hero, some commentary squarely if briefly indicates shortcomings and limitations in his character. Various witnesses (most of them his friends or teammates) refer to him as cold, moody, and given to harboring grudges for slight reasons. As a boy, for example, he snubbed one of his best friends because he failed to leave a game he was playing to accompany DiMaggio downtown to pick up newspapers. As a man he snubbed the loyal Toots Shor, because Shor passed a remark about Marilyn Monroe that DiMaggio didn't like. In his private life he is shown mostly as a good person whose flaws and misbehaviors are quite ordinary and unheroic. That is an angle on DiMaggio the purely adulatory and worshipful books and articles do not reveal, just as he did not supply that sort of insight about himself in his autobiography. Phil Rizzuto's comments about Joe and his wife Dorothy support a conjecture easily gained but rarely documented from reading much of the literature about DiMaggio, that he was most comfortable with men and that he did not really understand how to deal or live in any full way with the women he was romantically interested in. Rizzuto remarks that after the 1942 World Series the Rizzutos and DiMaggios dined and had drinks at Rizzuto's apartment. Rizzuto was to leave for Norfolk and the Navy the next day. "Cora and Dorothy got along real good, but Joe would get a little moody and leave for a few minutes every so often. He didn't like the idea of sitting and talking all night with the women." DiMaggio was so disgusted seeing Marilyn pose for still photographs in New York streets before the crowd howling for her to let her skirt blow high again, he "went to Shor's and drank heavily." These signs of frailty or incompleteness surely constitute no evidence of secret deviousness or viciousness in him, but only suggest that he behaved like an ordinary person, though one whom few ever thought of as ordinary.

Allen supplies relatively little information concerning DiMaggio's marriage to Dorothy Arnold though he provides more about their lives together than do most book-length sources. Surprisingly he prints no interview with Arnold or anyone who might know how she felt about her life with DiMaggio. Similarly, he pays scant attention to DiMaggio's war years.

The book's last quarter is downbeat because there Allen writes or presents interviews mainly about DiMaggio's declining skills and the bitter frustrations he tried unsuccessfully to keep to himself, and his involvement with Marilyn Monroe. Though it is clear that DiMaggio never permitted himself to sink into the retirement swamp that drags down so many star and average professional athletes after their playing days are finished, his remorse over Monroe pervades the stories Allen chose to fill the last pages of his book. This DiMaggio is a man who has coped fairly successfully with life after stardom, but he is not a happy man. To what extent this reveals the true DiMaggio and to what extent Allen is here portraying the standard melodrama of the unhappy aged hero is difficult to determine. Certainly the evidence Allen provides to bring out the shadows in DiMaggio's last years is effective. The picture is relieved sometimes by such testimony as that of Robert Spero, then a vice-president of the advertising agency Ogilvy and Mather, who tells how adaptive DiMaggio became to the demands of the Bowery Savings Bank commercials, how he loosened up gradually on the film sets and even began "making suggestions" to the director. His friend the lawyer and sportsman Edward Bennett Williams seems to speak for many when he calls DiMaggio "a very lonely man at times." DiMaggio told

Williams he "burned in" his "belly to be the best there was." Williams remarked that this "put pressures on DiMaggio as a player that were beyond belief. He wanted to be the greatest ever, and there was no settling for anything else." With that kind of greatness as his goal he would inevitably be unhappy, for in sports absolute greatness is evanescent even if amazingly enough it is achieved.

Many of the details Allen relates about DiMaggio's life with Monroe are in other books, but some are new and revealing. Again, Allen shows DiMaggio more fallible, and perhaps because of that more real and human, than most sources where he is the primary subject. Monroe's press agent Lois Weber Smith, even though as she admits she never met him, provides an astute view of DiMaggio that seems consonant with his passionate attachment to the woman he clearly could not possess for very long. Smith's comments are conjectural, but they seem worth pondering and even if uncomplimentary to him, also show better than the weekly gift of flowers on her grave the bitter depth of emotions Monroe apparently compelled in him. "I am sure Marilyn was afraid of him, physically afraid. She said Joe had a bad temper. He was obviously rigid in his beliefs. There must have been a great ambivalence in his feelings toward her."

DiMaggio has been presented like a comic book hero, in books such as Gene Schoor's he is like the hero of a film, and sometimes in Allen's book he has touches of a self-lacerating character from a Dostoevski novel. Allen saves his interview with DiMaggio for last. Here he is presented—or presents himself in a guarded fashion—as a successful but not satisfied man. Allen either asked him no questions about Monroe, or deleted them from his print account of their talk together while DiMaggio relaxed during a golf tournament in Florida. He looks good, but clearly nothing ever replaced baseball for him. "It was all I knew," he says, "It was all I ever wanted to know." The golf is fun, the commercials are all right, "but it's not like playing ball." To Allen there is "a brief sadness in DiMaggio's eyes" when he mentions playing the game.

When Allen questions him about Casey Stengel, DiMaggio's "face twisted in a strange smile. 'The old man had his ways and I had mine. I don't want to say any more about it,'" and he doesn't. (Earlier, Allen quotes Stengel for three pages mostly in praise of DiMaggio, including the ambiguous remark "What do you mean did I get along with him? I played him, didn't I?") DiMaggio also discusses at length his dissatisfaction that he never achieved his ambition to own at least part of a club. He adds that he had a "wonderful career" with "pleasant memories," but the interview does not report many of them. It ends with a fat bald man yelling to DiMaggio that he was there that night in Cleveland when Keltner robbed him. He says "I remember it, Joe, I really do." DiMaggio says "softly" that he does too, and that concludes the book. The ending seems to suggest that the young DiMaggio has vanished from himself, just as he disappeared from Mrs. Robinson and the rest of us.

Hank Greenberg says of DiMaggio early in the first half of the book that after forty years "I guess I really don't know him. I don't know him. I don't know if anybody knows Joe DiMaggio." That seems to sum up Allen's point of view, the message about the last American hero that he wants to deliver to his audience. In some ways the message is substantiated by the technique Allen employs, mostly permitting a variety of respondents to set forth their observations and opinions about DiMaggio with a minimum of author's comment. In this way it appears that not just one but many Joe DiMaggios are described. But of course Allen had guided the interviews into their final form, selected and arranged them, and thereby shaped the pictures they presented. If he is saying how can anyone understand Joe DiMaggio one reply could be of course, how can anyone be understood? How can one understand one's parents, children, husband, wife, self? Not to understand people in any final, clear, simple fashion is a characteristic of the modern intellectual world. Post-modern art abjures understanding frequently replacing it instead with pure presentation, which is what Allen has almost done. It seems appropriate that the modern hero is a person not to be understood.

Another sense in which Allen's last hero is difficult to understand is that he represents a time now gone. Throughout the text there is an undercurrent of the old against the new: in the old days you didn't have to play night games. In the old days you could travel more slowly on the train and live in a community of fellow athletes. Today the players carry briefcases and separate in each city away from home to see their brokers. How could a totally dedicated individual like DiMaggio, who as Phil Rizzuto remembered would talk volubly with his teammates only about baseball, be understood in the company of today's incorporated performers (though in an older incarnation he has become a handsome businessman himself: that is a different DiMaggio).

Yet there is much that Allen shows that is understandable about DiMaggio. He was a star and even though he has remained a bright star perhaps longer than any of his sports contemporaries (Ted Williams is still splendid but not nearly as often before the public; Joe Louis stayed around in the hearts of his countrymen but his real presence was an embarrassment when first his fortunes then part of his mind eroded), nothing will replace his active days of greatness. He aged gracefully and overcame the trauma of his experience with Marilyn Monroe, a woman he loved deeply whose suicide shocked him. He has a grown son and a more than comfortable income and the respect of his country, but he was playing on top once and never will again, and certainly that must bring him sorrow sometimes. People who are not stars or celebrities who have successfully developed in their own lives, ordinary people also often grieve for their youth or early maturity. It is part of the romantic tradition that seems ingrained in what was once called human nature. So to an extent, the idea that DiMaggio is not understandable or that he is discontent sometimes or in a mild fashion much of the time (if that is so) constitutes a very human part of his story. If the hero does not die young and at his or her peak, the trail of decline after greatness becomes inevitably part of their narrative, and it is a part Allen firmly fixes onto DiMaggio's myth. He shows convincingly that DiMaggio experienced a falling away from physical ability but not a sharp and disastrous fall. That there was eventually a parallel decline of the spirit, may be a valid observation and an important comment on the real life of a hero in America. But it could also be a conventional literary attitude imposed upon the story of a successful athlete and person.

George DeGregorio's *Joe DiMaggio* (1981) is not nearly so mythic or melancholy a figure as Maury Allen's last hero, though according to the opinion of a close friend in a section of the book describing DiMaggio's retirement "he is definitely a lonely guy. . . . A lot of it stems from not being really close to baseball. And . . . he still misses Marilyn Monroe." Nor is he the heroic film version of himself that Gene Schoor presents, a sportswriter's dream of almost seamless perfection. Neither is DeGregorio as powerful as Allen in depicting the narrative of his grand rise to fame not just as a baseball player but as a culture-hero. Yet this unpretentious book is a fresh and relatively accurate recitation of the details of DiMaggio's life, and arguably the most realistic of DiMaggio's full portraits. In this book people talk like people and not as though they were being recorded for a movie sound track or Smithsonian Institute archive, and DeGregorio provides details on many of the important events in DiMaggio's off-the-field history most other writers do not. One of the book's deficiencies as a story is one of its strong points as factual narrative: it lacks a clear point of view toward its material, and thereby seems more objective than the other biographies.

DeGregorio seems to have relied more on research into other books and particularly into newspaper files, including at least one San Francisco paper, than his predecessors. Though newspapers, even the ubiquitous *New York Times* can be notoriously inaccurate, especially concerning historical background, they are a rich source of detail on day-to-day matters. The book also gains from some oral interviews; Ernie Sisto, a *New York Times* photographer who knew DiMaggio from his earliest years with the Yankees, is the outside voice DeGregorio most often weaves into the description of events to provide helpful explanations. Sisto seems like an average fellow with good sense, and so he and a few others supply a sort of chorus of normative commentary.

DeGregorio presents new details or expands greatly on the old information concerning a number of events in DiMaggio's life or the life of his family. He is presented less completely as a star performer and more as a person who has to deal with everyday life like everyone else. A fuller version than any other of his 1938 holdout offers a realistic view of contractual confrontations; details about DiMaggio's armed service career reveal the dreary landscape of that episode and show how absolutely different it was for DiMaggio from his baseball years, suggesting why he might have changed so greatly as a performer when he finally returned to playing games. DeGregorio constructs a solidly three-dimensional view of DiMaggio's life. All the triumphs on the baseball field are shown, the wounds observed and comebacks retold, but these events occur surrounded by a fuller range than usual of private or unsensational activities that were also part of DiMaggio's life. Rosalie DiMaggio's trip back to New York in 1936 to see Joe star in the World Series, is described in considerable detail for the first time in a book; his life with Dorothy Arnold is presented at far greater length than usual. One photograph in the picture section shows Dorothy nibbling a pencil at one of Joe's games, bored but glamorously dolled-up, her sharply drawn eyebrows perfectly arched. Information about Toots Shor and George Solotaire clarifies their male, Broadway world DiMaggio found so comfortable. The problems Giuseppe DiMaggio faced early in World War II as an Italian who had never become an American citizen has little effect on the public's view of his son but everything to say about the real difficulties the old man had to face in his lifetime, and further demonstrates how distant in his way of life Joe DiMaggio had grown from his father. Equally unheroic but revealing as an insight into the problems even great stars must confront is the explanation of DiMaggio's meeting with Judge Landis in 1940 about possible outside meddling in Joe's contract negotiations. Usually DeGregorio simply narrates these stories. Sometimes he draws conclusions from them and these are ordinarily sensible, as when he comments on DiMaggio's failure to accompany his mother one night during her 1936 visit, because he had to go out with the boys. Mrs. DiMaggio accepted his decision without question. DeGregorio observes that the pampering shown Joe here by his mother, "the female acceptance of male preference," could be a reason for the failure of his two marriages.

DeGregorio does not sharply differ from most of the previous writers who presented versions of DiMaggio's life, and helped construct his image even while they were reflecting it, but he presents him in a more comprehensive fashion operating in more fully described surroundings. DiMaggio is shown as a player whose special "talents were gifts," who could perform great tasks "instinctively," a man of extraordinary achievements who lived in the ordinary world of haggling for salaries, failed marriages, submission to military routine, and was subject to the physical decline brought by age and injury. While not a completely balanced biography—far more is written about a two-month trip DiMaggio took late in 1951 to play ball in the Orient than about his life with Marilyn Monroe—it is an unusually substantial portrait. The virtual elimination of Monroe from the text constitutes a defect but not one that undermines DeGregorio's accomplishment in depicting a believable, real hero.

The book begins with DiMaggio's hitting streak occuring during a time of war preparations and Andy Hardy films. The streak is described again in added detail about a third of the way through the book. It is a central symbol of DiMaggio's greatness as a player and the event which according to DeGregorio more than any other made him "a symbol of cosmic masculinity; a creature of animal magnetism desired by women, approved by men." At the conclusion of the book DiMaggio has long since played his last game. He is reported still lamenting for Marilyn Monroe, lonely if not a loner, but also as a successful spokesman for commercial firms because he is a greatly known and respected man. On the book's last page his friend Ernie Sisto, a newspaper photographer and therefore in theory anyway a man who deals in accurate pictures, tells how bitter DiMaggio was that no good place was ever found for him in the Yankee organization. This hurt DiMaggio Sisto says, though he never admitted it. DiMaggio said "Ah, fuck them," according to Sisto, "Ah, fuck them," about the owners. The remark if made tells that DiMaggio still was not the kind to give up. The words are unheroic, but seem real enough. They are not found in any other account of DiMaggio and it is nice to think that even though he figured he was *Lucky to Be a Yankee*, he could say "Ah, fuck them" too.

DeGregorio concludes his book with the detail that "in January of 1980, Joe DiMaggio became a member of the Board of Directors of the Baltimore Orioles." Maybe this was just another business deal, or a symbolic gesture rather than a meaningful appointment. Still, it was a sign of success in the real world where men like Joe DiMaggio live only for a short time.

*   *   *   *

It is strange and intriguing that after so many years of often intense public attention, Joe DiMaggio still retains an elusive quality, a part of himself that seems always obscured from the view of his fans, fellow performers, and friends. He has not become the kind of person or hero whose character one feels can be encompassed. There remains a teasing incompleteness about his figure, as though one perhaps small but key piece to our understanding of him were absent, or beyond the camera's range. Possibly he has kept the piece hidden or perhaps it never existed, as though he were somehow in himself unfinished. Although the literature about him is filled with the reminiscences of those who knew him, no one seems to have been his intimate friend, to have felt they possessed deep understanding of him.

The reasons that he has achieved such great fame within and far beyond the world of sports seem relatively clear. There was his talent, which for a time focused attention on him as a dominating player, and which after he had passed the period when he could perform almost daily with superior skills, still enabled him to play usually at a level higher than most of his fellow performers, and even occasionally allowed him to hit peaks only few could attain. There were for much of his career his day-to-day skills at bat, in the field, and on the bases. There were his unparalleled major-league batting streak and his comeback against Boston in 1949. There was his leadership ability, hard to quantify but easy to register in the responses of his teammates.

Furthermore, he possessed personal attributes of birth and personality that made him particularly attractive to Americans at first in the 1930s and continuing until the present time. He fit snugly into the mold of the poor boy who makes good, the immigrant's child who reaps success in the new world. As an Italian-American he benefitted from the adulation of an emerging ethnic group particularly ready to create and reward heroes who could in turn symbolize the group's successful arrival on the American scene. He played for two teams based in cities with large Italian populations ready to offer him strong support, places able to provide him with unmatched opportunities for disseminating his exploits throughout the country. When he arrived at the training camp of his only major-league team, he was heralded as the man who would take the place of the greatest star his team had ever known, and he fulfilled the expectations of those who had announced and were awaiting his appearance.

As he matured from a rookie to a greatly respected team leader, from a veritable young man of the provinces (his North Beach Italian-American community) to a gentleman with at least a veneer of suavity and sophistication, as he progressed from the sandlots of San Francisco to the seemingly glamorous and tricky streets of Manhattan and Hollywood, he displayed admirable traits that always eclipsed the less attractive characteristics which were equally a part of his temperament, but that were—typically in the instance of heroes—often excused as the prerogatives of a great man under pressure. That he played with pain, came back again and again after he was hurt, helped make him a symbol of human courage. That he practiced his sport with the devotion of a craftsman and the sometimes inspired dedication of an artist, that he felt he should play both ends of a doubleheader with complete involvement even in sultry heat because some kid might be in the stands who had never before seen him perform, helped make him a symbol of almost priestly purity in a secularized and corrupt, highly commercial world. And that he was so often a winner made him even more attractive as a symbolic American: even when he lost, for example in his relationship with the doomed Marilyn Monroe, he seemed to emerge a winner, even more fixed as a hero who had to endure and could finally surmount a real and messy problem.

He seemed destined to play baseball the way Keats appeared to have written his odes, with easy grace (after much painstaking revision) and beauty. One writer viewed him as lazy and many as sullen, but these were also traditional characteristics of the hero, petulant, driven to excel, single-minded in purpose, smouldering inside to perform nobly, and either uncaring when he was not at his ordained task or bitterly angry when not succeeding at it: Grant rocking on his front porch waiting for the Civil War, or Gary Cooper brooding before the showdown at *High Noon.*.

When his playing days were over DiMaggio, unlike most sports figures, maintained an afterlife as a cultural symbol mentioned through song and story. The bright light these works have cast upon him has been augmented by the mellower afterglow he has projected as a commercial spokesman. Always it has been his dignity, his integrity, his success that have been emphasized as he evolved from a raw high school leaver with few apparent skills, to an internationally known hero.

Still, he seems more comprehensible as a symbol or hero than as a real person. Perhaps that is because from the start of his major-league career—almost from the beginning of his minor-league play—the audience of onlookers around him, fans and reporters, have not seen him as an ordinary person. After his 61-game Seals streak, and through his introduction as Babe Ruth's successor, he has been viewed in the heroic mold, as a special breed of competitor. But all along inside that hero was at first just another not highly educated young man from a good, loving, stable immigrant family. Numbers of writers knew that about him and passed the information along to the public, like scenes from the childhood of a legend. He was neither viewed nor treated as the ordinary young man he was without his rare gifts as a performer. Despite the glaring attention he received, he managed to grow up inside the hero's covering in which his talents and the praise sung about him had encased him, like the armor of a knight—that like a knight's armor made him seem bigger than life-size and less human looking too.

So what is perhaps most truly amazing about him is that cloaked in his legend he has retained his ordinary measure of basic decency and responsibility, mixed with ordinary measures of human frailties—his occasional ill-temper, his sulkiness, his residual, inviolate coldness. Were he the fellow down the street, he would doubtless be a likable if withdrawn person, not one you could ever get very close to. He had his ways: probably his first and second wives found that out. He liked to be with the Broadway boys, he was not good at small talk (or deep talk either), he was uncomfortable when not living in his own style. But then, he was loyal, reliable, and in his own way caring. It is not a part of his record that he ever exploited any relationship though he may have monitored his relations with the press more than anyone realized. He was great enough to meet presidents and be written about by important, idolizing writers who thought him a symbol of greatness, but inside he appears to have always remained an ordinarily good, humanly imperfect person. He grew a little lopsidedly like most people do, but he grew up. The faults he kept do not seem to have resulted from the adulation he received, from the successes he attained. He seems unwarped by fame though his image was fabricated mainly from adulation, and blemished only as probably all are who grow up in the bruising real world.

Immersed in the hyperbole, bloat, and falseness that admiration on a grand scale seems inevitably to accumulate, he has remained an ordinary man. That is often glibly written of celebrities, stars, and heroes, but it seems true of DiMaggio. He seems at heart the same person he would have been had he followed his father's wishes and become a fisherman getting up every day to work hard, hanging out in his spare time with the other fishermen. This is to his credit, but also suggests his limitations. Perhaps the piece that seems missing in him is actually an illusion based upon incessant misperception. Perhaps we simply do not want to see that he has remained his own real, bounded, essentially good but unglorious person. Or perhaps that view only reflects another shard, another fragment of his image: his mystery, that we do not wish to admit we have helped manufacture.

NOTES

1. I am indebted to Professor Gary Mormino of the History Department, University of South Florida, for his translations from the Italian here.

4

INTERVIEWS

INTERVIEW WITH VINCE DIMAGGIO

(The following edited interview with *Vince DiMaggio* took place June 25, 1984. Vince lives with his wife of over five decades, Madelaine, in a pleasant house with a lovely garden in the Los Angeles suburbs. He has been for many years a successful, self-employed salesman.)

I was three years old when I left Martinez. I remember, we had relatives that lived there and we'd go to visit. There was a railroad track, and we used to cross the railroad track, and there was a swimming hole, more like a creek of the Sacramento River, and a lot of fishing boats were set on the inside of the creek and in the mouth of the river on the outside. We used to play and swim there. My dad was a fisherman at that time. We'd go back very regularly because we had relatives there.

My dad's brother lived there. The two brothers married two sisters. The brother in Martinez was younger. There was one brother that lived in Pittsburg, California, not too far from Martinez, but he was older than Dad. I was named after him—his name was Vince. I believe he came to America later than Dad. My dad came first, set up and got into the business, and then called for the family in Italy.

Mom and Dad were born in Isola della Femmine. Palermo is the province. They never talked about living in Italy. The only thing was, people asked Dad if he ever played baseball, and he said no. They played actually in a sense, a game in Italy that's similar to what we call one-a-cat here. They used anything they could get their hands on, cans and sticks and whatever. He was born and raised a fisherman.

America was the place for opportunity. There was nothing he could do over there. He wanted to be a fisherman. There were friends here from Italy that used to write and tell him how good the fishing was, so he decided to come over and try it by himself to see, and when he found it was good, saved up enough money, and sent for the family. They lived around Collinsville. That was a little island right across the river from Pittsburg, California, in the middle of the river actually. The houses were on slats. The island would flood.

My oldest sister was four years old when she came over with my mother: my sister Nell. She was just newborn when he left Sicily. That I know because my dad, or my sisters, they said so themselves. I think I remember my mother told me too.

If he did something else when he came over other than be a fisherman, I didn't know.

Martinez is where he settled because all his friends and relatives were right there. My aunt who is my mother's sister lived right in Martinez. My mother's maiden name is Mercurio. My other aunt on my mother's side lived in San Francisco. One sister lived in Pittsburg, used to be called Black Diamond. They have a street named after that in Pittsburg. They all lived in the Contra Costa County area.

My sister Nellie was real nice. She kept more to herself. She didn't marry an Italian. Usually in the old Italian custom, matches were made for people before they made them for themselves. If they had a match for my sister she evidently didn't follow it, because she married Robert Helquist. My brother Tom, he didn't marry until late in life. My dad and mother had arranged a wedding for him and he said no way. When Tom didn't accept it, then they went to Mike with the same woman and he finally married her. There wasn't much difference between Tom and Mike. Tom married quite a few years later. His wife was not Italian.

You always spoke Italian when you spoke to the parents. But as far as we were concerned, among ourselves, we spoke English. As youngsters, we were more or less learning the Italian language at home, at the beginning, until we went to school. Our older brothers and sisters would more or less talk in English to us, and we would learn from them. It was easy to learn when you were a little baby.

Tom was a good baseball player, but he hurt his arm before he got into pro ball. He worked with Dad when he was young, then he got a boat of his own. In 1937 Joe, Tom, and my dad, they opened a restaurant. Then Tom was head of the organization. In the majority of Italian families it was the tradition that the oldest son actually had control of the family. The father would always have the oldest son see that everything was taken care of. And if there was any problem or anything that was to be done, if the parent didn't get up to do it, the son did it. He was the one that did the disciplining unless the parent got provoked enough to go and do it himself. Dad was more or less easy around the house, easy but firm, let's put it that way. Mom was the one that took care actually when it came to where the youngsters were concerned. She was in contact with them all the time. She was the one that had to be the boss. But then when she couldn't handle it, she would say, "when Dad comes home you're going to be in trouble." That's it. And he would do the disciplining.

Tom was with my dad to begin with. Then when my brother Mike was old enough, my dad got another boat, and my oldest brother Tom took over the other boat and he fished by himself. My brother Mike went with Dad. When my brother Mike got old enough to take over the boat, then my Dad retired and I went with my brother Mike. So we did fishing together. Once in a while Dad would go with us. He retired before I started playing baseball. He owned the two boats, and he got a percentage from the two boats. We were supposed to follow in his footsteps too. My dad had a thought in mind that he was going to buy one of the bigger boats and have the five sons with himself on this bigger boat.

He was pretty successful. He was one of the best fishermen. He may have been once with somebody else, but I don't recall. When my father retired, he would leave the house at a certain time and he would get a ride to the marina or he would go down to Fisherman's Wharf, otherwise he would take his time and go for a walk. They were very good parents, and Dad was proud, especially when it came to the fishing part of it. He had to be number one or close to the top. He was very competitive. So when we went fishing we had to be there at a certain time and that was it. I wanted to play ball and I was late coming down to the wharf to go fishing, and I would get in trouble a lot.

I was about twelve years old when I really started fishing. I went fishing a lot before then, but really started when I was about twelve. After school was out, then we went fishing. A lot of it was night fishing.

We would lay out the nets and it would be after school. We'd go out for a few hours and we would come back. Most of the time I would be sleeping out there. You'd lay the net out . . . and you make a drift and you are drifting with the net for an hour or so, two hours, depends on the tide, and we would be in places where the tide would take us down to a certain point, then the tide would stand still, then the tide would change and we would go back, and we'd make one to two drifts, maybe. That would be out in the bay. At that time we would catch everything that was there. We used to go for herring, then we used to go for bass and salmon. My oldest brother Tom was the crab fisherman, afterwards, and he stayed as a crab fisherman.

A poor family yes, but we were never without food or clothing. We had enough of that. Like all big families when the older ones grew out of clothes they passed them down to the ones that were next in line.

Unless we had some vocation to follow there was no strong pressure to finish school, but I don't think any of us had a vocation, really. We were more scheduled to go into fishing. That was Dad's point of view. We were going to be fishermen.

I graduated from junior high school when I was sixteen. They said in school I would have to go until I was eighteen. I said I can't. I have to go to work. It's a hardship. Joe and Dominic went to high school, Galileo, but I think Joe only got to the tenth grade. I don't think my older brothers went to high school. I don't recall about the girls.

We rented a house on Taylor Street, $25.00 a month, at that time a lot of money. The house had actually three big bedrooms, then it had a room that my dad figured he'd use for his nets. Instead, my brother Tom took over that room and put a bed in there and he slept in there by himself. He had nets that were new in there and he put them in a big closet. Then we had a couch that we used to open up in the dining room. It was a big house. We were all in that house. The only one that I think was missing to begin with was Nellie. I think she was married. Then my sister Mae left and then Marie left after that. One at a time they left. Then after that Mike, then me, and by that time there were only two or three left in the house. Then Joe bought the house down at the marina, close to the Presidio.

A lot of times I would speak to my dad in English, and in the beginning he'd answer in Italian. Then I'd know he understood. Then after a while he got to where he would speak to me a little in English. I would say, now you speak to me in English and learn the English language. It would make it easier because he would get a lot of questions asked, and if he didn't want to answer then he could say "no savvy." He could never read or write Italian or English, but he was able to read the box scores. Mom could read Italian, but not English. When we got into baseball and we would show Dad the box score we'd explain the different things to him and after a while we didn't have to tell him anymore, he knew how to read the box scores, he knew who got the base hits, he knew who made the errors, and then he'd read the summary and tell you exactly what went on during the ball game.

As far back as I can remember, the times were good. But of course they had their little ways. When I wanted to get married, they said well, you're too young. I was twenty and two months. I was supporting myself, but I gave them all the money. I had a hard time getting into baseball. I didn't think of fishing as a career. Not that I didn't like it. It was a good life. But then, I wanted to be a ballplayer. I wanted to be a singer before being a ballplayer, and I wanted to be a ballplayer before being a fisherman. So when I came out of it, from being a fisherman, I got into baseball, because that came easier than singing. I couldn't afford to get into paying for lessons. Dad thought, "That's crazy. That's a bum's game." To be respected he thought nothing but fishing was the thing. That's all he knew, and he was proud of that and he wanted all his sons to follow in his footsteps. I put a monkey wrench in that.

My mother wanted me to be with Dad as far as the fishing was concerned. But then the scout wanted to sign me to a contract, I passed it to my dad, and he said nope, and my mother said nope. And I said, "either you sign the contract, or I'll just take off anyway. Do you want me to go with your will or against your will? I'd rather go with your will, but if you don't give it to me, then I'm going to go anyway." I was pretty strong minded. I don't think Joe or Dominic were.

Well, they didn't sign the contract. They said no. They said you go out and don't come back. So I just said okay. I just took off, and went and played baseball.

From the San Francisco Seals I went down to Tucson, Arizona, for instruction. I was down there about three months, and they paid my salary. I figured with the money that I would be able to save, that my folks would know that there was more money in baseball than there was in fishing. So with all the bonuses and everything that I had coming from the club, when I came home I had $1,500.00. That was a lot of money. This was during the Depression, 1931. So I came home and I walked in. My dad—he didn't say much—but I knew he was waiting for an opportunity. My mother when she saw me, she put her arms around me. Dad was in the kitchen. He was having a little wine, and he had some peaches cut and he was dipping peaches in the wine. When I went in and greeted him he looked at me and greeted me more or less saying, what are you doing here?

So I said "Dad, I've come home. If it's all right I'd like to stay here," and I said "this is what I earned, and this is what I'm bringing home."

Right away before he could say anything—I brought it in cash, I didn't bring no check, I brought it in cash so he could see it was more than a piece of paper: he knows the cash but he didn't know anything about a check, so I had it all in cash—and the first thing he says when he saw the money, was "where'd you steal that money?"

I said I earned it. I said you come with me, I'll introduce you to my boss. So the next day, sure enough, he went and talked with the owner Mr. Graham, and they had a little conversation. Dad was talking broken English now, and he was talking broken English to Mr. Graham. Once in a while when Mr. Graham couldn't understand, he would ask me the question and I would explain it to him. When my dad couldn't understand, then I would explain it to *him*. So after a while, they got to be pretty good friends, my dad and Mr. Graham. So then Mr. Graham explained everything to him. And I said "Dad you ought to go out and watch the ball game." So from then on he wanted to watch the ball game. Then he says "I guess there is money in that. Well, if you can do that and make more money than you would be out fishing, you might as well stay here, at home."

So that broke the ice for Joe and Dominic. I really set the pattern for the family, as far as baseball was concerned. Joe didn't have any opposition, because I had already broken the ice. The scout that scouted me was Mickey Schraeder. Bill Essick had something to do with Joe. He's a Yankee scout. Ike Caveney was the manager of the San Francisco Seals. Now everybody wants to get the credit of bringing Joe into the Seals, but nobody brought Joe into the Seals, because in 1932 when Henry Oana was with the ball club, and

Augie Galan, I came back and was living at the house and playing with the Seals, and Oana was going to Hawaii and Augie Galan wanted to go with him. Ike came, and he said "I can't let you go, I don't have any more infielders. I can't let you go." I heard that. I told Ike "I got my kid brother, he's a shortstop and a good one. A good shortstop." So Ike said, "Can he really play short." I says "oh yeah. He's played semi-pro, lots of semi-pro. He's good." Ike said "if he's anything like you, bring him on. Okay, Augie, you can go. I'll take Vince's brother, put him at short, you can go ahead."

I don't know any part of that Spike Hennessy story. If that were so, then why would I be bringing Joe on? They all want to get the credit. They all have a story. But as far as getting credit for him joining the pro ranks, the only time that Joe got in, was I made the contact for Joe and I brought Joe in. He played three ball games, threw a couple up in the stands, made a couple of good catches, got a couple of good hits, and they liked him. They liked him so well that they wanted to sign him right then and there. But Tom was the boss, so it had to be under Tom's jurisdiction. Joe was still under age, so Tom took over. In all Joe's dealings as far as San Francisco is concerned, Tom was Joe's manager.

After the season they wanted to sign Joe to a contract immediately. So Tom did all the dickering back and forth. He was the boss, he did all the bartering and transacting that was to be done as far as baseball was concerned. They held out for this, they held out for that, but Tom did everything. So Joe couldn't have had much opposition from the folks. And I don't recall any opposition, as a matter of fact.

Another story is—I don't know who these different ones are that come up with stories—that Joe took my job. Well he did take my job but only when I couldn't throw hard enough to break a pane of glass, when any rookie would be able to take my job. I had hurt my arm diving after a catch and I threw the shoulder out. It took three years for it to come back. The Seals released me at just about the start of the season. Mr. Lane, he owned the Hollywood Stars, and I think the man just loved me and he watched me play and he saw me do a lot of things. So when I was up in the stands watching the ball game he came down and talked to me and he said look I know you can't throw and I know your arm is practically gone but I think I've got a man that could help bring your arm back. Now I'm willing to gamble and I'm willing to play you even though I know that a single is going to be run into a double if it's hit out there to you, and that any fly ball they're going to advance a base. All that I know. And I'm willing to put you back into baseball but I can't pay you much because I know I'm going to be abused when I sign you and then I have you out there playing and they're really going to ridicule me but, he says, I've got some pretty heavy shoulders. But this is all I'm going to be able to pay you, this is the salary.

Not that I wouldn't want to pay you more if you were in good shape, you'd be worth every bit of it but you're not right now. So I said okay, I agreed.

Any time I was playing ball was the best time. There were different games that were just as important as an All-Star game. In the course of a year, when it meant something, that game was as important as any All-Star game. I had a great 1943 All-Star game. That's where I got this watch. A Hamilton. I hit a single, a triple, and a home run, and my team still lost. Who wouldn't feel good after going three for three, off Hal Newhouser and Tex Hughson? The triple was a harder hit ball than the home run. The triple was a direct line drive that would have been a home run had it not been for the wire fence above a concrete wall. The ball hit the iron bar on top of the wire fence exact dead center and came straight back at the outfielder, past him, and the second baseman came out and got the ball and I was already on third.

The last old-timer's game that I played in was in San Diego and I think it was in 1975. And then I refused to play in any more old-timer's games and even to show up. You show up and they want to play you and I don't want to play anymore. The eyes are not the same. It was twilight. That's tough. I could see the ball, the ball was hit, I could see the ball hitting the bat, coming out, and I saw it go up, and then I couldn't judge it any more. I said that's it. I could still hit but I figured I'm not going to fool with this anymore.

As far as being a closely knit family, as long as Dad and Mother were alive then we would come once a year or sometimes twice a year and we would all get together. Especially when the restaurant was open. And they would close the restaurant for two or three days and that would be the reunion. After they passed away my older brother Tom tried to carry on the tradition but nobody would make the effort that they would for Dad and Mother. When they didn't show up finally after about three years, Tom said there's no sense when only two or three show up. We used to go up to the house where Marie lives twice a year. But every time we'd go, Joe would be off somewhere. He's on the move.

We were together quite a bit as kids. Joe was always shy. As youngsters, I think even I was a little shy myself. Maybe not as much as Joe. I don't think Dominic was shy. We all had that sort of tendency as youngsters growing up. As far as the neighbors were concerned, it didn't make any difference anyway. They never called us by our right names. There were so many of us, when they'd look at us they'd call us by the wrong name. They'd call me Joe, or Joe Vince.

I still sing. Tenor. All my life I wanted to be a singer, but I never got there. The only voice training I had was about fifteen years ago. I went and had a few lessons and the voice teacher said well, now we've got your voice set, but this is as far as I can go with you. I never had the opportunity to get lessons when I was a kid. I play piano with one hand. I got the piano and sit at it and I play with one hand and I sing. If I want to learn a new song I go over there and I can read the music.

As far as right now is concerned, I think I'm in the happiest part of my life.

INTERVIEW WITH SPURGEON CHANDLER

(The following edited interview with *Spurgeon* [*Spud*] *Chandler* took place in his attractive home in Clearwater, Florida. Chandler pitched for the Yankees 1937-47 [with reduced seasons in 1939 because of a broken leg, and 1944-45, because of Armed Services duty]. His .717 won-lost record [109-43] is the best of any Yankee pitcher with over 100 games pitched. He has been a major league scout for many years.)

I was a country boy all my life. I was known as the Carnesville plowboy. I was small, but I had a lot of wire and a lot of guts. I couldn't get a scholarship at the University of Georgia. The only concession they'd make to me was that if you come down and make the freshman team and look like varsity material we'll give you a full scholarship. Well, we didn't have much money back in 1928. I had a scholarship to Clemson, Vanderbilt, and Oglethorpe, and I'd already agreed to go to Clemson which was 35 miles east of my home and Athens was 35 miles southwest. So the day before I was supposed to leave and go to Clemson an alumnus from Georgia came up there and says "Why aren't you in practice down there, they've been practicing for a week?" And I said, "Just don't have the money to go to Georgia for a year." He said "Money? You're worrying about money?" He says "You turn that T-model Ford around and head it toward Athens because anytime you need money you let me know and you'll get it." I says "Do you mean that?" and he says "Hell yes I mean it. Once you walk on that football field, the University of Georgia belongs to you."

I could throw a football 85 yards, and I outran everybody in the backfield except one guy. I outran all of them for the position I was going out for which was left halfback, and I could kick the damn cover off the football. The only thing against me was my weight. I played in every game except one, for four solid years. I was starting left halfback my last two years.

I only missed one game, against the University of Florida, and they beat the hell out of me in 1929. I never will forget it. They had a big left end, I was back in short punt formation. I dropped back to quick-kick them, and, man, he broke through that line and got hold of me and he carried me back about ten yards and he threw me up in the air and threw me against the ground and then fell on me and knocked the damn breath out of me and liked to damn kill me. But I got up and I told him I says "I hope I have the chance and I'll give it to you," and so help me God I did. I got him catching a flat pass out on the left side and he had his back to me and I could run like a scalded cat and I hit him right in the center of the damn back, just as hard as I could run, and I left my feet and hit him and I folded him up. They took him off the field and I told him, "Well, I'll see you later." I guess I was a little cocky.

I never thought too much about playing professional baseball until my senior year. The Yankees were my first preference, Chicago was my second.

I got a $25.00 a month raise when I moved from A to Triple A. [Laugh] That George Weiss was a hard man to get along with. He'd say "take it or leave it, or we'll send you back to Newark."

In the Pacific Coast League in 1935 with Portland we opened against San Francisco in the first game and DiMaggio was on that club. I never will forget it. He came up and I tried to throw that ball by him and he hit a home run. Into left center field about ten rows up. I thought now I'd get a little smart with him, I wouldn't give him the same delivery, and he hit that one about the same spot for a home run. And the third time up I threw side arm at him and he hit a triple and it didn't lack but about two feet from going in for a home run. And the fourth time up I threw an under-hand cross fire and he hit it right back between my legs. Four for four. And I told him the next day "I hope you remember me when I pitch for the Yankees and you're playing center field. I hope you tee off on somebody the way you teed off on me." And he just grinned.

Joe McCarthy was one of the greatest. He was the type of manager who had respect for his players and he demanded respect from them. He didn't have any hard and fast rules, he just said, like, "if you're going to drink, don't drink beer. Drink whiskey. If you drink beer you'll get beer legs and you'll sweat and be sloppy and all that. It throws you down."

He didn't give much advice, but there was one thing he wouldn't do, he wouldn't second guess his ballplayers. I know I was pitching and somebody hit a home run about twenty rows back into right field and when I came in he said "what did so and so hit?" and I said "he hit a fastball." He says "tell you what I'll do. I'll bet you he can't hit a curve, that boy." He never held any meetings, and he didn't give much advice, but he knew baseball.

I roomed with Bump Hadley, and Atley Donald and I roomed together, DiMaggio and Gomez roomed together. They switched around some. I roomed with DiMaggio once, on the road. That was in 1937, my first year up. He was always quiet.

Bucky Harris was a good manager and a great man, but he was a little bit too slack on his players, and they'd take advantage of him.

When I came up, DiMaggio was already playing. He could have played in 1935 just as good as he played in 1936. I guess it's been quoted a thousand times, but I'm going to quote it one more time. He was a great leader, besides being a hell of a ballplayer. There's very few things DiMaggio couldn't do, playing. I locker'd side by side with him for years, he was very quiet and unassuming. He'd never get into an argument, he never had any criticism of anybody. I never saw him squawk in a ball game but one time. He could take the extra base, and you'd say he'll never make it, but he'd slide in safe. One time there was a real close play at second base and he was thrown out and that was the only time I ever heard him squawk at an umpire. And he didn't stand up and breathe in his face, he just gave the ground a kick or two and came on in to the dugout. He was a good guy on the field and off the field. We had other guys on the club like Gehrig and Lazzeri that were really established, and as quick as Gehrig became ineligible to play—his sickness kept him from playing—I would say DiMaggio became a leader then. But he didn't try to show anybody up. He wouldn't get up and make a speech in the clubhouse or anything like that. He just let his abilities do the talking. In hitting, making great plays.

He was a lot of people's idol. No, Gehrig wasn't a better power hitter, he just had a shorter fence to reach. Because left center in New York is a long damn ways out.

When he held out, there was no criticism. We realized, at least I did, that whatever he was holding out for he deserved it. I've often thought, how much DiMaggio would be making if he were playing today.

I was the highest paid pitcher in 1947, that had ever been on the Yankee club. And you'd be surprised how much it was: $28,000. You had to not only win twenty games but then try to get the money. One year I won twenty and lost eight, and had the lowest earned run average in the league, and the next year George Weiss sent me a contract for the same money as the last year. He'd feel you out. Once he sent me a contract, and said at the bottom of it, in the event you don't sign this contract, don't send it back, just keep it as a souvenir. He was just a tightwad. I think he was given just so much money to sign the minor-league ballplayers, and all under that amount that he could save, he'd get a percentage of that. That was the way he operated. He'd just give players an ultimatum. This is it. Take it or leave it. We can send you back down to a lower organization. You'd go in and try to get an appointment with him, at his office in New York, and his secretary would ask you, "What do you want to see Mr. Weiss about?" I'd say "This is a personal matter." She'd say, "Well, he's not in. He's in Terre Haute, Indiana." I'd say, "Do you know where he's stopping?" and she'd say, "No, he didn't leave a forwarding address where he can be reached." But do you know where he was? He'd be in his office, sitting right behind his desk. Three times I went up. The second time she said "He's still in Terre Haute, Indiana." The third time I said, "now don't tell me he's in Terre Haute." She'd say, 'Well, he's out of town."

Ruppert was a fine old man. He wasn't too demanding. I know Ruth held out one year, and he got $60,000, and Ruppert chewed him out and said, "What do you think I am, a millionaire?" George Weiss, he'd always give you this story, you don't know how tough times are. And you'd win the pennant and the World Series every year. I think they took the responstbility for winning themselves, not the players. When the Yankees let Weiss go, he came out with a story, he couldn't understand how an organization could let a man go who made over $6,000,000 for them. Now the shoe was on the other foot.

DiMaggio was a very quiet guy. I think he had his teeth corrected. You never heard him get in an argument, or any animosity about him. People didn't think DiMaggio was fast. He wasn't what you'd call a graceful runner, but he had a very hard slide. I've seen him run bases and you would think he'll never make it to second, and he'd always be in safe. He could run. He had great range in the outfield, and he had a lot of confidence in himself.

When he hit his streak, there was no change in him. He never showed any tightness or nervousness. He was just the same guy all the way through.

I've always been critical of Mr. Weiss. He's a great baseball man, he was a smart operator, but he was really tight with that money. He'd send out a letter to the scouts, "In the event that you've got to see a certain club play, if you'd write them for the information that you'd like to have, it won't cost you a long distance call." And the long distance call might cost you fifty or seventy-five cents, like from Atlanta to Birmingham. He made it rough. I think Ed Barrow was a rough operator too. I think George Weiss inherited all his tactics for signing players.

I know it was 1939, I guess it was. Barrow sent me a contract and I held out. It was the year I broke my leg. And he just sent me a wire saying, when you're able to play, report. And I thought I was about able so I went to New York. I know I was broke. I'd paid for my hospital bill and doctor's bill and operations. They didn't pay for that. It wasn't in the contract. I went down to his office to sign, and I didn't take the original contract with me. He brought out a contract just exactly like the one I'd left in my room. I said "Mr. Barrow, that looks just like the same contract you sent me and I refused, and I sent it back." He says, "Yeah, I know it," but he says, "if you don't want to sign for that we can send you back to Newark. $2,580 I believe it was you got there. And now you get $3,200 and you can't play." So I signed it. I had to. They sell you a lot on the idea of winning the World Series.

George Weiss was a good politician. He'd throw a party for the press, special people and spend 5 or 6 thousand dollars, and wouldn't give his ballplayers a quarter. But he stayed in the good graces of the public, and there was never any criticism of him in the press.

I want to tell you a little story about DiMaggio. I was in Murfreesboro, Tennessee, way back in Tennessee, and Tennessee State Teachers College was playing and I was sitting in the stands with Bill Marns, a scout from Milwaukee, and school gets out and here comes three college Joes and set down one two three beside us and about the time they set down this guy hit a ball to center field, hit it real good, and the center fielder went back and made a great play over his shoulder. And this one kid in the middle he jumped up and started clapping his hands and the guy next to me says "What's the matter, what are you cheering about?" And the other guy says "That's the greatest play I ever saw." It was a good play. And the guy next to me says "If you think that was a good one you should have seen the one that I saw one time." And I stopped him, and said "You mean you've seen a better play than that?" And he says "Yes sir." I said "I'll tell you what I'll do. I'll bet you a dollar I can tell you who it was who hit the ball, what the pitch was, and who made the catch." He looked at me as if to say well, this is a smart alec. I says "Was it in Yankee Stadium?" and he says "Yes sir." And I said "was it Joe DiMaggio that caught it?" and he said "yes sir." And then I told him what the pitch was. It was a fastball. And the man that threw it was me. That ball was hit to the left of the graveyard and he was playing shallow; where Ruth was and a couple more they had statues of out there, in straight-away center. The ball was hit to the left of those. And it had a wire on top of the stands and he ran right to the fence, on the dead run, jumped, and backhanded that ball and caught it and Greenberg's almost on second base. Of course Willie Mays made a great catch in the World Series but he didn't have to go near as far as DiMaggio did to catch the ball.

You know playing in New York and being a Yankee ballplayer, the name and all that goes a long way in a ballplayer's way of thinking. Who had you rather be with, the Yankees or somebody else? The St. Louis Browns? They had such an abundance of good material in the minor leagues, and a great ball club in the stadium, that it wasn't too easy to break in on that, unless somebody was really getting old. You were no young chicken when you got up to the Yankees. You knew how to play. They didn't bring you up to teach you how to play.

INTERVIEW WITH ROBIN ROBERTS

(The following edited interview with *Robin Roberts* took place January 25, 1983, at the Sundome, University of South Florida, in Tampa. From 1948 until 1966, mainly with the Philadelphia Phillies, he won 286 games, and was elected to the Hall of Fame in 1976. For many years, he has been Coach of the University of South Florida baseball team.)

Those that saw him will argue with you if you feel he was not the greatest living ballplayer.

That coffee commercial really did bring him back. A lot of people are more associated with him because of that, among the younger generation. They don't know he was a great ballplayer. Most people that know Joe were amazed that he did such a good job on the commercial, because he was such an introvert. For him to come out and be a commercial personality like that was as surprising as that he did such an excellent job of presenting the product. That was the biggest surprise to those of us that knew him, that he could go out and become a person who could do commercials and express himself like that. He was kind of almost bashful in a lot of ways.

My biggest disappointment that he brought on, was that he hit a home run and beat me in the only World Series game I ever pitched. That was interesting because I'd got him to pop up four times and the only time I really wasn't concerned about him was the last time, because I thought I was able to handle him. I was pitching him all fastballs. I do a few curve balls but I didn't throw them to a guy like Joe. I didn't want to give him a chance to get the bat around. This was in 1950. 1950 and 1951 were the last two years he played. He had a lot of problems with bone spurs and that sort of thing. Joe had a lot of injuries in his career. A lot of people don't realize that. He came up in 1936 and he had suffered a bad injury with the Seals. The Red Sox were more associated with San Francisco in those days than the Yankees and they had picked up three or four guys that had played with San Francisco, but he had had an injury so the Red Sox kind of steered away from him and the Yanks took a gamble that his leg would come around. He had injured his knee quite severely.

I was old enough in 1936 when he first came up to remember him. I think Joe was one of those perfect mixes. He was an outstanding player that came with an outstanding organization, and he played center field which is a real romantic position. You're a tremendous athlete if you can play center field. It's the easiest position to play if you can play it. If you can run, if you can see the ball off the bat. It's just got to be a fun position to play if you can play it. But it's not easy unless you can run. You've got to have certain particular skills. Joe could run. Joe was an exceptional baseball player. He ran well, he threw well, he slid beautifully. He shagged the ball. From my standpoint, I would have voted for Willie Mays myself as the greatest living baseball player, because I saw more of Willie. I have often said, if Joe was better than Willie, I wish I had seen more of him, but I wouldn't want to play against him.

Joe was quiet. He even played that way. He did everything so smoothly, where Willie had a lot of flair about him. Joe and Willie were different type personalities and players but they were both of them just tremendous.

Joe has that star quality that very few people have. Frank Sinatra has it. Laurence Olivier has it. They may be among the best of all time, but they're not that much better than the others. They just come across that way. I think it's an ability to realize that you can't do everything and you just do what you can do. A lot of us fall into the mistake of thinking we can do a lot of things. You *can* do a lot of things but you can't do a lot of things *well*. You can only do one thing really well and those guys like DiMaggio that were able to stay aloof from everything else and just keep his mind on what he was doing, well. . . . It's hard to imagine Joe DiMaggio as a flop. Maybe he was just destined to be a ballplayer.

I knew about him when he played in San Francisco. I was quite a fan. 1936 I would have been eight or nine years old, so I knew about him then. I graduated from high school in 1944. He was the enemy. I was never a Yankee fan. I was from Illinois. I remember the great respect everyone had for him, from listening to St. Louis Browns ball games, sometimes Chicago White Sox ball games. The Browns were pitiful in those days and the White Sox weren't much better. I was more of a National League fan because of the Cubs, they were my favorite team. But I remember following him. I think he held out after his first year. He had a tremendous rookie year. I think he was a very confident person, and he knew how much he meant to the Yankees. He must have, to have the ability to hold out with the Yankees at a young age. He must have felt he was a really good ballplayer. I know when he became a hundred thousand dollar ballplayer was a big day.

Joe had a tremendous press. I think New York really in those days was an asset for a player from that standpoint. Plus the fact that he must have been a whale of a player. I remember in 1950 Granny Hamner hit a ball, Joe was fairly old at the time, 35 or 36, Granny hit a ball to right center, that if it goes by Joe it's a triple. And he went over and cut it off and held Granny to a single. It was in a close ball game. He made a beautiful play, and it looked so easy. When it was hit it looked like it was going through there. For those who watched DiMaggio all those years, he did that all the time.

1950 was the first time I won twenty games. I was twenty-three years old. I was just starting. I never threw harder than I did that year. That was the tops as far as that physical part of it. I was basically a one pitch guy. So there wasn't a whole lot of talking about how to pitch to DiMaggio. Just keep the ball down and throw it by him. Get movement so he couldn't hit it square. Not blow it by him. I wasn't thinking of striking him out, I was thinking of good movement—I popped up a lot of guys. I popped Joe up four times that day, twice to right field and twice to second base. And really it happened to me so often in my career, if I was tense in a situation, had reason to be tense, I could handle that. But sometimes I would be lulled to sleep and I wouldn't really do what I should have been doing, and DiMaggio's home run was a perfect example of it. I remember distinctly how when he came up for that fifth time I thought now he did not present nearly the formidable opponent that he had the other four times, in my mind. And there was reason, because he had popped up. But I wish I had been a little leery of him.

I always tried personally to keep from being awed by the big stars, to do what I would do with any other hitter. I always thought that if I gave them too much credit I'd get behind them in the count and then they'd be an even better hitter than they would have been otherwise. So I tried to go ahead and treat them normally knowing that if you made mistakes with them, you'd really be dead—Musial and Mays and Aaron and those guys—as a pitcher I just tried to keep it in perspective and go with what I had and let everything else take care of itself.

I think it's because of New York that a player like Musial doesn't, his name doesn't have the impact of DiMaggio's. Musical was a player's player. He was a beautiful person. He's respected by people, and he played hard. But Stan gave you the impression that it wasn't life or death. Joe gave you the feeling that was all there was. Stan gave you the feeling he was having a hell of a time playing ball. Stan came across much differently than Joe. I think Stan felt very fortunate to play baseball. I don't think it was ever much of an effort for him—though later in life there were probably times when it was hard for him to go out there. But Joe, on the other hand, he was injured a lot. For some reason there was always seemingly pressure on DiMaggio. The same pressure was on Musial but Stan treated it differently. Somehow Joe was always under the hammer. I don't know why. I think his aloofness allowed people to describe him in that manner, under pressure. I think he looked sad. I don't think he was, particularly. I think he was probably having a hell of a time. But I think he looked sad and I think he had somehow along the line accepted the personal responsibility for New York's baseball team. I think Mickey Mantle did that too, later in his career. You can't keep them from it. But I do think that's part of Joe's name, the fact that he did assume such responsibility.

Ted Williams was never the complete ballplayer DiMaggio was. That's why Ted's not remembered like Joe. Ted was a hitter. Ted put on a show with the bat but Joe was a fantastic all-around athlete. Joe was fantastic at sliding. He ran the bases with grace and flair and speed. Of course to play center field at Yankee Stadium is exceptionally tough anyhow.

I remember the 56-game hitting streak. I remember them stopping it. Kenny Keltner made some great plays with Cleveland. One of the funniest stories I heard was the big contract with Heinz 57 Varieties, they were all set that if Joe could go to 57, he was going to be their lifetime spokesman. I remember when it was stopped. I remember Al Smith pitched against him, a left-handed pitcher, so it was surprising that he would stop Joe. Joe did hit two balls and Keltner made two great plays on them. The interesting thing about that was he was stopped that day and then I think he hit in sixteen more games.

I knew that the ball he hit against me was gone the moment he hit it. It really carried out of the ball park. It wasn't a fly ball that just dropped over. It was a line drive in the upper deck. I felt disappointed that I hadn't worried about him. We call it giving in. That's not quite the word. It was under-rating, I felt. I mean I knew as soon as he hit it I hadn't approached it with the same intensity. I was behind in the count.

I'll tell you an interesting DiMaggio story. Which kind of shows I think what makes some athletes better than others. It's the concentration connected with it. I was in St. Louis at an old-timer's game and a photographer from Springfield, my old hometown, wanted a picture of me and Joe. So I was sitting there and whenever that happens, they don't get Joe and bring him over to you, I go over to Joe, and I do it willingly and I don't complain at all. If they had done it the other way I'd have fainted. So I go over to Joe and say they want a picture and he's very cooperative and they're fixing, adjusting the lens and he said to me "you know Robin I can still see that pitch up over the plate. I could just see it, it seemed to tail away when I swung at it." Now that was 26 years ago, at that time. And I remember I said to him "Joe, you should have seen it from my angle, it didn't look so good." And I can still see the pitch. I guess those people who were not involved in something like athletics cannot imagine that kind of concentration and memory. But that was probably one of the reasons he was so good. When he sees me he associates me with that pitch, and vice versa.

At that old-timer's game my wife and son Jimmy who was about eight or nine or ten, they were with me and when we came down for breakfast there was a table for two but not for three. And we walked by Joe—he was sitting by himself and he saw our predicament, and he said "Robin, your boy can eat with me." So Jimmy sat down. It was so easy for Joe to do that. With most people, he didn't come across as that cooperative.

Joe had a way about him. You know I don't know all the problems he had, I don't know what his financial situation was, but he was so reserved, so much of an introvert that people don't know a lot about his life. A lot of people don't even know that Joe was married to a gal named Dorothy Arnold. Joe was completely closed about all that. I respected him tremendously for that: to be able to live in that fishbowl and to be able to keep his private life fairly reserved. Now the Marilyn Monroe thing, that was impossible to keep too quiet.

FOR THE RECORD

In his prime, DiMaggio was approximately 6 '2 " and weighed about 195 pounds, with brown eyes and black hair that turned silver-gray as he aged. He threw and batted right-handed. Though some early descriptions refer to him as "knock-kneed," generally his build was depicted as powerful and his movements graceful, with broad, sloping shoulders (that became rounded as he grew older), long arms, and particularly powerful thighs.

During his playing days, he held or tied the following records: tied American League record for highest fielding percentages for an outfielder (1947), .997; tied major and American League record for most extra bases on long hits, 8, and total bases in an inning, 8 (fifth inning, June 24, 1936); tied major and American League record for most three-base hits in a game (first game, August 27, 1938), 3; tied major and American League record for most home runs in an inning (fifth inning, June 24, 1936), 2; holds major-league record for hitting in consecutive games (1941), 56.

In World Series play, he held or tied the following records: tied, most times at bat in one game (October 6, 1936), 6; tied most times at bat in one inning (ninth inning, October 6, 1936, and sixth inning, October 6, 1937), 2; tied most hits in one inning (ninth inning, October 6, 1936), 2; tied most put-outs in one inning (ninth inning, October 2, 1936, and sixth inning, October 7, 1937), 3; held record for most put-outs in one five-game Series (1942), 20; only player to play in four World Series his first four major-league seasons; held record for games played in World Series with one club, 51; held record for playing in World Series with one team, 10; held record for playing in World Series most with the winning team, 9; held record for most World Series at-bats, 199.

DiMaggio was named the American League's Most Valuable Player in 1939, 1941, and 1947. The Baseball Writer's Association elected him to the *Sporting News*'s All-Star major-league team in 1937-42, and 1947-48. He was the *Sporting News*'s Player of the Year in 1939, and named the Greatest Living Player in a special poll of sportswriters as part of baseball's 1969 centennial celebration.

The following statistics present a clear record of Joe DiMaggio's performance at bat and in the field during his professional baseball career. A day-by-day outline of the progress of his famous hitting streak is included.

1

DiMaggio's 56-Game Batting Streak, 1941

Date		Pitcher	Club	AB	R	H	2B	3B	HR	RBI
May	15	Edgar Smith	Chicago	4		1				1
	16	Lee	Chicago	4	2	2		1	1	1
	17	Rigney	Chicago	3	1	1				
	18	Harris (2)	St. Louis	3	3	3	1			1
		Niggeling (1)								
	19	Galehouse	St. Louis	3		1	1			
	20	Auker	St. Louis	5	1	1				1
	21	Rowe (1)	Detroit	5		2				1
		Benton (1)								
	22	McKain	Detroit	4		1				1
	23	Newsom	Boston	5		1				2
	24	Johnson	Boston	4	2	1				2
	25	Grove	Boston	4		1				
	27	Chase (1)	Washington	5	3	4			1	3
		Anderson (2)								
		Carrasquel (1)								
(Night)	28	Hudson	Washington	4	1	1		1		
	29	Sundra	Washington	3	1	1				
	30	Johnson	Boston	2	1	1				
	30	Harris	Boston	3		1	1			

Date		Pitcher	Club	AB	R	H	2B	3B	HR	RBI
June	1	Milnar	Cleveland	4	1	1				
	1	Harder	Cleveland	4		1				
	2	Feller	Cleveland	4	2	2	1			
	3	Trout	Detroit	4	1	1			1	1
	5	Newhouser	Detroit	5	1	1		1		1
	7	Muncrief (1)	St. Louis	5	2	3				1
		Allen (1)								
		Caster (1)								
	8	Auker	St. Louis	4	3	2			2	4
	8	Caster (1)	St. Louis	4	1	2	1		1	3
		Kramer (1)								
	10	Rigney	Chicago	5	1	1				
(Night)	12	Lee	Chicago	4	1	2			1	1
	14	Feller	Cleveland	2		1	1			1
	15	Bagby	Cleveland	3	1	1			1	1
	16	Milnar	Cleveland	5		1	1			
	17	Rigney	Chicago	4	1	1				
	18	Lee	Chicago	3		1				

Date		Pitcher	Club	AB	R	H	2B	3B	HR	RBI
	19	Smith (1)	Chicago	3	2	3			1	2
		Ross (2)								
	20	Newsom (2)	Detroit	5	3	4	1			1
		McKain (2)								
	21	Trout	Detroit	4		1				1
	22	Newhouser (1)		5	1	2	1		1	2
		Newsom (1)								
June	24	Muncrief	St. Louis	4	1	1				
	25	Galehouse	St. Louis	4	1	1			1	3
	26	Auker	St. Louis	4		1	1			1
	27	Dean	Philadelphia	3	1	2			1	2
	28	Babich (1)	Philadelphia	5	1	2	1			
		Harris (1)								
	29	Leonard	Washington	4	1	1	1			
	29	Anderson	Washington	5	1	1				1
July	1	Harris (1)		4		2				1
		Ryba (1)								
	1	Wilson		3	1	1				1
	2	Newsom		5	1	1			1	3
	5	Marchildon	Philadelphia	4	2	1			1	2
	6	Babich (1)	Philadelphia	5	2	4	1			2
		Hadley (3)								
	6	Knott	Philadelphia	4		2		1		2
(Night)	10	Niggeling	St. Louis	2		1				
	11	Harris (3)	St. Louis	5	1	4			1	2
		Kramer (1)								
	12	Auker (1)	St. Louis	5	1	2	1			1
		Muncrief								
July	13	Lyons (2)	Chicago	4	2	3				
		Hallett (1)								
	13	Lee	Chicago	4		1				
	14	Rigney	Chicago	3		1				
	15	Smith	Chicago	4	1	2	1			2
	16	Milnar (2)	Cleveland	4	3	3	1			
		Krakauskas (1)								
		Total for 56 games		223	56	91	16	4	15	55

.408 Pct.

Strikeouts - 7; bases on balls - 21; hit by pitcher - 2

Stopped July 17 at Cleveland, night game won by New York 4-3. First inning, Al Smith pitching, thrown out by Keltner; fourth inning, Smith pitching, base on balls; seventh inning, Smith pitching, thrown out by Keltner; eighth inning, Jim Bagby, Jr. pitching, grounded to Boudreau to start double play.

2

Minor League Statistics

Year	Club	League	Pos.	G.	AB.	R.	H.	2B	3B	HR	RBI	B.A.	PO.	A.	E.	F.A.
1932-San Fran.	P.C.	SS	3	9	2	2	1	1	0	2	.222	4	7	1	.917
1933-San Fran.	P.C.	OF	187	762	129	259	45	13	28	169	.340	407	32	17	.963
1934-San Fran.	P.C.	OF	101	375	58	128	18	6	12	69	.341	236	11	8	.969
1935-San Fran.	P.C.	OF	172	679	173	270	48	18	34	154	.398	430	32	21	.957

3

DiMaggio's Major League Statistics

Year	Team	LG	G.	AB.	R.	H.	TB.	2B	3B	HR	RBI	B.A.	S.A.
1936	N.Y.	AL	138	637	132	206	367	44	*15	29	125	.323	.576
1937	N.Y.	AL	151	621	*151	215	*418	35	15	*46	167	.346	*.673
1938	N.Y.	AL	145	599	129	194	348	32	13	32	140	.324	.581
1939	N.Y.	AL	120	462	108	176	310	32	6	30	126	*.381	.671
1940	N.Y.	AL	132	508	93	179	318	28	9	31	133	*.352	.626
1941	N.Y.	AL	139	541	122	193	*348	43	11	30	*125	.357	.643
1942	N.Y.	AL	154	610	123	186	304	29	13	21	114	.305	.498
1943-44-45						IN MILITARY SERVICE							
1946	N.Y.	AL	132	503	81	146	257	20	8	25	95	.290	.511
1947	N.Y.	AL	141	534	97	168	279	31	10	20	97	.315	.522
1948	N.Y.	AL	153	594	110	190	*355	26	11	*39	*155	.320	.598
1949	N.Y.	AL	76	272	58	94	162	14	6	14	67	.346	.596
1950	N.Y.	AL	139	525	114	158	307	33	10	32	122	.301	*.585
1951	N.Y.	AL	116	415	72	109	175	22	4	12	71	.263	.422
CAREER			1736	6821	1390	2214	3948	389	131	361	1537	.325	.579

Year	TOB	TBP	TRP	LH	EB	1BH	BB	SO	HP	IP	OBA
1936	234	402	228	88	161	118	24	39	4	.253	.352
1937	284	492	272	96	*203	119	64	37	5	.327	.412
1938	255	415	237	77	154	117	59	21	2	.257	.386
1939	232	375	204	68	134	108	52	20	4	.290	.448
1940	243	383	195	68	139	111	61	30	3	.274	.425
1941	273	432	217	*84	*155	109	76	13	4	.287	.440
1942	256	378	216	63	118	123	68	36	2	.193	.376
1943-44-45					IN MILITARY SERVICE						
1946	207	322	151	53	111	93	59	24	2	.221	.367
1947	235	349	174	61	111	107	64	32	3	.208	.391

1948	265	431	*226	76	*165	114	67	30	*8	*.278	.396
1949	151	219	111	34	68	60	55	18	2	.250	.459
1950	239	388	204	*75	*149	83	80	33	1	*.284	.394
1951	176	242	131	38	66	71	61	36	6	.159	.365
LIFE	3050	4828	2566	881	1734	1333	790	369	46	.254	.398

TOB-Times On Base (H+BB+HP)   TBP-Bases Produced (TB+BB+HP+SB+SH+SF)
TRP-Total Runs Produced (R+RBI-HR)   LH-Long Hits   EB-Extra Bases
1BH-One Base Hits   BB-Bases on Balls   SO-Strike Outs   HP-Hit by Pitcher
IP-Isolated Power (EB/AB)   OBA-On Base Average (TOB divided by (AB+BB+HP))

YEAR	SB.	CS	SBP%	GDP	HR.%	SH	PLA	GIF	PO.	A.	E.	DP	TC.	F.A.	RFAC
1936	4	0	1.000	NR	4.6	3	668	138	339	*22	8	2	361	.978	2.62
1937	3	0	1.000	NR	7.4	2	692	150	*413	21	*17	4	*434	.962	2.89
1938	6	1	.857	NR	5.3	0	660	145	366	20	15	4	386	.963	2.66
1939	3	0	1.000	11	6.5	6	524	117	328	13	5	2	341	.986	2.91
1940	1	2	.333	16	6.1	0	572	130	359	5	8	2	364	.978	2.80
1941	4	2	.667	6	5.5	0	621	139	385	16	9	*5	401	.978	2.88
1942	4	2	.667	9	3.4	0	680	154	409	10	8	3	419	.981	2.72
1943-44-45							IN MILITARY SERVICE								2.51
1946	1	0	1.000	13	5.0	3	567	131	314	15	6	3	329	.982	2.51
1947	3	0	1.000	14	3.7	0	601	139	316	2	1	0	318	*.997	2.29
1948	1	1	.500	20	*6.6	0	669	152	441	8	13	1	449	.972	2.95
1949	0	1	.000	11	5.1	0	329	76	195	1	3	0	196	.985	2.58
1950	0	0	.000	14	6.1	0	606	137	363	9	9	1	372	.976	2.72
1951	0	0	.000	16	2.9	0	482	113	288	11	3	3	299	.990	2.65
LIFE	30	9	.769	130	5.3	14	7671	1721	4516	153	105	30	4669	.978	2.71

SB.-Stolen Bases   CS-Caught Stealing   SBP%-Stolen Base Percentage   GDP-Grounded into
Double Play   HR.%-Home Run Percentage per At Bat   SH-Sacrifice Hits   PLA-Plate
Appearances (AB.+BB.+HP+SH)   GIF-Games Played in Field   PO.-Putouts   A.-Assists
E.-Errors   DP-Double Plays   TC.-Chances Taken (PO.+A.)   F.A.-Fielding Average
(TC./(TC.+E.))   RFAC-Range Factor (TC./GIF)

NOTE: Fielding statistics are shown only for player's primary position unless otherwise
stated. In 1950, DiMaggio played one game at first base, made 13 putouts, 0 assists, 0
double plays, 0 errors. *Denotes lead or tied for league lead.

4
DiMaggio's World Series Statistics

	G	AB	H	2B	3B	HR	HR %	R	RBI	BB	SO	SB	BA	SA	Pinch Hit AB	Pinch Hit H	G at POS	PO	A	E	FA
1936 NY A	6	26	9	3	0	0	0.0	3	3	1	3	0	.346	.462	0	0	OF-6	18	0	1	.947
1937	5	22	6	0	0	1	4.5	2	4	0	3	0	.273	.409	0	0	OF-5	18	0	0	1.000
1938	4	15	4	0	0	1	6.7	4	2	1	1	0	.267	.467	0	0	OF-4	10	0	0	1.000
1939	4	16	5	0	0	1	6.3	3	3	1	1	0	.313	.500	0	0	OF-4	11	0	0	1.000
1941	5	19	5	0	0	0	0.0	1	1	2	2	0	.263	.263	0	0	OF-5	19	0	0	1.000
1942	5	21	7	0	0	0	0.0	3	3	0	1	0	.333	.333	0	0	OF-5	20	0	0	1.000
1947	7	26	6	0	0	2	7.7	4	5	6	2	0	.231	.462	0	0	OF-7	22	0	0	1.000
1949	5	18	2	0	0	1	5.6	2	2	3	5	0	.111	.278	0	0	OF-5	7	0	0	1.000
1950	4	13	4	1	0	1	7.7	2	2	3	1	0	.308	.615	0	0	OF-4	8	0	0	1.000
1951	6	23	6	2	0	1	4.3	3	5	2	4	0	.261	.478	0	0	OF-6	17	0	0	1.000
10 yrs.	51*	199*	54	6	0	8	4.0	27	30	19	23	0	.271	.422	0	0	OF-51*	150	0	1	.993

5
DiMaggio's All-Star Game Statistics

Year	League	POS	AB	R	H	2B	3B	HR	RBI	BA	PO	A	E	FA
1936--American		OF	5	0	0	0	0	0	0	.000	1	0	1	.500
1937--American		OF	4	1	1	0	0	0	0	.250	1	1	0	1.000
1938--American		OF	4	1	1	0	0	0	0	.250	2	0	1	.667
1939--American		OF	4	1	1	0	0	1	1	.250	1	0	0	1.000
1940--American		OF	4	0	0	0	0	0	0	.000	1	0	0	1.000
1941--American		OF	4	3	1	1	0	0	1	.250	1	0	0	1.000
1942--American		OF	4	0	2	0	0	0	0	.500	2	0	0	1.000
1947--American		OF	3	0	1	0	0	0	0	.333	1	0	0	1.000
1948--American		PH	1	0	0	0	0	0	1	.000	0	0	0	.000
1949--American		OF	4	1	2	1	0	0	3	.500	0	0	0	.000
1950--American		OF	3	0	0	0	0	0	0	.000	3	0	0	1.000
Totals*			40	7	9	2	0	1	6	.225	13	1	2	.867

*Selected for team in 1946 and 1951 but did not play due to injuries;
1943-45 in Armed Services.

I am indebted for supplemental statistics beyond standard totals to Neil Munro, SABR, who also provided help in checking standard career totals. I would also like to acknowledge the considerable help of other Society for American Baseball Research Members for their aid.

BIBLIOGRAPHY

BOOKS OR SECTIONS OF BOOK-LENGTH WORKS

Allen, Lee, et al., eds. *The Baseball Encyclopedia.* New York: Macmillan, 1969.
_____. *The Hot Stove League.* New York: A. S. Barnes, 1955.
Allen, Lee, and Tom Meany. *Kings of the Diamond.* New York: G. P. Putnam's Sons, 1965.
Allen, Maury. *Where Have You Gone, Joe DiMaggio?: The Story of America's Last Hero.* New York: E. P. Dutton, 1975
_____. *You Could Look it Up: The Life of Casey Stengel.* New York: Time Books, 1979.
Allen, Mel, with Frank Graham, Jr. *It Takes Heart.* New York: Harper & Brothers, 1959.
Anderson, Dave. "Joltin' Joe's Historic Stand," in *Yesterdays in Sport,* edited by Maitland A. Eddey. New York: Time-Life Books, 1968.
Anderson, Dave, et. al. *The Yankees: The Four Fabulous Eras of Baseball's Most Famous Team.* New York: Random House, 1980.
Andreano, Ralph. *No Joy in Mudville.* Cambridge, Mass.: Schenkman, 1965.
Angell, Roger. *The Summer Game.* New York: Viking Press, 1972.
Appel, Martin, and Burt Goldblatt. *Baseball's Best.* New York: McGraw-Hill, 1977.
Barrow, Edward, with James M. Kahn. *My Fifty Years in Baseball.* New York: Coward-McCann, 1951.
Boorstin, Daniel. *The Image: or What Happened to the American Dream?* New York: Atheneum, 1962.
Bortstein, Larry. *Great Moments in Baseball.* New York: Grosset & Dunlap, 1973.
Boyle, Robert. *Sport—Mirror of American Life.* Boston: Little, Brown, 1963.
Broeg, Bob. *Super Stars of Baseball.* St. Louis: *Sporting News,* 1971.
Brown, Gene. *The Complete Book of Baseball.* New York: Arno Press, 1980.
Cannon, Jimmy. "The Joe DiMaggio I Remember," in *Sport Magazine's All-Time All-Stars,* edited by Tom Murray. New York: Atheneum, 1977. (Originally in *Sport,* Sept. 1955, pp. 65-72.)
Cinel, Dino. *From Italy to San Francisco.* Palo Alto, Calif.: Stanford University Press, 1984.

Conlon, Jocko, and Robert Creamer. *Jocko*. Philadelphia: J. B. Lippincott,, 1967.

Connor, Anthony J. *Baseball for the Love of It: Hall of Famers Tell it Like it Was*. New York: Macmillan, 1982.

Creamer, Robert W. *Babe: The Legend Comes to Life*. New York: Simon & Schuster, 1974.

_____. "Ruth, Gehrig, and DiMaggio," in *The Game and the Glory*. Edited by Joe Reichler, Englewood Cliffs, N. J.: Prentice-Hall, 1975.

_____. *Stengel, His Life and Times*. New York: Simon & Schuster, 1984.

Daley, Arthur. *Inside Baseball*. New York: Grosset & Dunlap, 1950.

_____. *Times at Bat: A Half Century of Baseball*. New York: Random House, 1950.

Daniel, Dan. "Joe DiMaggio: My Friend—The Yankee Clipper," in *Sporting News Year Book*. St. Louis: *Sporting News*, 1950.

Danzig, Allison, and Joe Reichler. *The History of Baseball*. Englewood Cliffs, N. J.: Prentice-Hall, 1959.

Davis, Mac, *Baseball's All-Time Greats*. New York: Bantam Books, 1970.

De Gregorio, George. *Joe DiMaggio—An Informal Biography*. New York: Stein & Day, 1981.

Devaney, John, and Burt Goldblatt. *The World Series, A Complete Pictorial History*. Chicago: Rand McNally, 1972.

Diggins, John P. *Mussolini and Fascism: The View from America*. Princeton: Princeton University Press, 1972.

"DiMaggio, Joe," in *Current Biography*, edited by Maxine Black. New York: H. H. Wilson, 1941.

"DiMaggio, Joe," in *Current Biography*, edited by Anna Roth. New York: H. H. Wilson, 1952.

Durant, John. *Highlights of the World Series*. New York: Hastings House, 1971.

_____. *The Yankees: A Pictorial History of Baseball's Greatest Club*. New York: Hastings House, 1949.

Durso, Joseph. *Casey, The Life and Legend of Charles Dillon Stengel*. Englewood Cliffs, N. J.: Prentice-Hall, 1967.

_____. Whitey Ford, and Mickey Mantle. *Whitey and Mickey*. New York: Viking Press, 1977.

Feller, Bob. *Strikeout Story*. New York: Grosset & Dunlap, 1947.

Finlayson, Ann. *Champions at Bat*. Champaign, Ill.: Garrard, 1970.

Frick, Ford C. *Games, Asterisks, and People*. New York: Crown, 1973.

Gallagher, Mark. *Day by Day in New York Yankee History*. New York: Leisure Press, 1983.

_____. *The Yankee Encyclopedia*. New York: Leisure Press, 1984.

Golenbeck, Peter. *Dynasty: The New York Yankees, 1949-1964*. Englewood Cliffs, N. J.: Prentice-Hall, 1975.

Graham, Frank. *The New York Yankees: An Informal History*. New York: G. P. Putnam's Sons, 1943.

_____. *The New York Yankees, 1900-1946*. New York: G. P. Putnam's Sons, 1946.

Guiles, Fred Lawrence. *Norma Jean*. New York: McGraw-Hill, 1969.

Gumina, Deanna Paoli. *The Italians of San Francisco, 1850-1930*. New York: Center for Migration Studies, 1978.

Hemingway, Ernest. *The Old Man and the Sea*. New York: Charles Scribner's Sons, 1952.

Henderson, Robert. *Ball, Bat, and Bishop*. New York: Rockport Press, 1947.

Hill, Art. *I Don't Care if I Never Come Back.* New York: Simon & Schuster, 1980.

Hofstadter, Richard. *Anti-Intellectualism in America.* London: Jonathan Cape, 1963.

Honig, Donald. *Baseball Between the Lines.* New York: Coward, McCann & Geoghegan, 1976.

———. *Baseball When the Grass Was Real.* New York: Coward, McCann & Geoghegan, 1975.

Hoyt, Edwin Palmer. *Marilyn, the Tragic Venus.* New York: Duell, Sloan & Pearce, 1965.

Iorizzo, Luciano, and Salvatore Mondell. *The Italian Americans.* Boston: Twayne Publishers, 1980.

Kaese, Harold. "Joseph Thomas [sic] DiMaggio," in *Famous American Athletes of Today,* Fifth series, with LeRoy Atkinson et al. Boston: L. C. Page, 1937.

Klapp, Orrin E. *Heroes, Villains, and Fools: The Changing American Character.* New York: Spectrum Books, 1962.

———. *Symbolic Leaders: Public Dramas and Public Men.* Chicago: Aldine, 1964.

LeComte, Walter. *The Ultimate New York Yankee Record Book.* New York: Leisure Press, 1984.

Lipsky, Richard. *How We Play the Game: Why Sports Dominate American Life.* Boston: Beacon Press, 1981.

Lipsyte, Robert. *Sportsworld, An American Dreamland.* New York: Quadrangle/ The New York Times Book Company, 1975.

Lowenthal, Lee. *Literature, Popular Culture, and Society.* Englewood Cliffs, N. J.: Prentice-Hall, 1961.

Mailer, Norman. *Marilyn.* New York: Grosset & Dunlap, 1981.

Mann, Jack. *The Decline and Fall of the New York Yankees.* New York: Simon & Schuster, 1967.

Mantle, Mickey. *The Education of a Baseball Player.* New York: Simon & Schuster, 1967.

Marill, Alvin H. *Robert Mitchum on the Screen.* New York: A. S. Barnes, 1978.

Martin, Billy, and Peter Golenbeck. *Number 1.* New York: Dell, 1980.

Mays, Willie, as told to Charles Einstein. *Born to Play Ball.* New York: G. P. Putnam's Sons, 1955.

Mays, Willie, as told to Charles Einstein. *My Life In and Out of Baseball.* New York: E. P. Dutton, 1966.

McCallum, John D., *Ty Cobb.* New York: Praeger, 1975.

Meany, Tom. *Joseph Paul DiMaggio, The Yankee Clipper.* New York: A. S. Barnes, 1951.

———. *The Yankee Story.* New York: E. P. Dutton, 1960.

Merchant, Larry. *Ringside Seat at the Circus.* New York: Holt, Rinehart and Winston, 1976.

Miers, Earl Schenck. *Baseball.* New York: Grosset and Dunlap, 1973.

Moore, Robin, and Gene Schoor. *Marilyn & Joe DiMaggio.* New York: Manor Books, 1976.

Musial, Stan. *Stan Musial,* as told to Bob Broeg. New York: Doubleday, 1964.

Novak, Michael. *The Joy of Sports:* New York: Basic Books, 1976.

Obojski, Robert. *Bush League.* New York: Macmillan, 1975.

Pepitone, Lena. *Marilyn Monroe Confidential.* New York: Simon & Schuster, 1979.

Reichler, Joe, ed. *The Game and the Glory*. Englewood Cliffs, N. J.: Prentice-Hall, 1976.

Reinshagen, Gerlinde. *Doppelkopf: Leben und Tod der Marilyn Monroe*. Frankfurt, Germany: Suhrkamp, 1971.

Reiss, Steven. *Touching Base*. Westport, Conn.: Greenwood Press, 1980.

Ritter, Lawrence. *The Glory of Their Times*. New York: William Morrow, 1984.

Rolle, Andrew F. *The Immigrant Upraised*. Norman: University of Oklahoma Press, 1968.

_____. *The Italian Americans*. New York: Free Press, 1980.

Roth, Philip. *The Great American Novel*. New York: Holt, Rinehart and Winston, 1973.

Schoor, Gene. *Joe DiMaggio, A Biography*. New York: Doubleday, 1980.

_____. *Joe DiMaggio, The Yankee Clipper*. New York: Julian Messner, 1956.

_____. The Thrilling Story of Joe DiMaggio. New York: Frederick Fell, 1950.

Senzell, Howard. *Baseball and the Cold War*. New York: Harcourt Brace Jovanovich, 1977.

Shoemaker, Robert H. *The Best in Baseball*. New York: Thomas Y. Crowell, 1949.

_____. *The Best in Baseball*. New York: Thomas Y. Crowell, 1974.

Silverman, Al. *Joe DiMaggio: The Golden Year, 1941*. Englewood Cliffs, N. J.: Prentice-Hall, 1969.

Smith, Leverett. *The American Dream and the National Game*. Bowling Green, Ohio: Popular Press, 1975.

Smith, Red. *The Red Smith Reader*, edited by Dave Anderson. New York: Random House, 1982.

Sobol, Ken. *Babe Ruth and the American Dream*. New York: Random House, 1974.

Spink, J. G. Taylor. *Judge Landis and Twenty-Five Years of Baseball*. New York: Thomas Y. Crowell, 1947.

Sullivan, George, and John Powers. *The Yankees: An Illustrated History*. Englewook Cliffs, N. J.: Prentice-Hall, 1982.

Turkin, Hy, and S. C. Thompson. *The Official Encyclopedia of Baseball*. 5th rev. ed. New York: A. S. Barnes, 1970.

Voigt, David Q. *America Through Baseball*. Chicago: Nelson-Hall, 1976.

_____. *American Baseball, From Gentleman's Sport to the Commissioner System*. Norman: University of Oklahoma Press, 1966.

_____. *American Baseball, From the Commissioners to Continental Expansion*. Norman: University of Oklahoma Press, 1970.

_____. *American Baseball, From Postwar Expansion to the Electronic Age*. University Park, Penn.: Penn State University Press, 1984.

Wagenknecht, Edward, ed. *Marilyn Monroe: A Composite View*. New York: Chilton, 1969.

Wallop, Douglass. *Baseball, An Informal History*. New York: W. W. Norton, 1969.

Williams, Ted. *My Turn at Bat*, as told to John Underwood. New York: Simon & Schuster, 1969.

Young, A. S. *Great Negro Baseball Stars*. New York: A. S. Barnes, 1953.

SELECTED PERIODICAL AND NEWSPAPER ITEMS

(I have included newspaper items of special pertinence only and have excluded nearly all daily journalistic reporting, though, as my textual citations indicate, I have made use of a variety of New York and national newspapers of DiMaggio's playing day, and of course the *Sporting News.*)

Allen, Mel. "Who is the World's Greatest Ballplayer?" *Sport,* Sept. 1948, p. 20.

Anderson, Dave. "The Longest Hitting Streak." *Sports Illustrated,* 17 July 1961, pp. 36-41.

_____. "Those Sundry Yankee-Red Sox Deals." *New York Times,* 18 December, 1980.

Barbour, James, and Robert Sattelmeyer. "Baseball and Baseball Talk in *The Old Man and the Sea.*" *Fitzgerald-Hemingway Annual,* 1975, pp. 281-289.

Baskett, Sam H. "The Great Santiago: Opium, Vocation, and Dream in *The Old Man and the Sea.*" *Fitzgerald-Hemingway Annual,* 1976, pp. 230-244.

"Big Joe." *Time,* 14 July 1941, pp. 44-45.

Bishop, Schuyler. "Reminiscence. A Painful Snub by a Sports Legend Brings a Father and Son Together." *Sports Illustrated,* 1 Sept. 1983, pp. 8-11.

Boswell, Thomas. "At Last, DiMaggio Feels Comfortable in Public." *Washington Post,* 1 Sept. 1983.

"The Bright Lights." *Newsweek,* 24 Dec. 1951, pp. 44-45.

Busch, Noel F. "Joe DiMaggio, Baseball's Most Sensational Big-League Star." *Life,* 1 May 1939, pp. 62-69.

"Comeback." *Time,* 11 July 1949, pp. 41-42.

Daniel, Dan. "DiMag Really 'Wants to be Alone'" *Sporting News,* 7 Sept., 1949.

_____. "DiMag Benched First Time as Yank for Failure to Hit." *Sporting News,* 23 August 1950.

"Died: Mrs. Rose DiMaggio." *Newsweek,* 2 July 1951, p. 55.

"DiMag and Co.." *Time,* 14 July 1947, p. 45.

Durslag, Melvin. "Why Hasn't DiMaggio's 56-Game Streak Been Broken?" *T.V. Guide,* 18 April 1981, p. 22.

"Edward Lanning Paints Joe DiMaggio Tying Record for Hits." *Life,* 29 Sept. 1941, pp. 64-67.

"A Few Weeks or Forever?" *Time* 25 April 1949, pp. 76-77.

Frank, Stanley. "Yankee Kingmaker." *Saturday Evening Post,* 24 July 1948, pp. 108-10.

Gerrasi, Frank. "The Care and Feeding of a Dictator." *Collier's,* 5 August 1939, pp. 11, 42.

Gildea, William. "Meeting DiMaggio: A Journey in Time." *Washington Post,* 7 August 1984.

Gorkin, Michael. "The Yankee Clipper is Still a Great Hero." *50 Plus,* March 1979, pp. 10-15.

Graber, Ralph S. "Baseball in American Fiction." *English Journal,* November 1967, pp. 1107-14.

"The Great Yankee." *Time,* 8 April 1946, p. 47.

Gumina, D. P. "The Fishermen of San Francisco Bay: The Men of 'Italy Harbor.'" *Pacific Historian,* Spring 1975, pp. 8-21.

Haenle, Rudolf K. "The Athlete as 'Moral Leader.'" *Journal of Popular Culture,* Fall 1974, pp. 382-401.

Hollander, Zander. "When DiMaggio and Co. Took Hawaii by Storm." *New York Times,* 5 Dec. 1982.

Holway, John B. "The Pitcher Who Stopped Joe DiMaggio's Streak." *Baseball Digest,* March 1963, pp. 81-84.

"Joe Comes Home." *Newsweek,* 11 July 1949, p. 62.

"A Joe We Like." *Reporter,* 21 Oct. 1954, p. 6.

"Joltin' Joe and Big John." *Time,* 16 June 1947, p. 71.

"Joltin' Joe Via Radio." *Newsweek,* 6 Feb. 1950, p. 52.

Kaese, Harold. "Will Little Dom Lead the DiMaggios?" *Saturday Evening Post,* 3 August 1946, pp. 20, 97-98.

Lardner, John. "The Cream of the Cream." *Newsweek,* 3 March 1941, p. 48.

_____. "Public Love." *Newsweek,* 13 Dec. 1954, p. 88.

Lundquist, Carl. "I'll Always Remember the Man by the Fence." *Parade,* 11 Sept. 1955, p. 2. Supposedly written "by Joe DiMaggio."

McCallum, Jack. "For Better, For Worse." *Sports Illustrated,* 2 May 1983, pp. 70-84.

Meany, Tom. "Joe DiMaggio As I Knew Him." *Collier's,* 19 April 1952, pp. 66-70.

Milstein, Gilbert. "Why They Cheer Joe DiMaggio." *New York Times Magazine,* 9 July 1950, pp. 14, 41-43.

Monteiro, George. "Santiago, DiMaggio, and Hemingway: The Ageing Professionals of *The Old Man and the Sea.*" *Fitzgerald-Hemingway Annual,* 1975, pp. 273-80.

"Mr. and Mrs. Joe D." *Newsweek,* 25 Jan. 1954, p. 44.

"Never Saw a Report Like It." *Life,* 22 Oct. 1951, pp. 133-38.

"The 154-Game Question." *Newsweek,* 11 April 1949, p. 84.

Owen, Russel. "DiMaggio, the Unruffled." *New York Times,* 13 July 1941, pp. 9, 19.

"The Parting." *Newsweek,* 8 Oct. 1954, p. 32.

Rader, Benjamin G. "Contemporary Sport Heroes: Ruth, Grange, and Dempsey." *Journal of Popular Culture,* Spring 1983, pp. 11-21.

Reiss, Steven A. "Race and Ethnicity in American Baseball: 1900-1919." *Journal of Ethnic Studies,* Winter 1977, pp. 39-55.

Reynolds, Quentin. "About to Shine." *Collier's,* 7 Sept. 1935, pp. 18-19.

_____. "The Frisco Kid." *Collier's* 13 June 1936, p. 22.

Roberts, Randy. "Jack Dempsey: An American Hero in the 1920's." *Proceedings, North American Society for Sports History,* 1974, p. 47.

Robinson, Clarke. "Silhouettes of Celebrities." *World Digest,* Oct. 1941, pp. 47-51.

Schaap, Richard. "No. 5 Returns." *Newsweek,* 20 March 1961, p. 89.

Sher, Jack. "DiMag, the Man Behind the Poker Face." *Sport,* Sept. 1949, p. 16-17, 71-80.

Seidel, Michael. "May 15, 1941: And DiMaggio's Streak Begins." *New York Times,* 16 May 1982.

Smith, Red. "Mr. New York, Mr. Bowery and. . . ." *New York Times,* 8 Feb. 1979.

"Sports" category section. *Time,* 13 July 1936, pp. 42-44.

Stewart-Gordon, James. "Unforgettable Joe DiMaggio." *Reader's Digest,* August 1976, pp. 173-80.

"Strike 'Em Up DiMaggio." *Newsweek,* 26 July 1943, pp. 76, 78.

Talese, Gay. "'Joe,' Said Marilyn Monroe, Just Back From Korea, 'You Have Never Heard Such Cheering.' 'Yes I Have,' Joe DiMaggio Answered: The Silent Season of a Hero." *Esquire,* July 1966, pp. 40-45, 112.

"What About DiMaggio Now?," *Sport*, November, 1950, pp. 18-26, 83. (By the editors of *Sport*.)

BOOKS AND ARTICLES APPEARING
UNDER DIMAGGIO'S BYLINE

DiMaggio, Joe. *Baseball for Everyone: A Treasury of Baseball Lore and Instruction for Fans and Players.* New York: McGraw-Hill, 1948.

_____. "I'll Always Remember the Man by the Fence." *Parade,* 11 Sept. 1955, p. 2.

_____. "It's Great to be Back." *Life,* 1 Aug. 1949, pp. 66-72.

_____. *Lucky to Be a Yankee.* New York: Rudolph Field, 1946; with additional material, New York: Bantam, 1949; with additional material, New York: Grosset & Dunlap, 1951.

_____. "Pitchers I Have Hit," *Collier's,* 29 July 1939.

COMIC BOOKS

"Joe DiMaggio, The Yankee Clipper." *True Comics*, May 1948.

Fisher, Thornton, "The True Story of the Yankees." *Trail Blazers,* July 1942, pp. 1-16.

MISCELLANEOUS

The Michigan State University Voice Library possesses the following pertinent audiotapes: *Sports Illustrated* interview, 14 August 1964; Farewell to baseball (CBS broadcast), 11 December 1951; final appearance in New York Yankees Old Timer's game, 5 August 1975; with Hank Greenberg on the NBC Today Show, singing "Take Me Out to the Ball Game," 27 June 1970.

DiMaggio was on the cover of national magazines more than most sports stars. Among these were *Time*, 13 July 1936 and 4 October 1948; *Life*, 1 May 1939 and 1 August 1949. He was also frequently on the cover of various sporting publications, most notably on the first issue of *Sport* in 1946 and on the September covers the following two years.

INDEX

About the Author

JACK B. MOORE is Professor and Chairman of the American Studies Department at the University of South Florida, Tampa. His earlier works include two critical biographies, *Maxwell Bodenheim* and *W.E.B. Du Bois*, as well as numerous articles in publications such as the *Journal of Popular Culture* and *Studies in Short Fiction* and several short stories.